The MASTERY
of LEARNING

Melvin Lewis Thomas

Lulu Enterprises, Inc.
3131 RDU Center, Suite 210
Morrisville, NC 27560
(919) 459-5858
www.lulu.com

This book can be purchased in retail stores or via the web site www.themasteryseries.com, and in volume from the publisher, www.lulu.com

While every precaution has been taken in the preparation of this book, the publisher assumes no responsibilities for errors or omissions, or for damages resulting from the use of information contained herein.

Proofreaders – Rev. Douglas Buchanan, Dušanka Mitchell, Dr. Jeanne M. Quaid, Jim Saul, and Carol Thomas
Cover Design – LightWerx Media, www.lightwerxmedia.com
Cover Art – Carol Thomas
Composition – Melvin Thomas
Drawings – Trevor, Matthew, and Melvin Thomas

Printed in the United States of America
Distributed to the book trade by Lulu Enterprises, Inc.

First Edition
Library of Congress Cataloging-in-Publication Data
Thomas, Melvin Lewis
The Mastery of Learning.
ISBN 1-4116-1362-7
1. Book
2. New Age & Alternative
3. New Thought

Thank you for your interest in the

The MASTERY of LEARNING

*I hope that it is an answer to what you seek
and it helps you accomplish what you desire.*

Respectfully,

Melvin Lewis Thomas - CEO
The Mastery Series Inc.
POB 640
Beecher, IL 60401
Mel@themasteryseries.com

Web Site
www.themasteryseries.com

Packaged at the back of this book is

The MASTERY of LEARNING CD

*It contains important new information and guides
you through learning the essential exercises.
Also appended at the back
is a booklet that is the script used to make the CD.
Using the CD and booklet together will enable you to
quickly develop your own Mastery of Learning expertise.*

In spite of aging, you can learn at least 1000% faster using the techniques of

The MASTERY of LEARNING

LEARN TO:

➤ ACTIVATE THE LATENT GENIUS WITHIN YOU

➤ READ A MINIMUM OF 25,000 WORDS PER MINUTE (An entire book in only minutes)

➤ INCREASE YOUR LONG-TERM RECALL TO 90%

➤ ELIMINATE STRESS BY REPROGRAMMING YOURSELF FOR OPTIMAL HEALTH, MEMORY, and LIFESTYLE.

➤ OPTIMIZE YOUR BRAIN'S POTENTIAL WITH SPECIALIZED BREATHING, HYDRATION, NUTRITION, and EXERCISES.

Put the U in fun back into the YOU in study, $ST_FU^NDY!$ ®

And – the great thing is - everyone can learn to do this!

Learn to L♥ve to Learn®

You Learn Best at $Z^{est}R_{est}$®

This Book's Objectives:

WITH understanding comes trust. If you don't trust the foundation, how can you trust the house? The purpose of such an understanding is to build confidence in the structure built upon it. The first objective of **The MASTERY of LEARNING** is the demolition of the old house and developing plans for a new one. The second objective is the foundation, which you build by learning how remarkably capable your mind/brain/body and visual systems are. Preparations made, you are ready to build your new house.

You are ready to *Learn to L♥ve to Learn.*®

That is the objective of **Section III**. You will learn a new form of reading that is stress-free and ultra fast, yet paradoxically, yields long-term results. Your knowledge becomes a permanent record that will never fade and that will increasingly give you ready access, with photographic recall the eventual goal. Reading at 25,000 words per minute becomes not only feasible, but also reasonable. In fact, it is the beginning; it just gets better. Your mind and memory will become allies in all of your creative endeavors. All forms of reading, the conventional form that you already know, speed-reading if that is one of your skills, and the new ultra fast version you will be learning, will enhance each other in synergistic ways to make your life easier. You will also learn new, easy, and effective ways of molding your life to be the stress-free, creative, and happy experience you have always desired. To aid you in learning what this book presents, **information nuggets** are highlighted in ***bold script*** so that you can review and recapture key points rapidly.

AUTHOR'S BACKGROUND:

I grew up in one of the most beautiful places in the world Sedona, the heart of Red Rock Country in Arizona. We lived there because my father was a photographer who recognized a great setting for his work, and life in general. My lifelong pursuit of knowledge initially induced me to earn a bachelor's degree in physics from Northern Arizona University. I started my professional career as a scientific assistant at Wilford Hall, United States Air Force Medical Center and ended that four-year enlistment with a patent application and a master's degree in physics from Trinity University. Next I became a teacher at Texas Military Institute. My last year there I was honored by being selected as "Teacher of the Year" by the senior class. Then I had short stints as a computer programmer for Honeywell and Arizona Public Service. Next came my longest employment opportunity, as a research scientist and program manager at the United States Air Force Armstrong Laboratory. In this capacity I was the primary author, or a coauthor, on ten research papers in the display field, many of which I was fortunate enough to present to international audiences at conferences in the United States and other countries. I left that experience with two patents and numerous other awards and recognitions. I often spent transition times between jobs and weekends working in the construction industry, which eventually enabled me to act as the architect and prime contractor in the building of my own house. My next career was as a software engineer supporting information technology in the legal and aviation departments of one of the largest corporations in the world. My career has recently taken a new turn allowing me to work as a manager in the insurance industry in Nigeria for a short time, and more recently in sales in the United States. It has also come full cycle in that I teach math at a local college. Complementing my professional career has been more than a decade of intensive research in metaphysics and, more recently, learning about learning. I have also along the way, been certified as an enzyme therapist.[1, 2, 3]

My college education molded me as a scientist with things as my subjects. Working at medical and human research laboratories, and as a teacher, shifted my focus to people. Eventually I became a metascientist and life became my focus, with reality my laboratory. That path led to this book. Along the way I changed jobs and even careers when what I was doing was no longer of interest or the industry downsized. I grasped it, then moved on, stepping-stones in the process of education; the process never ends. It is my understanding now that my diverse career has been essential preparation for writing this book, and possibly others beyond it.

ACKNOWLEDGEMENTS:

I wish to express my gratitude and thanks to all who helped me in the writing of this book: those who took my first developmental workshops and gave me constructive feedback and suggestions; my parents and grandparents who imparted wisdom I am still discovering; my wife Carol, whose watercolor painting graces the front and back covers, whose Japanese kanji calligraphy provides an example with style for the paragraph on that subject, whose support was critical to my ability to find time to do this, and who served willingly as proofreader, insightful contributor, and first critical audience; my sons Trevor and Matt who contributed their own insights and many of the illustrations, and Trevor's graphic design work and development of The Mastery Series web site; critical review, proofreading, and key contributions by good friend Dušanka Mitchell; major contributor Rev.

Douglas Buchanan who allowed me to present his techniques and tell part of his amazing story, then proofread successive generations of the manuscript each time offering more invaluable insights on how to support the ideas presented; Jim Saul who proofread the final draft bringing to bear his more than twenty years of editorial expertise; Dr. Jeanne M. Quaid whose medical advice and proofreading has been invaluable; my friends at Wilford Hall United States Air Force Medical Center, Texas Military Institute, and the Armstrong Research Laboratory, whose inquiring minds taught me much and whose guidance and support were invaluable in helping me learn in the laboratory of life; and all of my other family and friends, dating back to my childhood, whose guidance and stories helped make this material understandable, and also interesting. When requested or warranted for the sake of anonymity, the names in these stories have been changed.

I would also like to thank the many hard working and talented people, in particular: Dr. Jeannette Vos, Gordon Dryden, Dr. Joseph Chilton Pearce, Dr. Carla Hannaford, Dr. Paul Welch, Paul Scheele, Dr. Dan Millman, Dr. Carolyn Myss, Barbara Ann Brennan, Drunvalo Melchizedek, and Dr. Lawrence Sajdecki; whose seminars or books helped to further develop my understanding. They, along with the many other authors I cite in the bibliography, have been critical to the development of a body of knowledge for all of us to learn from and build upon. I am indebted.

DEDICATION:

This book is dedicated to children everywhere, the young and those who still think young, who are striving to be who they are rather than what they are expected to be.

DISCLAIMER – Although this book contains information that can be used to augment one's health, none of it should be construed as medical advice. Any decision to follow what is advocated ought to be at your own discretion and where appropriate, with the consultation and advice of your physician or medical provider. Please do not discontinue the use of prescribed medication or treatments without getting professional advice.

BOOK COVER – The colors of mastery are white, gold, and violet. White and gold are typically used to depict the aura around masters such as Jesus. Violet is the color of the crown chakra and the associated master gland, the pituitary. The traditional symbol for the crown chakra is the lotus flower. The book's title is done in gold colored script. **MASTERY** uses Western print and **LEARNING** *is* calligraphic Eastern print that appears to have been painted with brush strokes. The title overlays the painting of a lotus blossom in shades of pink and upper charka with its large, circular green leaf providing the backdrop. The lotus blossom is viewed at an oblique angle thus giving depth and perspective to the cover, and by inference, the material. A mix of block and calligraphic print is used to mirror the merging of the left and right brains, and associated East and West cultures.

The phrase, **You Learn Best at Z^{est}R$_{est}$**® is done with block lettering transitioning to "lazy" script for the word "Rest," all in upper charka dark blue. The phrase *Learn to L♥ve to Learn*® is also done in dark blue calligraphic print with a pink heart for the letter "o" in Love. Pink is the secondary color of the heart chakra. The leaf of the lotus flower provides the primary heart chakra color of green. The super words (power words) from the book are used to form an undulating stream of script across the front of the book using indigo for the font color as that is the color for the third-eye chakra. The throat charka is represented by the color blue in the wash of water across the white field of the front and back covers. The cover is therefore designed to appeal to upper chakra development and full brain thinking in both the East and the West, hence globally.

The MASTERY of LEARNING – OVERVIEW

THIS book is meant to help you achieve your full learning potential. It addresses your mind/brain/body and vision as an integrated learning system. In order to do that, it is organized much like a high quality automobile dealership where your biological equipment is treated as they would an automobile. You take your car in to have it checked out. The first thing they do is a systems check in order to determine its current status. What is supposed to work and doesn't? As you sit in the waiting room your mind drifts back to what you always wanted in an automobile but were told you couldn't have. That is **Section I, Introduction and Your Systems Check**.

Next, with your permission, the dealership will replace the broken parts and repair all the malfunctions, then tune it up to factory specifications, clean, and polish it. That operation is generally at the back of the dealership because most customers never go into that area. We put it at the back of this book, in **Section IV, Rebuilding Your Foundation**. It is there for you to read when you are ready to make sure your equipment can handle what you discover in the previous sections.

While you are at the dealership, if you ask them, they will explain the buttons on the radio that you never understood, and why the lights stay on after you park the automobile. They will explain the positraction switch and antilock brakes. They will show you where the spare tire is hidden and how to operate the remotely activated locking and alarm system. That is **Section II** of the book where you learn **What Your Equipment Is Supposed to Do**.

Finally, you drive away feeling your new tires gripping the road firmly. The steering is tight and accurate, the way you like it. The brakes stop you firmly now without screaming in protest. Best of all, the engine is responsive and smooth – you're ready to go!

What I have presented so far is really an understatement. Most of us started our lives asking for a new red convertible Ferrari. Now we settle for driving on the wrong side of the road in a rusted-out secondhand station wagon with bent wheels, doors different colors from the body, and a couple of bashed-in quarter panels. The road is packed solid and most of our vehicles are propelled by an engine working with only one cylinder. It is dark out and only a few of the vehicles have even a single working headlight that is very dim because it is covered with mud. Consequently, we are all driving so slowly that the bumpy road we are traversing might as well be a parking lot. To top it off, most of us are almost out of gas and the road seems to stretch on forever with no rest stations in sight.

What all of us had in the beginning, but need to remember, was the professional driving class we attended and graduated from with the highest honors, the custom-built turbocharged convertible sports car we left sitting unused in our garage with the gas tank filled to the top, our glove box filled with gold credit cards, and cleared passage waiting for us on a superhighway weaving gracefully through beautiful terrain leading to the destination of our heart's greatest desire. Try to remember riding with your surround sound concert hall quality radio turned on while keeping track of your position with your state-of-the-art Global Positioning Satellite equipment coupled with electronic maps covering the entire world. Remember seeing great distances using your super-bright headlights, and resting luxuriously in the reclining bucket seats while leaving the driving to the full function autopilot. We are meant to be on the most comfortable and relaxing ride we have ever dreamed of. That is what **Section III** of this book, **Learning With MOM and DAD**, is structured to help you remember. Finally, **Section V** is a **Road Map** so you can take it with you whenever you need a quick review. The result of putting all of this together will be:

The MASTERY of LEARNING

The MASTERY of LEARNING – CONTENTS

The MASTERY of LEARNING – ILLUSTRATIONS AND TABLES

NOTES

SECTION I – INTRODUCTION AND YOUR SYSTEM CHECK

Chapter 1 – THE PROMISE OF A CHILD

Except during the nine months before he draws his first breath,
No man manages his affairs as well as a tree does.

Unknown

All children are born geniuses,
and we spend the first six years of their lives degeniusing them.

Buckminster Fuller

Every child has, at birth,
a greater potential intelligence than Leonardo da Vinci ever used.

Glenn Doman

We have no greater or lesser conquest than over ourselves.

Leonardo da Vinci

Adult rage shocks the child's system like physical shock,
While grief and depression swamp it like a fog.

Barbara Ann Brennan

50 percent of a child's ability to learn is developed in the first four years of life.
80 percent is developed by the age of eight.
Overwhelmingly the best learning methods are similar to those we use as infants.
Gordon Dryden and Jeannette Vos, *The Learning Revolution*[1]

The opposite of courage is not so much fear as it is conformity.

Wayne Dyer

Come to the edge, he said. They said, we are afraid.
Come to the edge, he said. They came. He pushed them… and they flew.

Guillaume Apollinaire

Sometimes we take a leap of faith, and grow our wings on the way down.

Unknown

It is never too late to have a happy childhood.

Wayne Dyer

Whoever welcomes a child welcomes me.
Jesus Christ in Matthew 18:5

The childhood shows the man, as morning shows the day.

John Milton

The child lives in the unconscious of the parent.

Carl Jung

IN order for you to achieve your full learning potential, first we need to examine how common belief systems as well as the typical understanding of reality can limit one's ability. That is a tall order. In order for this to work I ask that you suspend judgment. That allows me to do my job, which is to present convincing arguments that what this book advocates is not only plausible, but also possible, and that *you can do it. Then your job is simply to do it!* According to US Olympic pentathlete Marilyn Kink, *Passion + Vision + Action are the keys to success in any endeavor.*[2] It is best for you to get passionate about this, have a vision of what you want to do, and then know that you will do it! Marina Raye states that, "Passion is living at your edges and giving 100 percent. To do less is treason against yourself. Life is either a passionate adventure or it is nothing!"[3]

As an aid in understanding the process we are embarking on, it will help to cover a few examples of how most of us came to have some limiting belief systems that filter the reality we live. Dr. Joseph Chilton Pearce cites research regarding "the pointing phenomena." At around fifteen months children begin to point. At home this can be a request for the name of an object. Outdoors, at the park for instance, the meaning changes. If a child's parent reacts positively to what they point at they advance to investigate, interact, or engage in play. If the reaction is negative, they return to their mom or dad. However, they also point at things that seemingly do not exist. When there is no reaction they often go to their parent, tug on their clothing, point again, and sometimes name what they see, such as "man", or "dog." When there still is no reaction they eventually stop pointing at such phenomena. This behavior pattern is found worldwide and has also been observed as analogous behavior in the animal kingdom.[4]

Another researcher cited by Dr. Pearce provides a second example in their investigation of the drawings by seven-year-olds with odd colors around objects. When older students were asked if they had seen the same thing they replied, "Yes, but not anymore. Caused too much trouble." These examples are indicative of the mechanisms children use to filter their primary perceptions to be only that which is acceptable in their society. These examples also probably indicate how we as children first filtered our reality and thus developed core concepts that became imbedded in our belief systems. These are the perceptual filters that this book will help you remove if you choose for they are also some of the key ways in which most people limit themselves.[5]

Exercise 1.1 – REMEMBERING YOUR CHILDHOOD POTENTIAL

This is a self-guided meditation, a journey of remembrance to the closet, basement, and attic places where your childhood memories are stored. Please take a few deep breaths and relax. Let your mind drift back to the way your life began… What were you as a child that you have forgotten? What gifts and abilities did you abandon in your race for acceptance and understanding? If you observe babies you will see that they seem to look both at and around you, for along with the physical they see both the vibrant colors of your aura and the light of your being. Sensing thoughts and feeling emotions are natural for infants. Most mothers know that even in the womb their child is distressed by discordant conditions around them, or at peace and harmonious when that is the environment they are immersed in. Young children sometimes see the spirits of departed loved ones, fairies, or their own angel guides. If they can speak they may call what they see *birdies* among other names, being limited in how they can communicate.[6] Most parents are aware that their young children have exceptional memories. They only have to read a book to them to verify this. They usually will be corrected for any mistake or deviation from prior readings.

Time has no meaning to small children so they live in the ever present now which holistically includes the past, the present, the future, and portals most of us no longer see except perhaps in our dreams. Therefore, they can have awareness of past events, potential futures, and other realities. Sometimes in their reality the name they apply to themselves is different from the one you have given them. Three years ago Mike, my wife's 19-year-old nephew, fell four stories onto concrete thus sustaining major head injuries and a broken back. Even with full life support in a modern trauma center he was not expected to live for more than a few hours. Then a miracle changed that dire prognosis. After a few weeks he finally came out of his coma. As is typical of massive head injuries, he began the process of rebuilding his brain and mind much like a child. When he first awakened he asked, "Where is Giovanna?" and he thought his name was Tony. His mother and my wife then remembered that when he was very young he used to think that he was Tony. In the early stages of his recovery he could see a girl in the hospital room that the rest of us could not. His brain and mind quickly recovered and soon he answered to Mike rather than Tony, but he could still remember his refreshed childhood remnants and the girl none of us could see who sat with him. To this day we have no idea who she or Giovanna were. They were part of a reality different from the one we have in common with Mike, who nine months after his accident recovered sufficiently to run in Chicago's 5K Beverly Ridge run. Soon he was back in college and he recently graduated as a certified public accountant.

Because it is acceptable in their cultures much of the world's population has children who openly speak of their knowledge of other civilizations and times, and parents who do the same. My wife learned from a client about her son Randy who lives in the Chicago area and sometimes mentioned to his mom his Indian friends. She thought he was fantasizing. One day his class went on an outing to the Field Museum in downtown Chicago. His mom was one of the chaperones. When their guide stood in front of a grouping of Native American artifacts and asked if anyone knew what one of the implements was, five-year-old Randy spoke up with both its name and an explanation of its use. He then further astounded everyone by accurately naming and describing the function of everything else in the same display.

Particularly enchanting is the story told by Dan Millman of four year old Sachi, who wanted time alone with her baby brother when he was newly arrived. Her parents finally agreed, while wondering if this could be sibling rivalry. As a precaution, they listened at the crack of the partially open door to the baby's room. They were stunned to hear her earnestly ask her brother to tell her again what God felt like because she was beginning to forget.[7]

The movie *Fairy Tale, a True Story,* is about children who photographed real fairies at the Great Houdini's request. In the actual event this movie is based on, Houdini wasn't involved. The man who brought the affair into prominence was Sir Arthur Conan Doyle, the author of the Sherlock Holmes classics. The grownups that tried to witness the fairies could not see them, but were amazed by the photos. After seeing this movie both my wife Carol and our daughter Gina were visited by the fairies during the night. What they saw correlated well with the movie but went far beyond in vivid detail. Gina was so startled she screamed, thus scaring them away. My wife also saw the fairies in the twilight of awakening, but she likewise overreacted and has been visited only one time since then.

My wife and I have a doctor friend named Jeanne who remembers a precious moment years ago when she was flying a kite with her five year old son Charlie. The kite and string got so tangled in a tree that they couldn't free it. Charlie said, "Don't worry mom, I know I can get this kite out of the tree!" Then he closed his eyes, put his forehead to the ground, and moments later the kite floated gently away from the tree. Sometimes adults retain or regain such abilities. Using similar levitation techniques Edward Leedskalnin, who weighed only 100 pounds, single handedly quarried and raised blocks of stone weighing as much as 28 tons to build his residence, a Coral Castle on ten acres. Now his home is a tourist attraction just South of Miami, Florida. The fitting of the stones astounds engineers and is so precise as to remind one of the Great Pyramids and Machu Pichu.[8]

When Uri Geller demonstrated on national television his ability to bend a spoon with his mind, what was never brought to the nation's attention were the thousands of children, and a few adults, who duplicated this feat because they saw him do it. A well documented case was that of eleven year old Juni who is Japanese. Just hearing the broadcast was all the impetus he needed.[9] A few years ago my son Matt met James Twyman, the author of *Emissaries of Light* and ten other wonderfully enlightening books. He learned in his travels how to bend a spoon with his mind and personally taught Matt the same skill. If you go to his web site: www.emissaryoflight.com, you can also learn from James Twyman how to develop your own spoon bending ability. China has recently begun to openly support the development of such abilities and now has hundreds of thousands of children with extraordinary capabilities because they are not limiting themselves.[10]

Many books, TV shows, and prominent personalities are giving us an expanded understanding, such as medium James Van Praagh, who has been on more than 5,000 radio and TV shows. In April of 2002, he was portrayed by Ted Danson in a made-for-TV movie that was broadcast by ABC. In 1997 I was at the Whole Life Expo in Chicago. While I was there James was scheduled to address a randomly assembled audience of thousands, much as he has done more publicly on his recent nationally televised show, *Beyond*. I arrived with the auditorium one third filled, but ended up seated in the front row because friends had unexpectedly saved me a seat. James started off by relaying the words from a man who was killed in a fire that was a surprise to him. I stood up because when I was very young, that is how my father died. After I gave him permission to come to me, James proceeded to describe scene after scene he was seeing, all recent incidents in my life. Then he described a handsaw I had used a month earlier that had my family's name marked on it. I learned for the first time that this tool had actually been my father's, and not my grandfather's as I had thought until that moment. At the end of my public session with James Van Praagh, it was obvious that my father had been watching over me for the more than 40 years since his body died. Maybe during the early stages of his recovery my wife's nephew Mike could see as James Van Praagh sees thus revealing to him the presence of a young girl who was invisible to the rest of us. In his initial childlike recovery Mike could articulate what it is possible many children sometimes see. Unlike Mike they cannot explain their perception to the grownups around them nor the greater reality they experience.

These gaps in comprehension limit in other ways. My wife was born with a knowingness that her hands were meant to heal. As a child she would pretend to be a doctor, with local cats and dogs as patients, because she didn't know of any other form of healer or healing. Now she is a clinical esthetician and Reiki master, both professions where you "heal" with your hands.

At one of his *Magical Child* seminars, Dr. Joseph Chilton Pearce had a man share what for him had been a "disorientating and confusing" experience. His eight-year-old son had been whittling with a knife, slipped, and cut the arteries in his left wrist. He was screaming as the blood sprayed. Without thinking the panicked father grabbed his son's face, "looked into his eyes, and commanded, 'Son, let's stop that blood!' The screaming stopped, the boy beamed back, said 'okay,' and together they stared at the gushing blood and shouted, 'blood, you stop that!'" The blood stopped, the wound healed quickly, and the father nearly came unhinged by the unexpected assault on his reality.[11] The Menninger Foundation has scientifically documented adult Jack Schwarz, who retained his childhood ability such that he can heal deep wounds instantly.[12] It is my hope that this journey via the exceptional experiences of a few adults, and the childhoods of others, has awakened memories of your childhood reality and the potential you began with.

There are many prominent examples coming forth today to enlarge our concept of reality. Dean Kraft discovered his healing abilities during the non-thought action he took upon witnessing an automobile accident resulting in a mortally injured woman. To his surprise he healed the woman! Dean was thoroughly researched scientifically. He tells his story in his book *The Touch of Hope,* which was also made into a TV movie first broadcast on NBC on October 10, 1999. Other examples are: John Edward in the UPN channel 50 hit *Crossing Over,* which is broadcast out of New York daily thus demonstrating his ability to communicate with our departed loved ones; local Chicago celebrity, author, and teacher Carolyn Myss, who has been on the *Oprah Winfrey* show and made numerous other appearances demonstrating her ability as a medical intuitive capable of reading our energy field as easily as we read books; Barbara Ann Brennan, who founded, and for more than 20 years with 5,000 graduates, has run the prestigious Barbara Brennan School of Healing in New York. It takes four years to graduate as a hands-on healer from this institution.[13] Then there is my friend Rev. Douglas Buchanan, whom many are aware of as having photographic recall and an encyclopedic knowledge of every subject we have ever queried him on. Douglas reads a book in only a few minutes and despite a busy schedule, fits in seven books a week. These people are here to help us remember that there are some who retained a portion of their childhood potential.

We are born as seagulls, or maybe even golden-winged, white-unicorn horses in a penguin world, yet few of us retain the ability to run and fly. Like a penguin we settle for waddling awkwardly on earth and being able to swim, our wings no longer capable of flight. We are creative enough to do something with even these limitations, so we laugh at Charlie Chaplin's waddle, marvel at Fred Astaire dancing in a tuxedo, and thrill to Julie Andrews as a nun singing in the *Sound of Music.* Those among us who manifest additional abilities are often the ones we penguins cannot stop, the savants of the world who are autistic or distanced in other ways so society cannot effectively "educate" them; or those who are just plain stubborn or so enchanted they retain their childlike nature into adulthood so that a few of their magnificent Pegasus gifts cling like wonderful remnants.

Figure 1.1

Stories of Santa Claus, the and so on are society's limited imagination and sense of wonder. reluctantly burst the illusion by telling them

Figure 1.2

Tooth Fairy, Peter Pan, Tinker Bell, attempts to help children retain their When they are around seven or eight we that Santa Claus does not exist, and that mom and dad really put the quarter under their pillow at night when they lost a tooth.

As a penguin, remember the times you felt frustrated taking tests. Remember the courses you took and grades you received that left you with a feeling of failure through not having met your own expectations or those of your parents and peers. Even if you are one of the rare super achievers who never felt a sense of failure, remember the pressure of cramming for exams and for many, the long overnighters. By the time a person graduates from college they will have taken an average of 2,600 tests.[14] Remember the sense of loss of knowledge as it all decayed into forgetfulness once you passed the tests and went on with your life. Those failures were the product of a system and not an indication of who or what you are.

What I have presented so far suggests that *you are but a dim reflection of what you could be.* As a child you made all of the sounds necessary to speak any language spoken on this planet, were telepathic with yours, other species, and even sometimes other dimensions or realities, could sense and feel perfectly the emotional climate around you, had marvelous creativity, and potentially had the ability to do extraordinary phenomena including spoon bending, telekinesis and other reality manipulations. Penelope Smith, who has written a number of enlightening books on animal communication, retained the ability to communicate with animals telepathically because they brought such joy into her life, even though she knew she was different. She never talked about her abilities when she was growing up.

In subsequent chapters this book will also discuss some of the indicators that you had perfect pitch, perfect memories, and could see into the subtle realms including auras and other entities such as our departed loved ones. In addition, you probably had a host of other abilities that penguin culture graduates such as myself cannot imagine or even understand.

As you grew up you pruned down until your abilities became a minuscule subset of your true potential thus making you what you are now, around average in most aspects and occasionally challenged or gifted. I contend that who you are now, even if you are another Michael Jordan, Mozart, or Einstein, is a pale shadow of your unbound potential.

My objective in this first chapter is to help you remember what you long ago suppressed and denied, even if only a small portion of it, and to assist you in making a conscious decision to reawaken this potential. The rest of this book documents pertinent information and develops techniques for reawakening your dormant legacy. You have an immense depository of personal wealth that for all intents and purposes, has only seen withdrawals in the nickel and dime range. As part of this process we will explore a holistic approach to our planet incorporating both Eastern and Western sciences in order to develop holistic thinking and full-brained potential. I believe that a balanced blend is necessary and that scientific inquiry is meant to be a tool for understanding, not a container for limiting. I once again ask you to *remain as open as you possibly can* because to be effective, my presentation must overcome or bypass the endless permutations of barriers and fears all cultures are built upon.

The basic purpose of this book is to give you the tools and opportunity to rebuild yourself naturally using your own talents and unique combination of abilities. *Now is the time to remember what you as a child forgot while becoming a penguin.* Penguins dress alike, congregate in groups that chatter a lot, and spend a lot of time sitting on their eggs looking around at a barren black and white landscape. They live in a world where the vast ocean they swim in can also consume them, therefore one penguin being the same as another they make sure that there is always a plentiful supply of penguins. By becoming a penguin most abandon 99 percent of their abilities and join the courageous survivors who are really the walking wounded, the dysfunctional competent who dominate and mold society. The few really exceptional people who slip past society's filters are often labeled as "gifted," "weird," or a "freak of nature."

Your are not a "freak of nature." You are you! *You are unique, one of a kind with a combination of abilities found in no other.* You are not a penguin; you have only made yourself appear to be a penguin to fit in. *You have abilities far beyond the penguin mold: abilities such as being able to read an average book in less than five minutes at a minimum rate of 25,000 words per minute with perfect recall, plus genius level creativity.* So, make a new contract! Get rid of that which isn't you and reunite with that which you have been all along. Remember that child who was so richly endowed. Release the penguin accouterments. Let go of the suit you donned to fit in. Quoting Gita Bellin, "Be outrageous! People who achieve mastery have the ability to be outrageous."

Exercise 1.2 – RELEASING AND CLEANSING YOURSELF

Write a list of the limitations and failures that you wish to let go of and ceremonially burn it. This is sometimes done as a burning bowl ceremony. However, a fireplace, pan on the stove, or outdoor bonfire will all do nicely. This is an act of releasing, a parting with old clothes and actions that no longer fit your true form.

Exercise 1.3 – YOUR LETTER OF RENEWAL, GROWTH AND EXPANSION

Now write a letter to yourself as a new contract of renewal, growth, and expansion that you wish to invoke without limitations. This is a return to the promise you were as a child. Place it in a secure area that has meaning to you such as: where you meditate, the top of your chest of drawers, Your private garden area, or in a safe place such as your diary where it can serve as both a bookmark and a constant reminder. Reunite with that which you really were all along but forgot. Now is the time to remember!

So let it be written, so let it be done!
Yul Brenner as the Pharaoh Rameses in *The Ten Commandments*

**Grown-ups never understand anything for themselves,
and it is tiresome for children to be always and forever explaining things to them.**
Antoine De Saint-Exupery, *The Little Prince*

Know you what it is to be a child?
It is to be something very different from the man of today.
It is to have a spirit yet streaming from the water of baptism;
it is to believe in love,
to believe in loveliness,
to believe in belief;
it is to be so little that the elves can reach to whisper in your ear;
it is to turn pumpkins into coaches,
and mice into horses,
lowness into loftiness,
and nothing into everything,
for each child has its fairy godmother in its soul.

Francis Thompson Shelley

The human mind-brain system is designed for functions radically different from and broader than its current uses. An astonishing capacity for creative power is built into our genes, ready to unfold. Our innate capacities of mind are nothing less than miraculous, and we are born with a driving intent to express this capacity.

Joseph Chilton Pearce: *Magical Child* [15]

I have discovered the secrets of the pyramids, and have found out how the Egyptians and the ancient builders in Peru, Yucatan, and Asia, with only primitive tools, raised and set in place blocks of stone weighing many tons!

Edward Leedskalnin [16]

Don't try to bend the spoon, because that's impossible.
Just realize the truth, that there is no spoon.

From the movie – *The Matrix*

All gifts spring from the desire and longing for Love

James Twyman – *The Spoonbenders Course*

I love the story of a little girl who showed her teacher a picture she
painted of a tree. The tree was purple. The teacher said,
"Sweetheart, I've never seen a purple tree, now have I?"
"O?" said the little girl. "That's too bad."

Marianne Williamson, *A return to Love* [17]

I do not understand what it meant to be Dalai Lama.
As far as I knew, I was just one small boy among many.

Dalai Lama

We begin life in-spirit seeking physicality
We end life in-carnate seeking spirituality

Melvin Lewis Thomas

To see a World in a Grain of Sand
and a Heaven in a Wild Flower,
hold infinity in the palm of your hand,
and eternity in an hour.

William Blake, *Auguries of Innocence*

SECTION II – WHAT IS YOUR EQUIPMENT SUPPOSE TO DO?

NOW you are ready to hear the automobile dealership's explanation about what your equipment is really capable of. The purpose underlying the next five chapters is to give you some idea of the awesome majesty and potential you are born with, and which occasionally a few have even demonstrated. You do not aspire to build the Parthenon by studying tract housing, nor a Ferrari by mimicking pickup trucks. Look instead to the monuments of greatness for your starting point. They rose only a little above the crowd yet shone brightly for it. Think what would happen if the crowd chose to shine thus inspiring all to express their brilliance as their starting point, then built from there!

Chapter 2 – YOUR BRAIN

> *The human brain is an enchanted loom where millions of flashing shuttles weave a dissolving pattern, always a meaningful pattern, though never an abiding one. It is as if the Milky Way entered upon some cosmic dance.*
>
> Sir Charles Sherrington

> **Intuition is the clear conception of the whole at once**
>
> Johann Lavater

> **An Occidental slip on an Oriental Rug**
>
> Gerard Wilkins

IN her book *Mansfield Park*, Jane Austin says,

> *If one faculty of our nature may be called more wonderful than the rest of it, I do think it is memory. There seems to be something more speakingly incomprehensible in the power, the failures, the inequalities of memory, than in any other of our intelligences. The memory is sometimes so retentive, so serviceable, so obedient – and at others so bewildered and so weak – and at others again, so tyrannical, so beyond control!*

Although the basis may be debatable, it used to be commonly estimated that *we use effectively between 3 percent to 7 percent of our brain's capacity.* I believe that Tony Buzan is more accurate when he cites *modern estimates indicating that our effective utilization is less than 1 percent.*[1] Given that the average intelligence quotient is suppose to be 100 while using less than 1 percent of our brain's capacity, then we have a potential IQ vastly beyond the current average. Until recently the highest recorded IQ was attributed to Maria Vos Savant with a score of slightly over 250. However, according to the book the *Indigo Children,* which characterizes the recent changes in our children and their associated "Indigo" nature, the average IQ for the children arriving on the planet today is 130. My generation had an average IQ of 100 and only one in a thousand had an IQ as high as 130. For the Indigo Children, one in a thousand is a genius, while only one in a million was at that level for my generation. In addition, Indigos are full-brain thinkers whereas my generation was trained to be predominately left-brained thinkers. I believe that the rapidly arriving Indigo Children will increase the record IQ considerably, as we have a lot of room to grow. In so doing, they will be resisting society's programming attempts to mold them in the "safe" penguin form of being like everybody else.[2, 3, 4]

As the new children arrive, where does that leave the older generation? *All of us used our brains more completely as a child than we do now, as evidenced by the abilities we have abandoned along the way.* I assure you that the rest of it is not there solely to serve as an even substrate for your hair! To see how we can reactivate that which we have allowed to atrophy, let us look at the human brain in greater detail. In no way will we explore the full complexity of what is known of how the brain functions, but it will help if we at least understand the different components and departments, their functions, and how they relate to each other.

8

YOUR BRAIN'S BUILDING BLOCKS

Let us begin with the smallest units that are the building blocks your brain works with. The cells of your brain are called neurons. You have about as many as there are stars in the Milky Way galaxy. That is 100,000,000,000, or 1 with 11 zeros after it. If you take your home computer as an example, it may have a gigabyte of main memory, that is 1 with 9 zeros after it. Your brain therefore has one hundred times the memory of even a well-endowed personal computer.

Personal computer memory sites have only a few electrical connections that allow access to them. The memory sites of your mind, the neurons, are connected with as many as 20,000 dendrites to other neurons forming a net of enormous power with combinations that vastly exceed the number of atoms in the known universe. Dendrites are like computer hyperlinks. The dendrites in this book are the stories and metaphors, such as penguins and automobiles, plus the references to other books and workshops, which provide continuity throughout the narrative to help string together the concepts that, like neurons, hold specific thoughts.[5]

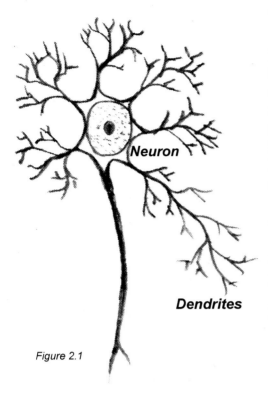

Neuron

Dendrites

Figure 2.1

When your home computer retrieves information it does so from one memory site at a time in a methodical sequence until all that was requested is retrieved. When your brain retrieves memories all the applicable neurons fire in a cascade that quickly avalanches to canvas·your entire mind. Rapidly retrieved are all applicable and related data, from all locations, organized and ready to use as needed. Computers are a toy next to the awesome processing power of your brain. *Your brain has been called the enchanted loom, the most astoundingly complex, beautiful thing in existence.*[6] You were not, however, born with this power at your command.

When you were a newborn baby your brain was only slightly organized. Developing it into a functional reasoning unit was one of the major tasks you had to perform. Every action and associated thought that was reinforced by repetition built your brain's neural net structure via a process called myelination. In essence, you wove patterns of thought, emotion, and feeling in what was initially a blank slate of gray matter. Each repetition added another strand until you had rope forming a well-established neural path, a well-myelinated structure. Thus you developed your brain into a reflection of your experiences, behaviors, and accompanying thoughts.

YOUR BRAIN'S MAJOR DIVISIONS

Human brains are inherently adaptable and can rewire to compensate for losses, even large ones from strokes and accidents. From my stint working for the government, there is an excellent example of how flexible our minds can be.

Pilots are an elite community. The best are selected to be fighter pilots. When I worked at the USAF Armstrong Research Laboratory in Mesa Arizona, the fighter pilots I worked with told the story of the F-15 pilot named Joe who sustained a blow to his head in an accident at home and lost consciousness temporarily. Joe was rushed to the hospital for a compete physical examination and placed on the Duty Not to Include Flying (DNIF) list until it could be shown that he was okay. This is standard procedure because the military watch their pilots with great care as a consequence of the million dollars in training invested in them. The magnetic resonance image (MRI) of Joe's head revealed that he had only half a brain, the other half being completely missing, apparently from birth. Other than this physical aberration, he was found fit to fly and returned to duty. The story, jokingly told after that, was that anyone could be a fighter pilot, look at Joe, he only has half a brain. No right brain/left brain dilemmas for Joe; he has the problem solved. What this example illustrates is that left brain/right brain delineations are ones of function and not anatomical placement. However, the question this raises is, how was it possible that Joe could function at elite levels, the best of the best, with only half a brain? Could it be that we are not really living up to our full brain potential? Maybe we ought to investigate the brain further.

*As depicted in **Figure 2.2**, your brain is actually three specialized layers. At the base is the reptilian brain or brain stem. It controls many of your instincts such as breathing and*

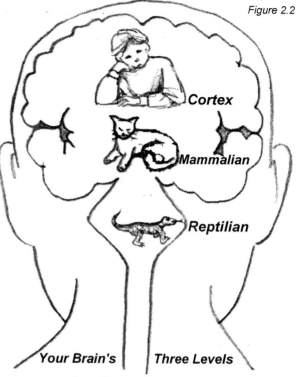

Figure 2.2

Cortex

Mammalian

Reptilian

Your Brain's | **Three Levels**

heartbeat. It, along with the old brain or the cerebellum, is the means by which you connect to the earth matrix, our perception of reality.[7] *The next layer is the limbic or the early mammalian brain, which wraps like a collar around the brain stem and controls emotions. The cortex is at the top of the stack and it enables you to think, talk, reason, and create.* **Figure 2.3** illustrates how it is typically divided functionally. Both figures have been reprinted with permission from *Your Child's Growing Mind*, written by Jane M. Healy and published by Doubleday, a division of Random House.[8, 9, 10] *At the back of the head located under the cortex is the cerebellum. It is vital for storing muscle memory and higher reasoning functions.* On the next page, **Figure 2.4** is a description of the parts of the brain and the functions they perform.[11]

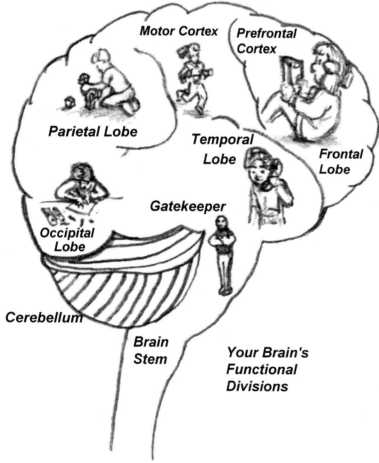

Motor Cortex

Prefrontal Cortex

Parietal Lobe

Temporal Lobe

Frontal Lobe

Gatekeeper

Occipital Lobe

Cerebellum

Brain Stem

Your Brain's Functional Divisions

Figure 2.3

Figure 2.4 – OVERVIEW OF YOUR BRAIN'S FUNCTIONAL DIVISIONS[12, 13]

YOUR CEREBRAL CORTEX'S FUNCTIONAL DIVISIONS (Command Central)

- **Prefrontal cortex** – (Forehead area) – Thinking, muscle control, and foveal control for your eyes.
- **Motor cortex** – (Top of the head) – Activity.
- **Temporal lobe** – (Located by the temple) – Listening, speech, vestibular, and smell.
- **Parietal lobe** – (Toward the back of the head) – Sensory, including taste.
- **Occipital lobe** – (At the back of the head) – Vision.

THE TWO HEMISPHERES OF YOUR CEREBRAL CORTEX

- **Left brain** – The masculine side for most people because it emphasizes academic thought – logic, words, numbers, mathematics, and sequencing.
- **Right brain** – The feminine side for most people because it emphasizes creative thought – intuition, rhyme, rhythm, music, pictures, daydreaming, and imagination.
- **Corpus callosum** – Links the left and right brains together for holistic thought.

YOUR BRAIN'S FUNCTIONAL LEVELS

- **Top** – Your **cortex** for thinking, talking, seeing, hearing, and creating.
- **Center** – Your **limbic** or "old mammalian" brain – which is similar to the brains of other warm-blooded mammals. It controls your emotions such as fear, rage, sexuality, love, and passion, and has a key role to play in your memory.
- **In back** – Your old or fourth brain, the **cerebellum (little brain),** for managing muscle memory, learning and speech. It and the brain stem are also your connection for some nonordinary phenomena.[14]
- **Bottom** – Your **brain stem** near the top of your neck, also called the **reptilian brain** because it is similar to the brains of cold-blooded reptiles. Part of it is the **medulla oblongata.** It controls instinctive functions such as breathing, heartbeat, and defensive reactions.

YOUR BRAIN AND EMOTIONS WORK TOGETHER

It is significant to note that the emotional and sexual center of the brain also controls memory, thus *you remember better when you are emotionally involved.* Do you remember the first time you ever saw a nail? Do you remember the first time you stepped on a nail? *Another way to increase memory is to activate the entire brain as with singing, for the left brain will process the words while the right brain processes the music thus making songs easy to remember,* a fact the advertising industry often capitalizes on with their jingles. Hence people who typically stutter can often sing words without a problem.

When we are conceived and have developed far enough to have a brain, nerve nets are developed first in the reptilian brain. Five months after conception the vestibular system develops. It's the motion detector for the body. Building this part of the brain requires motion as stimulation for further development. That is why children love to spin and ride on amusement rides while grownups are not as enchanted having already developed their neural nets.[15]

Central to our development is also our emotions, which are neurochemically woven with our mind. Computer scientist David Carpenter sums it up nicely by stating that emotions are inseparable from thought and are "inextricably tied up with bodily states. The bodily state is part of the emotion, feeds it and helps define it. This means that ultimately you don't think just with your brain; *you think with your brain and body both." The point in the body where most emotion processing originates is the junction between the body and the brain, known as the limbic system. That is the area of the brain that lies between the reptilian brain and the neocortex.*[16]

YOUR BRAIN'S TWO HALVES AND HOW TO UNIFY THEM ☯

By plucking her petals, you do not gather the beauty of the flower.

Rabindranath Tagore

Japanese Kanji for: *Figure 2.5*

The MASTERY of LEARNING

学識を究める

Gakushiki   wo   kiwameru

Gä kö shē´ kē   hwō'a   kē wä mir´ěr ö

The top processing jobs for your brain are reserved for the cerebral cortex, or "bark" of the brain as it translates literally. For this part of the brain, the development of language itself sets up associated patterns in the cerebral cortex. If you grow up in China or Japan, you learn to write a picture language, called kanji, which will be largely learned through the right side of the brain. Growing up in the western "alphabet" cultures you learn how to take in information through all of your senses, but to communicate using linear writing, which is usually a left brain function.[17] The marriage of the two halves of your brain, the gestalt with the logical, the right brain with the left brain, mirrors the coming together of the intuitive–based East with the logic–based West, a process that is happening both internally with the learning revolution and externally with world events.

The East has long specialized with going inward, having fewer resources for expressing outwardly, which more typically happens in the resource-abundant West. However, if both paths have the same goals of truth and unity, then they will have the same destination. The marriage of the East's inward and the West's outward paths is more than just the mating of intuition with cognition; it is a marriage of the two halves of our brain and body, and the sexes. Understanding the partners in this marriage is essential for understanding the resultant union. *Paramahansa Yogananda said that, "In the course of world travel I have sadly observed much suffering: in the Orient, suffering chiefly on the material plane; in the Occident, misery chiefly on the mental or spiritual plane."*[18]

In the West, epitomized by America, cattle are a mere commodity. They are treated as dumb animals only useful for their by-products. In the East, epitomized by India, they are worshipped. In the West, we focus only on the single known lifetime. In the East, there is holistic awareness of multiple life-times. Babaji, an avatar who is considered to be the Yogi-Christ of modern India, advises that, "The East and West must establish a golden middle path of activity and spirituality combined."[19] In the joining of the East with the West, the Orient with the Occident, the right brain of the Earth with its left brain, we have hope of ending suffering on all planes. My opening

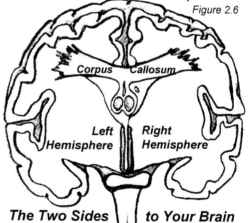

Figure 2.6

Corpus Callosum

Left Hemisphere   Right Hemisphere

The Two Sides   to Your Brain

statement for this chapter cited Maria Vos Savant as currently the individual with the highest known IQ. The title of one of Maria's books is, *The Power of Logical Thinking*. One reason I believe her IQ will soon be surpassed is based on **Figure 2.7**. It is a half brain title. Although it is likely that she is full brain functional her emphasis is not balanced. Those who surpass her certainly will be. She has in fact, probably already been eclipsed, by Greg Smith, whose IQ is so high that having maxed out every IQ test he has ever taken, is so far unmeasurable. Oprah Winfrey featured Greg and a few other child prodigies on her October 10th, 2002 program. At that time Greg was 13 and a senior in college with the objective of getting four Ph.D's. He has already been nominated for the Nobel Peace Prize for his humanitarian work during his summer vacations. **Figure 2.6,** reprinted from *Unicorn's are Real* by Barbara Meister Vitale with permission from publisher Jalmar Press, depicts the brain's hemispheric divisions.[20] **Figure 2.7** lists the key known differences between the two halves of our brain and body.[21]

Figure 2.7 – **SUMMARY OF DIFFERENCES BETWEEN YOUR BRAIN's HEMISPHERES**[22,23]	
♂- left for LOGIC -♂	♀- right for GESTALT-♀
Usually left half of brain	_Usually right half of brain_
Typically controls right side of body	_Typically controls left side of body_
Masculine/Western side	_Feminine/Eastern side_
Splitter - starts with the pieces first	_Lumper - sees whole picture first_
Parts of language, syntax, semantics	Language comprehension, Image, emotion, meaning
Letters, sentences, consonants	Rhythm, flow, dialect, vowels, signature
Details, numbers, analysis, linear	Images, intuition, estimates
Looks at differences, planned – structured	Looks at similarities, spontaneous – fluid
Sequential thinking, controls feelings	Simultaneous thinking, free with feelings,
Language, past-future oriented	Feelings/experiences, now oriented
Technique	Flow and movement
Sports (Hand/eye/foot placement	Sports (flow and rhythm)
Art (media, tool use, how to)	Art (image, emotion, flow)
Music (notes, beat, tempo)	Music (passion, rhythm, image)
Growth spurt from ages 7-9	_Growth spurt from ages 4-7_

The part of your brain that unites the two halves is called the corpus callosum, which marries your brain's hemispheres and associated body halves to facilitate full brain and body potential. People with attention deficit hyperactive disorder (ADHD) have a corpus callosum that is markedly smaller than people with normal attention spans. _Females typically have 10 percent overall, and as much as much as 33 percent more fibers in the frontal portion of this area than males._[24,25] _It is the opinion of Dr. Hannaford that these differences are not genetic but are the consequence of environment. The freedom that women have to express emotions and engage in rich dialogue, as opposed to men who concentrate primarily on left brain activities while controlling their emotions, results in a greater holistic brain capacity than in males._ Likewise, people with ADHD come from an environment that does not allow them to express themselves adequately either emotionally or verbally.

However, the masculine has to contend with a problem that does not exist for the feminine. The masculine aspect does not experience oneness when it looks out into the world; it sees only division and separation as opposed to the feminine side, which automatically sees unity and oneness. When the masculine side begins to see unity, it relaxes and the corpus callosum opens in a new way, allowing integration. This process also turns on the adjacently located pineal gland, or third eye. The significance of that event is discussed more fully in **Chapter 5**, which covers vision.[26,27]

Cross-lateral movements such as babies crawling, walking, yogic alternate nostril breathing, the Brain Gym® movements discussed in **Chapter 15**, _juggling, and sports in general, help develop the corpus callosum and foster whole brain abilities such as creativity and linguistics._[28] It is worth noting that in the West we typically begin teaching printing the alphabet at the age of five, or first grade, yet according to the growth data, the brain's logic circuitry to support this doesn't grow to accommodate such activities until between the ages of seven to nine.

Similarly, _inner speech development doesn't occur until around the age of seven, so prior to that age children naturally think out loud and write cursive. Being forced to read silently, and write in block letters, will handicap most._[29] Dr. Joseph Chilton Pearce relays the experience of watching one of his sons begin unfolding as a music prodigy. By the age of five and a half he had perfect pitch and composed music. By the age of six he played Bach, Clementi, and Bartok on the piano. Yet all of these skills diminished when went to school and began learning to read and write. By the time he was eight no vestige remained.[30] In general then, the consequences of the mismatch between how we raise and instruct our children and how their minds work, is a high failure rate and associated low self-esteem. These are more examples of how we squander the vast potential our children have, while turning them into penguins.

Exercise 2.1 – ACKNOWLEDGING YOUR BRAINS ATTRIBUTES

Write a list of your attributes - your strengths and weaknesses. Focus on your brain's functional divisions as outlined in **Figure 2.4** and what abilities and challenges you find in your brain's two hemispheres as outlined in **Figure 2.7**. By doing this exercise you become more aware of who you are and internalize the understanding of how your brain is built. Such knowledge helps you become who you wish to be.

He that is good with a hammer tends to think everything is a nail.

Abraham Maslow

I felt a cleavage in my mind
As if my mind had split;
I tried to match it, seam by seam,
But could not make them fit.

The thought behind I strove to join
Unto the thought before,
But sequence raveled out of reach
Like balls upon a floor

Emily Dickinson

In each of us two powers preside, one male, one female; and in the man's brain, the man predominates over the woman, and in the woman's brain, the woman predominates over the man…. If one is a man, still the woman part of the brain must have effect; and a woman also must have intercourse with the man in her. Coleridge perhaps meant this when he said that a great mind is androgynous. It is when this fusion takes place that the mind is fully fertilized and uses all its faculties.

Virginia Woolf [31]

When you make the two one, and when you make the inside like the outside and the outside like the inside, and the above like the below, and when you make the male and the female one into the same… then you will enter the kingdom of God.

Gospel of Thomas

If you are relaxed, I think your brain functions more effectively.

Dalai Lama

Left Brain, Right Brain - By Dr. Jean Houston [32, 33]

Left brain, right brain * get your head together
Left brain, right brain * get your head together
Get * * your head * * together.

The left brain discusses what your eyes can see
Teaches you to read and the one, two, three.
The left brain helps you structure your day,
If you didn't have a left brain, you couldn't say
That the right paints pictures,
Right brain loves stories,
Right brain makes scriptures,
And right brain dreams glories.

The right brain intuits things as a whole,
Synthesizes, integrates, believes in the soul.
The right brain visualizes patterns so strange,
If you didn't have a right brain, you'd never change.
And the left brain clock watches,

Left brain loves order,
Left brain hates blotches, and the
Left brain makes borders.

Left brain, right brain * get your head together
Left brain, right brain * get your head together
Get * * your head * * together.

And the corpus callosum acts like a road
For the two brains to share each other's load.
In one given second there's a quadrillion things
That the brain puts together and that's how it sings.
Whole brain wants teaching.
Whole brain needs learning.
Whole brain's out reaching.
The whole brain is yearning.

Left brain, right brain * get your head together
Left brain, right brain * get your head together
We'll get * * our heads * * together

Chapter 3 – YOUR MIND

We need to be more balanced, not always in our analytical minds…
It is up to you to choose the thoughts that remain in your mind…
Allow nothing to prevent you from accomplishing your mission…
Any belief becomes reality the moment it is accepted…
We bring about what we think about…
We can make the choice to create our own reality…
Hold onto your dream no matter what happens…
Dreams give birth to reality…
Life as you have ordered it has arrived…
Marina Raye

In shallow men the fish of little thoughts cause much commotion,
In oceanic minds, the whales of inspiration make hardly a ripple.
Saying from Hindu scriptures

The greatest discovery of my generation is that human beings
Can alter their lives by altering the attitudes of their mind.
William James

The antecedent to every action is a thought….
Once you know that what you think about expands,
You start getting real careful about what you think about.
Wayne Dyer

Thoughts are things!   *Thoughts are reality!*
Edgar Cayce   Daniel R. Condron

Thought is force, even as electricity and gravitation.
Lahiri Mahasaya

You may control a mad elephant;
You may shut the mouth of the bear and the tiger;
Ride the lion and play with the cobra;
By alchemy you may earn your livelihood;
You may wander through the universe incognito;
Make vassals of the gods; be ever youthful;
You may walk on water and live in fire;
But control of the mind is better and more difficult.
Thayumanavar

Imagination is the door through which disease as well as healing enters.
Disbelieve in the reality of sickness even when you are ill;
An unrecognized visitor will flee.
Sri Yukteswar

When we quiet the mind, the symphony begins.
Anonymous

IN the Fifth Gateway of his book, *Everyday Enlightenment, the Twelve Gateways to Personal Growth,* Dan Millman admonishes:

Tame Your Mind: You perceive the world through an obscure window of beliefs, interpretations, and associations. The world is therefore a reflection of your mind. As your mind clears, you perceive reality simply as it is. What does your experience of life reveal about your filters of perception?

Your brain provides a valuable function for your mind. Quoting Napoleon Hill, "More than forty years ago, the author, working in conjunction with the late Dr. Alexander Graham Bell, and Dr. Elmer R. Gates, observed that *every human brain is both a broadcasting and receiving station for the vibration of thought.*"[1]

Your brain is often compared to hardware, and your mind software. However, your mind is not limited to your brain, for your consciousness transcends your body. The literature on near death experiences (NDEs) confirms this. The first researcher to investigate this field extensively was Dr. Raymond Moody. He worked with people who had near death experiences and documented repeatedly that consciousness is independent of the body. He found compelling evidence that those having this experience were viewing reality from a different perspective than their body. Examples would be people who could describe what was "on top of the lights" in the operating room where their NDE occurred, or others who knew the names of emergency personnel who worked on them and could describe them accurately, despite having encountered them only while "unconscious." Dr. Moody chronicles story after story where people found themselves observing what was going on from a vantage point outside of their body. Their descriptions sometimes even included the thoughts of the people working on them and Dr. Moody's investigations confirmed their observations. The body, including the brain, is therefore just a vehicle for your consciousness, including your mind.[2]

The gurus and sages tell an even more expanded story. They indicate that *the brain is a logic machine and a communication device while the mind is independent and eternal.* A better analogy then would be to call the brain the hardware/sender/receiver unit and the mind the eternalware and great central library.

From the sleep research that has been done we learn that our brain cuts itself off from the body at night by gating (turning off) the reptilian brain so that no sensory input comes in. Isolated from your body, the brain goes into cycles of deep sleep alternating with periods of rapid eye movement (REM) during which we dream.[3]

From the foundation of modern psychology by Carl Jung and Sigmund Freud, great significance has been attributed to dreams. They recognized that the information conveyed symbolically by dreams could be critical to understanding an individual's behavior. Carl Jung in particular had a phenomenal memory that included reading books in libraries in his dreams and remembering them when he awakened. Years later he would sometimes come across the book that he had seen in his dream.[4] When my older son Trevor first received a draft of this book to read, he sent me the following email the next day:

> *I had a dream about reading your book. I never actually got around to reading your book last night, but I had to think twice this morning because the dream was so real. I no longer remember much about the dream, but I read a portion of your book (in the dream) and it was very well written. It flowed nicely, and I forgot you had written it... I remember thinking, "Oh yeah, my DAD wrote this!"*

Obviously, the dream state is a source of information independent of the body, yet all along we have been demonstrating that the mind/brain/body combination accounts for holistic thought. The conclusion is that the dream state does not need the body as a source of inspiration for the imagery it conveys to us. Therefore, based on the fact that the body cannot be the source of these dreams, and knowing from the near death literature that our mind is capable of ranging outside of our gated (incapacitated) body, the origins of dreams and what they tell us then becomes an important point to explore. Douglas Lockhart in his book, *Savazius – The Teachings of a Greek Magus*, explains dreams this way:

> *The dream world is like a simulator. It teaches you the correct attitude to have by presenting your attitudes in visual form. It shows you how to think clearly by visually presenting your thoughts with all their inner discrepancies on the surface. When a man dreams, his history is played back like a roll of cleverly edited film, and each frame contains some aspect of the man's character which requires his attention.*

Dreams can address the body, mind, or spirit thus coming from levels both internal and external to extend to the vastness of all creation. Understanding the imagery they provide has long been a source of guidance and insight for indigenous cultures. Dream interpretation is also given great significance in the Bible and other holy books around the world. Learning how to interpret and work with your dreams is therefore critical to holistic living and natural learning. Aborigines actually think of wakefulness as dreamtime, and sleep as reality time. The *Talmud* says that: **"*A dream not interpreted is like a letter that is not read.*"**

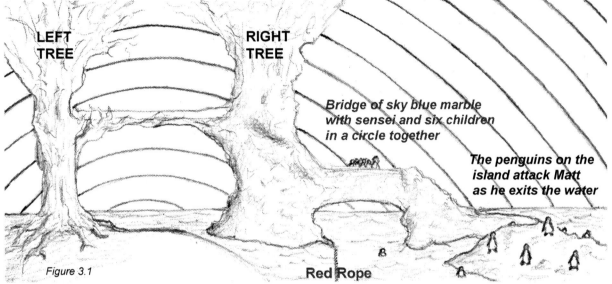

LEFT TREE

RIGHT TREE

Bridge of sky blue marble with sensei and six children in a circle together

The penguins on the island attack Matt as he exits the water

Figure 3.1

Red Rope

MATT'S DREAM

While reading a rough draft of this book my son Matt dreamed that he was walking out of a cave. He found himself in a large valley with a biodome over it. To his left, only 10 feet away, was a big tree. Matt had a compelling urge to climb it, but it was unclimbable. Looking up he saw that at the top it joined with the tree on his right, which was climbable as it sloped off to the right. Part way up the slope was a bridge of shimmering sky-blue marble. There was a sensei sitting on it teaching six children arrayed in a circle with him. When Matt tried to get to the base of the right tree he found it surrounded by water. Then he saw further to the right an island from which he could begin his ascent. Desiring to be on the island he was instantly across the water finding himself at the island's shoreline. Before he could advance and start his climb penguins stepped in front to block him. An authoritative voice in his head warned him that the penguins were dangerous and that they will attack in groups. The penguins worked together attacking from the front and behind to push him back toward a red rope barrier just above the shallow water. This time the authoritative voice in his head warned him, "Do not go under the red rope, avoid the red rope!" He stopped at the red rope and noticed that beyond it was an old and crumbling approach to climbing the right tree. It was too dangerous to climb. Seeing no way around the penguins, and having his back to the red rope, Matt had a sense that fighting was hopeless. He woke up.

MY INTERPRETATION OF MATT'S DREAM

Matt's dream "placed him" inside his skull with two large trees representing the masculine left and feminine right halves of his brain. As with the trees, the two halves of his brain were bridged together in unity at the top, the corpus callosum. The only way to climb to unity was via the feminine side on the right as it sloped gently. Then Matt came to water that he must traverse, the emotions being the way on the feminine side of the brain. His thoughts instantly transport him across the water to the island where he wished to be. On the island penguins attacked him in groups, as our penguin society typically does, thus blocking his way. His Higher Self began to advise him as to what to expect. The penguins pushed Matt to the red rope of anger that he was advised to not cross over. He observed that crossing that boundary would only lead to a false solution of great danger. He found himself losing the battle to the penguins as he awakened knowing that fighting was useless because he was so outnumbered.

Dreams typically present both the problem and the answer. The key in Matt's dream was how he got across the water, via his expectations. He thought his way across. The sensei and six children represented Matt's chakras, which are the primary energy centers of the body, the guru being the crown chakra. They were on the shimmering marble bridge of blue-sky thinking. Had Matt been able to change his thoughts he would have instantly been above the battle he placed himself in and on the bridge to unity. Then his chakras would have been in a perfect circle of childlike innocence, the circle being the ancient representation of God, or Matt's Higher Self in this instance.

Douglas Buchanan indicates that he knows of people who dream about penguins whom they immediately recognize as symbolizing the nuns from their school days. If you have a dream like this it is best to thank the nuns for the honorable duties they performed and to work to overcome the limitations all of our penguin cultures gave us along with their many gifts. Matt's dream conveys an impression of what penguin society represents and how dreams can support and reinforce us in our learning as Matt was learning, via reading this book. His dream is also clearly giving the message that *fighting the penguins, or getting angry at them, is not the answer. The only way above it all is to change your thoughts in a peaceful and loving way. The way to know what to do is to listen to your inner voice. The only path up is via the right side of the brain* and being above it all as the guru and children were in their circle of peace and enlightenment. They were showing *the way to unity is through the path of a child.* That child is in each of us, as is the unified circle of youthful wisdom.

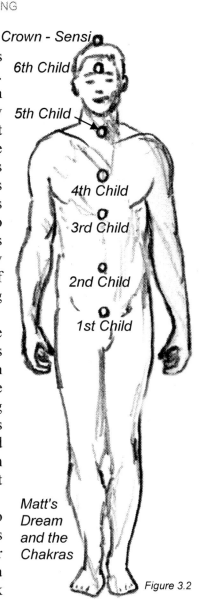

Crown - Sensei
6th Child
5th Child
4th Child
3rd Child
2nd Child
1st Child

Matt's Dream and the Chakras

Figure 3.2

Figure 3.3

Penguin Nun

Exercise 3.1 – JOURNAL YOUR DREAMS

If you are not already doing so, begin journaling your dreams. One technique to aid you in remembering them is to take a glass of water and place it on your bed stand. Drink half of it upon retiring while setting the intention to remember your dreams upon awakening when you drink the other half. When you awaken, whether in the morning or the middle of the night, avoid moving until you can remember enough detail to be certain that you captured the essence of the dream(s). You might have to have someone awaken you in the morning rather than use an alarm clock if you wish to avoid moving. If you don't remember your dreams at this point, drink the remainder of the water in the glass to refresh your memory. Don't be discouraged if at first you don't remember. Persistence pays off, usually within a week. *Keep a pencil and notepad or your journal next to where you sleep.* When you begin to remember, write it down. More will come to you as you write and understanding will likewise come. *After recording your dream, try analyzing it.* For resources in analyzing your dreams I suggest: *Mary Summer Rain's Guide to Dream Symbols,* or *Dreams – Your Magic Mirror,* by Sechrist, *How to Interpret Your Dreams,* by Mark Thurston, and *Edgar Cayce on Dreams,* which are all based on the highly informative Edgar Cayce material.

Your mind doesn't know anything,
Not any more than a book on a bookshelf knows anything.
It's soul of itself that knows.
Phil Morimitsu quoting Paul Twitchell

According to some of my dreams, I have some very close connection
with the Thirteenth Dalai Lama as well as the fifth Dalai Lama.
Dalai Lama

You cannot play with the animal in you without becoming wholly animal,
play with falsehood without forfeiting your right to truth,
play with cruelty without losing your sensitivity of mind.
He who wants to keep his garden tidy doesn't reserve a plot for weeds.
Dag Hammarskjold

Every good thought you think is contributing its share to the ultimate result of your life.
Grenville Kleiser

In dream time I never feel I am Dalai Lama.
Dalai Lama

We become what we contemplate.
Alphonse de Chateaubrillant: *La Réponse du Seigneur*

Your mind will be like its habitual thoughts:
For the soul becomes dyed with the color of its thoughts.
Marcus Aurelius

The mind is like a seed;
when cultivated it gives rise to many other good qualities.
Dalai Lama

Imagination is the unicorn that lifts us above the mundane chains
that bind the minds of many and flies us on fantastic wings
to a place where dreams DO come true.
Poem by V. Bassett [5]

Chapter 4 – YOUR STATES OF BEING

> There are a hundred and one arteries of the heart,
> one of them penetrates the crown of the head;
> moving upwards by it a man reaches the immortal.
> Khandogya Upanishad

> Leaving the old, both worlds at once they view,
> that stand upon the threshold of the new.
> Edmund Waller

> Do not take life's experiences too seriously. Above all, do not let them hurt
> you, for in reality they are nothing but dream experiences....
> If circumstances are bad and you have to bear them, do not make them a
> part of yourself. Play your part in life, but never forget that it is only a role.
> Paramahansa Yogananda, *Par-a-gram*

> In an instant, rise from time and space.
> Set the world aside and become a world within yourself.
> Shabestari (c. 1250-1320, Persian Sufi poet)

> Behold I am within all things, centering them.
> And I am without all things, controlling them.
> But I am not those things which I center and control.
> Walter Russell

> Nothing real can be threatened. Nothing unreal exists.
> Herein lies the peace of God.
> *A Course in Miracles*

> There was a child sent forth every day,
> and the first object he looked upon, that object he became,
> and that object became part of him for the day or a certain part of the day,
> or for many years or stretching cycles of years.
> Walt Whitman

> The snow goose need not bathe to make itself white.
> Neither need you do anything but be yourself.
> Lao-Tze

FROM the masters, sages, and seers who have come throughout all ages to help us remember who we are, and from modern science, we learn that *our mind/brain/body system has been built to operate in many different modes. These modes are what allow us to function as a spirit having a human experience. The purpose of being both awake and asleep on a daily basis is to transition through this range of states-of-being,* as our spirit finds incarnation difficult, much like being a puppeteer trying to put on a play. The sleep mode allows your spirit to put down the hand puppet and do other things both educational and of a repair nature for your puppet body, to enable you to keep functioning optimally. According to author, scientist, teacher, and healer Barbara Brennan:

> *The process of incarnation takes a lifetime.* It is not something that happens
> at birth and is then finished. To describe it, we need to use metaphysical terms.
> Incarnation is organic soul movement in which higher, finer vibrations or soul
> aspects are continually radiated downward through the finer auric bodies into the
> more dense ones and then finally into the physical body. These successive energies
> are utilized by the individual in her [their] growth throughout her [their] life.[1]

Another important author and teacher, Drunvalo Melchizedek, further adds that:

The human spirit's main focus starts at the bottom of the chakra system when you're born, then moves up during your life through the various stages.[2]

Our true purpose in being here then, is to learn to bring all of these stages and states of being into a unified whole, or state of oneness. When we attain that goal we graduate from Earth School. We are therefore much like Pinocchio who had free will and could go where he wanted. In *A Course in Miracles* it is explained thus: "Free will does not mean that you establish the curriculum; only that you can elect what you want to take at a given time." Learning how to freely operate and move between these states of being is an important step in achieving the unified state where the puppet attachments and their illusion of control are no longer required.

The immediate practical benefit of this understanding helps us cope with what mankind is currently experiencing. The rate at which mankind is acquiring knowledge is increasing exponentially such that in only a few years we double what we know. In the past few years we have learned as much as it took all of recorded history to acquire prior to that. The current way most of us learn is woefully inadequate to cope with this explosion of knowledge. By learning how to use our subliminal learning mode where we directly tap into the subconscious, we accelerate our learning to match this trend. More importantly though, we tap into our wisdom, which is critical if we are to conscientiously use this knowledge and the power that mankind possesses for either creation or destruction.

We are accompanied in this journey by Mother Earth who has a history of vibration modes much like our brain exhibits and thus can be thought of as going through the same stages of awareness as we are. According to physicist and author, Gregg Braden, the Schumann Frequency is the base frequency at which the earth resonates. It has historically hovered around eight cycles per second with such stability that the military once used it to calibrate their instruments. A cycle is a complete wave going past you transitioning from crest to trough and back to crest again. Eight cycles per second would be eight complete waves going by every second. This is a low vibration, so low that it is below normal hearing, a much lower note than any bass singer could ever hit. When a person meditates, or a healer attunes to heal, it has been scientifically demonstrated that they synchronize to this resonant earth frequency.[3]

A few decades ago the Schumann Frequency began increasing. Gregg Braden presents evidence that it is moving from the key Fibonacci series number of 8 to the next Fibonacci series number of 13. Based on the frequency ranges and associated states of being depicted in **Figure 4.1** on the next page, this could be interpreted as meaning that *the Earth is moving towards the high end of the subconscious alpha state transitioning to the low end of the beta state. By so doing the Earth integrates all the states it has experienced thus making them more readily available to us.* Douglas Buchanan believes the speedup of vibrations is an indication of the way we are processing karma (the consequences of past actions both individually and collectively) more quickly.[4]

From his experience Drunvalo Melchizedek states that: "*Mother Earth is a young child about two to six years old, depending on who you talk to. She is always a child, because she is a child.*"[5] The Kahuna's of Hawaii put that information into perspective when they tell us that humans are divided into three parts, the higher self (which connects to all that is), the middle self (duality consciousness), and the lower self (our primitive, basic, or child self). In order to contact your higher self you must first go down and contact your lower or basic self. Drunvalo states it as, "spirit must first move downward before it can reach to the heavens." Your lower self is your unconscious, or your subconscious, subliminal mind. It is part of the collective unconscious as stated by Jung.[6] *The subconscious mind is connected to all life on earth – past, present, and future.* The collective unconscious mind that Carl Jung speaks of is therefore coming from a single source, the matrix of Mother Earth. That is why your lower self, your subconscious, is like a child.[7]

Figure 4.1 – TREND ANALYSIS OF YOUR STATES OF BEING

STATE	BETA - β	ALPHA - α	THETA - Θ	DELTA - Δ
Cycles-per-sec	25 to 13	12 to 8	7 to 4	3 to 0.5
MIND	Conscious	Subconscious	Transconscious	Omniconscious
BRAIN	Calculates	Sends/receives	Passive	Auto pilot
BODY	Active	Restful	Quiescent	Rebuilding
BEING	Incarnated	Less incarnated	Out-of-body	Spirit (like death)
AGE	Adult	Child of 5	4 years to Baby	Embryo
SENSING	Five-senses	Intuitive listening	Trans-sense	Omnisensed
VISION	Two-eyes	One-eye (third eye)	Trans-eyes	Omnieyed
INTELLIGENCE	Normal	Intuitive/insightful	Genius/supermemory	Omniscient
AWARENESS	Wide awake	Relaxed alertness	REM dreaming	No memory
SEPARATION	Duality	Union	Oneness	Omnipresent
VEIL	Complete	Partly down	Mostly down	Gone
THINKS WITH	Words	Pictures	Holism	Transcendental
BEST FOR	Doing	Learning	Inspiring	Unknown tasks

YOUR MODES OF OPERATION

I created **Figure 4.1** to show how *your mind/brain/body system operates much as a radio that can be tuned to different stations. By learning how to dial down to a lower frequency a Zen-like anomaly occurs where as your mind goes slower, you get smarter.*[8] Metaphysical pioneer Ram Dass observed that: *"The quieter you become the more you can hear."* Socrates said: "Think less and feel more." This concept has been known for years in martial arts. For example, author and Zen expert Robert Linssen states that: "In judo, he who thinks is immediately thrown. Victory is assured to those who are physically and mentally nonresistant." Martial arts icon Bruce Lee said: "The less effort, the faster and more powerful you will become." As with your body, so with your mind. *True thinking begins where conscious thought ends. The point of nonresistance is the beginning of true power.* **Figure 4.1** is also a trend analysis of our mind/brain/body states in order to make these concepts easier to understand.

Figure 4.2, reprinted with permission from *The Learning Revolution*, graphs actual human brain wave patterns. What this information indicates is that from the practical perspective of trying to learn, the beta state is where your mind/brain/body is at its highest frequency of operation, and this is the state-of-being where you typically use your knowledge. The next lower state, the alpha state, is still a conscious state and is the best state-of-being in which to acquire your knowledge. The theta state, during which you usually sleep and dream, is the best place to go to seek inspiration. Finally, the delta state is when your body rebuilds while your spirit is elsewhere. Edgar Cayce noted that as the conscious mind is lulled to sleep, our senses collapse into a single sense, your "sixth sense," which closely resembles hearing. It is a state of pure intuition via listening.[9] Therefore, BETA is for doing, ALPHA is for insight, THETA is for inspiration, and DELTA is for renewal. To state it another way: *being awake is for doing, meditation is for insight, dreaming is for inspiration, and deep sleep is for rebuilding. Note that in school most of us were told to not day-dream, thus cutting off a vital source of creativity.*

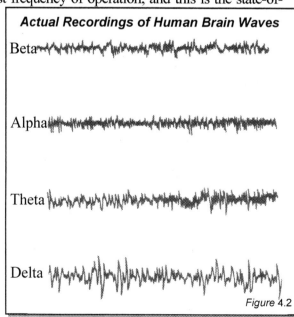

Actual Recordings of Human Brain Waves

Beta

Alpha

Theta

Delta

Figure 4.2

Another way of looking at your different states of being is to interpret this as scrolling back the clock and becoming more like a child as you move from the beta into the alpha and lower states. You are therefore reversing the process of birth and growth, which gradually transitions you as a newborn baby in delta to theta, then alpha, and finally as early as age five, to the beta state. You follow the same cycle every night on about an hour and a half schedule where you begin your sleep going deeply into the delta and every hour and half come up to the theta and rapid eye movement (REM) sleep, then back down into delta. This cycle follows the same pattern throughout the night, becoming shallower until you emerge from theta into alpha, and awaken having that moment as a golden opportunity to remember your dreams. This is the time to record them while you are still not consciously analyzing. Give yourself enough notes so later you will recall your dreams in sufficient detail.

THE PURPOSE OF DREAMING

Your dreams will be a source of inspiration and guidance letting you know how you are doing while giving you answers to the questions foremost on your mind as you went to sleep. *Learning how to analyze your dreams is like gaining a wise grandparent who counsels you every night.* Dreams are one of the primary feedback mechanisms your puppeteer uses to help you. When you awaken you emerge anew from the depths of sleep with your dreams as the gifts of the night like the stars that accompany the darkness.

In his book *Everyday Enlightenment, the Twelve Gateways to Personal Growth*, Dan Millman devotes his Sixth Gateway to working with this state, saying of it:

> *Trust Your Intuition: Below everyday awareness is a shamanlike, childlike consciousness – weaver of dreams, keeper of instinct. Your subconscious holds keys to a treasure house of intuitive wisdom, clear insight, and untapped power. All you have to do is look, listen, and trust, paying attention to dreams, feelings, and instinct. If you can't trust your inner senses, what can you trust?*

YOUR CIRCADIAN RHYTHM

Your circadian rhythm is your body's twenty-four hour clock cycle of rest, restoration, awakening, activity, shutting down, and rest again. The Chinese characterize this as a time when you cycle through the twelve meridians, each meridian addressing a different body system. *The importance of the daily circadian rhythm cannot be overstressed. Not only is sleep a critical state-of-being, but the sleep pattern is also critical.*

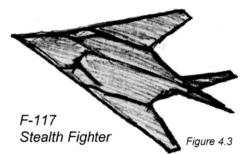

F-117
Stealth Fighter

Figure 4.3

Disturbing this pattern is what causes jet lag when people cross multiple time zones in a short period of time. People off pattern can become so traumatized that they cannot function properly. When the United States Air Force was still developing the F-117 Stealth fighter, and even after the plane first became operational, its flights were stringently guarded secrets. Flights were scheduled only at night over the highly classified and closely guarded airspace North of Las Vegas, Nevada. The pilots who flew these planes were the crème de la crème, the very best of the best. Typically they spent weekends with their families in Las Vegas during which time they tried to follow normal sleep patterns, then on Monday mornings they were bussed up North to spend their work week flying missions throughout the nighttime hours. Despite high motivation and exemplary skills, two pilots and the planes they were flying were lost due to pilot error. Even the threat of death didn't keep these pilots alert enough to prevent making either a fatal error, or possibly outright falling asleep. After investigating these accidents the Air Force was forced to modify procedures to accommodate the flying schedule to the pilot's circadian pattern.

All of us have probably experienced the same loss of functionality when trying to drive through the night because of some compelling reason to get to our destination. Some don't make it just as the pilots didn't make it. We become slaves to our technology rather than the way it was intended, our machines being slaves to us. In the process we sacrifice the circadian pattern that is fundamental to our ability to function. It needs to be honored in a consistent fashion. When you are zoned out you are not in alpha, beta, or theta, you are brain zoned out. You are as much as anything in the delta carrier tone and consequently only weakly incarnated. Zoned out people are therefore disconnected, uncoordinated, "out of their body." That is the danger of messing with your circadian rhythm. Hence, the F-117 pilots crashed, and so do many others on our highways.

YOUR DAILY BIRTH TO CURRENT AGE CYCLES

Why is it called morning after sunrise and mourning after death? Are these then different sides of the same door, a threshold you cross going in different directions? Why do we say something dawns on us, and say that it is a newborn day? Are all of these word usages playing off the same theme? For adherents to Siddha Yoga, 3 a.m. is the optimal time for meditation from the perspective of the central nervous system, which follows this same cycle on a daily basis.[10] *Every day is really like a birth. When we cycle through all of our states of being coming from deep delta sleep to full consciousness in the beta, we are really coming from in-spirit to in-carnate, to begin anew the task of running the body.* When we first awaken we begin the day much like a child in the subconscious. In this state-of-being, the alpha state, we answer with childlike honesty questions put to us, which sometimes strains marriages and other relationships. In this state-of-being we are also closer to our source of creativity so, prior to the first cup of our favorite caffeinated beverage, we often take a bath or shower and find ideas flowing like the water. It is no coincidence that in dream analysis water is often associated with our subconscious and emotions. You can find inspiration during this time. As with sleep in general, this is a good time to keep a pad of paper available to jot things down while they are still fresh in our mind. Later, such thoughts become vague and their recall unreliable because they were stored in short-term memory.

I was recently on a camping trip with a group of close friends. Being the first up on a somewhat cold day, I was attempting to build a fire for the camp. My friend Betty emerged from her tent and went immediately to the camp's kitchen area in order to start the coffee. My stack of paper, kindling, and logs was ready to light but I couldn't find the lighter so I asked Betty if she knew where it was. She said yes and without looking at the picnic table where the kitchen equipment was stacked, picked up something with a red handle and handed it to me. I looked at it and matter-of-factly stated to her, "these are the tongs!" She apologetically went back to the table, found the red-handled fire starter and handed it to me. As I walked away I heard her chastising herself for her stupidity. Later I realized that she had been in the alpha state during this interchange between us. In response to my request for the lighter she had internally asked for the red-handled thing. Her subconscious instantly responded such that searching wasn't necessary; it knew exactly where a red-handled thing was lying.

That is the way it works. *The subconscious will answer a request literally, without judgment, and give you exactly what you ask for. You must therefore be careful in how you ask your questions, then treasure and nurture the time with your subconscious,* for here you can receive answers of greater import than just where the red handled lighter is. *You can discover the answers to questions that have vexed your life.* Remember though, that the subconscious is like a five-year-old and will answer with honesty that is sometimes hard to take, even admonishing you as my friend Betty experienced when her mumbled requests sought such responses.

Some grownups are like this much of the time. Because of childhood traumas blocking their development, they never grew emotionally past the age of five even though intellectually they might have earned their doctorate. Like a five-year-old they emote and act with gusto, yet often because of their strong inner connection to the five-year-old, they can answer with great creativity when asked the right question.

There are many forms of therapy aimed at recapturing the early moments in our life and healing the traumas sustained there, such as rebirthing, experiential therapy, and even past life regression or Rohun if you really want to explore back to the source. Rebirthing, which was developed by Leonard Orr and is currently being shepherded by Bob Frissell, employs long, hot baths to return a person to something approximating the womb.[11] *By taking long baths, or right after awakening choosing to lie in bed basking in the quiet and solitude, you can maintain the alpha state and lengthen the time you spend with your inner child. When you learn to ride the alpha wave you surf the vast sea of your subconscious.* I get up before the rest of the household to garner private bath time. That is primarily how I found the inspiration for this book. I call it my tub thoughts time. Others may prefer thinking shower streams. While writing this book I had a dream where the chrome overflow disk on the bathtub I typically use transformed into a five-inch silvered buffalo nickel with a feather design on the perimeter so it looked like a shield. A voice spoke to me and told me that it was the transfer disk, thus reinforcing my perception of my morning bath as a time of knowledge transfer to my conscious mind. Author James Twyman is another who reports having his ability to receive inspiration greatly augmented by being in the bath.

I have had a good many more uplifting thoughts, creative and expansive visions while soaking in comfortable baths in well-equipped American bathrooms than I have ever had in any cathedral.

Edmund Wilson

Rossini, the brilliant Italian opera composer, was thought of as being lazy. There are apparently many stories that "substantiate" this judgment. A classic one relays how he was working on an overture in bed one morning when his sheaf of papers spilled off the bed onto the floor. The bed being warm while the floor was very cold, he chose to remain in bed and start a new composition, which turned out to be even more brilliant and lively than the one strewn on the floor.[12] Possibly those who labeled him as indolent would have withheld their judgment had they understood the need for an artist to delve deeply into intuition for inspiration. In the morning prior to getting out of bed is the time that Gordon Dryden spends reading an entire book.[13] This is reading that is highly intuitive and hence very productive, plus the knowledge gained is long-term. He is spending time with his five-year-old and in a society struggling to have enough time to do what is asked of us, that time is often sacrificed. That sacrifice is more significant than most realize.

PENGUIN SCHOOL

In the industrialized West we sacrifice even more. *It is not a coincidence that the age of five is when we start school, and suddenly lose our ability to learn quickly. Ground breaking author Dr. Joseph Chilton Pearce contends that most five year olds are traumatized by this experience in much the same way as a violent birth!* [14] Douglas Buchanan, whose scholastic achievements are noted in *Appendix H*, makes an excellent case that for Americans the damage is even more pervasive,

The reason that Korea, China, and Russia are beating us hands down in the production of scientists is simply the cruelty of the American school playground. American children are trained by the media to think that being tough and rude is cool. Children who are natural scholars or good at science and mathematics are taunted and given names like "nerd" or "twee" or whatever. Thousands of gifted children give up learning at a crucial point because of their more aggressive and less competent peers. In Korea, China, and Russia, gifted children are regarded by their peers as heroes. The result is obvious. America is now a nonintellectual country relying on immigrants for its

Nobel prizes. I won't even mention how Ritalin is given to gifted children who get bored with school. We use five times as much Ritalin in the U.S. as the rest of the world combined. I think this country is doomed to less than mediocrity because of the way it treats its children, and how "hero" or "heroine" is automatically linked to a uniform.

This loss isn't just limited to American children around the age of five. Entire cultures can lose abilities when they are no longer exercised or honored. In the mid 1970s a *National Geographic* special aired which depicted an African tribe in the process of becoming "civilized." This culture had a strong oral tradition and no written language when civilization first impacted them. From their initial exposure to Westerners, they learned to play checkers. They had such strong visualization abilities that members of the tribe would typically play a game in less than sixty seconds. Most in the tribe could tell who was going to win in the first few moves. A few years after they had been "educated" to read and write, most members of the tribe lost this ability along with their strong oral tradition.

The same thing happened to virtually everyone on the planet after the invention of the Gutenberg press in 1454, which meant that books could be printed rather than copied by hand. The Chinese and the Koreans had a similar device centuries earlier but were handicapped by the complexities of a picture-based language using thousands of symbols. Gutenberg had to make only 26 reusable characters that he could assemble in a sequence to make any word required.[15] Prior to the widespread dissemination of printed material, reading and writing was primarily limited to the royalty and aristocracy, plus the priests, monks, and scribes who laboriously created handwritten copies of older manuscripts. Dave Meier in his excellent book, *The Accelerated Learning Handbook,* developed an enlightening chart, **Figure 4.4**, showing the impact of the Gutenberg press, which publisher McGraw-Hill has given us permission to republish.[16]

Figure 4.4 – EDUCATIONAL EMPHASIS	
Before Gutenberg	**After Gutenberg**
Concrete experience	Abstract concepts
Images	Words
Whole-brain learning	Left brain learning
Holographic processing	Linear processing
Learning by doing	Learning by reading
Learning in context	Learning offline
Learning with others	Learning by yourself

Douglas Buchanan contends that the beta state is a relative newcomer, being the consequence of widespread education via reading. He feels that the alpha state is properly named because it is the state where all of the best work and thought occur. Like the alpha male in nature, it was first, or dominant. With the advent of the beta state after the invention of the Gutenberg press, there was hypertrophy of the left brain. When alphabets were pictures, as in Sumerian or Egyptian hieroglyphics, the right brain was much more involved in reading, which was still connected to the real world. When writing became cuneiform-type scratches on clay or paper, the whole inner meaning of reading began to divorce the reader from the natural world, and segregate thought in the left brain. Hence, the destruction of the environment by people who regard a tree as a word, not a living thing.[17] Even the word alphabet is composed of alpha-bet(a) hence inferring taking you from alpha to beta.

It is also worth noting that the symbol chosen for each state-of-being indicates a deep understanding of their significance. The foundation, or first state experienced, is the delta – Δ, a symbol both of the trinity and of solidarity in structural engineering. The next state, the theta – Θ, looks like a representation of the two halves of the brain and hence symbolically represents duality at the mental level. The alpha state is represented by α, which is suggestive of an incomplete infinity sign. Finally, the beta state – β, looks like a staked infinity sign thus firmly grounding it in duality, or this reality. Each symbol therefore represents a step away from the trinity toward duality as an infinite experience. Such patterning, however, is probably essential to effectively immerse us in "reality."

MASCULINE SEEKS DOMINANCE OVER FEMININE

The immediate result of the advent of the Gutenberg press was an attack on the feminine, or right brain aspect. One of the first uses for printing was the mass distribution of information about witches. The subsequent witch hunts were predominately against women who were often brutally tested with devious means to confirm their guilt, tortured until they confessed and gave a list of their conspirators, then ultimately dispatched either by hanging or burning along with those they implicated. Over a duration of more than 50 years the masculine left brain aspect became dominant as intuitive thinking fell prey to the madness of the times. It was replaced by logical processes led by Sir Isaac Newton's codification of the natural physical laws the universe runs on, and Descartes' *Cogito ergo sum*, "I think therefore I am." The pre-eminence of scientific logic therefore ended the witch-hunt madness with masculine finality. This in turn led to the Industrial Revolution and the elevation of scientific logic and the worship of the mind as a new religion eventually surpassing even religion in its emphasis and power in the West. Another big boost for logic came with Darwin's theory of Evolution and survival of the fittest. An initial consequence of its logic was more madness; the assertion by many that, "because of their smaller heads, women must be less intelligent than men."[18]

Today we find that only eight percent to nine percent of the population is left-handed and hence typically right brain dominant.[19] If a person is right-handed, they are also, by inference, right! There is a widespread cultural prejudice against the left hand and associated right brain. Examples are expressions such as: left out, leftovers, left-handed compliment, left in the lurch, and being the creative ones in our society, often being called absent-minded. In many Eastern cultures the left hand is used to wipe yourself after going to the bathroom, and the right hand is the one you eat with. In Italian the word for left is *sinistra*, from the Latin root of the English word sinister. In French *gauche* is left and it translates as clumsy while the word for right, *droit*, means correct. Maladroit in English means awkward and translates from the French as *not right*.[20]

That which is holy, is holistic, or whole. All are derived from the same root word and are feminine attributes. Archeological evidence indicates that thousands of years ago our worship was plural with deities who were female in a feminine dominant culture.[21] Because the sun is considered masculine and the moon feminine our spin directions became associated with the motions of these celestial bodies. Spinning clockwise mimics the apparent movement of the sun and counterclockwise mimics the apparent movement of the position of the moon phases from new to full. When our deity became masculine and singular, we consequently spun in the masculine direction, clockwise. The Church even banned counterclockwise, or *widdershins*, circle dancing because of its goddess association.

Prior to the digital watch era, watches mimicked the body having hands that went *deosil* to follow the movement of the sun.[22] Likewise, merry-go-rounds, music boxes, washing machines, and anything else that spins in an earth or body frame of reference direction is typically given a clockwise spin. The Northern Hemisphere is predominately masculine being dominated by land masses. It is the birthplace of Western civilization. Because of the Coriolis Effect storms and ocean currents also typically exhibit clockwise motion. The Southern Hemisphere, considered feminine, is dominated by water, the birthplace of all life. It contains Africa, generally considered the birthplace of humanity. Its fluid masses typically spin counterclockwise. Previously noted author and teacher Drunvalo Melchizedek adds important information to our understanding of the gender spin associations with this statement:

SUN

Pocket Watch with Sun Orbiting It.

Figure 4.5

There are two primary ways the energy (prana) can move up through the body, one male and the other female. First, the energy always moves in a spiral, and when it spirals counterclockwise relative to the body, it's male; when it spirals the other way, it's female, which is clockwise relative to the body.[23]

Based on the information Drunvalo provides, clockwise spinning is internally in the feminine direction and externally interpreted as masculine. The converse is true of counterclockwise spinning, thus imparting a mixed gender balance to either spin direction. Society has long attributed great significance to spin direction, yet when all of the options and sometimes-contradictory evidence and beliefs are examined, the differences are probably moot at this point. A healthy consequence of this may be that people be allowed to spin the direction they choose rather than what society says they should. It is also important to note that clockwise and counterclockwise are not as meaningful expressions as they used to be for children raised with digital timepieces. Digital timepieces are inherently left-brained while analog timepieces, ones with hands, are inherently right-brained.

REMNANTS OF THE FEMININE ASPECT

An often-distrusted remnant culture in the Western hemisphere is the Romanies, the Gypsies. Their origin can be traced back to India and their name to Egypt. Gypsy is derived from Egyptian.[24] Even today they have no written language and in their healing work exemplify the shamanic practices associated with the right brain. For the majority of the people in the societies they move quietly through, the dominance of the right hand and associated left brain is a natural consequence of block writing. Hieroglyphics are holistic while block letters are left-brained, iterative. Hence, understanding comes only from reading the sentence in sequence. The desire for understanding via pictures is still with us though. A remnant of picture-based writing can be seen in English and other European languages. For instance, the words *water, wave,* and *whoosh* all begin with a *w* having its origin traceable to a representation of water waves. Another example is Mississippi, the name for the river and associated state as it mirrors the serpentine nature of the river in the use of S's, with Missouri likewise following form. It is likely then that the Gutenberg press did not completely squelch the desire for form to embody function; however, the remnant is a barely detectable vestige when compared to true picture-based language.

Another remnant is signatures, which being cursive and highly individual, are decidedly right-brained. In Western civilization cursive is the closest we have to a right brain language. In many advanced education systems, such as that found in Holland, cursive is taught to children first, thus matching the natural order where the right brain matures prior to the left brain. It is not a coincidence that in Holland children start school at age seven or eight, and graduate from high school with a level of competence closer to a college graduate in the United States.[25]

PARADIGM SHIFTS

With the advent of the Gutenberg press the widespread availability of printed materials resulted in the education of the masses. There was a great hunger for knowledge and education made for smarter workers. An educated population eventually led to the downfall of kingdoms and priesthoods as their subjects began to question the autocratic or dictatorial rule being imposed on them. Examples are the French Revolution which beheaded the monarchy, the Bolshevik Revolution leading to the downfall of the czar in Russia, the populating and rebelling of the United States of America, and the loss in power and splintering of the Holy Roman Church into many disparate factions. All are the result of people attempting to escape oppression using the power of the written word to educate and incite the general public. In this regard *the Gutenberg press can be seen as a uniting factor helping mankind to act in concert when the reasons are compelling enough. Still, Dave Meier's comparative analysis shows that, along the way, mankind in general also lost something important in every nation whose people became literate. Their gain in masculine-based logical knowledge caused them to lose contact with the right side of their brain, the feminine aspect.*

The invention of the Gutenberg press was therefore globally a defining moment in history, a watershed event that led to a sequence of new paradigms, such as the Industrial Revolution and the Emancipation Proclamation. The ramifications of the Industrial Revolution took hundreds of years to unfold. More recently the invention of the mainframe computer similarly revolutionized management with an information revolution; but that event took only decades to lead to a new paradigm. Even more recent watershed events have been the invention of personal computers that led to the computer revolution based downfall of the mainframe priesthood who were the computer gurus, then the Internet, which allows everyone access to global information, and now the learning revolution which is already leading to significant changes in only years rather than decades.

THE RESURGENCE OF THE FEMININE ASPECT

The scientific revolution eventually began aiding the right brain in an unexpected manner. Although first described as a device by Leonardo da Vinci, the first functional camera was developed in 1837 by Louis Jacques Mande Daguerre, whose technique fixed images on metal. It captured an image at a moment in time and preserved it. *Photo-graphy* meant literally, "writing with light," the opposite of writing with ink for interpreting an image is inherently a right brain function. Photography, therefore, started a cultural shift back from the written word to perceived image. Although artists and their art have always served this function, the majority of the population didn't have significant exposure to art. Because images were widely disseminated by the Gutenberg press, perception changed. By disseminating art to the masses, people learned the language of art.[26]

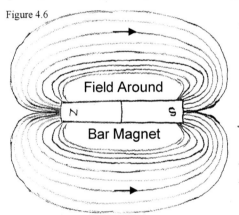

Figure 4.6

Field Around

N S

Bar Magnet

The next perceptual change came with the discovery of the magnetic field by Michael Faraday. Being an invisible field of energy, feminine metaphors were used to describe it, such as "web," "matrix," "wave," and "strands." These and the common descriptor, "field," are all terms borrowed from agriculture and nature. Poets were able to expand the vocabulary of love beyond *flames*, to include, in the words of Leonard Shlain, "the *spark of love*, an *electrifying kiss*, a *compulsive attraction*, a *magnetic personality*, an *aura of sensuality*, a *repulsive person*, and the *pull of polar opposites.*"[27] Being invisible, the magnetic field resembled the spirit and hence, the feminine aspect. It gave attention to that which cannot be seen and easily analyzed, but which forms a unified presence, all feminine aspects. Taken together, photography and the magnetic field began shifting left brain society toward a more balanced perspective.[28]

The world's current energy base is petroleum, a masculine endeavor from the extraction of the oil from our Earth Mother via phallic drilling, to the use of its products in cars and roads built predominately by male work forces using left brain logic. Jeanne Manning's book, *The Coming Energy Revolution,* gives good evidence for the source of the next major paradigm shift. If Manning's premise is correct we are poised to change our entire energy focus from a masculine base to a feminine base. That is a significant shift as few objects are as worshiped as the energy-hungry automobile and the freedom it provides. Manning presents a variety of zero-point-energy based inventions that focus on harnessing an invisible energy field. She cites one case where a zero-point-energy device has for decades been providing reliable energy for a small community. The evidence is mounting that even though many of the yet to be proven claims in *The Coming Energy Revolution* are speculative, there is enough solid evidence to establish credibility and a reasonable expectation that if only a few of the approaches listed pan out, their impact will be revolutionary.

THE LEARNING REVOLUTION

The book *The Learning Revolution* sold 7.5 million copies in only 25 weeks making it last decades best selling international non-fiction book in the world. These impressive sales figures occurred in China, not the West, where it eventually sold 10 million copies. ***The country that leads the learning revolution will eventually lead the world.*** Combine that information with the knowledge that China is encouraging the development of super children capable of nonordinary phenomena and you see a country fostering massive change building toward a well-endowed future by posturing for excellence. You will then understand the prediction in the book, *Megatrends 2000*, that China will be the largest economy in the world by 2030.[29]

Contrast that model with the West. ***The West in general, and the United States of America and England specifically, have one of the worst educational systems in the world.*** Education is a broken leg that we keep covering with a Band-Aid labeled "Public Education System." The dominant educational system in the West is a product of puritanical thinking that was tailored to produce factory workers at the beginning of the Industrial Revolution. This model is hardly applicable today when so few workers earn their living via muscle power. The minimal teaching of the three R's – reading, writing and arithmetic – may have been appropriate centuries ago, but it hardly prepares students for the continuing education requirements rampant in the modern work force.

For an excellent example of how early childhood development can yield what most would think of as rare talents, I quote *The Learning Revolution*:

> *It's significant that youngsters in the Pacific islands of Polynesia, Melanesia, and Micronesia almost invariably grow up with the ability to sing in harmony – an almost perfect sense of pitch. Every Polynesian also seems to be a natural dancer....They grew up in a culture where singing and dancing play a major part. And they patterned all that information in the vital early years.*[30]

PENGUIN ENTERTAINMENT

In the West we added to our learning dilemma by the invention of progressively compelling mass entertainment via radios, movies, televisions, video games, and most recently, surfing the Net. Mass entertainment is really mass patterning although unfortunately, what is patterned is not the skills being displayed. Talents such as those of Gene Kelly, Fred Astaire, and Ginger Rogers were not products of the medium that made them famous. Musicals are no longer popular having been supplanted by action movies as competition drove entertainment toward more exciting subjects. Today's movies employ massive amounts of computer-generated imagery in order to present rapid pace sound byte action for an audience accustomed to sitting rather than experiencing. In order to experience true learning with others via physical activity, our children have to be driven to sports events, gym class, dance, music, and art lessons. For most of the young minds in the Western population, the emphasis is too little too late.

When I was eight years old I lived in Los Angeles and typically watched three hours of television every day. Then my family moved to Sedona, Arizona. I was initially devastated finding nothing to do in a sleepy little town of fewer than 4,000 residents. To make matters worse, there wasn't even any broadcast TV available. However, I soon learned to entertain myself and spent many hours riding my bike, climbing, and exploring the forests and hills around Sedona. I also learned to read. When a few fuzzy nationally broadcast stations became available six months later it no longer mattered, I was hooked on reading and doing things. My grades went from C's and D's and slowly climbed until I was the top student in the school when I graduated to go on to high school (reality check – my graduating class in eighth grade had only seven kids in it). In moving to Sedona from Los Angeles I was really moved from operating primarily with my left brain to my right brain, from Western upbringing to Eastern upbringing. It made all the difference; it made possible the person I am now by retrieving some of what was lost in my personal Gutenberg paradigm shift.

Western science learns by going outward via dissection. Eastern science learns by going inward via integration. This book draws from both approaches to present a unified view. The same union is occurring in the world today. Mixing via immigration, the fall of boundaries such as the Berlin Wall from peaceful consequences of the cold war and apartheid due to the peaceful courage of Nelson Mandela, the coming out of seclusion by China and many other countries, Mahatma Gandhi's freeing India while retaining relations with England, and the Dalai Lama leaving Tibet to spread his wisdom worldwide, are all examples of how the West and the East are groping to join.

THE PRICE OF FEAR

Most children today are not given the same opportunities I had, or that the children in Polynesia and elsewhere have. *Most kids today have to contend with another state-of-being, many forms of fear.* Fear of failure, of gangs, of terrorism, of abduction, of diseases and getting sick, plus gut reactions to the constant fear messages they are bombarded with on radio, television, and the movies. From the last chapter's discussion about our brain remember that fear, or survival-based reactionism, happen in the most primitive part of the brain. That is the reptilian brain or the brain stem, and the sympathetic nervous system. Sexuality is rooted in the next level up, and the highest levels are reserved for the most sophisticated thinking and feeling. *When we become fearful we largely abandon rational thinking. In addition, the production of adrenalin causes the production of the neurotransmitter cortisol, which decreases our ability to learn and remember.*

Today's movies and television often activate the fear reaction of fight or flight via both the action they are depicting and by making many quick scene changes that stimulate our peripheral vision while compelling us to watch. The result is the constant production of adrenalin that is not healthy as it was originally intended to stimulate our muscles to maximum capability in case we needed to fight or flee. Our blood becomes a cocktail for action while we are immobilized in a growing state of tension.[31]

Carla Hannaford explains the situation very well, *"when children sit and watch the movie or TV screen, their eyes go into ocular lock (staring) and disassociative hearing (no connection between words and pictures). As a defense, the brain goes into lower alpha brain wave activity where active thought and reasoning cannot occur."*[32] It is important to realize that this is the perfect state to put a person in to pattern them, so the use of the term programming for the TV schedule is most appropriate. Edgar Cayce and others have indicated that the subliminal mind is telepathic.[33, 34] It also therefore absorbs the thoughts associated with what is being viewed and listened to. Author/therapist Marina Raye says, *"Most media programming is like a bucket of garbage dumped into our minds on a regular basis. We take better care of our carpets than we do our minds."*[35]

We are therefore programming our children with violent thinking and the resultant stress, which is really pervasive fear, produces a reduced attention span and learning capacity. Children, or adults who are under a lot of stress, are poorly postured to perform well in learning tasks. How well can you read a book right after you have been frightened, let alone remember what you have read? According to Carla Hannaford, fear drives a person into the high beta state of frenzied thought, our least intelligent state-of-being. She makes the compelling argument that *there are no forms of learning disability, only forms of stress.* In order to avoid all of the other labels, the term she prefers is SOSOH: Stressed Out, Survival-Oriented Humans. She believes that chronic exposure to stress inhibits full brain development. That applies to any form of stress: physical, emotional, mental, or even spiritual.[36] *Stress leads to hyperactivity, kills brains cells, and decreases memory.* The words of Marina Raye are particularly applicable: *"There are no learning disabled children, only learning disabled teaching methods."*[37]

THE PENGUIN FILTER

The compelling conclusion is that most of us, and in particular our children, live very unhealthful lifestyles. It is also apparent that, *at whatever point a life style and educational systems is imposed, on either an individual or a group, at that same point begins the process of pruning abilities.* Quoting Dr. Jill Bolte Taylor, a brain specialist of national renown, "When we are born, 50 percent of the nerve cells die almost immediately… at puberty, 40 to 60 percent of the dendritic connections disappear. The connections are pruned."[38] For example, a baby is both telepathic and according to the *Learning Revolution,* naturally makes all 70 of the sounds from which all languages are composed. English takes a maximum of 44 sounds to speak so a baby born to an English-speaking family rapidly stops being telepathic and making any but the 44 reinforced sounds. *As the child grows its brain becomes optimized to its environment while those skills that are not required either atrophy from lack of use or are blocked.*[39]

Once we have habituated, the parts of our brain that are used the most, generally only the left side of the brain, are usually in the frenzy of high beta state while the rest of our abilities are in the deep sleep of delta state. This is much like driving an automobile with a V-8 engine functioning on only one cylinder. This may be why advanced species such as the dolphins do not talk to us. They perceive us as having so little of our brain functioning that we appear to be asleep. As with all animals, they communicate telepathically and we are, for all intents and purposes, deaf and possibly dumb, or at least disturbed if they are subjected to the typical chaotic thought stream most humans radiate.[40, 41] As it is with sounds it also is with a myriad of other abilities thus enabling us to fit into our "penguin" population. Children can learn a language more quickly and perfectly than any adult no matter how brilliant or well educated. That mode of learning can be reacquired, but the older we are, the more challenging this process tends to be.

HOW TO RECOVER YOUR CHILDHOOD POTENTIAL

Our brain is pliable enough to accommodate our efforts to awaken it if we are insistent enough. That is what this book is about. For a start, Carla Hannaford says that there are three things we can do to immediately help our children: [42]

Exercise 4.1 – RECOVERING CHILDHOOD POTENTIAL

Do as many of the recommendations listed below, for yourself and your children, as is reasonable. Even doing only one helps. Implement others as you can in a march towards healthy living. You can record your progress in your journal that you began for your dreams.

1. *Ban TV and video games prior to the age of eight, and restrict it for older children in order to avoid adrenaline-producing violent programs.*
2. *Institute a daily integrative movement program.*
3. *Decrease or eliminate simple sugars in your diet because stress, coupled with high dietary intake of sugars, causes the production of alcohol that affects frontal lobe functioning.*

You can go much further though. If you are not already doing so, you can *begin listening to the wise teacher available to each of us,* our puppeteer! *This teacher is known by many names around the world. Names such as: Your Higher Self, Higher Power, Christed or Buddha Self, Guardian Angel, Mahatma, Brahman, Conscience, Monad, and the Divinity within.* Douglas Lockhart had this illuminating statement to make about the subject:

> *When the energy level of a man is sufficiently high, a singular Intelligence will then take on the task of helping, or showing that man how to refine his Being further. And eventually, when the man's being has reached the necessary level, the Intelligence which has adopted him will use that energy to manifest itself through sound, vision, or both.*

Greek playwright Aeschylus stated it this way: "When we feel willing and eager, the gods join in."

THE "MOUTH OF GOD"

The puppet also has free will so the attachments are really ones of support and not control. The main attachment is called the antahkarana, an ancient word from the Sanskrit that combines antar (interior) with karana (sense organ) to convey *interior sense organ*. *It is the energy cord or pillar of light by which our body receives all of its energy and through which we are connected to our puppeteer, which I will call the Monad, and from there to God.* Theosophist Madame Blavatsky indicated that it was "the path that lies between thy Spirit and thy self, the highway of sensations, the rude arousers of Ahankara," that is, the sense of egoity. What it connects to is, the "Mouth of God."

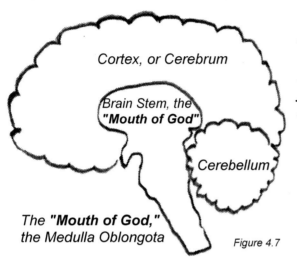

Cortex, or Cerebrum

Brain Stem, the "Mouth of God"

Cerebellum

The "Mouth of God," the Medulla Oblongota

Figure 4.7

Quoting Paramahansa Yogananda, *"The 'Mouth of God' is the medulla oblongata [Brain Stem] in the posterior part of the brain, tapering off into the spinal cord. This, the most vital part of the human body, is the divine entrance (Mouth of God) for 'word' or life energy by which man is sustained."*[43] In John 4:4 in the Bible it states that, "Man shall not live by bread alone, but by every 'word' that proceeds from the 'Mouth of God.'" Ruby Nelson, in the extraordinary book, *The Door of Everything*, makes this statement about the energy flow known as the antahkarana, "Your body is the vessel which receives it, your mind controls the angle of the vessel, and your heart determines how much of this River of Life you will let in."[44]

The "Mouth of God" is part of the reptilian brain, the most "primitive" part of your body. It is the dividing part between your mammalian brain and your body. It controls your most fundamental functions, your breath, heart, reflex actions, energy flow, and connection to the earth. When you speak a great truth that is a revelation, sometimes confirmation of the truth in the words spoken, by yourself or others, will come in the form of good feeling chills, sometimes called "angel hugs," that originate at the top of the backside of the neck, and run down the spine.

My wife Carol had her first child, a girl, almost 30 years ago. Both she and child were gravely ill. Carol struggled out of the hospital bed a week after delivery to walk down the hall to the neonatal room because she knew intuitively that her baby had just died. That was, and has remained, very difficult for her to accept. Five years ago we were discussing this period in her life while we were driving in Chicago. Without thinking, I said that her third born child, another girl, was the same soul as her first born who had died. We both got chills down the back of our necks as I said this, thus placing emphasis on our truth just spoken. What we discovered is something that might be fairly common. If a soul tries to incarnate in a family and for whatever reason, is unsuccessful the first time, then it tries to be a subsequent birth in that family. A second example is J. Z. Knight, who had a sister who drowned before she was born. J. Z. eventually remembered being that little girl, and the experience of looking up through the water prior to drowning.[45]

Likewise, when the hair stands up on the back of your neck and you get chills of fear as a cold shiver runs down your spine, these chills are also originating in the "Mouth of God." In Europe this feeling is said to be due to someone walking over your grave. Maybe what really accounts for this feeling are different types of energy qualities and fluctuations to get your attention.

My cousin Penny had an experience like this when she was a young woman. She was horseback riding with a girl friend. They come to a fork in the trail with one path leading up a canyon. As she and her friend started to ride up this path they both had cold chills radiate through their bodies. They decided to turn around. As they rode back, along came two other young women on horseback that ignored their warnings and continued up the canyon. They learned later that the two women were pulled off their horses by a group of men and raped.

The "Mouth of God" is also the entry and exit point for your consciousness when it separates or returns to the body, and the means by which the body is maintained in your absence while you are in the theta and delta states-of-being. Your free will determines where you go based on your last thoughts. An example is when you go to sleep. If you choose thoughts that are fear-based, you go to places that are frightening. Thoughts that are love-based take you to loving places. It is that simple.

My brother Mark was going through a rough time in his life such that he really did not want to be here. One afternoon while driving home from work he suddenly found his vantage point separated from his body and rising rapidly upwards. Realizing that this fascinating experience was a decision point he rose thousands of feet above his vehicle. Then loving thoughts of not wanting to abandon his children elicited the thought, "I want to go back!" thus returning him to his body which had moved safely down the interstate highway nearly half a mile. Another friend had a similar experience but didn't fare as well. Although he walked away from the resulting accident without being harmed, his truck was totaled.

THE ILLUSIONS OF DEATH AND LIVING

Many believe that the same rules govern so-called "death." Your last thoughts determine where you go, for this is a transition point to another state-of-being that is really more like a punctuation mark in the book of life. A famous example of how to deal with this is Mahatma Gandhi. As he lay dying at the feet of the assassin who shot him, Mahatma Gandhi forgave him, and with his last breaths repeated the name of God, which for him was Rama. In death, he followed a pattern he had all of his life by performing japa, the constant repeating of the name of God as a mantra.[46] Where do you suppose he went after transitioning from here? Douglas Lockhart answers that question this way, "When a man dies, he enters into what he believes." Mother Meera says that, "Wherever we want to go we will go. The wish at the time of death and the past actions of the lifetime determine future experience."

Our current issue though is still with living. *Edgar Cayce described sleep as a "shadow of that intermission in earth's experiences of that state called death."*[47] While your spirit is on these excursions during sleep in the theta and delta states of being, it is still connected to the puppet by the silver cord, which the Bible speaks of in connection with the process of death, in Ecclesiastes 12:6,

> *Because man goes to his lasting home,*
> *And mourners go about the streets;*
> *Before the silver cord is snapped*
> *And the golden bowl is broken,*
> *And the pitcher is shattered at the spring,*
> *And the broken pulley falls into the well,*
> *And the dust returns to the earth as it once was,*
> *And the life breath returns to God who gave it.*

The silver cord is what allows your spirit to return to your body, which in the same Biblical passage is referred to as the "Golden Vessel." When you transition out of deep sleep to alpha state wakefulness, your resulting dreams are interpretations of your adventures and the guidance you were given in order help you. The importance of dreamtime cannot be overstressed. Dreamtime is characterized by rapid eye movement (REM) so it is easy for researchers to identify.[48] It has been shown in laboratory settings that if, over a period of days, you consistently awaken a person during their dreams thus robbing them of that necessary state-of-being, you rapidly drive them crazy.

Alexander Solzhenitsyn writes in *The Gulag Archipelago* of his experience in the Russian prison system in Siberia. The Russians broke him, along with all of his fellow prisoners, in only days using intensive interrogation with bright lights and total sleep deprivation. According to Solzhenitsyn, of the more than 17,000,000 prisoners who were incarcerated in that archipelago in a frozen wilderness, the only one who wasn't broken had the unusual ability of being able to sleep while standing with his eyes open. Hence one might want to rethink doing all-nighters in order to pass a test, thus once again emphasizing the importance of daily cycling through all of your states-of-being.

The important thing to remember is the concept of "non-attachment," for you are not the puppet. Your brain is of the puppet but your mind is of the puppeteer. Your mind is therefore independent of the puppet. This is why sleep, during which you return to who you really are, is of vital importance to your well-being. This is also why Ram Dass said, "Never take your life personally." *Theta/delta state sleep is therefore an important rest period for both your body and your spirit, which finds incarnation difficult. This is why disruption of your circadian cycle is so devastating.*

HOW TO CONQUER FEAR – A PUPPET'S SOLUTION

Love your fear, and it will release you
Marina Raye

Love is letting go of fear
Gerald Jampolsky

So, if you establish a regular sleep pattern for yourself, how do you control the fear states patterned into you that can awaken you in the middle of the night and at other times can erupt as panic attacks for people who have much to contend with. To combat the fears modern life tries to instill in us, Depak Chopra advises in his ninth key of *Ten Keys to Active Mastery*:

> *Replace fear-motivated behavior with love-motivated behavior. Fear is the product of memory, which dwells in the past. Remembering what hurt us before, we direct our energies toward making certain that an old hurt will not repeat itself. But trying to impose the past on the present will never wipe out the threat of being hurt. That happens only when you find the security of your own being, which is love. Motivated by the truth inside you, you can face any threat because your inner strength is invulnerable to fear.*

Therapist Marina Raye states that, *"There are no barriers to those who release their fears."*[49] In John 4:18 it says, "Perfect love casteth out fear." As with myself, many of us are now seeking a closer connection to the puppeteer. When you become aware of the puppeteer in your life it draws closer and strengthens your ties to it. Depak Chopra's tenth key addresses this very well:

> *Understand that the physical world is just a mirror of a deeper intelligence. Intelligence is the invisible organizer of all matter and energy, and since a portion of this intelligence resides in you, you share in the organizing power of the cosmos. Because you are inseparably linked to everything, you cannot afford to foul the planet's air and water. But at a deeper level, you cannot afford to live with a toxic mind, because every thought makes an impression on the whole field of intelligence. Living in balance and purity is the highest good for you and the Earth.*

What each of these teachers is really telling us is to **master your different states of being. As you cycle through your daily awake and asleep pattern you likewise cycle through being in-carnate and in-spirit.** During your waking hours you work on mastering the incarnate state-of-being. You enter wakefulness in the calm of the alpha state and your descent into alertness is at its deepest during the beta state, which is characterized by high brain activity thus allowing you to focus on only a small part of the reality around you. Psychiatrists indicate that many adults can be characterized as frightened children compensating for the fears they learned from the adults who raised them by using high thought activity in order to "keep on eye and ear" on their world and its many suspicious activities. Quoting Joseph

Chilton Pearce, *"Once anxiety over safety becomes a child's orientation, s/he will use his/her long-range sensors (sight and sound) as buffers between self and experience."* [50] By releasing our fears we eventually achieve freedom incarnate while broadening our ability to sense, experience, and create. According to Phil Morimitus who quotes Sri Gopal Das, "What man wants most in life is freedom. And if this is denied in his waking state, he'll fulfill it on the astral plane while he's asleep... The essence of freedom is expression, and freedom is measured by the degree that one is able to express oneself." [51]

Balancing the incarnate state of wakefulness is the light sleep of the theta state and the deep sleep of delta state when you are connected to your puppet body via the silver cord. The silver cord is the one significant difference between what we call death and sleep. While in the delta state your spirit is free thus allowing you to encompass all of creation while being tethered only by the silver cord, which pulls you back to incarnation and this reality. That cord is strong, but it can be broken when it is meant to be broken. Thus when someone dies we say that "his time was up" or "she was meant to die." That choice is sometimes made by the puppet if it was too frayed, worn out, or discouraged to continue its tasks, or sometimes by the puppeteer if the purpose for the puppet has been fully accomplished. Then the puppeteer prepares for the next puppet act. When the puppet and the puppeteer become one, then the need for the puppet act no longer exists. That is graduation to another state-of-being and associated level of awareness where the veil is no longer required, nor is sleep for that matter - another chapter in the volume of life.

YOUR STATES OF BEING IN CONTEXT

What this chapter has covered is how your consciousness engages in many different modes of operation. *As states-of-being your beta/alpha/theta/delta, love/fear, and life/"death" modes provide a rich palate upon which to paint a panorama on the canvas of creation. The same is true of mankind collectively as we shift paradigms, and of the planet. Mastering your modes of operation enable you to greatly increase your effectiveness including learning rate, and significantly decrease the stress of living. You will make significant progress by not allowing TV or video games to become the focus they often are, engaging in healthy movement such as the Brain Gym® exercises covered in* **Chapter 15,** *and restricting the intake of processed sugars. For your children, avoid premature literacy and ensure that they are well connected to the earth matrix. Your progress helps everyone advance for from your example, all become empowered. Your ability to control your thoughts and memories become the key.* That key is the focus of section III of this book. But first, **Chapter 5 will explain** how your vision modes complement what you have learned so far, and **Chapter 6** how your unique combination of abilities make your life priceless beyond compare.

> **Teach me your mood, O patient stars; who climb each night the ancient sky,**
> **Leaving no space, no shade, no scars, no trace of age, no fear to die.**
> Ralph Waldo Emerson

> *Be like a very small joyous child living gloriously in the ever present Now*
> *without a single worry or concern about even the next moment of time.*
> Eileen Caddy, *The Dawn of Change*

> **Some of your beliefs originated in your childhood,**
> **but you are not at their mercy unless you *believe* that you are.**
> Jane Roberts, *The Nature of Personal Reality*

> **Eastern and Western – yes, there are differences.**
> **I think at the mental level, the intellectual level, the emotional level we are the same.**
> Dalai Lama

> **Eternity is in love with the productions of time.**
> William Blake, *Proverbs of Hell*

Chapter 5 – YOUR VISION

Our senses are guarded by sentinels of belief, censored by comfortable prejudice.
When I am honest with myself I can see, when I am dishonest I am blind … it is that simple.
Douglas Lockhart

When one sees eternity in things that pass away, then one has pure knowledge.
Bhgagavad Gita

Use the light that is in you to recover your natural clearness of sight. . . .
There is no need to run outside for better seeing, nor to peer from a window.
Rather abide at the center of your being; for the more you leave it, the less you learn.
Search your heart and see if he is wise who takes each turn. The way to do is to be.
Lao-tzu

Darkness and light are both of one nature, different only in seeming,
For each arose from the source of all.
Darkness is disorder, light is order; Darkness transmuted is light of the light.
This, my children, your purpose in being; the transmutation of darkness to light.
The Emerald Tablets of Thoth, Tablet 15

You have to believe it in order to see it… Believe it and you'll see it. Know it and you'll be it!
Wayne Dyer

I practice seeing the Christ in everyone, no matter how ugly the disguise.
Mother Teresa

The sense of sight discerns the difference of shapes, wherever they are…
Without delay or interruption, employing careful calculations with almost incredible speed.
Ptolemy, *Optics*

If therefore thine eye be single, thy whole body shall be full of light.
Matthew 6:22

The eyes have it!
Jeannette Vos and Gordon Dryden, *The Learning Revolution*

OOwl-eyes are allies in learning!
Melvin Lewis Thomas

Enlightenment consists not merely in the seeing of luminous shapes and vision,
but in making the darkness visible.
The latter procedure is more difficult, and therefore, unpopular.
Carl Jung

The single eye, the telescopic gaze of intuition.
Paramahansa Yogananda

The clearest way into the universe is through a forest wilderness.
John Muir

The real voyage of discovery consists not in seeking new landscapes, but in having new eyes.
Marcel Proust

We are at the mercy of influences over which we are consciously unaware
and over which we have virtually no conscious control.
Robert Rosenthal, *Pygmalion in the Classroom*

YOUR visual system begins with your eyeballs, a set of compact organic optics which, in many regards, are not nearly as good as that of most cameras. *Each eyeball has a sensor array at the back, called the retina, which works effectively across a tremendous range of light levels with a high acuity foveal capability and very sensitive peripheral motion detection system. Their performance is incredible, plus your mind/brain as the processing unit making the end result absolutely brilliant with capabilities far beyond anything man-made.* We have the technology to build something better than most of the individual characteristics of your visual system, but we cannot even come close to matching the package. In order to understand the purpose of your foveal and peripheral visual systems, try this simple exercise:

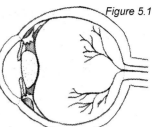

Figure 5.1

Your Eyeball, Part of Your Visual System

Exercise 5.1 – YOUR FOVEAL AND PERIPHERAL VISION:

Position your right hand extended in front of you with your thumb pointing upward in what is often referred to as the "artist's stance." When you are looking directly at your thumb, you view it with your foveal vision. Notice that you are able to see your thumb and thumbnail in high detail, or high acuity. Now, without moving your eyes, slowly rotate your right arm to your right keeping your thumb pointing upward. Somewhere past extending your arm straight out to your side your slowly moving thumb will disappear. Bring it just back into view, and then move all your fingers. Notice that they are much easier to detect when moving than when still. Also notice that you can detect no details such as colors. In fact, when your thumb is motionless you cannot detect whether it points up or down. Now you have a sense of feel for what your *detail-oriented foveal and motion-detecting low-resolution peripheral vision* are capable of.

Exercise 5.1 should have given you a better understanding of what the 130 million receptors in the thumbnail area of your retina, your mundane peripheral and foveal vision, are built to do.[1] Let us go a step further. Based on what we have presented so far, it is likely that we are demonstrating only a small percentage of what your visual system is really capable of. That is because most people use it in a conscious linear fashion. It becomes much more capable when you use subconscious processing.

A few examples might help. Tom Brown authored many trail-blazing books about how to develop a relationship with nature and read her signs as easily as you read this book. When analyzing footprints Tom has approximately 600 characteristics he checks for. Because of his abilities he is often called upon by the authorities to track children and adults lost in a wilderness. Tom was taught by his mentor, an Apache scout he called Grandfather, how to move through the forest with *relaxed alertness*, or *eagle eyes*. The key was to keep his eyes primarily oriented forward in a relaxed state with his peripheral vision opened out to maximum so he would be aware of everything going on around him, but seldom need to focus on it. The description of what Tom Brown was asked to do for *relaxed alertness* correlates well with what ***Exercise 15.1*** in **Chapter 15** describes as *open focus viewing*. This is wide-eye viewing without focusing on anything. The Japanese call the foveal vision *Ken*, the peripheral vision *Kan,* and learning their use is part of *Bushido*, the way of the *Samurai*.[2, 3] An explanation for the proper use of the peripheral vision is in *The Book of Five Rings*, written by Japanese Master Miyamoto Musashi in 1645.[4]

The United States Military teaches peripheral vision technique at sniper school. The oldest cultures on the planet, the Aborigines of Australia and Kalahari of Africa, are masters at using their peripheral vision. My brother Mark learned this as a Yaqui Indian technique by reading about Shaman Don Juan Matus in Carlos Castaneda's books. Don Juan called it *the proper way of walking*. By practicing this way of walking, which includes avoiding holding anything in your hands, talking while walking, and seldom talking in general, Mark astounded his friends with his ability to detect what was going on around them while they hiked together in wilderness areas. *I call this visual mode "owl-eyes," and they are allies in rapid learning.* The question is - how does your visual system support this ability?

OOwl-Eyes

Figure 5.2

 If you speak with the human factors experts who study the visual system, they will tell you that the visual acuity of your eyeball falls off rapidly as you move away from the light-sensor-rich fovea, which often has better than 20:20 visual acuity, to the peripheral of your visual field where the light sensors are sparse and your acuity is less than 20:200, or legally blind. Your mind/brain combination compensates for the gaps in your imagery presenting the impression that you see in full color with high acuity across the entire field of your vision. The reality is that your peripheral vision is not even in color, it is black and white, yet you perceive color. The hole in your vision, caused by the exit point of the optic nerve in the back of the retina, is also filled in, thus giving you the overall feeling that everything you are looking at is rich in full color detail.

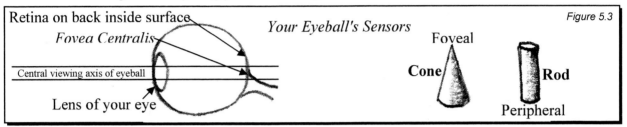

Retina on back inside surface.
Fovea Centralis
Your Eyeball's Sensors
Central viewing axis of eyeball
Lens of your eye
Foveal
Cone
Rod
Peripheral
Figure 5.3

 Your light-detecting retina, which wraps onto the back inside surface of your eyeball, is populated with two different types of cells with specialized functions – cones and rods. Cones are found in the central part of your retina called the *macula,* and they are concentrated in the *fovea centralis.* Your foveal region, having the highest concentration of cones, is concentric with the central axis of the lens of your eye and hence, your visual field of view. ***Cones are color sensitive and built for clarity.*** They need a lot of light in order do their detecting function as they achieve clarity only by stopping down light input with pupil constriction. ***Although your cones are wired to both halves of your brain, the left brain is typically best suited for processing the focused perception of cone vision while you are in a state of doing.***

 Your rods are also concentrically arrayed around the central axis of your eye, but concentrated in the peripheral vision and very light sensitive, so they operate over a larger range of light levels than your cones do. They work best with your pupils dilated, or wide open, to let in the maximum amount of light. They are distributed evenly and work well even in dim light, but are restricted to black and white with no color capability. ***Your rods are arrayed for total acquisition of your field of vision as a single picture. Even though your rods are wired to both halves of your brain, they acquire viewed reality as a gestalt and hence are naturally processed by your right brain while you are in a relaxed state-of-being.***

 Therefore, your foveal vision is typically left brain masculine vision and your peripheral vision is typically right brain feminine vision. Your masculine vision is wired to look at detail and your feminine vision is wired to look at the big picture. Your masculine vision works best in high light conditions with your pupils constricted, and your feminine vision works best with your pupils wide open thus giving you low light capability. Your masculine brain, paradoxically, is short-term memory and therefore able to remember only now, while your feminine brain retains the long term future and past memories as it does not realize that there is a future or a past. Therefore, your masculine brain is your short-term details memory, and your feminine brain is your long-term big picture memory.

 Rod vision is found in all vertebrates while cone vision is found in abundance in only a few animals, the predators. As carnivores, predators had to focus on fast-moving prey while herbivores, the plant eaters, dealt with plants that didn't move and predators who typically attacked from peripheral vantage points. Logically, predators were a later development because what they ate had to develop first. ***Cone vision, masculine vision, is therefore evolutionarily a more recent development.*** The same theme is played genetically with the x- and y-chromosomes where the root is feminine with the masculine a more tenuous development that is overlaid later.[5]

The same developmental sequence is found in babies who acquire rod vision within days of birth and cone vision months later. Because your cones are built to look at detail, or sections of the visual field, your associated left brain processing has to deal with the sequencing of images in a rapidly moving tunnel vision fashion. It is therefore built to deal with time sequencing. Hence, it handles the concept of past, present, and future in a tunnel of timed events. Your rods are processed by the right brain as a total input of the space around you, and hence are evolutionarily best suited to deal with space as a unified enveloping field experienced in the now.[6] Because the alpha state is associated with your right brain, and the beta state with your left brain, the alpha state is therefore the one you first begin processing with as a baby and evolutionarily was likewise the first state used by all animal life on this planet. This is why Douglas feels that the beta state is a relative newcomer as asserted in **Chapter 4 – Your States of Being.**

The best thing about the future is that it comes only one day at a time.

Abraham Lincoln

Investigating further the possibilities inherent in your alpha state based peripheral vision is therefore warranted. As with being left handed/right-brained, peripheral issues may have more potential than what we have "focused" on in modern industrial societies. Your supposedly black and white, legally blind in resolution, peripheral vision is the purview of both your subconscious and your reptilian brain. It is sensitive to motion and hence is your early warning system whenever objects are moving rapidly toward you on a collision course. Quickly reacting to situations like this is what your reptilian brain is built to do. That is however, generally a fear-based reaction.

A HIGHER PURPOSE FOR VISION

A higher purpose for your peripheral vision is therefore waiting to be explored. Tom Brown was trained to use his peripheral vision for acquiring a total knowledge of what was going on around him as he moved through the forest. Your peripheral vision therefore accounts for far more information input than what, based on the human factors research, it appears to be capable of. In the words of Douglas Lockhart, "All objects are obscured by our ideas about them. Seeing strips away the ideas with which we surround objects, melting the factuality, and allowing the actuality to surface." A good example of this occurred historically with explorer Magellan in the Yucatan. At first the natives could not see his ship. When their shamans finally made contact with it and relayed it to the tribal consciousness, the tribal community lost its bearings completely and disintegrated. The culture shock was too much and the tribe became apathetic.[7]

Developing wide-eyed relaxed alertness allows your subconscious to take in that which you cannot possibly process consciously. When awareness of this faculty is developed you become much more sensitive to subliminal advertising, and hence consciously aware of this form of manipulation found in most mass media, from magazines to TV. Subliminal advertising is filled with subconscious messages such as death skulls in the ice cubes of liquor ads, the word sex and sexually suggestive patterns in art work, low contrast messages in TV and radio ads compelling you to "buy, buy," and much more.[8, 9, 10] Once attuned, your peripheral vision will allow you to be more aware of your environment. Consequently, while driving your rear view mirrors will give you information about what is going on behind you without having to focus on them. By developing this awareness you both increase your ability to detect this information and your ability to block that which you do not wish to be programmed with. The key question for us is: What physical condition are your eyes in when you assume the relaxed alertness state that Tom Brown was trained to use?

When you look at objects up close your eyes rotate inward toward your nose so both eyes are foveating on the same object thus giving you stereoscopic vision, depth focus, and a sense of volume for the object and space immediately around you. Your internal eye muscles also distort the lenses of your eyes so they focus at the distance your eyes are being asked to view. When you look farther away your eyes focus out farther and the axis of vision for each eye moves outward toward being parallel. When you look at something around 20 feet or farther from you, the axes of your eyes become parallel to each other and your focus goes to infinity. If you relax both your eye muscles for focus, and those that move the eyeballs, your eyes focus at around a meter from you and pivot to become parallel to each other for viewing at infinity. This is the physical position for the state of relaxed alertness that author Tom Brown's mentor was asking him to develop. *This is also the state of soft focus that many talk about as being necessary in order to view auras around objects, and see with what Barbara Ann Brennan called higher sense perception, or your subtle vision as opposed to your mundane vision.*

Exercise 5.2 – RELAXED ALERTNESS AND YOUR THIRD HAND

Looking at something in the distance, at least 20 feet away, allows you to easily experience the state of relaxed alertness where you are focused near infinity with your eyes parallel. Maintaining your distance focus, put your hands together in front of you held upright in the "praying hands position," then keeping them parallel, separate them by about an inch. As you pull them apart from each other, you will see form between them the image of a third hand that will come into sharp view by adjusting the separation between your hands inward and outward until the image becomes solid. *Viewing past an object like this where double imaging occurs is the state your eyes assume in the relaxed alertness mode. Your eyes are relaxed and your focus is at infinity.*

Figure 5.5

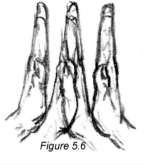

Figure 5.6

My wife and I have a charming friend who can see auras. Her name is Willow and she has degenerative eyesight such that her foveal vision no longer functions. Having only her extreme peripheral vision to see with she views the world as a child does from an oblique perspective without dissecting it with judgment. Consequently she sees not the details but the amorphous forms as we all did prior to developing high acuity focus vision. Hers is the world of energies and entities that children live in but which most adults seldom retain an awareness of. It is a world filled with multicolored auras around vaguely seen objects, the spirits of those who have passed on, and sometimes the gnomes and fairies of lore.

Learning how to see the energy of auras, and possibly the energies of entities around us, is not difficult to do. As with any skill, it only takes practice. Drunvalo Melchizedek covers this subject very well in Volume 2 of his *Ancient Secret of the Flower of Life Workshop*. Drunvalo indicates that the military trains some of its special forces to see auras as they use this information to know exactly what a person is feeling and hence, thinking. He is also aware of a physician at the Human Dimensions Institute who teaches courses on diagnosing human illness using this skill. Teaching how to see auras is beyond the scope of this book, but it can be learned by anyone who has a partner who can work with them, and a room that can be darkened with an adjustable incandescent light so the illumination level can be controlled. Drunvalo explains this procedure in his section on *Energy Fields Around the Body* on pages 337 through 341.

YOUR SUPERVISION

In order to see auras and other subtle energies you have to be in the alpha state. That is also the state where your mind becomes open for rapid information patterning. Quoting *The Learning Revolution*, "*Many researchers are now convinced that we can absorb information much more quickly and effectively when our brains are in a state of 'relaxed alertness.'*"[11] This is a meditative state whereby we are not judging what we see, just taking it all in. We look at nothing and therefore see everything. The ancient texts stated this as a Zen-like conundrum – that which is looked at is not seen. Author Paul Scheele states it this way, "to see it without looking at it."[12] One way of interpreting these statements is that they mean using only your peripheral vision, which is where higher sight occurs thus allowing you to perceive auras as previously noted. This state-of-being is what the sages and masters talk about when they advocate moving through life in a constant state of meditation. You lost this state-of-being as a child when you first went to school. There you were taught to read, told to keep your eyes on the book, and *to not look around!* Now is the time when you can return respectfully to this state-of-being. ***When your focus is soft, your vision at infinity, and you are in the alpha state, then your ability to learn approaches infinity, as it was when you were a child. This is the alpha zone. It is all encompassing covering A to Z, the alpha and the omega, the beginning and the ending.*** Based on the discussion so far, I compiled ***Figure 5.7*** as a listing of the characteristics of your visual system.

Figure 5.7 - Characteristics of Your Visual System		
	Peripheral	**Foveal**
Acuity	Low	High
Approach	Gestalt	Logical
Reasoning	Intuitive	Linear
Attitude	Accepting	Judgmental
Age	Child	Adult
Gender	Female	Male
Child Develops	First	Last
Ancestry	Oldest	Youngest
Sensor	Rods	Cones
Light Input	Open	Constricted
Viewing State	Relaxation	Concentration
Brain Hemisphere	***Right***	***Left***
Brain State	***Alpha***	***Beta***

According to the experts then, your eyes are not that good; it is really your mind/brain that is that good. However, testing of human vision has been largely limited to people operating in the conscious beta state rather than the subconscious alpha state. Subconscious vision is largely unexplored territory. Your eyes are really much more than two coordinated sensors that operate in a couple of different modes, only one of which is fairly well understood by the scientists.

The arts, and everyday experience, tell far more in this instance than science has gleaned so far. The eyes have been called the windows of the soul. Looking into someone's eyes can tell you much about their soul, and their state of awareness. Douglas Lockhart stated it this way: "The complex personalities which look out of the human eye are, for all to see, the complexes, or complexities of conscious intention, or tension."

In his book *Ageless Body, Timeless Mind,* Depak Chopra talks about this state-of-being in his third key to mastery: "***Take time to be silent, to meditate, to quiet the internal dialogue. In moments of silence, realize that you are recontacting your source of pure awareness. Pay attention to your inner life so that you can be guided by intuition rather than externally imposed interpretations of what is or isn't good for you.***" Addressing the same subject author Dan Millman says: "The complete practice of meditation involves a three-fold process of 1) attention, 2) insight [to look inward], and 3) surrender."

YOUR THIRD EYE

As we explore this territory it is worth asking the question about what eye is being used. Medically documented is an instance when Padre Pio prayed for healing for a woman who had no eyesight. Her vision returned despite the fact that she had no pupils in her eyes therefore making vision "impossible!" The doctors in Italy noted her physical condition and the fact that she could see, and were at a loss to explain how this was possible. [13]

Drunvalo Melchizedek tells of a woman that NASA worked with. Her name is Mary Ann Schinfield. She is capable of viewing at a distance whatever they asked her to. She is legally blind and when they requested it, could view and tell them the current status of the instruments located on a NASA satellite in earth orbit. [14]

Author Mary Summer Rain had an Indian shaman teacher who lived alone in a small cabin in the forest. She was called No-Eyes because she had been born with no eyes. As demonstrated by her ability to discern what was going on around her, and even walk the woods freely collecting herbs for her craft and all the food needed for her table, she apparently was able to "see" despite her handicap. Obviously she saw and perceived differently. However, she functioned as effectively as a person who had normal eyesight.

What is most apparent is that all of these women transcended the penguin culture. They didn't need to have two eyes as the rest of us think we do, because, as with all of us, they also have *a third eye, which takes vision to another level.* This is summarize in ***Figure 5.8*** which enlarges on ***Figure 5.7*** by adding a third-eye column between the peripheral and foveal columns.

Figure 5.8 - The Addition of Your Visual System Third-Eye Characteristics			
	Peripheral	***Third-Eye***	**Foveal**
Acuity	Low	***Infinite***	High
Approach	Gestalt	***Unity***	Logical
Reasoning	Intuitive	***Oneness***	Linear
Attitude	Accepting	***Omniscient***	Judgmental
Age	Child	***Infinite***	Adult
Gender	Female	***Androgynous***	Male
Child Develops	First	***Born with***	Last
Ancestry	Oldest	***Unknown***	Youngest
Sensor	Rods	***Pineal gland***	Cones
Light Input	Open	***Total***	Constricted
Viewing State	Relaxation	***Attuned***	Concentration
Brain Hemisphere	Right	***Both***	Left
Brain State	Alpha	***Low alpha/High theta***	Beta

Being able to see without the normal two eyes, or at great distances, or without pupils in your eyes, could be called miraculous. A Course in Miracles has this to say about miracles: "There is no order of difficulty in miracles. One is not 'harder' or 'bigger' than another. They are all the same. All expressions of love are maximal." However, instead of attributing them to miracles, maybe they really are functions of a higher law; forms of higher vision. Barbara Ann Brennan calls it *higher sense perception* (HSP) as it is above and beyond our normal vision, and other senses for that matter.[14] It is also called third eye vision. Mother Meera says that: "This [third] eye comprehends all things. It sees the whole picture – for example, it can see the background to the actions of others. At what stage it opens varies with the individual. It is not intuitive, it SEES everything clearly."

The ability to see being referred to by Mother Meera, is via the pineal gland which is located between the two hemispheres of the brain just below the corpus callosum. Externally it looks something like a pinecone which is how it got its name.[16] There are indications that as a major chakra it nourishes and governs the upper brain and right eye.[17] According to *Gray's Anatomy*, in some reptiles it has a lens and is constructed like an eye having color receptors. In one species of fish it is even at the surface of the skin and situated as an eyeball would be. In humans it is characteristically less well developed. At age seventeen it typically begins accumulating grains of sand known as "brain sand," hence making it particularly easy for radiologists to identify in X-rays.[18] Anatomically the pineal is pointed backward, which possibly accounts for the expression, "Having eyes in the back of your head." It is also pointed somewhat upward so it is focused more on "heaven" than earth. A healthy, fully functioning, pineal gland would be closer to the size of an eyeball. For most humans it has atrophied to around the size of a dried pea.[19] We naturally try to access this eye, and to a certain extent do so fairly often, even if for only relatively minor feedback. For instance, whenever a person is seeking inspiration, trying to visualize, or just plain feigns not knowing, they usually look up. This can be interpreted as an attempt to align their two eyes with their third eye, and hence the transcendent information it provides.

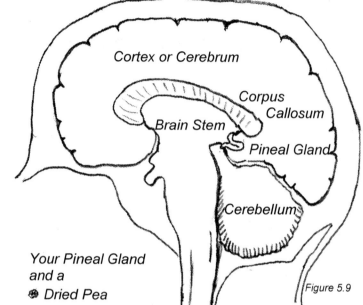

Cortex or Cerebrum

Corpus Callosum

Brain Stem

Pineal Gland

Cerebellum

Your Pineal Gland and a
🌑 Dried Pea

Figure 5.9

According to the book *Super Learning,* the Soviets were successful in their experiments to cultivate third eye and associated abilities.[20] Their work inspired an American study in 1973, called Project Blind Awareness, which was conducted in Niagara Falls, New York. 20 blind people volunteered to participate. Over the course of a year they learned how to "see" in a new way. Quoting from *Super Learning:*[21]

Some started to recognize colors far across the room. The world began coming back into "sight" in a way they found very hard to express... There seemed to be a light in their heads... One man retired his white cane.... A completely blind woman "saw" a photograph. As relaxation and training continued, these solid citizens started learning how to travel in their minds' eyes to distant rooms, houses, offices – places they had never been to – yet they were able to describe the layout.[22]

Such abilities are not limited to the blind. Anyone can develop them. My wife Carol is normally sighted yet very capable in third eye sight. She often "sees" in her mind's eye images that later turn out to be verified as correct. For instance, when our friend Dušanka was a human relations manager for a *Fortune 100* corporation, her office was in a downtown Chicago skyscraper. One workday she and my wife were talking on the phone and my wife spontaneously "saw" her office, and was able to describe it accurately to her including the arrangement of the desk and other furniture. Another time, Dušanka was searching for her misplaced passport and Carol "saw" that it was in a manila envelope. Dušanka is also capable in this regard and she "saw" a box that she then realized was one she had forgotten about in the back of one of her closets. In that box was the manila envelope containing the misplaced passport.

If you are interested in developing such abilities on your own, pages 226 through 238 in *Super Learning* describe the techniques the Soviets used, which were also employed in Project Blind Awareness. However, this book is leading up to teaching you a process that naturally awakens this faculty. Referring back to **Figure 5.8,** the conclusion to reach is that *your visual system really has three different modes of operation: foveal vision that is high acuity and low information content, linear, logical and judgmental as an adult; peripheral vision that is low acuity, high information content, gestalt, intuitive, and accepting as a child; and third eye vision that transcends both of these. Each of us has all of these abilities and if so desired, can cultivate them. True seeing transcends all.*

YOUR MUNDANE AND SUBTLE SENSES

Do not, however, limit your third eye to purely visual tasks. True perception is unity perception for all of your senses. According to therapist Marina Raye, around 10 percent of the population is not capable of visualizing in the sense we have been using the word.[23] They are visually impaired finding their strengths in the auditory and kinesthetic arenas. They are not, however, left out; because the work of Barbara Brennan and others indicate that your mundane senses become a single sense at the subtle level of the third eye. Your mundane senses are arrayed in duality as is reality around us as reflected in the dual particle/wave nature of light, thus "male/female" at the root of creation. We have two eyes, two ears, two hands for feeling, two sides of our tongue for tasting, and two nostrils for smelling. Each division maps to a hemisphere of the brain and hence is steeped in duality. Based on what Mother Meera tells us, the third eye transcends duality. Therefore, *when you perceive with your third eye your senses become one. You see with one unified eye, hear with a unified ear, and likewise taste, touch, and smell with unified senses.* That's equal opportunity for all the ways that people perceive although there is an infinite variety of mixes in which these different abilities are combined. We tread now in an arena where what we can fathom is but the tip of an enormous perceptual iceberg. Douglas Lockhart sums it up well:

> *The human body is an energy generator greater than anything man has ever built or conceived of. It has the ability to supply an infinite amount of energy if and when an organism wakes up to the meaning of its existence through continuous acts of seeing. An act of seeing stirs this generator into action, and the energy supplied stirs acts of seeing into perception. When enough energy is available, the acts of seeing expand and carry the seer far beyond the normal confines of conscious recognition, for if the generator is not allowed to run down, the psyche eventually penetrates itself as energy. All this is possible if a human being will only stop for a moment and look at the world properly. It is, as you know, that simple, and it is this very simplicity which makes it so profound. This is why it is not understood.*

**Time and space are real beings, a male and a female.
Time is a man and space is a woman.**
William Blake[24]

**It is in vain that we say what we see;
what we see never resides in what we say.**
Michel Foucault[25]

**I saw Eternity the other night
like a great *Ring* of pure and endless light, all calm, as it was bright,
and round beneath it, time in hours, day years driv'n by the spheres
like a vast shadow mov'd, in which the world and all her train were hurl'd.**
Henry Vaughan

*Perception can be insight or blinders, such is the nature of free will.
To see clearly is to see beyond.*
Melvin Lewis Thomas

*I know I'm not seeing things as they are,
I'm seeing things as I am.*
Laura Lee

The difference between a flower and a weed is a judgment.
Susan Hayward, *A Guide for the Advanced Soul, A Book of Insight.*

A change of world view can change the world viewed.
Joseph Chilton Pearce[26]

Chapter 6 – DIVERSITY IN LEARNING

Because of the infinite variation in the way individuals are assembled, it must be assumed that the sentient properties of any one person, like his or her fingerprints, could never be identical with those of another. It is probable, therefore, that there does not exist or ever will exist one person exactly like another. If uniqueness were an indispensable requirement for an evolving society, every person would be indispensable.

Paul MacLean

If we are to achieve a richer culture, rich in contrasting values, we must recognize the whole gamut of human potentials, and so weave a less arbitrary social fabric, one in which each diverse human gift will find a fitting place.

Margaret Mead

Know Thyself!
Aristotle

He who knows others is wise, he who knows himself is enlightened.

Lao-tzu

Be Yourself – Who else is better qualified?
Frank J. Giblin

**Though he should conquer a thousand men in the battlefield a thousand times,
Yet he, who would conquer himself is the noblest victor.**

Buddha

**You cannot transcend what you do not know.
To go beyond yourself, you must know yourself.**
Sri Nisargadatta Maharaj

*Why do people take the world as real?
Because they concentrate on things, and see diversity rather than unity.*

Mother Meera

THE book *The Learning Revolution* raises the mark for all of us with this observation: "Until she was 10, Helen Keller was deaf, blind, and mute. But by 16 she had learned to read in Braille, and to write and speak well enough to go to college. She graduated with honors in 1904." Desire can overcome enormous obstacles. However, without specialized instruction to help her get started, Helen Keller probably would never have accomplished anything.[1] It is important to note that scarlet fever at the age of 18 months robbed her of sight and hearing while leaving intact cognitive development to build upon in the future.[2]

Understanding learning styles is critical to one's ability to learn effectively, and the supporting foundation of a teacher's ability to teach effectively. Dr. Paul Dennison developed the concept of dominance profiles in order to characterize the different types of learning. His work is based on the fact that we have dominant brain hemispheres and sensory mechanisms. *Because the left hemisphere of the brain controls the movement of, and sensory input from, the right side of the body, and vice versa, knowing your dominance profile becomes critical for knowing how you learn best. Cross-lateral dominance profiles work well because sensory and brain dominance match up. Homolateral profiles require the two halves of the brain to communicate across the corpus callosum. Under stressful conditions this connection is poor.* **Figure 6.1** lists the different dominance profile combinations and associated learning strengths and weaknesses. It, along with the concept of the Brain Dominance Bug on page 48, has been taken from Dr. Carla Hannaford's book *Smart Moves, Why Learning is Not All In Your Head,* with permission from Great Ocean Publishers, 294 Lone Pine Road, Alexander, NC 28701.[3,4]

Figure 6.1 – DENNISON DOMINANCE PROFILES

Dominant Sense	Dominant Hemisphere	Preferred Learning Style
Cross-Lateral Dominance Profiles		
Right eye	Left	Visual
Left eye	Right	Visual
Right ear	Left	Auditory
Left ear	Right	Auditory
Right hand	Left	Verbal
Left hand	Right	Kinesthetic
Homolateral Dominance Profiles		
Right eye	Right	Visually limited
Left eye	Left	Visually limited
NOTE: Prefer to learn through their other senses		
Right ear	Right	Auditorially limited
Left ear	Left	Auditorially limited
NOTE: Tend to tune out of heavy talking (lectures)		
Right hand	Right	Communication limited
NOTE: See the whole image, may have difficulty expressing it		
Left hand	Left	Kinesthetically limited
NOTE: May have difficulty manipulating objects to communicate their ideas		

Exercise 6.1 – DETERMINING YOUR DOMINANCE PROFILE:

Determining your dominance profile can be done via energy kinesiology. The process is explained in **Appendix A.** However, it takes time to develop expertise and confidence in your answers. If you are already proficient at energy testing, or develop your proficiency after reading **Appendix A,** then you are ready to test a person's brain hemisphere dominance and likewise which eye, ear, and hand is dominant. Some people will not be dominant in either hemisphere or, stated another way; they will test as having both hemispheres dominant. A balanced profile is a natural consequence of full brain development and a stress-free environment. People with balanced dominance have a larger variety of answers to choose from when working problems than people with only one hemisphere active. If both hemispheres are equal in use then potentially that person can learn well visually, auditorily, and kinesthetically.

On the next page the Brain Dominance Bug and question answers are boxed for an *example* person who is right brain and right hand dominant, and left eye and left ear dominant.[5] **Figure 6.1** was used to determine their learning profile. In this *example* we find that this person has cross-lateral dominance for visual and auditory learning because their right brain naturally controls their left ear and left eye, but they are communication limited because they are right-handed with right brain dominance. Based on **Figure 6.1,** they would be classified as a visual and auditory learner. When you are ready to test someone, or have someone test you, ask the associated questions and fill in the blank Dominance Bug on the next page. There are two more blank Dominance Bugs for you to copy and work with in **Appendix B.** Alternatively, If you have Internet access, you can go to www.emode.com and take *The Brain Test.* For a modest fee you will be told your learning style and receive a 23-page report including a self-improvement program. For additional understanding, obtain a copy of Carla Hannaford's excellent book, *The Dominance Factor.* Carla covers the subject in greater depth including characterizing the 32 different dominance profiles.

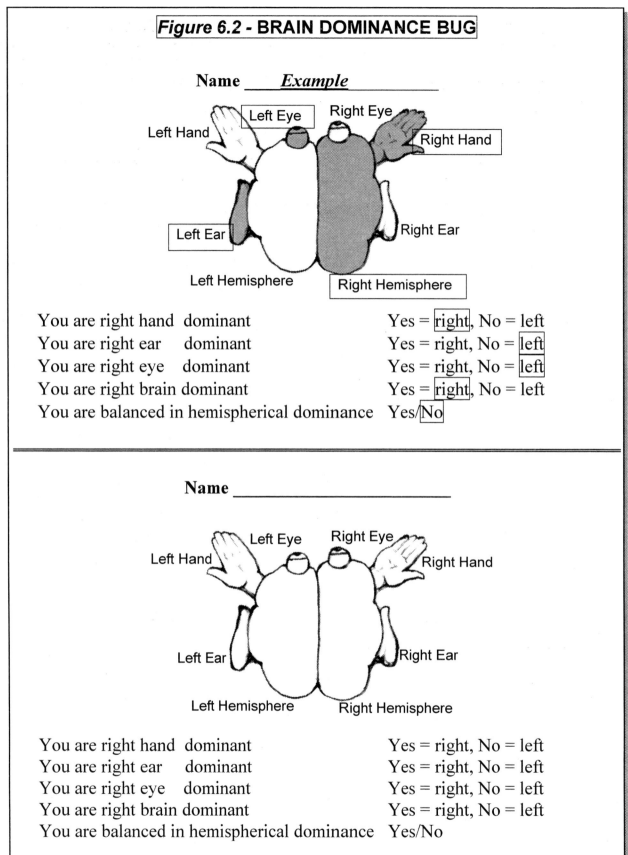

Figure 6.2 - BRAIN DOMINANCE BUG

Name ___Example___

You are right hand dominant   Yes = right, No = left
You are right ear   dominant   Yes = right, No = left
You are right eye   dominant   Yes = right, No = left
You are right brain dominant   Yes = right, No = left
You are balanced in hemispherical dominance   Yes/No

Name _____

You are right hand dominant   Yes = right, No = left
You are right ear   dominant   Yes = right, No = left
You are right eye   dominant   Yes = right, No = left
You are right brain dominant   Yes = right, No = left
You are balanced in hemispherical dominance   Yes/No

The bottom two-thirds of **Figure 6.1** is a listing of homolateral profiles that are limited in some sense. As previously noted, the reason for each limitation is due to the dominant brain hemisphere and sense being on the same side of the body thus making communication difficult. This is particularly evident under stress because even with a well-developed corpus callosum, stress limits your brain's ability to communicate this way. There are professionally administered techniques developed by Paul Dennison and others for reprogramming the body when dominance factors like this are a problem. One simple technique is to rub your hands together as this action brings the brain hemispheres into balance.

Once problems associated with homolateral profiles have been taken care of, there is still the problem of how to effectively teach such a broad range of learning preferences. ***In Western schools the schooling approach generally used is aimed at only 15 percent of the student population.*** In order to address the other 85 percent, Carla Hannaford notes that Sandra Zachary, a third grade teacher in Hawaii, arranged her students in the following fashion in order to accommodate all their learning styles:[6]

- *BRAIN GYM® activities (**Chapter 15**) for five minutes at the start of the day, after recess, and after lunch.*
- *Visual learners in front*
- *Right ear dominant auditory learners in the next row on the room's left side and the reverse for left ear learners.*
- *Gestalt fully limited in the back of the room with clay or wax to manipulate kinesthetically during class.*

Figure 6.3

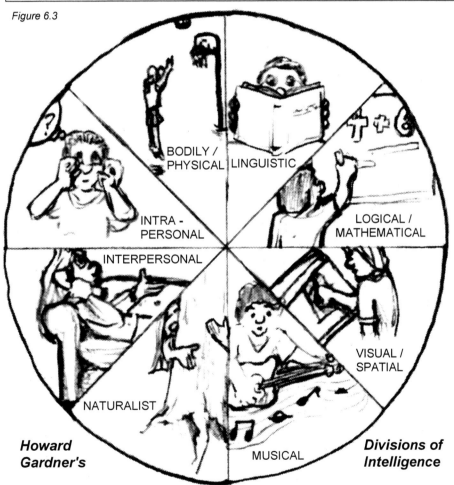

Howard Gardner's **Divisions of Intelligence**

Sandra had her students tape their dominance profiles on the front of their desk. She taught the class what these profiles meant thus fostering self understanding and compassion for others. The stress levels in the class dropped significantly and by the end of the school year every student was achieving at higher academic levels than they had ever achieved before.[7]

Diversity goes much deeper though than just Dominance Profiles. Chapter 10 of *The Learning Revolution* is a good overview of the different learning styles and intelligences that humans employ. For instance, Howard Gardner divides intelligence into eight categories as depicted in **Figure 6.3**: *Linguistic, Logical/mathematical, Visual/Spatial, Bodily/Kinesthetic, Musical, Interpersonal (Social), Intrapersonal (can access own feelings), and Naturalist. Unfortunately, Western school systems typically cater only to the first two of these eight categories.*[8]

Dr. Jane M. Healy characterizes people as either lumpers or splitters thus reflecting which brain hemisphere is their dominant one.[9] *Carl Jung categorized people based on how they perceived things thus developing another diversity metric. He classified them as feelers or thinkers, sensors or intuitors, and of those combinations, either extroverted or introverted, for a total of eight possible combinations.* Carl Jung also said:

> *The great decisions of life usually have far more to do with the instincts and other mysterious unconscious factors than with conscious will and well-meaning reasonableness. The shoe that fits one person pinches another; there is no universal recipe for living. Each of us carries his own life-form within him – an irrational form which no other can outbid.*

Exercise 6.2 – YOUR MIX OF ABILITIES IN THE DIVERSITY SPECTRUM

Based on Howard Gardner's divisions of intelligence, how would you characterize yourself? Record your observations in your journal. In which of these divisions of intelligence are you gifted, average, or challenged? Going further, are you a lumper or a splitter as Dr. Healy has observed? How would you assess yourself based on Carl Jung's divisions of people as feelers or thinkers, sensors or intuitors, and of those choices, either extroverted or introverted? These introspective actions will add to your understanding of who you are, where you shine, and where you might want to apply a little more polish if you desire to achieve a more rounded set of abilities.

Chapter 10 in *The Learning Revolution* states that there are at least 20 different methods for characterizing learning styles. Beyond that plentiful mix, a few more ways in which we differ are: working styles, thinking styles, managing styles, life styles including biological preferences such as being a morning or evening person, and so on. It is worth noting that most school and college students are not morning people.

Another take on diversity was developed by James Redfield in his best seller, *The Celestine Prophecy,* which characterized all people as operating via one of four different control dramas: Intimidators, Interrogators, Aloof People or Poor Me's. In her comprehensive and well researched book *Light Emerging, the Journey of Personal Healing*, Barbara Ann Brennan presents evidence that the basic body styles people come in are a result of early traumas in their lives, and associated with body shapes are three different methods of dealing with relationships, plus five defensive strategies which she names as: Schizoid, Oral, Psychopathic, Masochistic, and Rigid.[10]

Each approach enlarging the concept of diversity is analogous to a different way of slicing an apple. None are really the apple, which is far more complex than a slice reveals, and only truly itself when whole. The methods of classifying human diversity presented so far, plus all of the other combinations that the genetic code allows for, provide more than enough combinations to preclude any duplication. It is therefore ludicrous to formulate one dominant approach to teaching based on some subset of this diversity. *The successful education systems around the world cater to the differences in humans by invoking learning with a variety of mediums; sound, vision, motion, hands on, experiential, and so on, so that learning becomes a whole brain activity giving everyone a path to success.*

Penguin Patterning

Carla Hannaford relays the experience of having an older woman student who never took notes in her class. While listening she spent her time knitting. She earned an A and left with nine sweaters. In Europe, knitting is part of the curriculum.[11] If education in general, or our own individual learning in particular, is to be truly successful, it has to address diversity while honoring individuality. This process is most effective if it begins with the parent's newborn child, and continues with peers and in school thus avoiding the current overshadowing of penguin patterning.

Figure 6.4

Quoting David Riesman from his book, *The Lonely Crowd*,

The idea that men are created free and equal is both true and misleading: men are created different; they lose their social freedom and their individual autonomy in seeking to become like each other.

THE ANIMAL SCHOOL   By Dr. R. H. Reeves, Educator

Once upon a time, the animals decided they must do something heroic to meet the problems of a "New World," so they organized a school. They adopted an activity curriculum consisting of running, climbing, swimming, and flying. To make it easier to administer, all animals took all subjects.

The duck was excellent in swimming, better in fact than his instructor, and made excellent grades in flying, but he was very poor in running. Since he was low in running he had to stay after school and also drop swimming to practice running. This was kept up until his web feet were badly worn and he was only average in swimming. But average was acceptable in school, so nobody worried about that except the duck.

The rabbit started at the top of the class in running, but had a nervous breakdown because of so much makeup time in swimming.

The squirrel was excellent in climbing until he developed frustrations in the flying class where his teacher made him start from the ground up instead of treetop down. He also developed charley horses from overexertion and he got a C in climbing and D in running.

The eagle was a problem child and had to be disciplined severely. In climbing class he beat all of the others to the top of the tree, but insisted on using his own way of getting there.

At the end of the year, an abnormal eel that could swim exceedingly well and also could run, climb, and fly a little had the highest average and was valedictorian.

The prairie dogs stayed out of school and fought the tax levy because the administration would not add digging and burrowing to the curriculum. They apprenticed their children to the badger and later joined the groundhogs and gophers to start a successful private school.

**Some people break precedent and establish a new paradigm,
others break wind and establish a new atmosphere.**
Melvin Lewis Thomas

Those who are not busy being born are busy dying.
Bob Dylan

**There was a child sent forth every day,
and the first object he looked upon, that object he became,
and that object became part of him for the day or a certain part of the day,
or for many years or stretching cycles of years.**
Walt Whitman

*There is no such thing as "best" in a world of individuals....
All I want is for you to accept me as I am.*
Hugh Prather [12]

Even if your body cannot move, you can still think and meditate.
Dalai Lama

SECTION III – LEARNING WITH MOM AND DAD

NOW it is time to apply what the owner's manual says your equipment is capable of doing! Now is the time to recall that professional driving class you mastered long ago but forgot about somewhere along the way. As you do this, remember what Plato said, "All wisdom is remembering."

Chapter 7 – NATURAL LEARNING

Those who can teach, teach. Those who can't, lecture.

David Perry

To learn anything fast and effectively, you have to see it, hear it, and feel it.

Tony Stockwell

Learning is experience. Everything else is just information.

Albert Einstein

UNDERSTANDING the modes our mind/brain/body and visual systems operate in, and our own unique combination of learning abilities, gives us the opportunity to understand how to learn in a manner that is natural for us as individuals, and thus efficient. The failure of the public school system in America is in the attempt to make everyone fit what is the dominant learning style for only 15 percent of the population. The school system in America, and England's from which it was derived, force children to sit without moving in relatively sterile classrooms while they are taught the so-called three R's from age five on. Thus, they cater to only one learning style providing instruction primarily by teachers who are dominant in that learning style. Carla Hannaford characterizes this as "students who can process linearly, take in information auditorially and visually, look at the teacher, and restate pieces of information in a logical, linear fashion."[1]

The problem is further exacerbated by the fact that it isn't until around age eight that the logic circuitry in the brain is functioning well enough to support this approach for even the students it works well with. The end result is a lack of successful diversity in capabilities and a high failure rate. As *The Learning Revolution* points out, our school systems are optimized for failure and not success. This is hardly a good business model for turning out a consistent high quality product. In the United States, and many other countries, only the lack of federal support for the competition has allowed this system to survive for as long as it has.

If you were educated in the West it is therefore likely that you were taught to read silently while subvocalizing your words so that you didn't disturb the other students.[2] You were also told to "sit still and keep your eyes to yourself!" We know now that movement facilitates brain development. To make up for this forced inactivity as a child, the Brain Gym® movements and other forms of physical therapy help us overcome the damage inflicted at an early age by school and our other dominant form of inactivity, the television. School also forced us to accelerate our brain into the beta state, or high activity, thus cutting us off at the alpha state pass. The differences between these two states can more easily be understood from a practical learning perspective, by looking at **Figure 7.1**, which summarizes reading types based on the discussion in this and previous chapters.

Figure 7.1 shows us that *most of us having been taught to subvocalize our words. Reading thus becomes linear, logical, stressful, and results in an average of 200 to 240 words per minute.*[3] That limitation is based on the speed with which most people can speak. *Because we use our conscious mind, the information is retained using short-term memory.* This form of reading is useful for analysis or pleasure, but not for reading volumes of information for long-term retention. *Using it in that mode is what makes it stressful.* It is best used for the narrow-focus tasks like road signs and analytical arguments, or for the pure pleasure of reading something like a good novel. That is why *I characterize this as focus mode reading.*

**I took a speed-reading course, then I read *War and Peace*.
It's about Russia!**

Woody Allen

The next form is speed-reading. It is useful in a different way. It is great for consciously covering a lot of material for quick analysis by seeking out the key words in each paragraph. It is much faster than conventional reading using an expanded visual field, but still typically engages the conscious mind with key word guidance so you can quickly move through the material while looking for sections to delve into with analytical focus.[4]   However, *neither linear nor speed-reading techniques are aimed at long-term retention of information. Using your short-term memory for long-term memory tasks can be compared to trying to mow a two-acre lawn with a pair of scissors. By the time you finish it is time to start over again. If you learn to absorb volumes of material more naturally, the way you did as a child using the alpha state and your subliminal system, then reading is without sub-vocalization, intuitive, relaxing, and begins at 25,000 words per minute with retention in long-term memory.[5] Now you are mowing with acre-wide swaths. That is SuperScanning.*

Figure 7.1 – COMPARISON OF READING TYPES			
Reading Type	**Linear**	**Speed**	*SuperScan*
Visual Mode	Focus	Hybrid	*Peripheral*
Words Subvocalized	All	Key	*None*
Speed in Words per Minute	200-240	2000	*25,000+*
Brain Mode	High beta state	Beta/alpha state	*Low alpha state*
Brain Hemisphere Used	Logical left	Both	*Gestalt right*
Reptilian Brain State	Active	Less active	*At rest*
Memory Used`	*Short term*	*Hybrid*	Long term
Long Term Retention	5 percent	Better than 5 percent	*Greater than 73 percent*
Typical Emotional State	Stressful	Stressful	*Restful*
Processing Function Used	Conscious mind	Both	*Subconscious mind*
Sense Used	Mundane	Both	*Subtle*
Best Use	Analysis or pleasure	Search & catalog	*Volume acquisition*
Emotional State with Best Use	*Creative*	*Intuitive*	*Restful*
Retention Ability with Best Use	*Low*	*Medium*	*High*
Analytical Ability with Best Use	High	Medium	*Low*

Exercise 7.1 – DETERMINING YOUR LINEAR MODE READING SPEED
    Including the quote at the end, the remaining text after this exercise box, to the end of this chapter, is composed of 2245 words. If you time yourself and read it in five minutes, then you read at 2245 divided by five, or 449 words per minute, which is very fast for that type of reading. If it takes you ten minutes to read, then divide 2245 by ten and you will find that you read at 220 words per minute. If you take longer than ten minutes, you read at less than 220 words per minute. This exercise will give you a rough indication of what your conscious mode reading speed is. Most people will require between five and fifteen minutes to read the 2245 words. At SuperScanning speeds it would take only about five seconds to read what probably takes you more than five minutes to read.

The advantage of knowing all three reading techniques is that they are complementary and without stress when employed properly. Once you decide that you want to read a block of text, the best way to energize it for conscious forms of reading is to use your peripheral mode to SuperScan it with your subconscious mind and associated long-term memory. Here we are discussing only what SuperScanning does, not how to do it. SuperScanning technique is discussed in detail in the next chapter.

Once you have SuperScanned the information all of your reading modes will become enhanced in both their intuitive grasp and the immediacy with which you perceive the material. You will find increased understanding when reading the same material again with your conscious linear mind in focus mode. In hybrid mode you will "skip and dip" as Paul Scheele states it, "skim and scan" as Tony Buzan phrases it, or to borrow from pilot lexicon, "yank and bank" quickly through the material speed-reading it as you search for areas to explore more deeply in focus mode.[6, 7] As you speed read you search and catalog the material. This mode can also be used prior to SuperScanning the material if you are attempting to determine whether or not it is worth committing to permanent memory. *The stress of using both focus mode and hybrid mode is associated with the unreasonable expectation that you have to remember long term what you are reading. When your objective changes to only short-term tasks such as analysis, searching, and cataloging, then the stress level is greatly reduced and as your comprehension develops, will eventually effectively disappear.*

If you are interested in reading a novel for pleasure, by SuperScanning it first you will find that the story takes on vibrancy and increased presence thus enhancing both your pleasure and comprehension. You will be able to visualize the scenes more readily, see characters more easily, and have an intuitive feeling for the action and emotions being portrayed. As you become proficient in all three modes, you will eventually find that they begin to merge as your ability to navigate among them becomes transparent. *Restful replaces stressful as your subconscious becomes an ally for analytical tasks.* Information and understanding merge into a gestalt of greater ability. One success piles on top of another. When this happens you will have at your command an immense logical capability, intuitive grasp, and encyclopedic understanding, as my friend Douglas Buchanan does. As they merge into a smooth functioning unit your associated genius potential will take off.

MUSIC HELPS

What the mother sings to the cradle goes all the way down to the coffin.
Henry Ward Beecher

By rhythmical breathing one may bring himself into harmonious vibration with nature, and aid in the unfoldment of his latent powers.
Yogi Ramacharaka: *The Science of Breath*

Those who danced were thought to be quite insane by those who could not hear the music.
Angela Monet

By harmonizing altered states of consciousness, rhythms of recitation, breathing, and music, we spiral into the reserves of the mind. Once this connection is made, awareness follows.
Sheila Ostrander and Lynn Schroeder [8]

Music attracts the angels in the universe.
Bob Dylan

In the latter half of the last century in Bulgaria, psychiatrist Dr. Georgi Lozenov furthered our understanding of the effectiveness of subliminal learning by studying people with extraordinary memories and their techniques for memorization. A similar path was also followed by L. Alfonso Caycedo, a Colombian doctor.[9] Both found many of their answers by studying *Raja Yoga, which translates as "ruler joining" or "royal union." The adepts in this discipline, and likewise in Japanese Zen as researched by Dr. Caycedo, and the Maoris in New Zealand as researched by Dr. Lozanov, developed hypermnesia, or supermemory.* An example of the practical benefit was the memorization of the sacred Hindu texts by many yogis. In the event of a major catastrophe, this provided the ability to recapture that knowledge as long as even only one yogi survived. Metaphors, poems, and songs are easier to remember. *To aid in the memory process, many Hindu sacred texts are written as poems.* Both men met many people who had developed supermemory abilities.[10]

Dr. Lozenov also had the artist Mikhail Keuni to work with. Keuni had supermemory along with the ability to do calculations incredibly fast. As an artist, by inference, he was right-brained. His supermemory was extraordinary. Anything that entered his mind he could retrieve effortlessly in whole chunks. When sent to Japan by the Soviets to demonstrate his abilities, he learned fluent Japanese in a month. Japanese is considered one of the hardest languages there is to learn, defying the attempts of most Westerners to master it. Sent next to Finland, he learned their language in a week.[11] From their research, including studying stellar examples such as Mikhail Keuni, Dr. Lozenov and Dr. Caycedo both concluded that *such abilities were the products of entering a state-of-being through which knowledge flowed unimpeded.* They also proved that *when such supermemory feats were performed, the person was in the alpha state and alert but relaxed, which I express with the made up word,* $Z^{est}R_{est}$®.[12]

They concluded that anyone could learn to do this if they are put into the alpha state, subjected to information in a synchronized rhythm including their breathing, and immersed in a positive and relaxing learning environment![13] *The key was to achieve a state of relaxed alertness where the conscious and subconscious minds were both operating to facilitate conscious acquisition of the material in a stress-free environment.*[14] *The other key component was breath control.* Both developed comprehensive programs of accelerated learning techniques based on these key ideas. Both programs have demonstrated an ancillary benefit of healing illnesses in those enrolled in the process as a natural consequence of meditation-based accelerated learning.[15]

Dr. Caycedo's program was called Sophrology and it is centered in Barcelona, Spain. Sophrology uses the human voice to present the material using special rhythm and intonation much like singing. A similar approach that is well-known to most Westerners is the ABC's song used as a mnemonic aid for learning the alphabet. Dr. Caycedo's first name is Lozano, an interesting coincidence![16]

Dr. Lozenov's program was called Suggestophobia® and it is centered in Sofia, Bulgaria, where in the 1970s, one out of every 17 Bulgarians did yoga.[17] *Dr. Lozanov used music to place people in the subliminal learning mode, specifically baroque largo movements because of their slow, steady pace, to put people into the alpha state* and while in this state, have foreign language instruction read to them. The reading of this material is broken down into eight- to ten-second segments with silent portions built in to give the brain cells a chance to build a new "charge" again for the next learning sequence.[18] Eight-second spacing of sound bytes of information was found optimal for learning. This, coupled with learning how to relax, yielded spectacular results. An exception to the sound byte principle would be when learning something like grammatical rules, which were absorbed best if kept as long chunks. Dr. Lozanov was able to optimize this instruction to teach children 1,200 new words per day.[19] In follow-up tests, Dr. Lozanov also found that even when not used for as long as two years, the language instruction given was still retained at the 57 percent level.[20]

To put this in context, although the English language has 550,000 words, you can understand 90 percent of everyday English with a working vocabulary of only 2,000 words. While attempting to further explore Dr. Lozanov's approach other researchers have been able to achieve learning rates of only 500 words per day, but that is still impressive. ***The slow 50 to 70 beats per minute pace of largo movements, which mimics the pace of the heartbeat babies hear while in the womb, is what is thought to induce the alpha state, and hence Super Learning® rates.*** Many modern foreign language instruction systems are based on this principle and are worth seeking out if you want to optimize your learning rate. The one presented as a recommended example in the *The Learning Revolution*, is from Accelerated Learning Systems in the United Kingdom.[21] There are also branches of the Accelerated Learning Systems organization in the United States in Denton, Texas and Encinitas, California.[22] Complete contact information is listed in **Appendix K**.[23] This highly effective teaching system has its roots in the work of Doctor Lozanov. **Appendix C** is a listing of the music recommended by Georgi Lozanov. **Appendix D** is a listing of more recent music by Dr. Jeannette Vos, who is in the process of publishing her latest research in a book titled, *The Music Revolution.*

OTHER EFFECTS FROM MUSIC

Music can also have the opposite effect. As reported by Carla Hannaford in *Smart Moves*, **Dr. Tomatis discovered that upper range vibrations have an important effect for maintaining alertness and energy.** Quoting Dr. Hannaford:

> *When monasteries in France dropped their Gregorian chanting in an attempt to modernize in the 1960s, they discovered that these chants provided the upper register vibration and harmonics that maintained alertness. As a result, the men in these monasteries needed more sleep, were less productive, and tended to get ill more often.*[24]

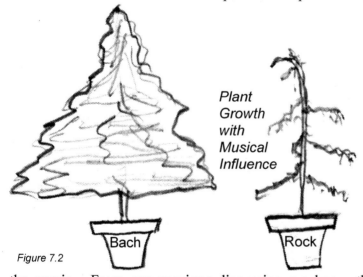

Plant Growth with Musical Influence

Bach

Rock

Figure 7.2

Another effect observed with music is that of either augmenting or stunting plant growth. Baroque music by Bach and Indian music by Ravi Shankar, caused plants to grow much more rapidly, and with thicker growth, than control plants grown without music. Likewise, rock music caused plants to shrivel and die. Country and Western music had no effect, and jazz had a small positive effect.[25]

One problem with listening to music in the subliminal state is that you are absorbing far more than just the music. From our previous discussion we know that ***the subliminal mind is telepathic.*** Therefore, *a listener in the alpha state absorbs the thoughts of the musicians who performed the music, the engineers doing the mixing, the stage hands who set up the show, and so on. **You absorb all of it.*** This might account for the differences seen by researchers who tried to duplicate Dr. Georgi Lozanov's 1,200 words per day learning rates, but were able to achieve only 500 words per day. Even using the precise same music would only approximate the result Georgi achieved because the thoughts of the researchers affect the outcome. Scientifically this is known as the Rosenthal effect, named after Harvard psychologist Robert Rosenthal, who first described it. Although initially discovered in psychology, it has since been demonstrated as applicable in physics and chemistry. *The Rosenthal effect is a verifiable consequence of the fundamental metaphysical principle that our thoughts create our reality.*

From a practical perspective then, it is essential that you choose healthful music to listen to. Many people have instincts that are pretty good in choosing music, or any other item for that matter, based on whether or not they impart a good feeling. Developing and reinforcing that feeling is important. If you cannot already tell instinctively, then the only way I know of to test for such intangibles is applied kinesiology, which is discussed in **Appendix A**. When seeking to purchase music, go to a concert, or while listening to background music or commercials with catchy tunes, use self-applied kinesiology to test how positive the subliminal content is. Avoid or block any music or commercial that flunks your testing.

This approach gives you a mechanism to test anything in your environment that you suspect might have a detrimental subliminal content. For instance, when you put your socks on in the morning you assume that they are just socks. However, if the person running the loom in the factory where they were woven was angry that day, then that anger is in those socks. They have a negative subliminal message that you become open to whenever you put yourself into the alpha state. This is why it is good advice to buy automobiles built during the middle of the week and not Monday or Friday; hangover and anxious-for-the-weekend days respectively

You are bombarded with such messages every day. *The majority of the feelings and thoughts that you process every day aren't even your own. Just setting the intention that they be blocked is a powerful first step. Become mindful of the environment you are in when you slip into the subliminal state.* For this reason, falling asleep with the radio or TV on is not advised as you open yourself up to absorb an unmonitored stream of subliminal broadcasts and their associated telepathic thought systems. If you need noise to sleep or meditate, use a sound source such as a fan, air conditioner, bubbling indoor fountain, or an appliance specifically built to generate white noise. The ideal is of course, nature. If you live next to a stream, waterfall, ocean surf, or where the wind in the trees predominate, you already have a white noise generator more healthful than anything manmade. There are many commercial recordings available that capture natures' magnificent auditory ambiances thus providing restful backdrops for sleep and meditation in the comfort of your own home.

Music heard so deeply that it is not heard at all,
but you are the music while the music lasts.
T. S. Eliot

We adults face a signal-to-noise ratio problem. Our semantic reality, kept intact through our roof-brain chatter, makes an awful din, but we grow afraid of silence.
Joseph Chilton Pearce - *Magical Child* [26]

Chapter 8 – SUPER RESULTS like SuperScanning

**The habits of a vigorous mind are formed in contending with difficulties.
Great necessities call out great virtues.**

Abigail Adams

Music can do in minutes what weeks of meditative practice strive towards.
Colin Rose and Malcolm J. Nicholl, *Accelerated Learning for the 21st Century*

I never worked a day in my life. It was all fun.

Thomas Edison

Imagery, as we use it, is another way to harness the extraordinary power of your mind.

Dr. Herbert Benson

**The most beautiful experience we can have is the mysterious.
It is the fundamental emotion that stands at the cradle of true art and true science.**

Albert Einstein

*The secret of making something work in your lives is, first of all,
the deep desire to make it work, then the faith and belief that it can work,
then to hold that clear definite vision in your consciousness
and see it working out step by step, without one thought of doubt or disbelief.*

Eileen Caddy, *Footprints on the Path*

WHEN I was growing up in Sedona, Arizona, I went to the local school there from third through eighth grade. When I was in fifth grade a new student by the name of Dean showed up. We soon became friends. When our class was given the assignment to memorize and recite the *Midnight Ride of Paul Revere* by Henry Wadsworth Longfellow, I struggled with trying to learn this poem, and ultimately was able to recite only about half of it in front of class. Dean effortlessly recited the entire poem without mistakes. After a few years his parents moved elsewhere and he didn't return until I was in high school. By then I could remember only the first line of the poem while Dean still knew it. Even though I was one of the top math and science students in a large school, I was still not able to outperform Dean. When we were both seniors, during a casual conversation I asked him how he could memorize so easily. He told me that he had a photographic memory. He read something only once and had it memorized. He never studied as far as I could tell and had plenty of time to pal around with his friends. I studied many hours every day and had to work to not be envious of his ability.

When I was in college going to Northern Arizona University in Flagstaff, Dean and I met again one day. I rode in an automobile with him and another friend named Mo to where Dean was staying while attending college. I was in the back seat while Dean was driving, and Mo rode up front, as we navigated the streets of Flagstaff that night. Mo was teasing Dean because his car was old and the left headlight was aimed down as it should be, while the right headlight was aimed so high that you could inspect treetops with its light. Dean shrugged it off. I had a good laugh and thought nothing of it at that time. That was the last time I heard from Dean until around 25 years later. I was living in Phoenix, Arizona, when he called me from Michigan where he lived, just to get reacquainted again. After catching up with each other's lives I asked about his photographic memory. He said he lost it around the age of 40 and that it was his understanding that many with this ability lose it at about that same age.

Dean's ability always fascinated me. The next person I met who had something like this ability was Richard. Rich has close to a photographic memory. He told me that this is the result of having positively affirmed himself for perfect memory ever since high school. I concluded that this ability can be both destroyed and developed for Dean had lost his, possibly because it atrophied for lack of use, or maybe because of a desire to not remember any more; while Rich had acquired and retained his because of his desire. I expect that Dean's automobile now has both headlights aimed straight ahead as do most of our automobiles.

More recently I met Rev. Douglas Buchanan. He has a photographic memory and a nearly encyclopedic knowledge of every subject I, and many others, have ever queried him on. When you ask him a question he sometimes seems to be scrolling down an invisible page of text with his eyes prior to giving you an extemporaneous answer of greater depth than most experts can in whatever subject you ask about. *Douglas said that years of practice and positive affirming gave him his extraordinary abilities. He also said that his abilities are based on absorbing material while in the alpha state.* He generously shared the basis of his abilities.[1]

HOW TO DEVELOP A PHOTOGRAPHIC MEMORY

Douglas developed his photographic memory by using the following technique:

DOUGLAS' TECHNIQUE
  For RETAINING and RECALLING SUPERSCANNED MATERIAL
1. Be clear as to your purpose for studying whatever you intend to SuperScan.
2. Start with deep breathing in order to relax. On the inbreath subvocalize **Re**, and on the outbreath subvocalize **LAX**. Repeat until you have entered a meditative state of relaxed alertness known as the alpha state, and are ready to SuperScan the material you have chosen.
3. Start your SuperScanning by saying **Re** sub vocally on the inbreath. Continue deep breathing while you read the material by SuperScanning it without using your conscious mind to analyze it so that you move quickly. When you finish, end by saying **TAIN** with your final outbreath.
4. When you need to recall the material you have SuperScanned, use deep breathing once again to get into the alpha state via **Re-LAX**
5. Affirm to yourself **Re** (inbreath) **CALL** (outbreath) and you will recall the material you previously SuperScanned.
6. Follow this procedure consciously with everything you SuperScan with the intention of developing a photographic memory.

What the Douglas technique relies upon is the state of relaxed alertness that is characteristic of the alpha state. This state-of-being is the way you operated all the time as a young child. Remember that child, wide-eyed, alert and smiling, free of judgment, and open to all. That state-of-being is what you wish to return to if you want to learn rapidly. In that state your penguin accouterments and labels will fall away to let the untarnished child come through. *Thus your penguin handicaps disappear. For instance, dyslexia is no longer a factor and glasses are no longer required.*

NATURALLY OCCURRING ALPHA STATES

In order to develop a sense for what the alpha state feels like so that you can start becoming mindful of the times when you are naturally in this state, a few examples might help. Many are circumstances you will naturally cycle through on a daily basis:

EXAMPLES OF NATURALLY OCCURRING ALPHA STATES:

- During the night when you get up to go to the bathroom.
- When you first awaken after a night's sleep.
- While taking long baths or showers, particularly the first thing after awakening.
- Quietly doing repetitive or boring tasks you are proficient, or even highly skilled at, where you "zone out," such as knitting, washing a stack of dishes, or polishing your golf clubs or other treasures.
- The quiet times during long automobile trips either as the driver or a passenger.
- Nature walks or if you're a runner, long runs.
- Listening to boring talks that drone on as you listen, listen, and listen to them.
- Rocking, sucking, and playing with objects, or other infantile habits.
- Humming a steady note much like a cat purrs.
- Being sick and feverish, which incapacitates the conscious mind.
- Drinking alcohol and getting hit on the head, however, neither is recommended.[2,3]

From these examples you can see that whenever you "zone-out," you typically are in the alpha state because your conscious mind has shut down and the subconscious has taken residence. Rocking, sucking, and playing with objects tend to put a person into the alpha state as all three are reminiscent of the behavior of babies. Hence rocking in a rocking chair or hammock, sucking on a drink through a straw or a small stone while hiking in order to allay thirst, and working clay or bread dough can all induce the alpha state if one is quiet during these activities.

Poets spend a lot of time in the alpha state as poetry is a full-brain activity. Likewise, music, painting, business, dancing, and mathematics are full brain activities. ***Breaking your circadian pattern can induce you to spend protracted times in the alpha state.*** The recent wedding of my daughter was so popular that young and old stayed up until the country club the reception was held in was closed at 1:00 a.m. thus shutting the party down. The next few days after this event everyone was wiped out, or more accurately, zoned-out. All of us spent a lot of time in the alpha state during this time. There are rituals, and even entire cultures, that are mindful of this principle of circadian disruption thus using the alpha state productively.

CULTURAL PRACTICES THAT FOSTER THE ALPHA STATE

In the West, Native American cultures engage in many alpha state inducing practices. For instance, the *I-ni-pi* (purification ceremony or sweat lodge), which places people in darkened, claustrophobic confinement under the stress of intense rounds of sauna-like conditions thus simulating being in a womb. A sweat lodge combines the four elements of earth, air, fire, and water. You sit on the earth under a light-tight shelter. Rocks heated red hot on a fire

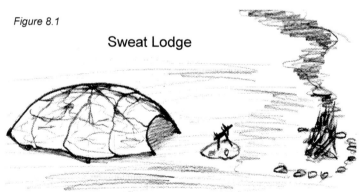

Figure 8.1

Sweat Lodge

near the small entrance are brought in one at a time and placed in a central pit. When all of the rocks for a round have been brought in, the entrance is closed and the ceremony begins. Herbs are placed on the hot rocks thus generating a lot of smoke. Then, water is poured on the rocks to fill the lodge with steam. Typically four rounds are done, which accumulatively have a heavy emphasis on cleansing, forgiving, and prayer. When the lodge is over it is followed by an emergence that simulates a birth. Another ceremony often practiced during sweat lodges, or independently, is smoking the sacred *C'anupa*, the pipe. Whenever this sacred ceremony is practiced it is also likely to be alpha state-inducing as it is a ceremonial meditative practice where words are seldom spoken.[4]

The *Han-ble-c'I-ya* (sacred rite of the vision quest) is another example. This rite is also referred to as, "going up on the hill." Vision quests can last from one to four days, dependent upon the form of the practice. They involve deprivation of sleep, food, and water, coupled with singing and praying to help induce the alpha state. The *Wi-wanyang wa-c'I-pi* (sun dance ceremony) incorporates the same elements for four days and has similar results for large groups of dancers. There are also communal drumming and dancing rituals that induce altered states of mind, particularly the ones that use slow tempos, thus inducing the alpha state. Most of these rituals elicit superhuman responses that for the longer four-day trials of vision quests and sun dances, are essential for survival.[5]

It is of some interest that sleep deprivation was the primary means with which the Soviets broke people in the Gulag Archipelago, yet when combined with positive affirmations and intentions, the states of deprivation practiced by the Native Americans are successfully survived with lasting positive benefits. The intention of the practice may be the only significant difference, yet it yields a profoundly different result.

From the East, repetitive and meditative martial arts practices such as tai chi chun, are also alpha state inducing and hence conducive to reprogramming the body for high energy states and glowing health. Many other martial arts forms are also aimed at achieving an altered state, including kung fu and qi chong, (chikung). All of these practices are whole brain activities and thus conducive to integrating the mind for greater levels of awareness and achievement.

All cultures have daily practices and some rituals that are alpha state inducing. Becoming mindful of these times allows you to begin to get a feeling for what is happening and to start using this state-of-being productively. Your conscious mind can maintain awareness, and hence control, while your subconscious mind performs what it does best, the storage and retrieval of a wealth of information from your magical cave. *When you can keep your conscious mind quiet, but still enthused with your objectives, you are postured to "learn with zest while at rest" as Jeannette Vos states in her seminars. I coined the word* Z^{est}R_{est}® *to describe this state-of-being.* Z^{est}R_{est}® *is having your rudder in the water while you sail the freshwater sea of your subconscious so if you need a drink of knowledge, you easily dip in to fill your cup. Likewise, you can also easily pour in more buckets of knowledge to merge with the rest.* What you are learning here is your own form of meditation by capitalizing on the times during the day when you are naturally meditative. To aid in returning to this state at will and using it productively we will explore other techniques that support this objective.

DEVELOPING YOUR ALPHA/THETA STATE INDUCING TECHNIQUE

As an optional first step, *use a few drops of lavender oil placed on your third eye and under your nose on your lip as this oil puts you into the alpha state. Then visualize a golden ball of light over your crown chakra as depicted in* **Figure 8.2** *on the next page.* Douglas Buchanan has obtained his best results by placing the ball eight inches back and a little above the top of the skull. L. Ron Hubbard used to say that the most efficient place from which to drive the body was a foot and a half behind the head.[6] Experiment with this in order to determine your personal optimum placement. The golden ball opens you up and keeps your conscious mind partly occupied so it does not interfere with what you are trying to do. Keep this ball there while you Re-TAIN or Re-CALL. As you do this **affirm that you will have wide-open eyes and expanded awareness of what is going on around you.** The marvelous thing about this state of awareness is, your conscious mind is working allowing you to navigate while your subconscious mind takes in the greater view. In this state the memory you access is your long-term memory, and you no longer need to focus on what you are reading, using your focus instead to just relax and flip the pages.

Your eyes are aligned at infinity, relaxed and at rest focus beyond the pages or screen. Your mind is therefore focused with the left headlight low allowing you to navigate, and your right headlight aimed high taking in the greater view just as my friend Dean did with his car. I suspect now that one of the reasons Dean had a photographic memory in the first place was because he was so fun-loving thus giving him good access to his inner five-year-old.

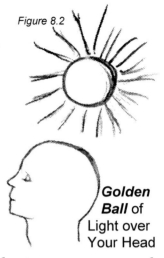

Figure 8.2

While in the alpha/theta state your speed of acquisition is limited only to the speed with which you can put the information in front of your eyes, either by flipping book pages or computer screens. As you flip past material, keep a steady beat going using whatever you have chosen for your alpha/theta state reading mantra. The mantra I suggest helps you "purr" with the alpha/theta state as a cat does while reinforcing positive memory and recall:

Golden Ball of Light over Your Head

> I learn with zest! I am in my gen ius zone where I am per fect mem o ry and I am per fect re call be cause I am at rest.

With this memory mantra each syllable is a page turn at a pace of about one page per second. Affirmations of this nature help reprogram your subconscious for perfect memory. Because of the holistic nature of the subconscious, you can SuperScan a book in any manner you wish including reading backwards.[7, 8] You therefore can read right side up, upside down, sidewise, or even from the middle toward the back end and from the front to the middle if that makes it easier to turn the pages. People with left-eye dominance will probably prefer scanning from right to left and hence, find it most natural to read books from the last page to the first page in reverse of the normal reading pattern.[9]

Posture yourself so you can sit holding the book with your eyes looking past the top edge at objects much farther away. This is the same situation that allowed you to see your third hand in **Exercise 5.2**. In this instance, rather than the way an opened book normally appears as shown in **Figure 8.3**, you will also see a third page which, like the binder of a book opened and viewed from the back side, forms a middle area, or arching page which joins the left- and right-hand pages. This is depicted in **Figure 8.4**. This middle page is analogous to the corpus callosum in joining the two halves of your mind. In this visual state, your perception is unified as your third eye unifies it, and your mind follows suit.

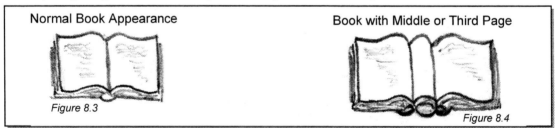

Normal Book Appearance

Figure 8.3

Book with Middle or Third Page

Figure 8.4

This visual state, *the state of relaxed alertness* previously discussed, *helps keep your conscious mind from trying to read the words or focus on the pictures. The objective is to use your conscious mind to set up the situation, then get it out of the way to allow the subconscious to perform its patterning task. Orienting the book in an unusual fashion, like upside down, helps you accomplish this.* You then read backward from the norm in the West thus mirroring the East, and likewise if you are in the East, the result is the same. This is useful in the beginning, but not essential once you have established the habit. Reclining with the book resting high in front of you so you can see off into the distance is one way of doing this. Because watching TV fosters being in the alpha state, you can even develop this skill to the point where you can watch TV while reading a book. This is possible, but probably not desirable unless you are very selective in what you view.

However you decide to SuperScan, the key is to first use your natural alpha state times to develop your ability to freely go into the alpha/theta state at will, then make certain you do not disturb your alpha/theta state while you are SuperScanning. When you finish whatever you have SuperScanned, take one final look at the title, author, or some key phrase or concept that will help you pattern this information for easy retrieval. Then, either continue with the next book or transition to the beta state for fully conscious action.

One way to have fun with this is to adopt a policy of SuperScanning a book whenever you have to get up in the middle of the night to go to the bathroom. Notice how easily you navigate your bedroom and its various obstacles in the dark because the subconscious is aware of where everything is and will advise you if asked. In order to maintain the alpha state avoid talking, turning on the lights, and looking at your clock, as these actions will tend to activate your conscious mind and wake you up. These precautions will also facilitate falling asleep again quickly after you finish this exercise.

Have a book already in the bathroom so all you have to do is pick it up and start SuperScanning as you subvocalize the memory mantra. Only very dim light is required as your alpha/theta state vision, being rod based, is much more acute than your normal mundane vision, being high light level cone based. Experiment with this if you like. Try SuperScanning books to moon- or starlight, or in other dim light conditions where your conscious mind is blocked from being able to see well enough to try reading the words. Not only will you develop a wealth of new knowledge, but you will also teach your conscious mind to feel comfortable with this procedure and not interfere. Thus you are using your oowl-eyes as a night owl, something many artists already understand.

The French linguist Joseph Justus Scaliger, born in 1544, apparently never forgot anything he learned once. He would awaken during the night and read in the dark. He spoke sixteen languages and never used a dictionary or grammar to acquire them.[10] When my son Matt tried reading in the dark in Phoenix, Arizona, he was at first startled, then delighted by the flash of a static electrical spark generated by the pages rubbing together in the low humidity. He experienced yet another enchanting surprise often lost in the bright hubbub of conscious living.

HOW TO CONTROL MONKEY MIND

One of the purposes of visualizing the golden ball over your crown chakra is to tie up the conscious mind. That ensures that the sea is calm for your alpha state sailing. In Hindu terms, the conscious mind is known as the chattering monkey that leaps from tree to tree never staying in one place very long much as our mind leaps from thought to thought. In order to meditate, one technique that is particularly effective for Westerners is called "meditation with seed." You give the conscious mind something to do so it is fully occupied and cannot get in your way during meditation. The memory mantra you subvocalize, and the visualizing of the golden ball over your head, therefore serve the double purpose of occupying the mind and reprogramming the subconscious at the same time.

There are historical instances of great composers who demonstrate this principle. Leonard Shlain cites two examples:

> *Alexander Luria, the Russian neurologist, reported the case of a composer who created his best work after he was rendered speechless by a massive stroke in his left hemisphere. [This case] history lends credence to the tale that Mozart asked his wife to read stories to him while he composed. By distracting his left brain with spoken language, the stories may have freed his music-oriented right brain to compose.*"[11]

I submit that in both cases cited, a means of tying up the beta state monkey mind was found, one via stroke and the other via distraction.

When I worked for the United States Air Force, it was generally acknowledged that no fighter pilot could keep track of more than around seven aircraft at one time during air-to-air combat. Above that number most pilots lost track of what was going on. The same would be true of the number of cars around you on the highway, or the number of football players you can track on a field. Your conscious mind therefore has a limit of how many tasks you can give it. When you are SuperScanning using the technique just outlined, flipping pages, maintaining an alert-relaxed state, visualizing a golden ball over your head, and following a memory mantra, your intentionality coupled with these tasks is enough to tie up the conscious mind so the subconscious is not interfered with. Once you establish a pattern of getting into this state without your conscious mind interfering, you can truncate the procedure to something shorter. Soon your memory mantra will become ingrained and the rate at which you flip pages can become independent of the mantra so that you can go faster or slower as appropriate for the medium you are working with.

SUPER WORDS – POWER WORDS

What we are calling super words are known historically as power words, and the concept has been around for a long time. Some words carried such power that people were not even allowed to speak them. Examples are some of the names of God and the Platonic Solid called the dodecahedron, which were thought to have great power. To give you another example from history, from Arabia there is the story of "Ali Baba and the Forty Thieves." While in hiding near the cave entrance Ali Baba sees the thieves approach their hidden cave. The head thief opened the magical entrance by saying the words "open sesame." After all of the thieves entered the cave, Ali Baba slipped in after them hoping to steal from them. When the thieves departed, closing the door behind them, Ali Baba ended up trapped inside because even though he said the same words, he didn't get the same results. What Ali Baba didn't know was that previously the head thief had done a longer ritual beginning with "open," and ending with "sesame." This longer ritual is the magic that opened the door. He repeated this longer ritual 100 times. After that all he needed to say was "open sesame" thus invoking the longer magical ritual with only the key words.

This parable is the key to how your subconscious can be programmed. In it your subconscious mind is the cave, and the treasure is the knowledge your mind stored there. Once you have programmed a ritual, all you need are the key words and your subconscious, like the magnificent vast cave of wealth it represents, follows the commands of the conscious, which is the leader much like the head thief was. "Yabba dabba doo," "I yam what I yam," "Scooby Dooby Doo," and even "Feel the force" and "To infinity and beyond!" are examples of other rituals that various generations grew up with that invoke strong images and feelings just by hearing the words.

This technique can also be used for your daily prayers and other rituals. All you have to do is insert a word like "abra" at the start of your morning prayers, "cadabra" at the end, and after 100 repetitions you invoke the intent of your morning prayers with only abracadabra. Abracadabra actually means, "As I say, so it becomes," and hence is a powerful affirmation. *Super power words* like this were usually drawn from other languages in order to ensure they weren't likely to be spoken in one's own community. In Europe the words chosen were often Arabic or Hebrew. You can choose from Sanskrit, Greek, Russian, Chinese, Navajo, Hopi, Lakota, Watusi, Swahili, Mayan, or any other language foreign to where you are. In Western cultures the use of Latin probably wouldn't be advised because so many of our words are drawn from this language. However, in China, Latin might be an excellent choice. Choose a language that you know others are not likely to use around you. This way you could avoid having someone say a power word in your presence at a moment of unawareness. In whatever language you choose to draw your words from, it would be best to try to choose words whose meaning supports what you are trying to do.[12] Power words can be used to allow you to cover praying over your food, water, and other sacred rituals you wish to have at your command.

You can also use power words to bracket physical rituals such as exercises. By doing this you capture the state-of-being exercise puts you into without having to do the regimen. The famous guru Yogananda had many disciples who never practiced sports, yet his students had super sports abilities such as great strength and coordination, because they used meditative techniques to achieve the same results. Power words can be built around physical, mental, emotional, or spiritual rituals thus giving you the same benefits in only a few seconds.

Power words can also be nested inside each other. For instance, Re-CALL can be nested inside abracadabra to form abra Re-CALL cadabra thus inserting in the middle a prayer or script that you wish to incorporate as a new addition to your abracadabra ritual. You can also program a power word in segments as you go through the day. Your prayers in the morning might be one segment, and later on you add another segment during your walking meditation through the forest. All you have to do is open your power word, add, subtract, or modify what you wish, and then close your power word. Your subconscious knows only the infinity of the now so it will holistically integrate it.

HOW TO STOP SUBLIMINAL PROGRAMMING AIMED AT YOU

The other side of the coin is also important. Without conscious control of your subconscious anyone can steal into your cave of wealth much as Ali Baba did. It happens to you all the time. Every subliminal act of programming you encounter in the form of printed and broadcast advertising is an Ali Baba slipping into your subconscious cave. The subliminal advertising business is multibillions of dollars in scope and little known by the general public, yet daily it influences all of us in a thousand ways that we are not consciously aware of. Hence, during the intermission at movie theaters we crave soft drinks, popcorn, and candy because we were subliminally influenced, both visually and auditorily, to do so. Likewise, after watching television commercials our subconscious has a wealth of new slogans and songs to contend with. Printed material is also filled with subliminal messages that are cleverly airbrushed into photos and other artwork so you have to search to find it with your conscious mind, but capture it easily with your subconscious.

Subliminal advertising, coupled with prominently displayed brand names and catchy music, is used to sell virtually everything on the market, and it works very well. This is because music accesses the right brain patterning ability. My son Trevor told me, "Sometimes when I listen to songs when I first wake up, they are stuck in my head all day." That is precisely the objective of subliminal advertising, to get it stuck in your head. I advised my son to not use the radio part of his clock radio to wake up. Because of this problem, and the fact that an alarm can cause you to forget dreams, I trained myself more than a decade ago to wake up automatically when I needed to without the use of a clock. All you have to do is ask your puppeteer, or guides, if that terminology is more familiar to you, to wake you at a certain time. They will also awaken your when it is best for you to be up if you do not want to set a time. Likewise, I also do not wear a watch. So many timepieces abound in modern society that it is easy to find out the time if I really need to know it. If I don't, why concern myself with time, which is all that a wristwatch tends to reinforce.

When I worked for the Air Force I traveled a lot. Because of my familiarity and comfort with being on airplanes, I would fall asleep before the plane took off and would wake up just as the drink or food cart arrived at my row. I knew of another person whose thought system was that he would always have clear passage on roads. On freeways cars parted for him like water before the bow of ship. These are simple examples of how to program the reality around you to reflect what you desire, not what you fear.

Another form of subliminal programming occurs when you look up at someone. ***Looking up puts you into the alpha state.*** This probably happens because that is the only direction you can look which also aligns your two eyes with your third eye, thus causing you to assume the natural meditative state of the third eye. You have to look up to see around, for a round is a sphere and thus sees in all directions at once. Hence, it is not just - keep your head up to be aware, but also - keep your eyes up to be able to see. You really do have eye(s) "in the back of your head."

However, while in the subconscious mode precipitated by looking up, you are inclined to speak with the truth of a five-year-old, plus you are open to patterning. This fact is often employed, although seldom with knowledge of what they are really doing, to great effect by royalty, clergy, lecturers, teachers, judges, police, politicians, and parents, all of whom often try to have their heads higher than those they are addressing. My third grade teacher often looked at her class over the tops of horn-rimmed glasses in order to get us to be quiet and sit still. Now I understand that she was employing the energy of her third eye, coupled with the power available in the alpha state, to maximize her control over us.

The most prominent example of the use of this technique is Adolph Hitler, who captured a powerful nation using his knowledge of the alpha state and hence was able to terrorize the entire world. The podiums and platforms he used were allied with the Hitler salute so people looking at their own raised hands subconsciously went into alpha. Anyone can practice going into alpha by keeping their head level and looking through their eyebrows at the ceiling, or at an imaginary Hitler salute. This is one of the secrets of the amazing effects of his oratory. He used voice rolling as an aid, starting softly to attain concentrated listening and then raising pitch and power as the Sieg Heils were orchestrated, sometimes in synch with the lighting.[13]

The way to combat these subliminally based control dramas is to take conscious command of your subconscious mind, and program it the way you want it to work. Become aware of the Ali Baba lurking around the entrance of your cave. You do this by exercising your subconscious, however, when you open the cave to put your wealth in to it, you also open it for intruders. Consequently, ***as you develop your abilities you have to be increasingly vigilant about stopping subliminal intruders by actively blocking or avoiding their messages. You block undesirable subliminal messages by issuing a conscious counter message to your subconscious that explains to it why that information is incorrect and that it is to be disregarded.***

ACCUMULATING KNOWLEDGE AT SUPER RATES

Because his time is very filled, Douglas takes only minutes and reads an average of one book a day. He can easily read many more in a single day if he chooses to, and have photographic memory levels of recall. With his technique you can read ten books in only an hour. I don't know about you, but even though I have a fair-sized personal library, there is no way I have the storage space or the desire to spend that much money on books in order to feed a knowledge appetite that is that prodigious. When you have progressed to that point, you might consider getting a library card as I have.

Electronically SuperScanned material needs to be viewed only once. However, most books are not yet available on line. www.projectgutenberg.com is a repository containing hundreds of books online. Seeing as most books are not yet available electronically, in order to be really effective at SuperScanning, you will need to be able to handle pages. Books may need to be SuperScanned multiple times because flipping pages is not a skill you are likely to be perfect at. Occasionally you will flip more than one page. Do not be concerned about this. Just keep going. Maintaining the cadence is what is critical for maintaining the alpha state.

Notice that one page a second is in the 50-70 beats per second range that Georgi Lozanov worked with, thus it mimics a mother's heartbeat. Sixty pages per minute is the cadence for the song you sing to yourself using a memory mantra like the one I recommend (I learn with zest! I am in my gen ius zone where I am per fect mem o rey and I am per fect re call be cause I am at rest) for maintaining the alpha/theta state. You flip pages at this rate because it reinforces this mantra. If you are electronically "flipping" through material you can go at much faster "flipping" rates. However, still maintain the sixty syllables per second pace with your memory mantra in order to support your alpha/theta state. If you who have watched Data on Star Trek, or Number 5 in the movie *Short Circuit*, then you have an excellent visualization of what true alpha state ultra fast reading rates might look like when computer systems become optimized to support this inherent human capability. The speed with which you can go is limited only by the speed with which the equipment can go. This may be one of the true untapped potentials in the Internet, and computer technology in general.

When flipping the pages of books, manual dexterity becomes important. The rubber finger covers secretaries use can help you flip single pages at a time. For an average page flipper, in order to get more than 90 percent of the book, you will need to SuperScan it three times. With a pace of four minutes for an average book of 100,000 words with 240 pages, you can SuperScan it three times in 12 minutes. Therefore, in an hour you can SuperScan five books three times each. Use your mantra to sing a song of memory to yourself until you can effortlessly maintain alpha state patterning mode. When you look with a song, it stays with you the best. Your mind, it will hold on!

Alpha state photography, or ASP, is an alternative name for SuperScanning that is more accurate scientifically. You can think of ASP as a mix of as soon as possible (ASAP) and extra-sensory perception (ESP) that yields spectacular results – an alpha state pronto way of taking in information. For instance, books with bigger pages filled with more words would still be SuperScanned at the same 60-cycle rate, only now you would be absorbing information at much greater than 25,000 words per minute. With Encyclopedia Britannica-sized pages you would SuperScan at closer to 100,000 words per minute. That ought to fill your cave of wealth fairly quickly as depicted in *Figure 8.5*, or, to hark back to an earlier metaphor, now you are flying as a golden-winged white-unicorn Pegasus. Remember though, intent is very important or else your mind will not grab it.

Before you commit to ASP or SuperScan anything, make sure that it is worth your while. Flip through the material using your conscious mind in hybrid mode to determine if it is subject matter that meets your needs. After you have SuperScanned, you can also read the same material conventionally with your conscious mind by looking for the sections you want to delve into more deeply for analysis with your logical, or focus mode mind.

Figure 8.5

The Subconscious - Your Cave of Knowledge Wealth

However, *if you want to go for the gold, remember Carl Jung's ability to read books in libraries in his dreams.* That is what my son Trevor will be able to do after he perfects his book reading dream recall. By setting the intention prior to going to sleep, you can go to whatever source contains the information you require. Edgar Cayce began his education poorly, but quickly caught up when he developed the ability to acquire knowledge from books he slept on under his pillow. Toward the end of his lifetime, he had only to hold a book and the knowledge it contained was instantly his. A book is a thought. As a thought it is accessible by tuning into the information as part of the collective unconscious, which your subconscious easily accesses.[14, 15]

RECALLING KNOWLEDGE

Your peripheral patterning and focused investigative minds need to work together so you can probe and study your wealth of SuperScanned information. One acquires, the other analyzes. They must work in harmony in other to reach your full potential. Initially your recall of SuperScanned material will probably be in the form of intuitive hunches. A knowingness will lead you to certain pages of already SuperScanned books when you wish to look something up, or ideas will "come to you" that you are able to expand upon. You might discover yourself making spontaneous statements during a conversation, yet recall no conscious source. As you perfect your technique you will begin to recall in greater detail whole sentences, paragraphs, then sections and whole pages as you require them. It will be as if you are using your narrow beta state foveal vision to pry open the big picture view your alpha state peripheral vision gives you. Think of it as great recall of alpha state photography, or GRASP. Now you will be able to GRASP that which you SuperScanned ASAP.

A photographic memory is an excellent long-term goal, just not something most of us can reasonably expect to experience in the short term. When you begin affirming yourself for a photographic memory, use an affirmation such as "I am willing to have a photographic memory." This gets around the subconscious fear of success that would reject the outright "I have a photographic memory." There are those among us who may indeed develop photographic recall in only a few weeks; for others it may take 20 years. This is dependent upon many factors, two critical ones being how developed your third eye vision is and how much you practice. If you are starting with a shriveled pea for a third eye don't necessarily expect to "leap tall buildings in a single bound" anytime soon. Likewise, *to develop proficiency practicing a minimum of half and hour a day is required. More practice yields results more rapidly.* However, right from the beginning, all who develop subconscious awareness will have a better intuitive feel for what they have SuperScanned along with a better conscious familiarity with the material.

What we are developing here is a program to enable you to absorb printed information completely. You can activate the program with whatever words you choose. Likewise you can also invoke recall with your own activation techniques. The foundation here is consistency. If you prefer other wording than what has been suggested so far, then select techniques you like, then stick with it. *After about 100 repetitions they will become part of your universe, being deeply imbedded in your subconscious. After that only your key super power words are required to open your cave so that you can deposit or retrieve a wealth of knowledge.*

Do not limit your thinking in terms of developing only visual memory. Although we have concentrated on printed information, the ability to remember comes in a variety of forms. We previously discussed that people have different modes of learning that we characterized as visual, auditory, verbal, and kinesthetic. Everyone tends to be dominant in one of these forms and have a mix of abilities in the others. Few people are good at all. A photographic memory infers a visual memory, but the term perfect memory is superior as it includes all forms of memory.

During my tenure with the Air Force Research Lab, one of my friends, a fellow scientist named Liz, was tasked with the job of briefing a four-star Air Force general. Because he was so intelligent, this man had a formidable reputation for being difficult to brief. Not only could he read and absorb view graphs at a speed such that a briefer was in danger of boring him, but he also had a perfect memory such that he remembered everyone he met and what they said verbatim, including conversations years earlier. Liz did very well by making sure that she was thoroughly prepared.

My second father (adopted as my mom remarried after my biological father died when I was five) told the story of an elder American Indian who was reputed to have a perfect memory. One day, during the annual PowWow held in Flagstaff, Arizona, my father happened to meet him. Knowing his reputation Dad decided to test him, so he asked him what he had for breakfast ten years earlier. With only a moments pause, he answered, "Eggs." My father then realized that there was no way of verifying this information. Before he could ask a more insightful question, the venerated elder had to leave to perform other tasks. Two years later Dad was walking down the streets of downtown Flagstaff when he saw the same Indian coming toward him. Raising his right hand in traditional Hollywood style, he greeted him by saying, "How!" The Native American elder answered, "Fried," as he walked by. There is the possibility that this was an old joke my father was passing along.

Humor is yet another form of memory along with many other variations that account for the richness of human diversity. Occasionally dancers, singers, martial art students, and other professionals, have perfect auditory, verbal, and/or kinesthetic memories thus giving them a considerable advantage over the competition. For instance, perfect pitch has a less easily characterized equivalency in perfect smell, taste, and even touch. All of our senses are candidates for perfect recall and the ability to access a flawless comparative memory for assessing new information. As you develop the channel for one, you increase your sensitivity across the full range of sensing and likewise your ability to recall in a variety of forms.

THE PENGUIN PRICE

In his review of this material Douglas Buchanan observed:

> *I used my system because until I was fifty I could not make pictures in my head. This connects with a previous cogent paragraph of yours. When I was very young, I am told, I too could see into the subtle world. In a desperate bid to avoid freaking people out, and to have normal friendships, I rejected the ability to see, around the age of seven. Unfortunately, because of my magical heritage I did too good a job and developed poor mundane vision at the same time. The inherited ability could not be erased and went up into the top chakra. So, where other people see, I know. Same program, different outlet. Quite a few children do this around age seven, I have found, though not always for the same reason.*

Douglas's observation that **many children limit themselves at around the age of seven** correlates well with an observation by Barbarra Ann Brennan that the age of seven is when children typically become less connected to mommy and more open thus beginning to see their similarities to others. She also indicates that not coincidentally, seven is the age when all of a child's chakras finally have protective screens over them.[16] According to Joseph Chilton Pearce in his book *Magical Child*, "Ernest Hilgard of Stanford University found that children become highly susceptible to suggestion at age seven." Dr. Pearce also found that after age seven is the point when the birth of individuality is complete and the brain assigns specialized functions to particular areas thus partitioning tasks. He presents good evidence that age seven or eight is the point when children lose their perfect pitch ability, their extra sensory perception (ESP) abilities, and their art begins to conform to cultural influences.[17]

This is the price many of us paid in order to be penguins. It is important to remember that the alpha state is also a heightened state of awareness for all five senses and more, not just your vision. You may indeed eventually be able to sense the touch of molecules or the color of paper in front of you with your hand, and so on, as you did as a child. These are the types of abilities found in the hundreds of thousands of super children in China. These children demonstrate that their thoughts become reality and they do so in only seconds.[18]

There is nothing that these children do that you as a child were not capable of and still are. *By practicing the Douglas Technique in Exercise 8.1 on the next few pages you can take another step in the direction of restoring your own abandoned abilities and begin building a new unlimited reality for yourself. Exercise 8.1 first calls for putting your "seat of consciousness" in the middle of your body rather than your head. This follows from the holistic nature of the body as part of the mind and the understanding that the true seat of consciousness resides "in your middle."* That is the location where your prana and associated consciousness first enter and gather. This area is known in martial arts as the Tan Tien.[19]

Next, you put yourself into the alpha/theta region using a technique that does not involve counting, but instead uses the chakra colors, starting at the root chakra and ending with the crown chakra. Thus *you count the rainbow bridge as depicted in* **Figure 8.6.** Counting with colors is a right brain concept much like Disney's Pocahontas singing, "Painting with the colors of the wind." Metaphors and parables are inherently right-brained. The word metaphor combines the Greek word *meta,* which means "over and above," and *pherein,* "to bear across." Like the corpus callosum, they bridge the chasm between the hemispheres of the brain. For instance, Zen conundrums cannot be solved with the left brain.[20] A student had to be right brain functional in order to progress in his lessons. Jesus and all the other great teachers were inherently right-brained. As they integrated above duality they reversed their original descent into physicality and followed a right brain path toward oneness thus unifying all states of being. *Crossing your eyes simulates the path of oneness with a unified look inward.*

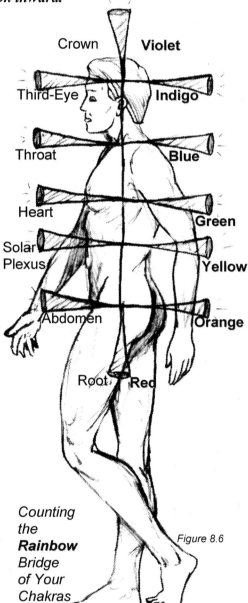

Counting
the
Rainbow
Bridge
of Your
Chakras

Figure 8.6

The technique of breathing out more slowly than the inbreath activates the parasympathetic nervous system, which is the body/brain brake pedal. Your breathing must be very deep using your diaphragm and pelvis, not the shallow breathing most people do by raising their collarbones or expanding their rib cage. *We will use the same breathing pattern that adept Jack Schwarz was found to use in scientific studies done at the Menninger Foundation. It was proven that this breath pattern allowed others who duplicated it to balance their brain hemispheres in the theta as Jack did while their corpus callosum remained in the alpha thus maintaining consciousness.*[21] Conversely, **Exercise 8.2** on the next page has you breathe out at the same rate as your inbreath. This special breathing pattern was likewise verified to anchor a person in the beta state just as Jack Schwarz was able to.[22] It stimulates your body's accelerator, the sympathetic nervous system.[23,24]

Finally, the affirmation, "I am in my SMART zone now!" is used to emphasize being in the alpha/theta region. SMART is an acronym standing for: "super memory alpha reaches theta." The SMART zone is where alpha reaches theta (ART) is accessed. The alternative affirmation, *"I am in my GENIUS zone now!"* is based on an acronym that you compose to your taste. The G in GENIUS is made from your choice of the following G words: generously, generally, globally, galactically, guy, gal, god, goddess (or any other G word of your choice). Your G word is combined with: encompassing now including the unconscious and superconscious (discussed in **Chapter 9**) to form GENIUS. You may prefer to begin learning how to SuperScan by using the SMART-based affirmation until it feels mundane, and then transition to your GENIUS-based affirmation when it feels appropriate.

The beauty of the SuperScan technique is that it activates both hemispheres, thus allowing left-brain script to be handled in right-brain holistic memory for long term retention. The effectiveness of SuperScanning is directly related to how deeply you descend into the alpha/theta region. It is only at the deepest levels of alpha, transitioning into the theta, that the collective unconscious is accessed and knowingness occurs. Quoting *The Learning Revolution,* *"It is in the alpha and theta states that the great feats of supermemory, along with heightened powers of concentration and creativity, are achieved."*[25] *This is the level where information patterns directly into your mind at thousands of words per minute, and recall becomes perfect.*[26] *This is the magical arena of the genie, the place of daydreams, inspiration, accessing other minds, knowledge of the past, and sometimes the future. It is the seat of pure genius, which combines genie with us. It is the bridge between the mundane world and the subtle world of true reality. The realm of poets and artists, and the doorway all sages, saints, avatars, and shamans pass through on their way to cosmic consciousness. It is the prize you seek!*

Now you are ready to use the Douglas technique with the *power words* Re-LAX and Re-TAIN, to SuperScan a book. It will take practice to become proficient at this procedure so be patient with yourself as you learn it. Once you are prepared by taping or memorizing this exercise, start by removing your glasses or contacts if you wear them, and make sure that you have a dictionary or thesaurus close by and ready to SuperScan.[27] It is essential that you seat yourself comfortably with good posture and shoulders back so that you can breathe properly. Listening to classical Baroque Largo music also helps.

Exercise 8.1 – SUPERSCANNING USING THE DOUGLAS TECHNIQUE.

1. Vocalize **Re-** with a quick inbreath, then with slower outbreath:
   Put your **eyes into soft focus or relaxed alertness, owl-eye mode.**
   Put your **consciousness at the center of your body,** behind and two inches below your navel.
   Put your **hands in a centering mudra** such as thumb+index+middle fingers together.
2. **Inhale** deeply for *4 seconds* with your nose using your diaphragm and pelvis while subvocalizing:
   I learn with zest!
   Hold for *8 seconds* while **crossing your eyes, looking up,** and mouthing:
   I am in my gen ius zone where
   Exhale slowly for *16 seconds* while you **look level, close your eyes, visualize your red**
   charka, and mentally track with the **memory mantra**:
   I am per fect mem o rey and I am per fect re call be cause
   Hold for *4 seconds* until the next cycle:
   I am at rest.
3. Repeat this pattern for each chakra color: **orange, yellow, green, blue, indigo,** and **violet.**
4. End by continuing **(4,8,16,4) breathing** and vocalizing **LAX!** with your **Exhale.**
5. Then transition to begin reading by vocalizing **Re-** for the inbreath and:
   Visualize a **golden ball of light over your crown chakra,** positioned where it feels best for you.
   Keep your eyes in **soft focus owl-eye mode while looking over the top of your book.**
6. Breathe in the **(4,8,16,4) pattern** as you mentally track with the **memory mantra** in a syllable per second cadence while you **turn the pages or view computer screens** with its metered pace:

   (Inbreath) **I learn with zest!** (Hold) **I am in my gen ius zone where**
   (Outbreath) **I am per fect mem o rey and I am per fect re call be cause** (Hold) **I am at rest.**
7. Upon finishing the book, on your **concluding outbreath** vocalize **TAIN!**

The next exercise, *Exercise 8.2*, incorporates a technique for putting you back into the beta, or focus-state, just to ensure that you are firmly planted in that state-of-being, or fully conscious after doing this exercise. As part of this technique I introduce the new trigger word Re-TURN using beta state breathing in order to develop a ritual that you can use to put yourself back into the beta state at a moment's notice. *The Re-TURN exercise is great for waking up quickly in the morning and likewise for accelerating your mind out of the alpha/theta state whenever that is required. Proper foursquare beta state breathing throughout the day reinforces this.*

Exercise 8.2 gives you practice in the elements of what Douglas does for Re-CALLing. The purpose of this exercise is to give you the perception of lighting up all parts of your brain, body, and mind while practicing recalling subliminal information. The next page of this exercise is a worksheet. It is a representation of the divisions of your brain and body. You will need a partner to work with you on this exercise. Have your partner read the exercise to you and when the time comes, randomly open the book you SuperScanned in **Exercise 8.1**, select a word, and read it out loud. On the worksheet the spaces for words have been numbered from 1 to 26, with the 26th space filled in with the word "*example*." Write down the word read to you in each section of the worksheet as you progress. Each section has room for two words. There is also a representation of an open book over each space where the word is to be written. During this exercise, after you write down the word, indicate with an "X" where the word is located on either the left or the right page of the open book pages above it as depicted in *example* **number 26** at the bottom right of the **Brain Bingo**® practice sheet.

If you require them for reading, you will need your glasses or contacts for this exercise. It is more typical that when doing **Exercises 8.1 and 8.2,** you won't be in a position to have background music so this time you can try this exercise without music. If you can dim the lights or work with only incandescent lighting, that also helps induce the alpha/theta state.

Exercise 8.2 – BRAIN BINGO®

1. Quickly re-enter the alpha/theta state from the last exercise by: Inbreath for 4 seconds and say **Re-**, hold for 8 seconds while looking up and crossing your eyes, exhale for 16 seconds while looking level and saying **Lax,** then hold for four seconds while you:
   Put your **eyes into soft focus or relaxed alertness, owl-eye mode**.
   Put your **consciousness at the center of your body**, behind and two inches below your navel.
   Put your **hands in a centering mudra** such as thumb+index+middle fingers together.
2. Begin information retrieval by breathing in the (4,8,16,4) pattern and vocalizing **Re-** on your inbreath. Visualize a **golden ball of light over your crown charka and concentrate on the material you wish to retrieve.** Vocalize **Call!** on your outbreath.
3. Breathe in the (4,8,16,4) pattern as your partner calls out each word. First write the word in the numbered blank space provided, then mark its location with an "X" using the area above it which represents the pages of an open book. Twenty-five randomly chosen words will be read to you.
4. Begin your return to the **beta state** by vocalizing **Re-**
5. Inhale deeply for a *4 second count* through your nose using your diaphragm and pelvis.
   Hold for a *4 second count* while **looking down.**
   Exhale via your nose or mouth and **look level** while **subvocalizing:** Cha kra 7 now!
   Hold for a *4 seconds count.*
6. Repeat this (4,4,4,4) pattern while counting down the chakras: **6, 5, 4, 3, 2,** and **1.**
7. Continue the (4,4,4,4) breathing pattern and subvocalize: "I am in my focus mode now!"
8. To conclude **vocalize TURN!**

To score yourself on this exercise, look up each word read to you in the book you SuperScanned. Put a circle around every **X** you placed in the correct position the word was located in as illustrated *example 26* on the next page. If you SuperScanned the book upside down, then you will have two correct positions for the word, the conventional location, and the location the word is in when the book is upside down. Either is accurate from the perspective of the subliminal mind. The purpose of this exercise is to give you the sense of lighting up your entire mind and brain while showing you that your intuitive capacity for word location is working even though you have only begun to reawaken your innate ability. Use the blank space provided below to write down the number of correct answers you had out of a possible 25. You multiply the number you got correct by four to get a percentage. Had you been randomly guessing, you would have gotten only a few of them correct or around 10 percent for a small two-column dictionary. Even the first time they do this exercise, most people do better than what random guessing accounts for. You now have a technique you can practice for strengthening your fledgling photographic Re-CALL ability.

	x 4 =	%

Exercise 8.2 – Continued

Name		**Figure 8.7 – Brain Bingo® Worksheet**		Date

Lighting Up the Whole Mind/Brain/Body

Front of brain · · · **Back of brain**

Prefrontal cortex	Motor cortex	Temporal lobe	Parietal lobe	Occipital lobe
1	2	3	4	5
6	7	8	9	10
Limbic		**Corpus callosum**		**Cerebellum**
11	Left-brain, right side of the body	12	Right-brain, left side of the body	13
14		15		16
Medulla oblongata		**Pineal gland or third eye**		**Brain stem**
17	18	19	20	21 x
22	23	24	25	**26** *Example* ⊗

Chapter 9 – WHAT LEARNING WITH MOM AND DAD MEANS

The human brain: A springboard by which you can leap into the magical world of genius.

Dilip Makurjea

The aim of education should be to convert the mind into a living fountain, not a reservoir.

John Mason

Now this, monks, is the noble truth of the way that leads to the cessation of sorrow. This is the Eightfold Way: namely, right views, right intention, right speech, right action, right livelihood, right effort, right mindfulness, right concentration.

Siddhartha Gautama – Buddha

Learning is finding out what you already know.
Doing is demonstrating that you know it.
Teaching is reminding others that they know just as well as you.
You are all learners, doers, and teachers.
Illusions, the Adventures of a Reluctant Messiah by Richard Bach

The true gentleman does not preach what he practices 'til he practiced what he preaches.

Confucius

Without this playing with fantasy no creative work has ever yet come to birth.
The debt we owe to the play of imagination is incalculable.

Carl Jung

A person who is an expert at languages is called a polyglot, which comes from Greek and translates as "many tongues." What do you call a person who speaks only one language? An American! This joke derives its humor from the elephant of truth in it. The West in general tends to focus on only one religion, Christianity, and to think in terms of only one lifetime. In America our communication is in terms of only one language. This is another reflection of our beta state focus taken to the extreme. Because of the extensive colonization by Great Britain and the current importance of the American economy, the world has adopted English as a standard for business communication thus allowing Americans to be lax in their learning of other languages. In many regions around the world multilingualism is common. In Europe it is a way of life. Those raised in such an environment are generally more tolerant of other ways of thinking and doing, having had to live with significant cultural diversity in often compact geographic proximity. Anyone seeking to achieve full brain activity will find learning other languages an excellent way to expand mental dexterity.

Superscanning techniques adapt quite well to learning other languages. The key is to establish a bridgework of understanding. Douglas Buchanan relays this of his experiences:

> *Before I went to France as a young man I bought a Collins pocket dictionary and learned it pretty well in a week, and then applied it to a French newspaper, so that I had several thousand words ready to be hooked into situations and scenery when I arrived in Northern France. I did a similar thing when I needed to know some physical chemistry and the book that dealt with it was in Spanish. I used a pocket dictionary and the chemistry text. Since I knew a lot of Latin and Esperanto at the time, this was no great feat.[1]*

One of Douglas' heroes is George Borrows, who wrote many books in the 1800s including: *Lavengro, Wild Wales, the Zincali,* and *With the Bible in Spain.* He worked for the British and Foreign

Bible Society and walked around Europe selling Bibles in various languages. When he encountered a country with a language new to him, he first learned a translation dictionary by heart, then began talking. With such simple techniques he mastered Chinese in three weeks, and twenty languages overall.[2]

Douglas also found a hero in another 19th century explorer, Captain Sir Richard Burton. Douglas noted that, "He was the best shot and the best swordsman in England, and one of the best horsemen. His career at Oxford was suitably scandalous." Sir Richard Burton's mastery of languages was so complete that he could pass as a native in Persian, Hindi, and some Arab dialects. He was the first European to enter Mecca and knew the Koran so well that he gave sermons on it to the Muslims. More than linguistic mastery was involved in this feat. The Muslims would have killed him had they had suspected that he was European. He translated the Kama Sutra from the Sanskrit, knew many Oriental languages, and wrote the book, *Arabian Nights*. His process for learning a language was similar to that of George Borrows; he began by memorizing a dictionary and a representative text of the language.[3]

The "King of the Polyglots" was the Italian Cardinal Mezzofanti, who lived from 1774 until 1848. By questioning galley slaves and criminals, and working with student linguists and foreign visitors, he developed his vast multilingual repertoire. In his meticulously researched biography Russell documents 72 languages that Mezzofanti knew, plus 39 dialects, for a total of 111. Thirty of these Mezzofanti mastered such that his fluency was indistinguishable from a person native to the language. Without prior knowledge he was observed to master one language overnight, and the Sardinian language of Sardo in 15 hours of study. Even Russell's conservative estimate of Mezzofanti's ability puts him heads and shoulders above all other known linguists. Russell noted that, "Children, as is well known, learn to speak a language more rapidly than their elders. I cannot doubt that Mezzofanti's child like simplicity and innocence were among the causes of his wonderful success as a speaker of many tongues."[4]

Mezzofanti, Richard Burton, Henrich Schliemann, and several other giants in the polyglot field all agree as to the method for learning a language. They used a dictionary and a text of the foreign language.[5] Russell notes that almost all great linguists have remarkable memories.[6] *Superscanning with supermemory recall therefore become the foundation upon which to build an understanding of a new language.[7] Committing the dictionary to memory gives you the connectivity, and the text example gives syntax. After that the polishing comes from interacting with people speaking the language, the best source being the country it is spoken in. Thus, with just minor preparation, tongue and ear adepts are able to learn in real time while accomplishing their mission.*

It is of interest that this field is dominated by men, and the giants are all European. Possibly the diverse European environment has fostered a singular excellence in this regard while the lack of opportunity has, for the most part, restricted success to the masculine gender. However, some women have achieved linguistic excellence. Of particular note is the dominance of queens. Russell lists Palmyra's Zenobia, Christina of Sweden, and Cleopatra who, among her other extraordinary attributes, seldom employed a translator when conversing with the diversity of ambassadors to her Egyptian throne.[8]

YOUR MAGICK LAMP

When I was a child my Mom's father, my Grandfather Ross, was the favorite with my brother and me, and all our cousins. He took as many of his grandchildren who could make it camping every year to marvelous places such as Yosemite, Redwoods National Park, and the Kern River. Around the campfire at night he would tell stories. One of our favorite stories was about the good things done helping other people by Aladdin and his magical lamp. We knew then that he was making these beautiful stories up but we just loved hearing them. Most people know the story about Aladdin and the genie in the lamp who could grant any wish. Aladdin would rub the lamp three times and out would pop the genie. Aladdin then commanded him to make the wish come true.

This is another story from Arabia that has a deeper meaning than most people realize. In this story the genie is your subconscious that is called forth by commanding it to make your wish come true. *The way to get the attention of your subconscious mind is to keep rubbing it until it appears and does your bidding. You rub it by programming it. We call this genie by many names such as "the power of positive thinking," "creative visualization," and "subliminal suggestion." Whatever the name used the results of this approach can be quite miraculous because the subconscious is both the way we store memories perfectly and how we manifest our own reality.*

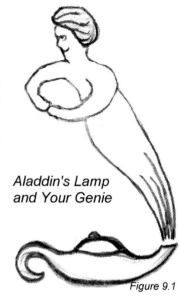

Aladdin's Lamp
and Your Genie

Figure 9.1

The East has had holistic medicine for millennia. However, Edgar Cayce is generally acknowledged to be the father of Western holistic medicine, which is less than a century old. When I first began studying metaphysics there were two passages written by Henry Reed in his well-worth-reading book: *Edgar Cayce On Mysteries of the Mind,* which reveal compelling information based on the Edgar Cayce material. The first one concerned multiple personality disorders. Reed had observed that people with this disorder could in one personality have severe allergies, require strong prescription glasses, or be right-handed, while the other personality could be allergy-free, have perfect eyesight and be left-handed. Analysis of the fundamental brain wave patterns, the delta waves, of persons with this disorder showed that they had changed. What you are is therefore, even at the physical level, a product of how you think, including the subconscious level, the level of the genie. Your thoughts create your reality; therefore the only limitation in life is your mind and how it is programmed.[9]

It was once thought to be impossible for someone to change their delta brain wave pattern other than under unusual circumstances such as multiple-personality disorder. In 1970 the Menninger Foundation in Topeka, Kansas, tested Swami Rama and found that he had absolute control over what state-of-being he was in. He could place himself in the delta state at will and remember perfectly statements spoken to him. He also had absolute control over his body functions to the extent that he could even stop his heart.[10] Similar experiments with adept Jack Schwarz also demonstrated his ability using metered breathing to freely place himself in beta, alpha, theta, or the delta state.[11] More recently, in a PBS special program, David Attenborough demonstrated an allied phenomenon by analyzing the delta brain wave pattern of master impersonator Rich Little who, upon assuming the personage of the difficult-to-impersonate Johnnie Carson, was shown to have assumed a similar brain wave pattern. Very accomplished actors, such as Robert DeNiro, may be at a level of expertise such that when taking on the persona of their character, their brain wave patterns change to support their acting. DeNiro's body seems to change as he changes roles, becoming almost plastic in his ability to alter it, another characteristic of mastership. Other actors in that class may be Meryl Streep, Alex Guinness, Ben Kingsley, Tom Hanks, Robin Williams, and Jim Carrey. Creative or determined individuals appear to be doing what used to be thought of as impossible.

A person can change literally in an instant if the reasons are compelling enough. After a significant emotional event, you SEE differently, and sometimes are even seen differently. Bob, our mechanic, recently gave me a ride home after I left our van off for routine maintenance. In transit we were discussing flying after 9-11. He relayed the story of his father, whom no one likes flying with even prior to 9-11, because he gets so nervous that he sits there wringing his hands. The reason is, during World War II he was a side gunner on a B-17. He was shot down over enemy territory in Europe. Between the time when he had to parachute out of the plane, and finally landing, his hair went from brown to pure white. That was a significant emotional event, a near-death experience, which forever changed his life. From that point forward we SEE him, and he SEEs life, differently. The 9-11 attack was such an event for this nation in particular and the world in general. We all SEE life differently now. However, such events are more in the purview of Providence and thus not a reasonable means to depend upon for changing oneself. Gradual change is more dependable and less traumatic.

The second passage Reed intrigued me with was an example of gradual change given to us by a mother and her child. It was taken from Cynthia Pike Ouellette's book, *The Miracle of Suggestion: The Story of Jennifer.* Jennifer was born premature by 11 weeks because her mother was very sick. Jennifer weighed only two pounds and was severely infected like her mother. Initially she nearly died and was saved only by a blood transfusion. Given no chance at survival her early weeks of life were a list of new revelations about how sick she was. The doctors said that if she lived she would be severely handicapped with damage to her eyes, brain, and lungs, and would probably be mentally retarded. She couldn't even be touched those first few weeks as it was so painful to her tiny body. The only way her mother could support her was with her voice. With just the power of her voice, her mother got her to gain weight. After nine weeks she was able to take her home. Then she learned that her child had cerebral palsy. Her mother despaired initially, then sought out expert advice and, finding material on the power of suggestion and the work of Edgar Cayce, she developed a program for positively programming her child by talking to her while she slept at night. She spoke to her only of how she was healing; how her spine was perfect, how she was a perfect normal creation, and other positive affirmations. Quoting Henry Reed, "Against terrible odds, having only the will to live, the atmosphere of positive suggestions, along with the massages and other forms of tender loving care, Jennifer gradually evolved into a healthy young girl."[12]

Another compelling example of what can happen was given to us by Napoleon Hill. His son was born without ears or any auditory, neurological organs. Using mental imagery, Napoleon worked on his son at the subconscious level until he grew the organs to support hearing. He did so by telepathically filling his son's mind with thoughts of hearing normally, and verbalized positive affirmations after he could hear well enough to respond to auditory support.[13]

Figure 9.2

Net of Eir Visualization

POSITIVELY PROGRAMMING YOURSELF

Douglas uses the power of visualization and suggestion to positively program his subconscious much as the mother did with her young child. To do what he does, first put yourself into the alpha/theta state, then use what has come from the Norse folk as the Net of Eir. Eir was the physician to the Norse gods. Her golden net was woven so fine that it had interstices of molecular dimensions and would hold water. It was used to extract mental and physical garbage by walking through it in spirit form. The dream catchers made by Native Americans mirror this idea. Their purpose is to catch the bad dreams and let the good ones through.[14]

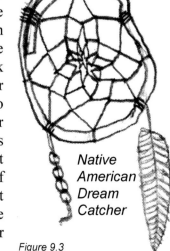

Native American Dream Catcher

Figure 9.3

Exercise 9.1 – THE NET OF EIR VISUALIZATION

Visualize yourself going to a great plain with mountains on the horizon. In front of you are two upright megalithic stones of different heights. The one on the right is the lower but it is still taller than you. Across these stones is a third megalith thus completing a construct forming the rune UR, the rune of healing. Thrown over this structure is Eir's ultrafine net of gold mesh. Holding the intention of healing while looking at the mountains beyond, walk through the net in spirit form. Then return to the front of the monolithic structure by going to your right around it. Collected on the net will be the dense, negative material that is lower in vibration than spirit so it could not get through. It often looks like black molasses. At the base on the right side of the structure is a stone or silver bowl. There is a flint knife lying to the left of it. Use the knife to scrape the gunk off the net into the bowl. Then point your power hand at the gunk and set it on fire in order to purify it, thus clearing it of all negativity. In moments the contents will be rendered into something looking like a collection of fireflies or sparklers. Empty the bowl over your head letting the points of light enter into your body to return to their original positions. Feel yourself balanced and at peace.

Traditionally the Net of Eir is woven of ultrafine gold, a metal of high vibration. According to Dr. Joshua David Stone, "Platinum is the highest-frequency color available to Earth. The only higher frequency is the clear light of God, which has no color."[15] An excellent alternative that uses the "clear light of God," is the waterfall visualization, which comes to us from Tibet.

Use the Net of Eir or Tibetan waterfall visualizations every time you are getting ready to SuperScan, meditate, or prior to going to sleep. Let them dictate the ideal you wish to be. Edgar Cayce indicated that ideals were like the rudder of a ship. Without an ideal, one would drift randomly upon the sea of life.[16]

Figure 9.4

Exercise 9.2 – TIBETAN WATERFALL VISUALIZATION

Visualize yourself transparent while standing in a waterfall of pure water filled with clear light that washes through all the levels of your being, taking with it all negativity, discord, and dross that no longer serves you. See yourself as becoming younger, happier, and having perfect radiant health while this shower bathes you in its perfection. After your cleansing shower you wade ashore and along the beach collect the black globs and weeds of negativity and discord you have released. You throw them up into the sun where they burn brightly and are transformed, bursting into a shower of sparks that rain down on you entering your transparent body. As they do so they embed in you the light of their divine love, wisdom, and power. Feel yourself filled with peace and contentment.

YOUR THOUGHTS ARE YOU

You can fly, but the cocoon has to go
1970s poster

It has been estimated that 80 percent of our thoughts are the subconscious, which is filled with the tapes programmed into it since infancy. With regard to your memories, the conscious mind is but a nail in the door of the subconscious, which remembers everything perfectly. Some heavily reinforced subconscious thoughts, dating from gestation and even before, are embedded as deeply as your bones. They are even more important in establishing your foundation. If the sages and wise teachers around the world are correct, then our thoughts create our reality and all thoughts count whether they are conscious or subconscious. The Pali Canon of 500-250 B.C. said, "*All that is comes from the mind; it is based on the mind, it is fashioned by the mind.*" Edgar Cayce's statement of, "*Spirit is the life, mind is the builder, the physical is the result,*" was speaking of more than just our physical body. Our great teachers knew this. The Buddha challenged individuals to do their own religious seeking. He put particular emphasis on thought, even opening his *Dammapada*, the most beloved of all Buddhist texts, with "*All we are is the result of what we have thought.*" Jesus put a similar emphasis on thought when he reminded us of our responsibility for our thoughts in the Sermon on the Mount, a sentiment previously expressed in Proverbs 23:7 "*For as he thinketh in his heart, so is he.*"

All thoughts can therefore be thought of as prayers that become empowered by the emotion that drives them. As you think and feel so you become. What is inside then becomes the resonator for what you draw to yourself by harmonic resonance, or, quoting Brian Adam's book, *How to Succeed,* "Like attracts like. Whatever the conscious mind thinks and believes, the subconscious identically creates." You create a world around you that reflects precisely that which is inside you. Richard Bach stated it this way, "Every person, all the events of your life are there because you have drawn them there. What you choose to do with them is up to you."

The current edition of the *The Ancient Secret of the Fountain of Youth* contains the recently rediscovered Part V that was lost for decades until a copy of the original book was found. Part V discusses the subconscious mind and how to program it, a practice well understood in Tibet long before Western civilization even existed. They use a mantram for programming the mind, something that Saint Germain's "I AM" activity calls a decree. It is a verbal command spoken out loud, from the conscious mind to the subconscious. Thus it differs from most prayers either thought or spoken in that prayers are generally supplication. A spoken command is a powerful statement for manifestation. *Of all the thoughts you can think, the most powerful thought you can have, or statement you can say, is an "I AM" statement for that preparatory phrase is directly patterned into your subconscious.* It tells the puppeteer what you desire to be. The puppeteer has the power to do what you command, and if the same thought is reinforced often enough, will do it.

However, *contradictory commands to your subconscious will effectively cancel each other out.* For instance, if you affirm consciously, "I always have the material abundance to fulfill my desires," then you would expect to have the resources to accomplish all that you desire in life. However, if you didn't do well in school because you are part of the 85 percent school wasn't crafted for, then your subconscious is probably still playing the tapes your parents and peers put there such as: "You will never amount to anything!" "Dummy!" and "You are no good!" You therefore end up in subconscious command limbo and go nowhere. To tip the balance in the direction you really want it to go, avoid as much as possible negative "I AM" statements. Instead, *use positive "I AM" statements to program the reality you want to live by patterning your subconscious for the success you desire.*

It takes equal and opposite programming for every unhealthy program or behavior to bring you back to balance. Then you can start to build a more positive behavior from that point. Keep in mind that you are challenging your comfort zone since your being is used to the old behavior. As a result, it will pull you back like a magnet until you overcome this attraction. Only time allows for that, or a significant emotional event leading to an epiphany or a satori, a word from Japanese Zen tradition that means a sudden awakening or insight, and associated change in behavior.

If you have negative tapes to overcome, and everyone does, you will probably have to consciously address them to nullify their intent, then reprogram until the positive statements outweigh the negative ones. *Setting the intention for doing this is the critical first step. Becoming aware of what your negative programming consists of is the next critical step. Nullifying it then becomes a process of acknowledging its existence, then wording a new thought system that you want to replace it and program yourself with.*

Dr. Lozenov calls this de-suggestion to reveal the unobstructed personality. His research indicates that there are three blocks that must be overcome in order to activate Super Learning®*. 1) The Critical/Logical Block: Super Learning*® *must be a put-on, and when convinced it isn't, 1a) It may work for others but it won't work for me. 2) The Intuitive/Emotional Block: Previous negative programming convincing the person that they are fundamentally a failure. I'm okay at geography, but math and I just don't mix. And 3) The Ethical/Moral Block: No pain, no gain. If learning isn't work, it isn't working. It was good enough for my parents; it must be good enough for me, and my children. All of these old programs have to be dealt with in order to achieve success.* According to Dr. Lozanov, *"The birth of knowledge should be painless."* Another significant point was that Bulgarian students tested after participating in Super Learning® exercises were found to be less suggestible. Thus, subliminally based instruction is one of the best defenses against being inadvertently programmed subliminally.[17]

This is an iterative process often compared to peeling an onion. As you become more sensitized to your subconscious you will find more layers of negative programming to deal with. One of the first programs to feed in is to command the subconscious to make you aware of all of your negative programs at a pace you can deal with so that you can nullify them and counter with positive tapes for the subconscious to focus on. Expect the unexpected. Be especially mindful of your dreams. Watch for the bear for according to *Animal-Speak*, its keynote is the awakening of the power of the unconscious, the subconscious.

GENIUS GUIDANCE

**Neither a lofty degree of intelligence nor imagination
nor both together go to the making of genius.
Love, love, love, that is the source of genius.**
Wolfgang Amadeus Mozart

Edgar Cayce said that nothing important ever happens to us without first dreaming about it. Dunne found evidence of this potential by carefully investigating his dreams.[18] Increased awareness like this is one of the results of working actively with your subconscious. Such awareness can save your life. Prior to a major tragedy such as 9-11, all who are involved and many others, will have dreamed about it. Those who have conscious awareness of that dream will have an important warning. Sometimes such dreams come long before the actual incident. The popular book and movie, *The Perfect Storm*, was based on the true story of how the Andrea Gail was lost off the coast of Nova Scotia in a monster storm on October 1991. Just prior to departing on their ill-fated fishing trip, the captain's wife dreamed that he would die at sea. She warned him months before the actual event occurred. The wife of the captain of the Arctic Rose also had a premonition dream and tried to warn him prior to his departure. His ship sank in the Bering Sea due to bad weather on April 2nd, 2001. Tapping into universal consciousness can go much further though.[19, 20]

TITANIC
Sinking

Figure 9.5

In 1898 Morgan Robertson wrote the novel *Futility* describing the maiden voyage of the largest liner every built. It was a British ship of exceptional size with three propellers, 24-knot top speed, watertight bulkheads making it unsinkable, and not enough lifeboats for the rich and famous people on board. On an April night it struck an iceberg on its starboard side thus causing it to sink, taking many people with it. This uncannily accurate novel presaged the *Titanic* disaster by 14 years. Robertson's ship was named the *Titan*, and it was far larger than any ship afloat when he wrote the book. Morgan also later wrote a book named *Beyond the Spectrum*, in which he described a futuristic war where airplanes carried sun bombs that could destroy an entire city. This was prior to World War I when airplanes could barely carry a single person.[21, 22]

J. P. Morgan and his wife cancelled their reservations on the *Titanic* when his wife refused passage after dreaming of drowning. Many heed such warnings. There was an uncharacteristically high cancellation rate for the maiden voyage of the *Titanic*, and research has shown that same phenomena whenever there is a major disaster. The airline flights involved in 9-11 were usually fully booked yet had occupancy about half the typical load. All of us have such information available to use as guidance if we so choose. We just have to listen to it.

EXAMPLES OF GENIUSES

If I were to ask you who was the greatest genius of last century, I would guess that most people would think of Einstein. So I ask you this – what genius was born in Boston in 1871, had his first epiphany at age seven subsequently becoming gifted as a pianist but was no longer functional in school and by age 10 was sent to work thus never attending school again; was pronounced dead of diphtheria at the age of 14 yet unexpectedly arose completely healed; was a musician and composer from 1884 to 1889; then an illustrator until 1898 during which he illustrated Mark Twain's magazine and was his friend; in 1898 added painting to his talents specializing in children's portraits subsequently having many prominent clients including President Theodore Roosevelt; from 1900 until 1926 became the architect of many notable structures in New York and Florida; then became a sculptor in 1927 producing many works including his masterpiece – the Mark Twain Memorial; finally, announced in 1926 a complete scientific description of matter which presaged our understanding of atomic energy? Here are more clues – at the age of 44 he won and held for four years a national championship in figure skating; was a gifted poet, philosopher, and writer publishing many books; and handled his own legal work. Give up? This internationally distinguished Leonardo da Vinci was Dr. Walter Russell, yet most Americans have never heard of him. I believe that the answer to that quandary is the fact that he attributed his abilities to working consciously with God and hence is not an acceptable figure for our education system to talk about just as Jesus is not discussed during the history of Rome.[23, 24]

How did Dr. Russell accomplish so much in one lifetime? *The historical record indicates that if you work long enough with the subconscious you eventually begin connecting with what*

Edgar Cayce called the superconscious. Carl Jung called this the collective unconscious or the archetypal mind. It has also been called the transpersonal mind and the Christ or the Buddha Consciousness. In previous times this consciousness was named after Akhenaton, Shiva, and Gogyeng Sowuhti, who also came as fully realized beings thus demonstrating a human being's unbound potential in order to plant the seeds of awakening in mankind.[25] That seems a more accurate description of the level that Dr. Russell worked at even though he was never educated in school, a distinct advantage if you have your superconscious mind as a teacher. Dr. Russell appears to have had this ability since birth so many people would call him gifted. Maybe "gifted" is a misnomer. Maybe those who display such abilities have really tapped into their uninhibited potential thus demonstrating a legacy all have available. I therefore assert that there are no gifted people, only people who draw from their rightful legacy rather than squander or limit it, as most seem to.

AWAKENING YOUR GENIUS POTENTIAL

An excellent path to earning your own ability for genius level creativity is the path of dreams. Your subconscious knows everything that has ever happened to you including every dream you have ever dreamed. It is also connected telepathically to all of creation which is why connecting with the subconscious eventually leads to connection with your superconscious. Dreams are therefore your genius level creativity path that you are granted access to nightly. In order to recall dreams, you use techniques similar to those used to recall other patterned material. *Being quiet and still are essential, at least initially. When you first awaken and try to recall your dreams, it is important that you not move until your have a conscious recall of your dream, or dreams, as complete messages.* Movement can "shatter the dream" thus making conscious recall more difficult. That is because dreams are right-brained, big picture holograms with a message. You dissect the message out of the hologram with your left brain in the conscious mode.

After you recall your dream, while still in the alpha state, you write it down so you will be able to remember it later in the beta state. This is the process of translation of the symbolic language of dreams into the linear language of civilization. That process may be more readily done in picture-based languages than in alphabet-based ones, but either way it is still a process of translation. A dream being holographic means that it is not something you can readily hold in your conscious mind. In order to retain the message, it must be translated into the terminology of Earth life, and specifically into the culture you have patterned yourself into.

In order to develop your own communication with your subconscious, and eventually the superconscious, you open the dialogue by asking questions prior to going to sleep. Whatever is on your mind as you drift off to sleep is what you will have answered. As an example, another person who received his education by home tutelage without going to school past the first three months, was Thomas Edison. He used to seek his inspiration by taking naps at work. He would pose a question concerning some problem with an invention he was working on, then recline in his desk chair with a steel ball in each hand. Upon falling asleep he would drop the balls, awaken and immediately write down what he had been dreaming about. He usually got the answer to the problem he was attempting to solve.

This light sleep range has also been used in other ways. TV star Art Linkletter used sleep learning techniques that were popular in the 60s to learn Mandarin Chinese in only ten nights. Others who tried such learning techniques were unsuccessful. The trick was apparently to stay in the alpha/theta state border zone experienced just after falling asleep, the reverie-like phase just as you are drifting off or waking up. Art was apparently good at achieving that optimal range. Dr. Lozanov, however, rejected sleep-learning because the person engaged in this practice is not in conscious control of the learning process, and also because it required a lot of specialized equipment.[26]

MORE GENIUS EXAMPLES

Once you tap into the superconscious, your answers can assume genius proportions and your techniques expand much beyond those discussed so far. Nicola Tesla is an example of a genius whose intellectual feats were of a superhuman dimension. He used to invent machines by going into the inner laboratory of his mind, make the machine, start it, and then come back months later to see how it was wearing. Everything he made worked first time in the physical world because of his inner testing system. He never needed blue prints either finding all the engineering details required instantly available three-dimensionally in his mind. That is genius-class visualization.[27] Tesla could also do instantaneous math in his head, had a photographic memory, effortlessly learned twelve languages, and was said by the men who worked with him to be telepathic. Tesla's mother worked with him as a child as she had some of these talents herself, including the ability to communicate with her son telepathically.[28, 29]

Other historical examples of geniuses who tapped into the immense intellect and wisdom of the superconscious mind are Albert Einstein, Thomas Edison, and Hans Christian Andersen, all of whom had to overcame dyslexia. Additional examples would be: Leonardo da Vinci, Mozart, George Washington Carver, and J. R. R. Tolkien, the author of *the Lord of the Rings* series of books along with 14 languages to support that masterful creation.[30] All of these geniuses demonstrated the ability to do both the logical and intuitive functions simultaneously, and were therefore probably full brain functional and hence, more capable than the rest of their contemporaries. By developing subconscious expertise, eventually you progress until you get answers while you are awake having learned to go through life in a meditative state. Now you are approaching the arena of the enlightened masters such as Buddha and Jesus.

You can also tap into your own genius by employing similar techniques. You have but to be open as a child and you will receive inspiration. In working with your subconscious and integrating your conscious, subconscious, and superconscious minds, you will find that you remember more of your childhood, sometimes even prior to being born. You will be more connected with your Inner Child, and it with the adult you have become

Now, so that you realize that there was more to your Mom and Dad than you as a child realized, I will now reveal to you my hidden meaning: *Learning with Memory Oriented Methodologies (MOM) and Dynamic Alpha state Development (DAD).*

MOM and DAD, the Queen and King of The MASTERY of LEARNING!

Melvin Lewis Thomas

Compare the restful approaches to learning that you have found in this book, to this quote from Albert Einstein, who admired Charlie Chaplin and longed to be a great comic actor:[31]

One had to cram all of this stuff into one's mind, whether one liked it or not. This coercion had such a deterring effect that, after I had passed the final examination, I found the consideration of any scientific problems distasteful to me for an entire year. It is in fact nothing short of a miracle that the modern methods of instruction have not entirely strangled the holy spirit of inquiry; for this delicate little plant, aside from stimulation, stands mainly in need of freedom; without this it goes to wrack and ruin without fail. It is a very grave mistake to think that the enjoyment of seeing and searching can be promoted by means of coercion and a sense of duty.

Chapter 10 – DEVELOPING YOUR OWN RITUALS

If I had six hours to chop down a tree, I would spend the first four sharpening the ax.
Abraham Lincoln

Champions, in any field, have made a habit of doing
what others find boring or uncomfortable.
Anonymous

Most people live, whether physically, intellectually or morally,
in a very restricted circle of their potential being.
William James

Our chief want in life is somebody who shall make us do what we can.
Ralph Waldo Emerson

It is an ever-fixed mark that looks on tempests and is never shaken.
William Shakespeare

WHEN you develop your own rituals with trigger words, remember that these are powerful prayers you are creating. When you do so, the words of Douglas Lockhart will serve as an appropriate warning:

Prayers are wordless thoughts, whole thoughts dropped into the universe. When such thoughts spin away from you Intelligences answer. But don't try to play with this, for such Intelligences cannot be fooled. They can see you as you cannot see yourself.

Seek to do good in what you do and good will come of it. Like attracts like!

HOW TO COUPLE YOUR RITUALS

When you develop your rituals I suggest using power words of your choice to bracket a ritual you compose like a script for a small movie. In it you combine all of the elements you want to use to put yourself into the alpha/theta region. One approach is to choose words you are never likely to use or accidentally hear. This approach is best if the ritual you are developing is one that you would like to avoid having invoked by accident. Examples would be prayers for others such as healing or abundance. It is best to have permission to pray for others prior to doing so, thus using obscure words makes sense. It is always a good practice when developing sensitive rituals to set the intention that only you speaking the word invokes the effect you desire. Memory tasks are less sensitive so Douglas uses common "Re" based words like Re-LAX, Re-TAIN, Re-CALL, and Re-TURN. *If we wish to make these words unique and further empower them, substitute Ra, an Egyptian name for God, for "Re" thus making **Ra-LAX, Ra-TAIN, Ra-CALL,** and **Ra-TURN.** Now you have put the power of a name of God as the central focus. Another approach is to use words that are pronounceable backward and forward, such as abra-cadabra, which you use to put yourself into the alpha/theta region, then use the backward spelling, arbadac-arba, to bracket a second ritual for returning to beta state focus.* This approach is also a good East/West combination in reading directions and hence, yin/yang for balance. Whatever your choice of words, if your ritual is short and simple you can probably remember it well enough to do live each time. If it is complex then record it in order to achieve consistency and precision in the results of your practice sessions. The rituals that I developed for you to use for programming your subconscious with the Douglas "Re" based words are complex enough that I packaged a CD with this book to guide you in the process of learning them.

Exercise 10.1 – DEVELOPING YOUR SMART/GENIUS MODE RITUAL

Figure 10.1

If you have chosen to do a simple ritual, you might still script it for consistency. All that is really needed is something like what you did to Re-LAX during **Exercise 8.1**. Even the music is not necessary once you have practiced it enough times. When dealing with anything, acting as if you have accomplished your goal puts you halfway there. If you expect it to work and act like it has, it will.

If you really want to include everything you can think of in your ritual, then I suggest recording it. The first step is to establish the perfect ambiance. Clear the space you intend to use by smudging it to cleanse it. You can use sage, *Flowers in a Vase* incense, or a campfire in an outdoor location. The preferred location would be *and Candles* where you usually meditate. Examples would be: Sitting cross-legged in your meditation area, on your bed, or in a hot bath or Jacuzzi. You can have playing in the background your favorite alpha/theta state-inducing music while you are taking a hot bubble bath with scented oils, bath crystals, and incense. **Appendix K** lists sources of supplies. Have fresh flowers in a vase nearby. White roses may be the best as white is the unity of all colors and roses are the flowers associated with the ascended masters. Or use aromatherapy floral essences along with your favorite divine photo or painting of a nature scene. For lighting I suggest using candles. Make sure you check out everything kinesiologically, as described in **Appendix A**, to ensure that it is subliminally positive.

Take the phone off the hook. Start by stating your intentions, then use deep breathing to relax yourself. Use cleansing and healing affirmations such as the Net of Eir or Tibetan Waterfall Visualizions plus positive affirmations such as those listed in **Appendix F**. For additional examples of what to use both Louise Hay and Shakti Gawain have excellent books filled with positive affirmations. You can use prayers if they suit you such as 1st Chronicles 4:10, *The Prayer of Jabez*, which is quite popular now as a small book describing the many people it has aided. Decrees can also be used such as Saint Germain's "I AM" Decrees listed in **Appendix G**. To center yourself, use balancing mudras such as putting together your thumb and first two fingers on each hand.

With a battery-operated portable music system you can even do all of this in the midst of your favorite meadow surrounded by a forest or next to a stream of running water or waterfall. Cultivate your feelings so the resulting emotions will be in the recording subliminally. The more feeling you put into this, the more energy you will put into the recording thus empowering your trigger words to take you there instantly. To precipitate going into the low alpha/theta state, incorporate counting the chakra colors from **red** to **violet** coordinated with **(4,8,16,4)** breathing and the memory mantra, crossing your eyes, looking up, then looking back level as illustrated in **Exercise 8.1**. Know that you are clearly and firmly in the low alpha/theta state and you will be.

Exercise 10.2 – DEVELOPING YOUR FOCUS MODE RITUAL

This ritual can also be kept simple. Looking down, touching the earth with your fingers, hugging a tree, visualizing yourself as a tree with roots going deeply into the ground, and doing your morning exercises while counting repetitions, all tend to ground you and bring you back to the beta state. Simply bracket these actions with *arbadac-arba* or Re-TURN and you have it. If you decide to record this ritual, then you can play invigorating music in the background. Pick something that for you represents being awake, joyful, alert, and fully in the beta state. Use positive affirmations such as: "I will remember and be able to recall perfectly everything I need whenever I need it"; "I will be clear, relaxed, and wide awake with all parts of my brain and mind fully functional and accessible when this recording ends;" or, "I AM healthy, happy, and whole." Then, if you wish, count down the chakras from seven to one using foursquare beta breathing **(4,4,4,4)** as done in **Exercise 8.2**. When you reach the count of one tell yourself: *"I AM fully awake, fully alert!"* which is what Douglas uses, or one used by the Unity Church: *"I AM awake, alive, alert, and enthusiastic!"* Now you only have to push a button and listen to your recording to return yourself to the beta state.

This is self-hypnosis using power words and strong feelings to induce the states you desire and pattern your subconscious for perfect memory. Make sure that anything you use for these rituals, such as music or props, has been checked out for positive subliminal content prior to using it. After around 100 repetitions you will find that your smart mode power word subvocalized instantly puts you into the learning state, and your focus mode power word brings you back to fully awake feeling refreshed with perfect recall of what you have just SuperScanned. When you say those words to yourself, remember the strong feelings they invoke and you will instantly put yourself in the place you desire. To reinforce this you can also hum or lightly sing the music that you used to place yourself in the state-of-being you desire. Eventually, just softly humming the tune can be your power ritual for inducing the alpha state, or returning to full wakefulness. One benefit of this process is, you will have better access to your dreams as a natural consequence of becoming more capable of moving among the alpha, beta, and theta states. *Recalling SuperScanned information is similar to how you recall a dream; you write it down while in the alpha/theta in order to transition it to the beta state. Writing acts as a bridge. When you have done enough dream recall you will remember them without writing them down. Likewise, you will develop the ability to recall SuperScanned material without having to write it down in the alpha/theta. It will come through the alpha/theta to enrich your beta experience.* You can also "open up" a power word at any time to modify it with additions or subtractions. Just say the preparatory part, your modification, and the concluding part of your power word, 100 times, and it is done.

YOUR SUPER MANIFESTATION LIST

Use your scripted rituals to form a contract with the universe, something that you can put in a secure area you have chosen, such as your bedstand, along with a prioritized list of everything you want to manifest in your life. SuperScan your manifestation list each time you are in the alpha state in order to program it into your subconscious so it will manifest. This is a letter to yourself about what you are to be and have in your life. Make sure you are specific about what will manifest without telling the universe how to do it. Be specific in the results but not the way it will come about so the universe will not be constrained in how it answers your request.

For instance, if you envision a new house, specify bedrooms, size, color, number of stories, the land including landscaping, and value, but not the price you will pay or whether you have to pay for it or receive it as a gift. If you desire a type of location then specify it without saying exactly where it has to be unless that is exactly what you want. You can specify how it will feel to you, or make you feel.

You can also include behavior modifications such as quitting smoking or eating in a balanced and healthful manner. Do not do this as a want or a wish list as then you will be asking to always be wanting or wishing. Say it as a decree, what you <u>will</u> to happen, and know has happened in the subtle realms! Say it with expectancy and hold that expectancy constant in your heart and head. Remember, the conscious mind is in command of the subconscious unless only the subconscious is active. In the excellent book, *Executive ESP, the following actions are listed as critical for problem solving:* [1]

1. *Visualize* **clearly the** *end* **result you desire**
2. *Accept* **that the creative mind can produce a solution – don't just hope or wish**
3. *Expect* **a solution – expect your mind to work for you and not against you.**

Your manifestation list can be any length you choose. I suggest a maximum of ten to twelve items. Shakti Gawain's book, *Creative Visualizations,* suggests you end with: *"This or something better, now manifests for me in totally satisfying and harmonious ways for the highest good of all concerned."* [2] *For intuitive or precognitive solutions,* Mihalasky Ostrander and Dean Douglas suggest: [3]

> 1. *Believe* – have a rock-hard belief that precognition and other psi channels can operate for you.
> 2. *Focus* – turn off the extraneous chattering of the logical mind
> 3. *Re-LAX* – let go of physical and mental tensions.

Thoughts, both subconscious and conscious, are the key. Change them and you change youself. Tap into them and you tap into all universal knowledge. Control them and you control what you manifest. A sustained thought of an apple would manifest an apple. Machaelle Small Wright describes in her book, *Behaving As if the God in All Life Mattered*, how to do proper manifesting. She manages to manifest exactly what she visualizes in only a few days. Eventually she manifests in only a few minutes. The key is sustaining a visualization of what you desire. By programming your subconscious with the thoughts of what you desire, you enlist the aid of your subconscious and thus, automatically program the reality around you to deliver what you require.

As you develop your expertise, bear in mind the advice of Harry Palmer, *"**Pretending is imagination without faith. Creating is imagination with faith. People who believe in their pretenses create them for real! Imagine no boundaries.**"*[4]

THE POWER OF EXPECTANCY

Expectancy can be a powerful manifester, even doing the seeming impossible, particularly when it is coupled with "trying to do good." When I was a teacher at Texas Military Institute, the chairman of the science department was my boss, mentor, and good friend. He was a man of considerable learning and understanding regarding how the world worked. He was also an icon at the school, having been there far longer than anyone else, more than two decades, and extremely popular with the students and alumni. He was known for his honesty and insightfulness, being able to see right through human-generated situations that most found too complex to deal with. He was a right brain thinker in his big-picture abilities.

Virgil Espino was his name and being Hispanic, he greatly honored his parents, only one of whom was still living, his mother. She still lived in the old part of San Antonio in the modest small house on the corner of the block that she had lived in for decades. Unfortunately this part of city had degraded over the years and was prone to crime. In order to honor his mother's strong desire to stay there, Virgil and his wife Linda searched for a company that would erect what they acknowledged as an illegal fence. Linda finally found one that agreed to do the job, if they were never mentioned or involved in any way. Once the six-foot chain link fence was up around the perimeter of the property, a hedge of prickly plants was planted to grow through it. Bars were also put on the windows and the front and rear doors were strengthened.

Eventually, one of the neighbors complained and because fences like that are illegal, they were told to take it down. The Espinos refused so the City of San Antonio took them to court. They hired a lawyer, and were promptly advised that there was no way they could win this lawsuit. The Espinos still wanted to go to court. They expected to win the case because in their prayers they had made a covenant with God stating that, if they won, while any family member lived on the land they would aid those who came to them needing a helping hand.

The first time they went to court they were being sued by the City of San Antonio in a local civil court. Virgil's mom had errands to run prior to the time she was to appear in court. She was late and consequently, was the last person to show up to register with the court bailiff. Courtrooms are run on a first-in, first-out basis, so Virgil's 87-year-old mother sat through all of the cases for the day waiting for hers to come up. After her vigil passed three hours, the judge finally took note and demanded to know who was responsible for making this elderly woman sit there for so long. He took one look at the court papers, said that the case was dismissed, and sent her home.

Again a neighbor complained. Now the case had to be tried in a higher civil court in San Antonio. Their lawyer once again advised them that they could not win. This time it was a cold and rainy day. They came before a new judge. Virgil's mom was learning so she purposely showed up late so she was the last case to be heard. Once again they were charged on three counts: building a fence without a permit, on city property, and too high. All of the cases ahead of her were for similar types of infractions, and all were found guilty.

When it was finally her turn, she told the judge how before they put the fence up, people were coming through all the time and stealing her things. She told him how she had five sons and a brother who had served in the military, and that she loved this country, but did not want to be raped in her kitchen. There was a young lady reporter who picked up on what was being said and started to interview her. The reporter decided to write about how unfair the city was being to this woman. The judge took note of what was going on – and dismissed the case.

Again the neighbors complained, and this time the case had to be tried at the state level. It was the state of Texas vs. the Espino's. Two lawyers were assigned to prosecute the case, both young and cocky yuppies. Their flippant attitude irritated the judge. They began arguing with each other, which further irritated the judge. The paperwork they submitted had errors, improper addresses and dates, which gave the judge more reasons to be unhappy. Then, as the judge was going through the paperwork, he discovered that none of the descriptions matched the pictures they had submitted as evidence. He was getting more and more exasperated as he tried to sort through the confusion. Finally, he discovered that all of the pictures had been developed backward so the images were reversed from right to left.

That was it! The judge said with finality, "I know how to take care of this nonsense; this is officially a case of not guilty!" Virgil, his mom, and their lawyer, were stunned. Their lawyer explained what this meant. Because the judge had rendered a "not guilty" judgment on all counts instead of dismissing the case, *it could never come to trial again, no matter who complained in the future!*

Their lawyer was named Gregory Luna and he was a Texas state congressman at that time. He expected to lose the case and had been concerned that he would have to contend with that negative mark on his permanent record as an elected official. He was so delighted with the win and learned so much from it, that he charged the Espino's only $50 for a case that had taken three years. Right after the case was finally over, eight people from Montana showed up at the Espino home. They all needed money to get back home. Virgil and his family scrambled to borrow money to help them. They were all fed and given a place to stay. They never determined who sent them, it was as if they just were told to come, and they did. It has been over 15 years now and Virgil's mom has passed away since then. The fence still stands and they have helped many people. Family members who live in the house must agree to honor their covenant with God. That is the power of expectancy, and what can happen when you seek to do good.

While on the train coming from Chicago one afternoon, a woman named Val told my wife and me another story that further illustrates this principle. This woman had her home broken into many years ago not long after she and her family moved in. What was taken was minor other than her jewelry, and all of that could be replaced except for one unique ring that was a family heirloom handed down from mother to daughter for a number of generations. Val kept thinking that if nothing else was recovered, she wanted that ring back. A few years later she went to a doctor's appointment, and there on the hand of the receptionist, was the ring. She reported this to the police and as the ring fit her description perfectly, she was able to prove ownership and recover it.

WORDS OF CAUTION

The examples of the Espinos and Val took a few years to manifest. *With powerful emotion driving it, manifestation can happen in less than a single day.* It is important to mention a cautionary point that is best illustrated by something that happened to a good friend of mine.

Bill and his wife Cindy were struggling in their marriage, and he was depressed. Their young son had been born autistic and the stress of contending with this as he grew had brought them near the breaking point. Bill was a fighter pilot in the Air Force. He was the flight leader that day for a four-ship flight of F-15's. As he and the men he commanded flew in formation in the spaces between large clouds like islands in the sky, a bolt of lighting suddenly arced from a nearby cloud to the nose of Bill's airplane. As blinding raw energy it crept up the nose, through the canopy, and into the confining cockpit right in front of Bill, who had no place to go. Bill's hands were raised up against the inside of the canopy while he pressed as far back as the seat would allow. The lightning ball was only a few feet in front of him. He thought he was going to be dead at any moment! Suddenly the supercharged energy field arced over to his left hand using his arm as a conductor, and from there into the plane, blowing all its antennas off with the force of the energy shunted into them. Declaring an emergency, Bill and his wingmen returned immediately to base. After landing safely he learned that his plane had sustained $300,000 dollars worth of damage. Bill, however, was unhurt, finding no damage except a small hole burned into the elbow of his flight suit where the lightning had exited. Upon returning home Bill bounced through the front door yelling loudly, "I'm alive, I feel great!"

Excitedly he explained what had happened to his startled wife Cindy. She blanched white, sat down and told him, "When you left this morning, I prayed to God to shock you out of your depression!" With a look of awe on his face Bill replied, "Next time, use different words!"

Cindy spoke her prayer in an emotional state such that her subconscious was programmed to respond, immediately! She expected a response and she got it. There was no hesitation here or second thoughts. That is the power of emotional outbursts that come from the heart, and not the head. Cindy attributed the lightning to a miracle from God. That was her truth and in one sense, that was correct. Another interpretation is that the mechanism is the universe God created and this is how it works. The response was inevitable as God made the universe such that it will give us anything we ask for. *When you program your subconscious, which is how you communicate with the universe using either the slow way of a manifestation list, or quickly as in an emotional outburst, you get a response as long as you do not program it with contradictory requests.* When you program for a response, as with Cindy and Bill, the cautionary point I wish to stress is, *be careful what you ask for!*

Now, you might think that you never use your expectancy to do anything to yourself that is "bad." However, I contend that most of us do it all the time in many different ways. It takes a while to root out all the things you ask for that you really wouldn't want if you thought about it. For instance, quoting therapist Marina Raye,

> *Whenever you hear yourself saying, "I should have," just say, "Stop!" You can't ever "should have" done anything. Should have's don't work because we can't go back and replay the past. When we delete the word "should" from our vocabulary, we will have come a long way toward controlling our dysfunctional self-programming and improving our relationships with others.*[5]

As another example, take your fears for instance. Dr. Wayne Dyer says that *what you get in life are: "What you really really really really really want, and what you really really really really really don't want." In other words, what you obsess about, your greatest desires and biggest fears.* Most have no objection to their greatest desires coming true but seldom understand that the same rules apply to their fears. What you put your energy into returns to you. If you fear being late, lightening storms, poverty, going bald which wrecks havoc with some men, lunar body cycles which wreck havoc with some women, or some particular illness such as cancer, then you are setting yourself up to experience that which you fear. Chose more healthful motives for your actions and release your fears. If you wear suntan lotion because you fear getting skin cancer, what is the message you are consistently sending out to the manifest in your life? The sun is usually considered to be the masculine energy for our solar system and the moon the feminine. The sun is the source of life and the moon choreographs life cycles for the entire planet. The sun becomes the source of death and the moon a monthly source of pain only if your expectancy breeds that outcome. Proof of that statement can be found in the fact that only some cultures have skin cancer and a woman's monthly period as significant problems. They are both therefore products of systems of thought and action culturally imbedded. It is worth noting what Leonard Orr states in his book on *Breaking the Death Habit, the Science of Everlasting Life,* "Staring at the moon all night can heal all the diseases of the mind and body. Watching the sun rise can give you cool strength the lasts all day."[6, 7]

Any time you don't want a thing, you get it.
Calvin Coolidge

I have met the enemy, and it is us!
Pogo Possum, created by Walt Kelly

Finally, even if you eliminate the negativity within yourself, you don't want to have to contend with the negativity within others. If you share with others what you are doing, that is what will happen! Many will quietly naysay your efforts, or openly put them down. Even a casual negative comment, or a joke at the expense of your endeavors, can introduce the element of doubt. Even if they don't consciously state their doubts, their subconscious will and it is telepathic with your subconscious.

I therefore recommend that you write down your rituals and manifestation list, on a 3x5 card for instance, as that can easily be carried in a pocket or purse. Then, don't tell anyone what you are doing, as that can cause you to fail in your objective. The apocryphal story about Jesus is that the first time he manifested an apple he was so astounded when it appeared in his hand that he doubted it for a moment and it disappeared again. It took him a few weeks to repeat the miracle as he had to overcome that doubt. He practiced in private as other peoples' doubts would have only added to what he had to overcome. It is only at the level of true mastery that the doubts of others have no effect. When you are there you will know it.

EXPLORE THE POSSIBILITIES

To aid you in manifesting the life you desire use the same techniques explained above to develop recordings for yourself that will allow you to, for instance, be at peace and rest despite contending with that which would normally stress you out. The library is an excellent source for books filled with positive affirmations you can record. The affirmations on this recording would be ones of loving yourself, of self-mastery, of being centered, and fully in command of your being.

You can also record your manifestation list and listen to it turned down too low to hear consciously as you go to sleep at night. If your recorder has a continuous play mode, then leave it on all night. Your hearing is much more capable subliminally than your mundane hearing just as your subliminal vision is much more capable than your conscious vision. As you do this you program new routines, healthy ones of your choice, into your subconscious rather than the old, dysfunctional ones most of us have as a constant undermining force in our lives. According to Dan Millman, clarity, duration, and desire are the keys to empowering your manifestation list, along with your life in general.

Exercise 10.3 – **WRITE DOWN YOUR MANIFESTATION LIST**

On a piece of paper, list 10-12 specific things you would like to manifest in your life. Be specific in what, but not in how. Prioritize it by listing first your fondest desires and deepest wishes. Write each item visualizing it as already part of your life. By accepting this in the "Now!" the future and the past become the illusions they are for only the now really exists. If you can dream it, you have it *now!* When you know it, you will see it *now!*

**Japa
mala**
with
27
Beads

Figure 10.2

JAPA MALA

There is one important tool left to make you aware of that has not been covered in the discussion so far. It is the fundamental tool for change being "bullet proof," as Douglas Buchanan says it. No matter how severely you have been limited by negative programming since you incarnated, this will work for you. In other words, no matter what your thought system is, you can reprogram yourself and overcome those limitations efficiently. A reflection of this technique can be seen in the Western world in the form of the Catholic rosary. The parent to that off-spring is found in the Eastern World and is known as a japa mala, which literally translates as a "Repetition using a garland of flowers." Japa means repetition and a mala is a string of beads in increments of 27, 54 or 108, that are used to count repetitions of a mantra. The number 108 is chosen because it is a sacred number that in itself imparts a deeper meaning to the repetition count.[8]

The Brain Gym® exercises, which are discussed in **Chapter 15,** are based upon the holistic nature of the body. They are physical activities that help your brain function properly. It is a small leap of faith to accept then that a physical action, employing beads for counting a mantra, can have a profound effect on the overall makeup of your being. In this instance, the mantra and the physical action are acting in concert. Scrolling the beads across different fingers stimulates the body on specific acupressure points thus supporting the mantra's chosen effect. This technique can significantly augment your meditation, healing, prosperity, self-help, memory, and much more. Japa mala is the most effective method I know for implementing desirable change. It works as long as you have a hand and fingers to work with. It could also be performed with the feet but few have the dexterity to pull that off.

According to Douglas, *in only a few days of doing japa mala a person can clear a lifetime's worth of negative programming and implement the desired program for ready access from that point forward.* However, the teaching of japa mala is beyond the scope of this class. Not to despair: Douglas Buchanan has written a monograph on the subject which you can easily procure. He also has many other monographs on various subjects that draw from the vast scope of his learning in order to clarify topics that are not well understood. In addition to *Japa Mala*, he offers other immediately useful monographs such as *Meditation* and *Health Matters,* which are directly applicable to the topics discussed in this book. The information for obtaining these monographs can be found in **Appendix H** along with a short biographical sketch of Rev. Douglas Buchanan.

SELF REPROGRAMMING OVERVIEW

Now you have a number of effective tools for getting yourself into the alpha/theta state and back into the beta state. The beta state is generally not a problem for most people who are on a regular sleep schedule. The primary objective for most is to learn how to shut down the beta state and reprogram via the alpha/theta state. From our discussions of our states of being, and associated visual and auditory mechanisms, it is apparent that low-level conditions incapacitate the beta state, whether they are low light or associated low sound levels. That fact is the basis for many subliminal advertising techniques.[9, 10] Background schema are therefore excellent ways to work with the alpha/theta state, and they can do their work nearly all of the time. One example is mantras, sometimes called japa in Hindu tradition, which means "repetition." The repetition of a positive mantra becomes the background schema that ties up the beta mind and reprograms the alpha/theta mind. Reinforcing this with hand mudras via beads gives you japa mala. One of the healthiest actions a person can take is to replace all empty thought moments in their life, and all negative reactions, with a positive mantra thus sowing the seed thoughts of success while reprogramming the subconscious for positive results.

Another example is your peripheral vision. It works all of the time but most do not consciously perceive it unless the beta-based foveal vision is incapacitated. An effective scheme for reading is to use a rheostat to turn light levels down, or use moonlight as a light source, because low light levels shut down the beta foveal vision leaving the alpha peripheral vision intact. The subliminal advertising business sometimes uses low level lighting to program the alpha state subconscious mind with thoughts reinforcing the buying of their products.[11, 12] You can do something more positive in your home with moving water, lights, and projecting nature scenes on a blank wall as the patterns generated are healing.

Low-level sound that is sub audible, or below conscious beta audibility, can also be used to reprogram the subconscious mind. You can make your own tapes, or use CDs such as *Om Namaha Shiva*. Use applied muscle testing, discussed in **Appendix A**, to check commercial music for safe content before listening to it; then, turn the sound down too low to hear it consciously. This will give your subconscious the positive programming you desire it to have.[13] There are many tapes on the market that are filled with positive affirmations. Keeping them going all the time in your home and car, or with earphones at work or while walking, is an effective way to quickly reprogram yourself.

Every moment of your life is infinitely creative and the universe is endlessly bountiful.
Just put forth a clear enough request, and everything your heart desires must come to you.
Shakti Gawain, *Creative Visualization*

What we are today comes from our thoughts of yesterday,
and our present thoughts build our life of tomorrow:
our life is the creation of our mind.
The Buddha

Your subconscious mind has the answer. If you are confronted with a problem and you cannot see an immediate answer; assume that your subconscious has the solution and is waiting to reveal it to you. If an answer does not come, turn the problem over to your deeper mind prior to sleep. Keep on turning your request over to your subconscious until the answer comes. The response will be a certain "feeling'" an inner awareness, whereby you "know" what to do. Guidance in all things comes as the still small voice within: It reveals all.
Brian Adams, *How to Succeed.*

You should always be aware that your head creates your world.
Ken Keyes Jr., *Handbook to Higher Consciousness*

If we want a beautiful garden, we must first have a blueprint in the imagination, a vision.
Dalai Lama

Chapter 11 – PUTTING IT ALL TOGETHER

**Doubt is the vestibule through which all must pass
before they can enter into the temple of truth.**
Charles Colton

If you think you can or if you think you can't, you're right!
Henry Ford [1]

If you can dream it you can do it.
Walt Disney

You teach best what you most need to learn…
Argue for your limitations, and sure enough, they're yours…
You are never given a wish without also being given the power to make it true.
You may have to work for it however.
Illusions, the Adventures of a Reluctant Messiah By Richard Bach

What you are is God's gift to you;
What you make of it is your gift to God.
Anthony Dalla Villa

Be the change you want to see in the world.
Mahatma Gandhi

To change yourself, look at what you fear and what you hate. Start there.
Wayne Dyer

Ultimately you will grow beyond the teachings of the outer masters.
The more of yourself that you know, the fewer teachings there will be.
The fallacy of the "path" is that there really is no path at all;
There is only your experience.
Gregg Braden

For the things we have to learn before we can do them, we learn by doing them.
Aristotle

One of the most responsible things you can do as an adult,
Is to become more of a child.
Wayne Dyer

THE PURPOSE OF THIS BOOK
THE objectives of this book can be summed up as two primary goals: programming your subconscious to work the way you want, and developing the ability to go into deep alpha/theta at a moment's notice. The result is mastery of your own mind and releasing it from the drudgery it now obsesses with to begin flowing with the intellect of the universe. In order to achieve those goals, there are five key steps that if followed, make the end result as inevitable as the rising of the sun.

Exercise 11:11 – **PUTTING IT ALL TOGETHER FOR YOURSELF**
   As you read the remainder of this chapter you will be reviewing what you learned. Record in your journal how you can implement each of the "five keys to success" that this chapter presents. It will help you integrate what you have learned and make it a part of your life. Practice it until you are living it.

1ˢᵗ KEY *– Awaken the child within and protect your inner child. Practice discernment!*

Quoting Dan Millman, "All the teachers of mankind have pointed to the same thing – that in order to grow truly, we must reintegrate the wisdom of our life experience with the open-eyed innocence of childhood."[2] Awaken the child within and practice discernment in what you allow your child to see, listen to, and experience in life. Especially practice discernment when you place yourself in the subliminal state. Fill up your infinite subconscious so that you have a gold depository, not a waste or toxic dump. Actively set up healthy boundaries to protect your child. Use affirmations to positively program your inner child to be always protected.

2ⁿᵈ KEY *– Develop your own, easy-to-do, healthful rituals.*

Establish the healthy routine you want, and make it easy to do so you will be willing to do it on a regular basis. Focus your routine on rebuilding your foundation, which is covered in **Chapters 14** and **15**. Start your day with deep breathing. Use healthful water for bathing and drinking to cleanse and hydrate your body. Choose the foods of the earth wisely based on what you determine is healthy for you. Get proper rest, and then exercise daily by some combination of walking, the Tibetan exercises, yoga, Dan Millman's Peaceful Warrior exercise routine, or something else of your choice. Before you employ your mind in the tasks of the day, do the Brain Gym® exercises to "tune up your engine." Get all eight cylinders firing so they will be there when you need them. Use positive affirmations and healing visualizations to build the body and life you want. Use japa mala to reprogram yourself with positive thought systems. Polish your golden vessel!

As part of your daily routine, take the time to develop your own alpha/theta and beta state inducing rituals, and your own Manifestation List. Use these rituals to firmly place yourself into the alpha/theta state while **SuperScanning** material, and to RE-CALL whatever you need when you need it. If you listen to your recorded rituals three times a day, in only 33 days your *super power words* will become activated and you will then be able to quickly and effortlessly enter or exit the alpha/theta state anywhere: a library, at work, over lunch, in the stall of a bathroom, and even in front of friends, coworkers, or an audience you are addressing.

Start filling your cave of wealth with key reference books, such as the dictionary, thesaurus, almanac, or a recipe book. Then tackle the books you already know and love as your feel for the material will help develop your ability to recall them perfectly. Next you can scan books you have always wanted to read but found so daunting that you never did, such as the *Bible*, *Koran*, *Dammapada*, the entire *Encyclopedia Britannica*, or all 12,000 pages of the *Pali Canon*. Let your successes build by SuperScanning that which you love and really desire to have a permanent part of your memory. Once your skills have developed to become a trusted friend, then branch out into the wealth of knowledge that mankind continues to stack higher and higher. This would be a good time to use your library card.

When you need answers to questions, seek them in your dreams and daydreams. The more conscious thought you put into something prior to sleep, the more likely it is that you will receive an answer in your sleep. Pre-sleep suggestion and imagery are the most critical ingredients for getting answers. By seeding your dreams with the questions that vex you, you awaken your fountain of creative inspiration.[3]

3ʳᵈ KEY *– Practice, practice, practice!*

The Third Key is best summed up this way:

A tourist on the streets of New York comes up to a native New Yorker and asks, "How do you get to Carnegie Hall?"

The New Yorker replies "Practice, practice, practice!"

4ᵗʰ KEY – *Keep your journal and manifestation list current.*

Keep a journal of your progress noting what books you have SuperScanned, words and key phrases you recalled when you needed them, dreams you had, guidance given to you by your puppeteer, what manifests in your life that you have asked for, and any other incidents that are significant to you because they mark milestones of progress. Be sure to say thank you whenever something on your manifestation list comes forth, then joyfully update your list with something new dropping off what you have realized in your life.

5ᵗʰ KEY – *Do it with imagination, visualization, passion, and LOVE, until you are it!*

Love is the pursuit of the whole.

Plato

Passion, vision, and action are the keys to success in any endeavor. Walt Disney was told no by more than 300 banks before he found one that said yes to his theme park idea. Get passionate about this, have a vision of what you want to do with it, then do it! Imagination and visualization are keys in this process. Beethoven composed his best symphonies after he went deaf.[4] Einstein discovered the theory of relativity by imagining what it would be like to ride on a ray of light. Walt Disney developed an entire reality around his abilities of imagination and visualization. Quoting Dr. Wayne Dyer, "The use of mental imagery is one of the strongest and most effective strategies for making something happen for you."[5] According to Elaine St. James, "Being effective there (in the alpha state) happens by *intention* and *imagination*."[6]

As a reader of this book you are part of a new learning culture. Share your failures and successes when such information will help others. Your answers may be the key to someone else's success. Douglas considers these techniques a handy tool set like a Swiss army knife you carry with you everywhere. They help you accomplish the tasks in your life more efficiently, and with better results. Many of these techniques are also crutches that adepts no longer require much as a temple, church, synagogue, or mosque isn't essential for piety. For example, the Re-LAX, Re-TAIN, Re-CALL, and Re-TURN rituals, all fit in that category and will ultimately become programmed thoughts imbedded deeply enough to activate by intentionality at a moment's notice.

I can be reached at mel@themasteryseries.com. Please send me your experiences as you progress in your learning. The Mastery Series web site is: www.TheMasterySeries.com. It addresses this book and associated workshop, and others as they become available. There is a chat room for sharing learning experiences and more information about these techniques, and a schedule of upcoming workshops. You can also find the core of this book available as an Internet course by going to www.ConsciousOne.com.

EMBRACE CHANGE

In numerology, the number 5 is the number of change. You now have five key steps to effect change in your life on the physical, mental, emotional, and spiritual levels. What we have called learning is really remembering as the puppeteer already knows all that you seek and much more. *A desire of your heart defines the experience and creates the path.*[7] You are molting from being the "penguin" to who you are meant to be. Seek the guidance of your own puppeteer and soon you will be more than the penguin, you will be the golden-winged white-unicorn Pegasus of your desires. This chapter is the 11th one because the number 11 is the sacred number for Christing. 11:11 is the considered to be the Christ gate.

From the video *Meetings with Remarkable Men, Gurdjieff's Search for Hidden Knowledge*, comes this empowering piece of advice, "*You have now found the conditions in which the desire of your heart can become the reality of your being. Stay there until you acquire a force in you that nothing can destroy.*"

"Who are you?" crooned the caterpillar.
Alice replied rather shyly,
"I – I hardly know, sir, just at present.
I know who I *was* when I got up this morning,
but I think I must have changed several times since then."
Lewis Carroll

Our deepest fear is not that we are inadequate.
Our deepest fear is that we are powerful beyond measure.
It is our light, not our darkness, that most frightens us.
We ask ourselves:
Who am I to be brilliant, gorgeous, talented, and fabulous?
Actually who are you to not be?
You are a child of God.
Your playing small doesn't serve the world.
There is nothing enlightened about shrinking
so that other people will not feel insecure around you.
We are born to manifest the glory of God that is within us.
It is not just in some of us; it's in everyone
and as we let our own light shine,
we unconsciously give other people permission to do the same.
As we are liberated from our own fear,
our presence automatically liberates others.
Marianne Williamson: *A Return to Love*

Between the stigma of your past,
and the enigma of your future,
lies your capacity for change.
For only in the present can you forge a new form,
wrought from the castings you inherited,
thus preparing for future molding.
Yet, despite these bracketing constraints
the sands of time always shift with you
allowing you to cut and fill at will.
While you move from churning to learning,
hesitancy to expectancy,
stressful to restful,
discord to harmony,
diversity to unity,
until you become a conscious one.
Formed from the ashes of your past
are the diamonds of your future.
Melvin Lewis Thomas

ReLAX, ReTAIN, ReCALL, and ReTURN ReWrite your ReAlity for ReMarkable ReWards
Melvin Lewis Thomas

Whenever any book claims to have all the answers,
then those who believe totally in that theory are not free,
But slaves to their book.
Marina Raye

Chapter 12 – EXCELLENCE IN THE CORPORATE WORLD

There is no real excellence in all this world which cannot be separated from right living.

David Starr Jordan

To understand truth one must have a very sharp, precise, clear mind; not a cunning mind, but a mind that is capable of looking without distortion, a mind innocent and vulnerable. Only such a mind can see what truth is. Nor can a mind that is filled with knowledge perceive what truth is; only a mind that is completely capable of learning can do that. Learning is not the accumulation of knowledge. Learning is movement from moment to moment.

J. Krishnamurti

Without an integrated understanding of life, our individual and collective problems will only deepen and extend. The purpose of education is not to produce mere scholars, technicians and job hunters, but integrated men and women who are free of fear; for only between such human beings can there be enduring peace.

J. Krishnamurti

I do not think that the measure of a civilization is how tall its buildings of concrete are, but rather how well its people have learned to relate to their environment and fellow man.

Sun Bear of the Chippewa Tribe

**The significant problems we face cannot be solved
at the same level of thinking we were at when we created them.**

Albert Einstein

*We are what we repeatedly do.
Excellence, then, is not an act, but a habit.*

Aristotle

*I know of no more encouraging fact
than the unquestionable ability of man
to elevate his life by conscious endeavor.*

Henry David Thoreau

**Sometimes when I consider what tremendous consequences come from little things…
I am tempted to think… there are no little things.**

Bruce Barton

**Man's perceptions are not bounded by organs of perception;
he perceives more than sense (tho' ever so acute) can discover.**

William Blake

IN his best-selling book, *The 7 Habits of Highly Effective People*, Stephen Covey says that:

We live in a primarily left-brain-dominant world, where words and measurement and logic are enthroned, and the more creative, intuitive, sensing, artistic aspect of our nature is often subordinated. Many of us find it more difficult to tap into our right brain capacity. The more we are able to draw upon our right brain capacity, the more fully we will be able to visualize, to synthesize, to transcend time and present circumstances, to project a holistic picture of what we want to do and to be in life.[1]

Many of the habits that Dr. Covey covers in his book are right brain dominant concepts that can be effectively employed only from that hemisphere. For instance: Habit 2: Begin with the end in mind; Habit 4: Think win/win; and Habit 6, Synergize. All of these concepts are essentially holistic.[2] Despite the dominance of left brain culture, the workforce is filled with "closet right brain thinkers" masquerading as left brain dominant. This farce is often necessary in order to function in a left brain dominant world. Most with this quandary do not begin with the awareness that they are conflicted. School reinforces a left brain behavior and from childhood helps develop a persona with effective coping schemes so that as an adult, the pattern is seldom questioned.

I am a right brain thinker but I only realized that after spending four decades of my life oblivious to what I was doing that was different. Fifteen years ago I learned that the label "attention deficit," could be applied to me. That label didn't exist when I was a child. When we moved to Sedona while I was in third grade; it took me until fifth grade to catch up because my new school was so much more advanced over the one I had come from. I usually found new subjects difficult to understand, making no sense to me as they were presented. When tackling a new subject I had to achieve a critical mass of understanding before I became effective. Sometimes that took weeks, or even months, to happen, particularly with subjects other than science and math, which I am good at.

Even today, despite an advanced college education, I sometimes find understanding auditory communication difficult. That includes lectures at work, sermons, and especially phone conversations. All are often difficult. When subjected to long lectures, I find myself tuning out the details being presented while letting the words go by without actually listening consciously. If what I hear subconsciously makes any sense at all, my right brain will eventually grasp it and often, I subsequently understand the big picture. When that happens I suddenly know more than most people who listen with their left brain. I am able to arrive at conclusions that allow me to extrapolate or interpolate the data thus deriving big picture answers. This is why I am effective in research environments. I am a puzzle solver and in so doing I arrive at new answers worth exploring. As a program manager, I often made my decisions by intuition; I knew that a certain line of inquiry, or approach to problem solving, was best.

However, I also know that almost no one will accept right brain justifications so I became good at backfilling the answer I felt was right. I would give a right brain answer with a left brain justification that my typically left-brain-oriented work environment would accept. The word for this is sophistry, the art of justifying an already arrived at conclusion with contrived arguments. This synergy works as it is in the left brain that one finds the details for implementation and in the right brain that one finds guidance for the major decisions. In working with both halves I often solve problems that seemed insolvable.

One other key ingredient: I am always optimistic that there is a solution. At the laboratory I worked at this was known as the Mel Factor. When I presented a program, even if I didn't know all of the answers, and in research that was the case all the time, if my instincts said "yes," then I presented what I had and gave a positive assessment of our chances for success. Even though the people I worked with knew that I was being positive without a fully logical basis, they went along with it because I was successful. What generally happened was some sort of solution would come along: more money, a new technology, an unexpected phone call that was precisely the answer I needed, something. Often the result was different and just as often, better because it lead to new answers. That is the nature of research. What my associates cared about was the fact that problems were solved, and sometimes they got more than they bargained for in the beginning. That sort of inquisitive environment, the willingness to be flexible on a grand scale, made for dynamic results – changing budgets and expectations, but great fun and unexpected triumphs.

Inflexible, left brain environments are unfun and I eventually leave such environments when I find myself in one. Consequently, throughout my career I have often changed jobs and even careers when what I was doing was no longer of interest. I achieved a gestalt understanding, then moved on. Thus, my professional career includes being a teacher who in my last year was selected as Teacher of the Year by the senior class; a researcher at a couple of major research laboratories with patents and numerous other awards and recognitions; a construction worker who eventually filled the role of architect and prime contractor in the building of my own home; and now my current status as a computer programmer and information technology engineer while drawing from all of these backgrounds to write books.

I am not alone, however in having a right brain approach in my corporate career. For instance, it is the educated opinion of Dr. Carla Hannaford that Albert Einstein was a gestalt learner, hence right-brained. As evidence for this assertion she points to the fact that his early school performance was riddled with academic failure. Later, as a scientist, his reliance upon visual imagery rather than linear logic is well known.[3, 4]

RIGHT BRAIN THINKING IN CORPORATE AMERICA

Although this fact is not well known, excellence in corporate America, and probably the world in general, is based on right brain leadership.[5,6,7,8] Dr. Charles Garfield has done extensive research on this subject and found that almost all of the world-class athletes and other peak performers are visualizers, a right brain characteristic.[9] At the heart of corporate leadership, many studies have shown that chief executive officers (CEOs) trust their intuition, including ESP, ahead of all other approaches when making decisions.[10] Examples are: Alexander M. Pniatoff, founder and chairman of the board emeritus of Ampex Corporation, William W. Keeler, chairman of the board emeritus of Phillips Petroleum; and John L. Tishman, former board member and executive vice president of Tishman Realty & Construction Company.[11]

A prominent example of right-brain thinking is Andrew Carnegie, who based his empire on visualization and intuition, and supported disseminating those secrets by backing Napoleon Hill in writing the book *Think and Grow Rich*.[12] The founder of General Motors, William C. Durant, was characterized by Alfred P. Sloan, former president of General Motors, as a man who "would proceed on a course of action guided solely, as far as I could tell, by some intuitive flash of brilliance. He never felt obliged to make an engineering hunt for the facts."[13]

Another prominent example is Conrad Hilton, the founder of Hilton Hotels. A documented instance of going with an intuitive hunch was a bid Hilton made for the Stevens Corporation. Initially he put in a bid of $165,000, but based on an intuitive feeling, he changed the bid to $180,000. His was the winning bid by $200 on a business prospect that eventually netted him $2 million. Those who worked for him called his intuitive leaps "Connie's hunches."[14]

Yet another example is Chester Carlson, the lawyer turned inventor of Xerox. He was so interested in the role intuition played, because of his own intuitive abilities, that he funded research in the field at the New Jersey Institute of Technology. One resulting study tested more than 7,000 executives for intuitive abilities in the form of precognitive ESP, or the ability to know ahead of time the card pulled from a deck. The scoring was above chance; however, what was most intriguing was the analysis of the results from 36 company presidents. Nineteen out of 21 of the company presidents who had doubled their firm's profits in a five-year span, scored high in precognition, almost a 90 percent correlation. For the remaining firms that had not done as well, only five out of 15 scored high, a 33 percent correlation.[15] One interesting sidelight to this study was the number of executives who came forward to comment on their belief in ESP. As Dean states in the seminal book, *Executive ESP*:

> *Executives kept coming up and saying, "I believe in ESP for one reason, because I use it."* Here were top-level executives, men with ultimate responsibility for the success of their companies, responsible for the stockholders' monies, men who almost all held engineering degrees, telling me they believed in ESP; they used it on the job. Surprisingly, they said they often went along with their intuition even though it was in flat contradiction to the supposed facts of a case. We certainly hadn't anticipated this. Executives came out three-and-one-half to one in favor of ESP. Their wives favored ESP seven to one."[16]

When asked how they were able to make decisions that in the future turned out to have been the wisest course of action, Dwight Joyce, president of Glidden Company, stated, "If a vice president asks me how I was able to choose the right course, I have to say, 'I'm damned if I know.'" Benjamin Fairless, former chairmen of the board of U.S. Steel said, "You don't know how you do it, you just do it."[17]

Likewise, I am certain that because the research laboratories I was involved in were group efforts involving a lot of creative people, many of them talked left brain lingo but secretly worked right brain creativity. **Buckminster Fuller tells of a study of prominent scientists' diaries where each listed their single most important item leading to their famous discoveries as intuition, and their secondary intuition that followed closely after their first realization thus giving them important improvement details.**[18, 19] Because of the prominence of ESP-based abilities in their work, many of the top scientists have been interested in psi including, Edison, Steinmetz, Marconi, Sir Oliver Lodge, Sir William Crookes, Madame Curie, Tesla, and Einstein.[20]

A well-known politician with this ability was Prime Minister Winston Churchill. His son Randolph documents many instances of his precognitive ability. For instance, during World War II:

> At 10 Downing Street, Churchill's precognitive flair served even more dramatically. Three government ministers were dining with the prime minister. The blitz began as usual, but the party went on and the cook and the maid continued working in the kitchen next to a 25-foot high plate glass window. Suddenly, acting on a premonition, Churchill got up and went into the kitchen. "Put dinner on a hot plate in the dining room," he instructed the butler and ordered everyone in the kitchen to the bomb shelter. Then he went back to his guests and his dinner. Three minutes later, a bomb hit the house, totally destroying the kitchen.[21]

During World War I Hitler was in a trench on the front line. Based on the urging of an inner voice, he moved around the corner a few yards away. A shell landed on the group he had just left. Incidents like this convinced him that he was being saved for a special destiny.[22] Abraham Lincoln, Franklin Roosevelt, and General George Patton in America, Prime Minister Mackenzie King in Canada, and Prime Minister Lord Balfour in England, can also be added to the list of prominent politicians who had psi experiences.[23]

THE ROLE DREAMS AND VISIONS PLAY

An allied process is that of dreaming. Thomas Edison used his dreams to provide answers to his inventions, thus accumulating the largest number of inventions ever conceived of by a single individual. Napoleon Hill was flying with one of the principal forces behind the building of the Hoover

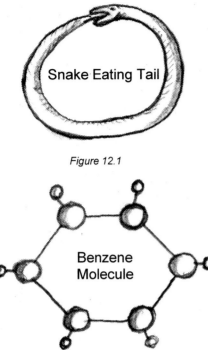

Figure 12.1

Benzene Molecule

Dam, Le Tourneau, when he partly awakened from sleep, jotted down an answer, slept again, and upon awakening discovered that his note was the answer to a problem he had been trying to solve for months. Elias Howe dreamed the answer to how to build the first sewing machine as a spear with a hole in the tip.[24] The unexpected circular structure of the benzene molecule, discovered by Belgian chemist Friedrich August von Kekule, was first seen in a dream as a snake swallowing its tail. [25, 26, 27] Dmitry Mendeleyev had an unusual dream where he saw a table with all the elements fall into place as required. Upon awakening he immediately documented his dream on a piece of paper thus creating the *Periodic Table of the Elements* that bears his name. Robert Lewis Stevenson indicated that his dreams were the source of much of his best work including the classic story *Dr. Jekyll and Mr. Hyde*.[28] After awakening from a light nap, Abraham Lincoln wrote down the Gettysburg address, a candidate for the single most effective speech ever given. Likewise, Darwin, Goethe, and Poincaré all gained insights via their dreams.[29]

The process of gaining insight appears to be directly related to the distraction, or shutting down, of the conscious mind; another Zen type conundrum: insight comes when you don't seek it. The key is the asking of a question, then distracting or incapacitating the conscious mind to let the subconscious flow forth. My adopted father once spoke of an incident in his life where he was bedridden with a high fever. He recounted it as great fun because as he drifted in and out of sleep, his dreams were precipitated by his thoughts prior to sleeping again thus giving him hours of entertainment. The fever apparently shut down his beta state conscious mind leaving him drifting in his alpha state subconscious mind. My father's experience is indicative of the general process by which creative ideas can be sought in daily life. Quoting the book *Executive ESP*:

> *French mathematician Henri Poincaré stated that creative ideas did not come to him while he worked at his desk, but frequently flashed into his mind while he engaged in other activities. The theory of relativity sprang into the mind of Albert Einstein after a lengthy period of work, while he was confined to bed because of illness. Later at Princeton, Einstein found his thoughts crystallized more readily while he drifted about aimlessly in a canoe.*[30]

The process of Eureka! breakthroughs has been investigated by Margharita Laski and was characterized by her as having six parts:[31, 32]

1. *Asking the question.* **The passionate seeking of an answer to a fundamental question.**
2. *Searching for the answer.* **All possible avenues of inquiry are sought out and pursued.**
3. *Hitting the plateau period.* **Stagnation sets in when no more materials can be found.**
4. *Giving up all hope.* **You quit and do something else while driving the thoughts from your mind.**
5. *Breaking through.* **With the mind cleared, the answer comes like a lightning bolt in the dark.**
6. *Translating the answer into the common domain.* **The critical step of transcribing the often-unusual nature of the answer into the context and terminology of the field it is applicable to.**

In his excellent book, *The Power of the Subconcious Mind*, Dr. Joseph Murphy tells about Prof. Agassiz, the distinguished American naturalist, whose wife relayed the following story after his death. Prof. Agassiz had been trying to decipher the zoological characteristics of an obscure fossil fish in a slab of stone in the Jardin Des Plantes. After weeks of frustrating and fruitless efforts, he gave up. In characteristic Laski-defined fashion, that night inspiration came to him in the form of a dream, which upon awakening, he realized had shown him the very fish he was trying to understand, yet he couldn't remember the details of what he had seen. He went to the stone slab again seeking inspiration, but was stymied. The next night he had the same dream and once again, could not remember the vision clearly enough to retain the needed details. On the third night, he slept with a pencil and paper by his bed and this time while it was still dark, he was able to record the details of his dream before they evaporated in the dawn of awakening. Returning to the stone slab his vision led him to chisel away more stone knowing that underneath must be obscured parts. When the fish was revealed in total, it was as he had seen and was subsequently easily classified.[33]

ELIMINATING LASKI'S PARTS THREE AND FOUR

The examples listed so far conform fairly well to Laski's list, with the possible exception of Thomas Edison, who supposedly never despaired in his search for answers. However, he also consciously sought inspiration in his dreams thus actively implementing the breakthrough via his subconscious. His example hints that the *giving up all hope* step might be a historical formulation and not a necessity. When physical sources are exhausted and the plateau is hit, that is the indicator that the subconscious is the next resource to poll thus eliminating the fourth step. In fact, **the subconscious is more appropriately the first source to poll, or the steady source to poll throughout this process, thus eliminating both steps three and four.** An example would be what happened to optical physicist Gordon Gould. While at home, during a weekend of casual activity, he saw as a flash a symbolic structure that took him the remainder of the weekend to write down and which constituted the totally unexpected discovery of laser light. The keys were a good technical understanding, an inquiring mind, and relaxation, since he was not consciously engaged in a search for an answer.[34]

A second example is Mozart who is another genius who never attended school.[35] Once his abilities had matured, he would hold a new commission for a piece of music as an "open-ended possibility." Sometime later the answer would suddenly appear in his mind as a "round volume of sound." It was therefore a holographic answer that he held in his conscious mind in his right-brain, similar to how one must hold onto a dream and translate it.[36] The translation phase was where he enlisted the aid of his wife. She read to him, thus freeing his subconscious mind to tackle the difficult task of transcribing the gestalt into linear-based notes, the musical language we can read and understand.[37] **Dreams can likewise be thought of as "a round volume of imagery"** which is why they have to be translated just as Mozart translated what he received.

During the discussion concerning the "Mouth of God," near the end of **Chapter 4**, I told the story of my wife's loss of her first child, Amy. Despairing after Amy's death my wife was desperately seeking an understanding of her loss, and her life. That night she dreamed a dream of understanding where she was shown how all the pieces of her life – past, present, and future, came flying in to fit together in holistic cosmic puzzle fashion as a "round volume of imagery," thus giving her understanding. Upon awakening she felt calmed knowing that everything fit together in a grand design. Despite being an excellent artist, and very visual, she was not able to transcribe this vision to paper as it didn't fit the constraints of the medium. Her dream indicates that there are limitations to our ability to translate holistic dreams to linear duality.

These examples also indicate that once a person is sufficiently attuned as Mozart was, obtaining information by submitting requests to the universe can become much like submitting your order at a new restaurant. You know what you want in general but what comes back and how long it will take is greatly variable. However, given patience and persistence you usually obtain what you desire while being surprised by the actual nature of the result. Most of the time what arrives is editable, and sometimes it is a masterpiece.

The majority of us already do this to a certain extent without realizing it. For instance, when you say that something dawned on you, those are code words for – your subconscious answered the question your conscious mind asked. Whenever you make a decision with less than 100 percent of the facts, which is most of the time, you are drawing conclusions that your subconscious supplies. Your subconscious is the mechanism by which you extrapolate and interpolate within the known to explore the unknown. My suggestion is that we realize what we are doing, and begin to consciously cultivate the subconscious, or unconscious, or alpha state. However you wish to name it, it is still a rose worth cultivating. The objective would be to become functional and balanced, at conscious and subconscious levels, in order to foster admittance to superconscious levels, the source of the truly creative and innovative solutions.

The evidence and approaches listed so far come from the individual level as our scientific and corporate leaders intuitive abilities have guided us despite our typical ignorance of the source for their leadership successes. The examples listed are drawn from those whose abilities represented the very pinnacle of human endeavor, with results matching the scope of their questions and comprehension of the answers. Their approaches were often eccentric, and tolerated because the ends justified the means. All of us are capable of creative problem solving with useful results. However, corporate America in general is not well equipped to handle people taking naps as Thomas Edison did or vision quests over lunch for creative problem solving while at work. Other countries foster this approach, the Mexican siesta or Japanese bathhouse for instance. In America we have generally had to rely upon "sleeping on it overnight" in order to obtain dream-based information. We may hope, as awareness of the importance of the alpha state grows, acceptance of the need to dip into it in various means will become common knowledge and eventually a cultural norm.

HOW TO DEVELOP ALPHA/THETA STATE FUNCTIONAL WORKFORCES

Besides the obvious benefits for all corporate continuing education programs in the form of accelerated learning techniques, there are steps that can be taken to foster subconscious, or alpha state level work in the everyday work environment, which is the realm in which intuition and all associated right brain activities blossom. *A first step would be to do the Brain Gym® exercises, found in* **Chapter 15**, *each morning and after lunch as a corporate sponsored activity much as Japanese workers begin their workday by doing tai chi. Another excellent step would be educating the workforce as to the importance right brain development has in achieving excellence in any field!* Positive labeling will help support such activities. For instance, rather than the negative connotation associated with zoning-out, replace that phrase with "zoning-in," or "being in the zone." How about, "right-brain, right-on!" as a slogan or bumper sticker, or, "Ride the Sub for Success!"

After education fosters acceptance, companies could have A to Z meetings, inferring both alpha and theta zones, and alpha to omega scope and depth. Alpha state proto (ASP) and great recall of alpha state photography, or GRASP, would become part of the everyday lexicon. Alpha/theta state facilities, alpha/theta teams, and α-θ team rooms could be developed. Scheduling regular alpha/theta meetings for the purpose of creative interaction would provide addition support. These specialized rooms could be populated with comfortable chairs, and alpha/theta state inducing music would be the prelude to a meeting as well as having low or subliminal volume level background during meetings. Many business meetings in Japan are silent. In the West, allowing moments of silence during meetings could likewise become acceptable, for it is during these moments that true creativity gestates. We would be working with: the wise elder within, or wise manager within, or wise mentor within. Then alpha/theta will be in, or AT is in, or as another variation, $\alpha\,\theta$ is in!

Some groups that are creativity-based, such as ad development agencies and cooperative artistic endeavors like those that Hollywood engages in, already have some of these elements in place. Every organization could benefit from thinking that draws from the deeper wisdom its employees carry as latent potential, particularly as international competition has raised the stakes for everyone while narrowing the profit margins.

Facilities like this would best be located in close proximity to natural settings such as gardens, or windows overlooking pleasant landscaping. Restful wall scenes of forests, streams, and nature in general could add or substitute for the availability of natural environments. Foreign countries are in many regards ahead of America in this arena. Denmark has a law making it mandatory that all children in school, and working adults, be able to see nature from their seat or workplace. Japan and England, despite limited space, are famous for their gardens. In Russia, classrooms have a wall of large windows and few light bulbs. However, in America we have tended to ignore such healthful role models and eliminate classroom windows in order to "reduce distractions." We have taken that philosophy with us into the workplace. This is unfortunate because most fluorescent lights have a 60-cycle-per-second flicker that is distracting because our peripheral vision, the subconscious vision, picks it up, thus stressing us. In Europe, the less perceptible 72-cycle per second rate is used. Newborn babies react adversely to fluorescent lights thus giving us a clue that they are discordant and possibly harmful.[38] *Wherever it is intended that people try to achieve alpha/theta state creativity levels of relaxed alertness, it is best that the lighting be natural if possible, and if not, then an excellent substitute is full spectrum fluorescent lighting with ballasts that switch at 20,000 cycles per second.*[39] If whole spectrum lighting is not available, then at least have lighting that is adjustable and incandescent-based. What is best is the elimination of as much of the stress effects associated with both the sources of light and the electromagnetic fields they emit.[40]

When corporate cultures begin to understand and support these activities with proper budgets, follow up by putting in reclining chairs for every desk and making available alpha/theta state music on multiple tracks as the airlines do for each of their seats. Then issue headsets to everyone and allow people to turn their telephones to non-ring messaging service modes while they engage in alpha/theta state activities. Have available beta state music on another track in order to help facilitate employees returning to that level when so desired. For long term planning, start building facilities with views of nature as Holland does.

Develop a culture of practical visioning. Let decisions based on feelings be as acceptable as those based on risk assessment, trend analysis, or spreadsheet accounting. Add feeling and intuition as categories to a white paper analysis of a problem. Add a company web site with pastoral scenes and alpha/theta state music. Start encouraging whole mind activities. Begin meetings with moments of silence to clear and center everyone. Establish a clear intentionality for each meeting or, if that direction is lacking, use the meeting to develop clear direction as the first step. Begin meetings with feeling assessments both for the individual, and for the problem at hand. If you have a lot of technical material to cover during the meeting, have everyone SuperScan the material prior to beginning discussions. Conclude the meeting with a statement of any remaining unsolved problems, and a request for any intuitive or dream based feedback people are given overnight.

Much can be done with information technology to support this activity. Provide reports, emails and other reading material in electronic media that can be paged through right side up and upside down with automatic paging rates in order to encourage SuperScanning. Solicit Microsoft to modify MS Office so material can be presented upside down at automatic paging rates, and in batch modes. Develop a common computer operating environment where documents can be scrolled through at rates equal to whatever the processor and local area network (LAN) is capable of. This material could be buffered locally on the LAN so a person could scroll through it at high rates, then dump it. Have a web site drop box for ideas for birthing corporate excellence. Expect the unexpected. Honor the unusual. Be open-minded!

When abilities and facilities begin to support the full human potential, lawyers will be able to absorb the million-document cases some of them work on; facility managers will intuitively know what every building on every site looks like and what it can accommodate in a rapidly changing environment; computer programmers will be able to memorize coding manuals and systems integration documentation with commensurate gains in efficiency and creativity; electronics engineers will absorb the circuit specifications for even multi-million component chips; marketers will be able to study potential clients at depth prior to pitching their wares, plus carry with them mental lists of the important details regarding existing clients; negotiators involved in international negotiations and personnel relocation to foreign countries will be able to learn the languages involved; and pilots will be able to remember in depth the technical information about their aircraft and have at their instant disposal key airport information, to name just a few potential gains in work force excellence.

RIGHT BRAIN WORK ALREADY UNDER WAY

In business, the process of rebuilding the business mind is already occurring in organizations aimed at excellence. For instance, during the first few decades of its development, software was considered more the purview of art as opposed to science. By the mid-80s it was apparent that this process had become the dominant cost in any information technology-based system, and said systems lived or died upon the success of an ill-defined software development process. In 1987 the United States federal government contracted with Carnegie Mellon to investigate the process of software development and see if the lessons learned could provide useful metrics whereby quality control measures could be applied.

Building on the pioneering work of Walter Shewhart, W. Edwards Deming, Joseph Juran, and Philip Crosby, the Software Engineering Institute at Carnegie Mellon created a Process Maturity Framework and associated questionnaire for companies engaged in software development. From this data they developed the Software Engineering Institute Computer Maturation Model (SEI-CMM®), which established five levels of sophistication in software development. The lowest level was Level 1, characterized by organizations using an immature process formed of ad hoc approaches yielding risky results. Hopes for success fell on the shoulders of heroes in the organization. This is sometimes characterized as "management by adrenalin," because of the long work-week requirements. Each maturity level above Level 1 could be compared to the growth of dendrites across the organization as processes become formalized first at the cellular level of the individual, then groups, and finally organization-wide as reinforced messages and associated processes myelinate to form a net of understanding.

Taking this analogy further, typically in business an individual starts out with left brain work like the mailroom, parts counter, component design, or software module coding, and ends up with right brain responsibilities such as system integration, process facilitation, team coordination, and management. The SEI-CMM® Level 5 takes this a step further by forming the organization into a whole-brain activity. Geniuses are whole brained, and so are genius organizations. In this model, processes form the brain cells and connectivity forms the dendrites by which such cooperative creativity occurs. Management, plus the contacts employees and groups make, form the corpus callosum, a predominately female function. In a Level 5 organization, management facilitates by providing information and resources where they are needed, thus nurturing a naturally evolving process of self-improvement and continued optimization.

The results of the Software Engineering Institute's analysis were startling, indicating that Level 5 organizations having whole-brain capabilities were more than ten times as efficient as Level 1 organizations, delivering products reliably in much less time for one tenth the cost. In addition, Level 5 organization employees were blessed with a low-stress environment. They were able to go home on a regular basis at the end of a normal workday having easily accomplished their goals. The United States federal government subsequently used this information to preferentially award contracts to organizations based on their SEI-CMM® rating. In 1991 there was only one Level 5 organization, NASA, and only a few dozen in aggregate down to level 2. The list has steadily grown with many foreign companies quickly developing expertise. In the summer of 2002 more than 700 CMM organizations existed including Telecorida Technologies in the West and Satyam in the East, which are Level 5 organizations along with more than 30 others that have achieved that distinction.[41, 42]

All of these impressive gains have been achieved *without employing anywhere close to the potential for excellence every person embodies*! **Think of what could be achieved if we began to develop the latent human potential to its fullest. The biggest productivity revolution was the Industrial Revolution, which moved people away from the fields of nature into the fields of manufacturing. In the 1890s, approximately 94 percent of all Americans lived on farms. In one hundred years that figure changed to 96 percent of Americans living in cities or towns, a profound change.[43] The next revolution on the horizon could well be the inspiration revolution, and it will move us out of left field logic work to right field balanced living and working.** Maybe then more people will be happy with their jobs rather than the less than 10 percent that most polls currently indicate.

Historically in the United States, major corporations have been the mainstay for employment. This past few decades, almost all of the new jobs are being created by young, entrepreneurial companies. Two-thirds of the 22 million jobs created in the 1980s were taken by women. According to analyst John Naisbitt, in medical and business schools, half of the freshman classes are women. Of even greater significance is the fact that women are creating new companies at twice the rate of men. Clearly the feminine aspect is rapidly rising to achieve parity with the established masculine aspect.[44]

As society integrates Eastern and Western, masculine and feminine, and all other dichotomies, it is likely that the resulting balance at organizational levels will also address the problem of dominance. It has been shown that the psi ability of the dominant group in an organization suppresses even superior psi ability in the minority group. For instance, if all of the executives in an organization are male, then the psi ability of the females is suppressed, and vice versa.[45] With balance, all will begin to contribute at a level closer to their unimpeded personality as characterized by Dr. Lozenov. *Cooperation has always been superior to competition, just nearly impossible to implement until now. Its time is coming. When it does the synergistic, win/win, keep-the-end-in-mind, leadership Stephen Covey found in stellar individuals will be applied broad spectrum to benefit everyone.*

**In seeking wisdom, the first state is silence,
the second listening, the third remembrance,
the fourth practicing, the fifth teaching.**
Kabbalist Solomon Gabiron, c. 1045

Eastern philosophy and Western science could be a good marriage, without a divorce.
Dalai Lama

Let us learn to dream, gentlemen.
Belgian chemist Friedrich August von Kekule[45]

Chapter 13 – YOUR SUPER POTENTIAL

He who knows, tells it not; he who tells, knows it not.

Lao-tzu

**Just because a person is young or small does not make him or her incomplete.
The truth is that we are complete at all moments in our life.**

Wayne Dyer

The conscious mind is narrow and fragile compared to the depths and power of the subconscious. The subconscious is an ally. It is like having a superman or wonderwoman at our side ready to assist us. Although hidden, it is truly a genie.

Henry Reed

You must come in contact with the empty space that lies within, not the form that encapsulates it.

Wayne Dyer

Look! Up in the sky! It's a bird! It's a plane! No! It's Superman!

DC Comics

*The seed of God is in us: pear seeds grow into pear trees;
hazel seeds into hazel trees; and God seeds into God.*

Master Eckehart

**They used to say to scientists, "Do you believe in God?"
And the scientist would respond, "No, I'm a scientist."
Today, in the '90s, if you ask a scientist, "Do you believe in God?"
The scientist will say, "Of course, I'm a scientist!"**

Wayne Dyer

What lies behind us and what lies before us are tiny matters compared to what lies within us.

Oliver Wendell Holmes

Things which matter most must never be at the mercy of things which matter least.

Goethe

THE historical perspective helps make discussions of super-achievement more reasonable to accept. Such achievements started out as the means whereby our super legacy was retained. The strong oral traditions of the storyteller used to foster remembering perfectly oral histories that were for most communities, the only means of retaining the legacy of their past. With the advent of the printing press, much of that tradition was lost. However, throughout history there have been individuals, often labeled as geniuses, who could accomplish amazing feats of memory and associated creative abilities. During the eleven years he was incarcerated, Alexander Solzhenitsyn was denied both pen and paper so in order to write, he memorized. He committed to memory the details of *The Gulag Archipelgo*, a major tome, along with 18,000 lines of a poem he wrote and published.

Nearly a century ago in France Dr. Maria Montessori first explored her theories about learning by working with the learning disabled. Her techniques were so effective that soon her disadvantaged students outperformed the average student of the day. Her pioneering efforts have grown into the widely disseminated Montessori Schools that perpetuate the excellence she gave birth to.[2] In the same time frame in Germany, Rudolph Steiner pioneered another excellent creative curriculum in his Waldorf Schools that have likewise spread worldwide. His intuitive genius personified what I hope this book is trying to foster in all of us. At the beginning of last century Napoleon Hill wrote what is probably the most famous and successful book of the super-achievement genre, *Think and Grow Rich*. Andrew Carnegie introduced him to many wealthy people so he could interview them and learn their secrets. The knowledge he distilled from this included an understanding of subconscious programming that many of his readers used to become wealthy. Everyone since, from Erhard Seminars Training to Sylvan Mind Control, has taught the same principles.

Dr. Lozenov is another pioneer in the subconscious programming field. His work found a receptive audience in Bulgaria, Austria, and to an extent Russia, and crossed the ocean with the label of Super Learning®, taking up residence in Canada and the United States where Pepperdine College in Los Angeles used it.[1] For whatever reasons, Super Learning® has not prospered with anything near the promise that Dr. Lozenov demonstrated. Nevertheless, his use of music to foster rapid patterning of information continues to grow in importance, particularly in the area of learning foreign languages. There are institutions worldwide that are exploring and using these concepts. Dr. Lozenov has a training institute for teachers, called Lozenov's Suggestophobia® Institute. If you are interested in learning more about what this true pioneer has done, his web site is http://lozanov.internet-bg.net, or you can email him at dr_lozanov@yahoo.com. The process he uses is more generally known as Neuro Linguistic Programming, or NLP. His institute teaches teachers via an apprentice system, who then use his techniques to help students access what Lozenov calls their functional reserves, the abilities lying dormant from childhood when most of us block them, or allow them to atrophy.

More recently during the last decade, Gordon Dryden and Jeannette Vos established a firm foundation for advancing education with their landmark book, *The Learning Revolution*. It is a world record best seller overseas with comparatively weak sales in America. The world currently has facing it major problems without clear solutions, such as global warming, the AIDS epidemic, depletion of the ozone, environmental genocide by toxic poisoning from the chemicals produced by industrial societies, and most recently, terrorism that can profoundly affect even the strongest of nations. Dryden and Vos contend that, ***given the rapid accumulation of knowledge and the problems facing mankind, only advanced education has the potential to lift us high enough to be able to see clearly our current situation and arrive at the best possible cooperative solutions.***

THE CURRENT FATE FOR THE WORLD'S CHILDREN

Despite the clear presentation by many individuals of the potential for greatness all humans have, America, and the rest of the world in general, continues to squander its children in largely unrewarding and outmoded educational systems. As we are the purported bastion for free thinking, that is unfortunate. Luckily, the best in corporate America are more aware. When Jack Welch was asked by Robert Slater whether GE would look like it does today in 20 to 30 years time, Welch replied, "I doubt it. I hope it will be the greatest learning institution in the world."[3] Unfortunately, what Douglas Buchanan has to say is probably more accurate:

> *America as a whole has no interest in education. It is even regarded as the way to a well paying job instead of the way to become an integrated person. There are bus drivers in England with PhD's because education is for what you do in your spare time. America has solved that problem by ensuring that the workers have as little spare time as possible. An increasing productivity is the only goal. Education is run by business as vocational training and is treated as a business in which the products are identical graduates. The major interests in America are court cases and wars of various kinds. Playing the role of the consensus mentality is more important than knowing who you are. Things you throw and things you catch are more important than things you know, particularly if the things you know are not obviously geared to earning or to make dollars. The abundant educational*

opportunities you mention are becoming more and more available only to the wealthy. Students abroad go to college to learn. Here they go to socialize, at enormous expense.

The potential being squandered in both America and worldwide, is enormous. For example, the father of modern day subliminal reading is Dr. Richard Welch. His work is presented under the title of *Dynamic Brain Management and Mental Photography.* **Appendix I** is a more complete description of his pioneering seminar. Since the late 1970s, when Dr. Welch began giving his seminar, more than 20,000 people have completed his workshop. He has many impressive success stories including people who, in spite of low IQ or other supposed learning disabilities, became super achievers. Unfortunately, from the perspective of America, foreign countries have proven more receptive to this type of instruction, fielding typical class sizes of around 100, as opposed to America where fewer than a dozen typically attend. Possibly this is an instance where the greater hunger for knowledge overseas drives their enthusiasm whereas the abundant educational opportunities in America obscure the true potential this incredible technique offers.

A more recent entry is Paul Scheele with his book, *PhotoReading: The Whole Mind System,* first published in 1995. It has sold more than 300,000 copies and is filled with excellent success stories demonstrating a wide spectrum of uses and benefits from PhotoReading®. His contribution helps further the work initiated by Dr. Welch. All of these groundbreaking efforts, from Dr Lozanov to Paul Scheele, deserve applause, and no doubt will someday receive acknowledgement for the importance of their contribution to mankind. Because of their efforts, *it is now understood that the extraordinary abilities of a few such as Douglas Buchanan, which until recently were considered aberrations, are accessible to almost everyone.*[4, 5]

The book you are reading was written by drawing from a broad spectrum of conventional and esoteric knowledge in order to extend our understanding of the alpha/theta state, and document simple techniques for tapping into it. Dr. Welch's "**Mental Photography®**," Paul Scheele's "**PhotoReading®**," and what I called "**SuperScanning**;" are all names for the same phenomena. The most accurate name scientifically is "**Subliminal Photography®**," which Dr. Welch trademarked along with his other references to his discovery. If you have already learned one of these methods and are proficient and comfortable with it, then you have nothing you need to change. The method I have presented is what Douglas Buchanan uses. All of these methods work far better than any conventional reading program aimed at the conscious mind.

OUR SUPER POTENTIAL

What all of these examples hint at is your true potential that I have only outlined in this book. This is an arena where unlike everyday advertising; the word Super becomes very applicable. *What we have covered is your potential for super intuition, super sight, SuperScanning, super memory, super recall, super abilities in general, and the Georgi Lozenov's groups, Super Learning® and Suggestophobia®. There is a real possibility that the comic book concept of Superman and Superwoman is derived from a deep knowing that the everyday abilities we all live with are not what we are truly capable of.* The book *Super Learning,* documents how great this potential is; and that such potential is not being totally ignored world-wide:

> *As of 1976, there were seventeen public schools throughout Bulgaria that had been using Lozanov's method for all subjects for several years. Supposedly, out of the scores of children in these Bulgarian schools, every one was a virtual prodigy. Supposedly, first graders read advanced stories. Third graders did high school algebra. Everyone covered two years of school in four months. Children learned to read in a matter of days. The 'supposedlys" began to soar off into the wild blue yonder.* **Everyone had fun. Everyone loved learning. Everyone was creative. No one failed. Sick children cured themselves in the new process of learning.**[6]

In his insightful book, *The Biology of Transcendence,* Joseph Chilton Pearce explores brain development. ***Figure 13.1*** presents his information on the developmental stages the brain goes through.[7]

Figure 13.1 – Brain Growth Spurts and Shifts of Concentration of Development						
					Prefrontal Lobes? 15 to Death	
				Cerebellum? 11 to Death		
			Left Hemisphere - 7 to 21			
		Right Hemisphere - 4 to 15				
	Limbic System - 1 to 11					
Reptilian Brain - Birth to age 7						

These stages are generally correlated with age brackets with the exception of the final stages of development, the cerebellum and prefrontal lobes, which probably account for the highest levels of cognition. The prefrontal lobe ability being referred to can be thought of as a secondary development stage as it will have already gone through one round of development along with the rest of the brain. The difference is that this secondary development gives us our civility thus allowing us to rise above our animal instincts with a cultured mind.

Only a small percentage of the population generally achieves this level of capability, each step in development being approximately a multiplication by a factor of ten. Quoting Herman Epstein, "*More than half the population of the United States never reach the Piaget stage of formal reasoning [thought is systematic and abstract]. We have knowers but few thinkers!*"[8] *As with all brain functions, few ultimately begin to use the full latent potential, thus making this a staircase of excellence. In order to progress, note that proper right-brain development is essential for proper left-brain functioning as each step is a foundation that the next increment depends upon. Therefore, advanced thinking generally can occur only if all the intermediary stepping stones are laid.*[9] *With proper development, advanced thinking occurs naturally.* **Quoting Bob Samples,** "*We discovered that if the right hemisphere functions are celebrated, the development of the left hemisphere qualities becomes inevitable.*"[10]

An interesting exception is those once known as idiot savants, who often have IQs in the range of 25, yet specialized abilities such as the capacity to calculate complex mathematical answers, or calendar manipulations to determine date/day correlations far in the past or future.[11] Such anomalies are rare and possibly instances of having all the stepping stones in place for a highly specialized staircase of reasoning, but nothing else around to make it a building.

What few realize is that we are all in the same predicament as the idiot savants. We are the products of unhealthy stress from our parents' first thoughts of us, the genetic material they used to conceive us, our gestation environment, our birth typically in a hospital, and our development in our chosen society. *For humans - normal, whether, physical, emotional, mental, or spiritual, is a stunted average culled from a dysfunctional field. Our concepts of intelligence, aging, heart rate, athletic performance, biochemical makeup, psychological profile, and any other factor we think we understand, have been developed and evaluated with blinders on all participants. We know ourselves to the same depth as we have explored the planets of the universe. It is only in the abnormal that we find hints of our true potential, some desirable and some not. Few if any achieve balance and the extraordinary at the same time. In each of us is the unexplored infinite potential waiting for permission to emerge. We still blindly waddle when we could soar. We do not just hide our lights under a basket; we steadily extinguish them from gestation until our faint glow matches the crippled ambient. Now is the time to rekindle our lights, throw off the basket, and begin seeing how brightly we shine! The children have already started down this path having agreed "in mass" to no longer adhere to our dysfunctional agenda. Either we grope blindly to extinction or follow their example.*

I submit that as we begin to exhibit our true potential what was once considered extraordinary will become the norm. An example of a normal well-rounded individual might then mime this historic example: in early 1500, Fernado di Cordova was born in Spain. By the time he was twenty-five he was an "installed doctor of all the faculties." Russell notes Feyjoo's observation that Fernando had mastered Latin, Greek, Hebrew, Chaldee, and probably all principal European languages.[12] Quoting Russell,

> *He could repeat the entire Bible from memory. He was profoundly versed in theology, in civil and canon law, in mathematics, and in medicine... He had at his command all the lights of the age in every branch of science... He was one of the most accomplished gentlemen and most distinguished cavaliers of his time. He could play on every known variety of instrument; he sang exquisitely; he was a most graceful dancer; an expert swordsman; and a bold and skillful rider; and he was master of one particular art of fence by which he was able to defeat all his adversaries, by springing upon them at a single bound of twenty-three or twenty-four yards!*

Figure 13.2

Properly established foundations can go even further. In the 100 years preceding the French Revolution, Count Saint Germain is documented as appearing in the courts of Europe doing demonstrations of seemingly impossible feats. For instance, he could write two letters at once, doing one with the left hand and the other with the right hand. The results could either be duplicates of each other, or separate thought streams. He never aged during that 100 years and would disappear and reappear at will. Given a royal sized gem with a flaw in it, he would return sometime later with the same gem now flawless. He was known as the wonderman, or "Superman" of Europe. Voltaire called him the "man who never dies and knows everything." There are scholars who believe that preceding that time frame; he was Sir Francis Bacon, who some scholars of the English language believe wrote the works generally credited to William Shakespeare.[13, 14]

Count Saint Germain

Knowledge of such super demonstrations of mastery are rare in the Western Hemisphere. They are far more common in the East where the strong yogic tradition has fostered such development. Paramanhansa Yogananda and Babaji are two Eastern examples that are better known in the West. Yogananda and Leonard Orr list many extraordinary examples in their books. For instance, Leonard Orr tracked down and met Bhartriji, who lives in the village of the same name in India. He does a public demonstration of what an immortal yogi is capable of. Every 108 years he has himself permanently encased in concrete. There are seven tombs in his ashram, all intact, because he has done this demonstration every 108 years for nearly eight hundred years. The last time he did this was in 1898, and the next time will be in 2006. All who choose to witness his mastery are invited. It is hoped that the Western press will broadcast this demonstration of mastery in 2006.[15]

A little research reveals dozens of examples. In the West, the Italian Saint Padre Pio, whom the Catholic Church recently formally beatified, performed many miracles including raising a child from the dead. He had all aspects of the stigmata and always smelled of roses.[16] Likewise, in the East, Sai Baba has done all of the miracles Jesus performed. You can have Darshan where he lives in Puttaparthi, India.[17, 18] Some of the names of other avatars are attached to the sayings sprinkled throughout this text. There are hundreds, if not thousands, of examples available for study if a deeper examination of the record is made. This is our super legacy, for the both the East and West. It is a legacy of examples of human potential that could more aptly be called Super Human. *Hu-man is actually Sanskrit for God-mind, a considerable legacy providing potential for unlimited growth. As we grow to manifest this potential, the super achievers that are today's anomalies will be tomorrow's standards.*

THE SUPER CHILDREN

Allow children to be happy in their own way, for what better way will they ever find?

Dr. Johnson

Except ye become as little children, ye cannot enter the Kingdom.

Matthew 12:13

*At the door of the Consciousness of every individual
should be engraved forever the words, be yourself!*

Saint Germain[18]

*Children can be conceptualized as mirrors.
If love is given to them, they return it.
If none is given, they have none to return.
Unconditional love is reflected unconditionally,
and conditional love is returned conditionally.*

Ross Campbell, M. D.

Don't limit a child to your own learning, for he was born in another time.

Rabbinic saying

A few decades ago, Gordon Michael Scallion prophesized that a new type of child would come into the world, "dark blue" children. Some ancient texts contain a similar prophecy. This prophecy has already been fulfilled.[20] Super growth is upon us now with the arrival in quantity of the super children, the Indigo children and the fantastic children in China, a few of whom are at the level of mastery of Quan Yin, the feminine aspect of divinity as Sai Baba is the masculine aspect. Another book dealing with the world's super children has been written by James Twyman who calls them *Emissaries of Love.*[21] The message conveyed by Twyman from these extraordinary children is a question, "How would you act or behave if you knew that you are an Emissary of Love this moment? Begin!"

All nations in varying degrees are experiencing the same phenomena although the less industrialized nations tend to have the children capable of nonordinary phenomena whereas the more industrialized ones are predominately composed of technically adept children like *the Indigo Children. All of these children are taking up the challenge of demonstrating humanity's potential.* Their impact has already been felt in the households and school systems they are challenging.

The authors of the book, *The Indigo Children*, have collected the input of teachers, counselors, and therapists who are trying to prepare the public to handle the changes in our children. Their conclusion is that *these children have one coordinated mission, to bring peace and unity to the world. As part of that process they will challenge any dishonest process whether it is found in homes, businesses, institutions, organizations, or nations around the world. Ultimately, that challenge will eliminate the concept of secrecy as a method of operation whether it is found in a family, financial, corporate, or national organization. How do you keep a secret from millions of children who read thoughts? The answer is, you don't! Only a free and open society worldwide is equipped to handle such openness in the children.*

As the barriers fall within us, they will fall around us. The foundation of this book is really one of learning how to control our thoughts, an essential prerequisite to being able to function in a society where reading thoughts becomes commonplace and openly accepted. I predict the obvious: that *the eventual outcome of this process will mean that the dominant form of communication for humanity will be telepathic communication.* Such communication already exists whenever barriers are eliminated. The typical example is married couples who often seem to read each other's thoughts and mirror each other's actions. Soon such coordinated thought and action will be far more commonplace, a natural consequence of the Indigo effect.

SUPER CHANGES HAPPENING NOW

This change is just around the corner. It is *the* paradigm shift poised to happen and it will probably eclipse all previous paradigm shifts in importance. Nancy Ann Tappe is the woman who first wrote about the Indigo Children as she could see the color a child incarnated with just as some people can see the Chakras. In 1999 she stated that, "90 percent of the children under ten were Indigo," the color of the third eye chakra, our unity eye.[22] ***They are not here to accept the status quo. They are here to change it.*** According to Tappe, about the age of 26 or 27 you will see a big change in these children when they "activate" to pursue their true purpose in being here.[23] Soon they will become an irresistible force "Seeking to do good!" ***It is up to the grownups in the world to see that they effect this change as savants who are honored rather than savages who are forced to rebel, for either way they will get our attention.***

Examples of Indigo Children getting our attention from extreme negative positions are those taking up guns in their homes and schools when they find themselves dishonored. You can often recognize them because, despite their predicament, they freely admit their guilt and accept their punishment. On August 2nd, 2002, young Andy Williams pleaded guilty and apologized after being sentenced to 55 years in jail for his multi-fatality shooting spree at his high school.

An example of an Indigo child getting our attention in a positive way is Mattie J. Stepanek, author of the *Heartsongs* series of books, featured on the *Oprah Winfrey Show* and endorsed by President Jimmy Carter, who is one of his biggest fans. Mattie began writing at the age of three. In 2003 he was eleven. *Oprah* and other television shows have occasionally featured Indigos who like Mattie, are reminding us of what true mastery looks like.

Joseph Chilton Pearce brings another prominent example of children with superior development to our attention in his book *The Biology of Transcendence*. He points out that the prefrontal lobe development previously discussed as typically occurring from age 15 on is increasingly being found in exceptional toddlers. The common parental characteristic in this case is mothers exuding inner security, confidence, and intelligence. Typically these children are born away from hospitals and they are often birthed in water and ideally, with dolphin assistance. They are nurtured in a breast-fed environment of loving support where they are "worn" for awhile. When grown, these children are exceptional, yet able to gracefully blend in without the need to challenge as seen in the Indigo Children.[24]

Throughout history there have been those who were born with knowingness and abilities similar to that attributed to Indigos. If taken singularly the extraordinary accomplishments of Leonardo da Vinci, Dr. Walter Russell, Fernado di Cordova, Count Saint Germain, Jesus and Sai Baba, tend to be discounted as either unreliable or unobtainable. Collectively these stellar examples establish a pattern of mind/brain/body mastery that cannot be discounted as they are found throughout history. They are examples meant to demonstrate to all of us our true potential. In the presence of such mastery there is a tendency for the older generation to think of themselves as "past their expiration date damaged goods." No one is being excluded unless that is their choice. What this book advocates is that the Indigo Child and super prefrontal lobe development is latent in all of us, and as each develops his potential that child will spring forth to demonstrate mind/brain/body mastery. That process will become easier as the children raise the stakes and urge us to join in. There is also the expectation that when a critical mass of humanity achieves this level, all will suddenly have this mastery at their command. This is generally known as the 100th monkey phenomenon. Those who have joined the unbound golden-winged white-unicorn Pegasus ranks will be discernable by their eyes, for in them will be wisdom and knowing. These are the attributes the children are already demonstrating. They are what the grownups carry either as a latent, or emerging force.

A nineteen generation old Lakota prophecy says that there would be born a white buffalo that would change to the different colors of the nations as it grows, and when its color returns to white, the world will be one nation of harmony and spiritual balance. Dave and Valerie Heider own a 43-acre farm in Janesville, Wisconsin. Despite nearly impossible genetic odds against it, they saw that white buffalo born on August 20th, 1994. Her coat has already changed colors to be black, red, and yellow. White is next. The Heiders named the buffalo "Miracle" and have watched as indigenous tribes from around the world have come to honor her. Defying the odds even more, an additional eight white buffalo have been born since then. [25, 26, 27]

Nineteenth generation Chief Arvol Looking Horse of the Eagle Butte South Dakota Indian Reservation carries the *C'anupa*, the sacred pipe of pipes originally given to the Lakota by *Pte-san win-yan*, White Buffalo Calf Woman, along with the white buffalo prophecy. Chief Looking Horse accepted this responsibility from his grandmother when he was twelve. She accepted the responsibility from her husband who broke tradition by giving it to a woman when he could no longer honor the path of peace the sacred pipe required. Chief Arvol Looking Horse strongly walks the path of world peace during this momentous time. [28]

Figure 13.3

Change is upon us. Currently we live in societies that are computer, food, sound, moment, and mental byte-based, but dwell on a world that can only be understood if approached at a much deeper level. The level of mitakuye oyasin – "all our relations," which honors the interconnectedness of all beings and all things. The child within us, as with the children around us, in our MASTERY of LEARNING *and their manifesting the love we are truly meant to be, are taking us to that level. Super penguins in one super society. The dominant signpost in this new paradigm: Expect a miracle for you are a miracle!* [29]

In the Indian way, everything is for the children. They learn respect because we show respect for them; we let them be free, but at the same time, there is always someone there to teach them how to act, the right way to treat people. When we get our land back, the first thing we will do is to make places for spiritual things and for the children, places where the children can learn the right way to live, to be generous, to be respectful, and to love all the living things. We believe in the Great Hoop: the Great Circle of Life; everything comes back to where it started. We believe this. That is the Indian way.

Matthew King

Softer than a flower, where kindness is concerned;
Stronger than thunder, where principles are at stake.
Vedic definition of a man of God.

You see things; and you say, "Why?"
But I dream things that never were; and I say, "Why not?"
George Bernard Shaw

What if you slept, and what if in your sleep you dreamed,
and what if in your dream you went to heaven
and there you plucked a strange and beautiful flower,
and what if when you awoke you had the flower in your hand? Oh, what then?
Samuel Taylor Coleridge

Lord, we know what we are, but know not what we may be.
William Shakespeare: *The Tragedy of Hamlet, Prince of Denmark*, Act IV, Scene V

The mythos leads the logos.
The language of fantasy goes before the language of fact.
Joseph Chilton Pearce

SECTION IV – REBUILDING YOUR FOUNDATION

MANY people treat their automobiles better than their own bodies, yet the automobile is much more easily replaced than the vehicle your soul drives. Vehicles require good air, water, and fuel in order to run properly. A vehicle that is overworked gets run down, and likewise never used to its potential tends to break down when it is really needed and those untried systems are called upon. The purpose of this section is to make sure that your vehicle is being properly maintained and supplied so its ability to perform optimally can be relied upon.

Chapter 14 – AIR, WATER, and FOOD

YOUR body runs on air, water and fuel. As important as these elements are to your body, they have ten times the impact on your brain. Your brain comprises only 2 percent of your body weight, yet it uses 20 percent of the air and energy from food and is 90 percent water. For a 100-pound person, the brain weighs two pounds and uses air and fuel as if it weighed 20 pounds. *When you skimp on any of these essentials, the brain suffers first.*

AIR

True awareness is observation without evaluation.
True awareness just happens, and so does correct breathing.
The body knows how to breathe properly and completely, it is we who stop it.
Douglas Lockhart

The mind and the breath are the King and Queen of human consciousness.
Leonard Orr, *Breaking the Death Habit, the Science of Everlasting Life*

The ancient yogis discovered that the secret of cosmic consciousness is intimately linked with breath mastery.
Sri Yukteswar

Deep breathing techniques which increase oxygen to the cell are the most important factors in living a disease free and energetic life.
Dr. Otto Warburg - Nobel Prize winner

20 minutes a day of deep breathing exercises clearly, dramatically escalates athletic performance and is the single most important factor in the effectiveness of all exercise.
U. S. Olympic Training Committee

Breath is life. You can last only a few minutes without air. In a single day however, you consume six times as much air by weight as you consume food and water, around five thousand gallons, or 35 pounds worth for an average person.[1] Air is vitally important to your brain because it is the first of your organs to die if you are deprived of oxygen. Carla Hannaford says that "*The brain comprises one-fiftieth of the body's weight yet it uses one-fifth of the body's oxygen…The whole system tends to take care of the brain's needs first.*"[2] Leonard Orr says that the body, and the mind in particular, are greatly energized and cleansed by doing 20 deep breaths daily. When done properly these breaths will involve the complete diaphragm and be circular in a continuous rhythm. Think of an infinity sign looping in and out of itself as you breathe. Most of us have forgotten how to breathe. If you want expert instruction on this vital function, watch a baby breathe. That is the way you breathed until you were taught by a penguin culture to halt your breath in order to stop feeling your emotions, and thus control them.[3]

Exercise 14.1 – EDGAR CAYCE ENERGIZING BREATHING

When you are ready to wake up in the morning, a very invigorating exercise is to stand up with your feet flat on the floor, gently rise on the toes while inhaling and bringing your arms high above the head and as far back as possible in a "Rocky Balboa stance." Then gradually bring your arms toward the front letting them down as you lower yourself and exhale. Do this slowly three or four times and you will feel greatly energized. This exercise is great for balance and posture.[4]

Yoga particularly stresses breathing and one of the most beneficial approaches is alternate nostril breathing. According to Leonard Orr, this practice yields physical and spiritual purification. You inhale through the left nostril, hold your breath comfortably long, and exhale gently through the right nostril. Then reverse the process for the next breath. Until you gain enough body control, you may have to use your fingers to close off the nostril you are not using during each portion of this exercise. You can hold your breath as indicated, or do twenty continuous connected breaths. Do this exercise once, three, or nine times daily.[5] Leonard Orr also recommends doing four short breaths and one long one, then repeating that pattern four times for a total of twenty breaths. This is just one breath exercise of seven listed in his book, *Breath Awareness*.[6]

Another extraordinarily healthful breathing activity is full breathing via your MerKaBa or light spirit body; an Egyptian term describing the energy field which surrounds all matter from individual atoms, to cells, to your entire body as a composite field, and likewise the Earth and other planets, solar system, and so on eventually aggregating to encompass galaxies in composite fields similar to the ones seen at every level. The aura typically seen around a person is really only the inner circle of this vehicle which, based on height, is an average of 54 feet across. MerKaBa is not just an Egyptian word. It is pronounced the same way in English, and in Zulu. In Hebrew it is Mer-Ka-Vah, the point being that this word can be found, with little variation, worldwide in many disparate cultures.[7]

Teaching how to fully activate your MerKaBa with breathing techniques is beyond the scope of this discussion. Drunvalo Melchizedek's organization provides accredited teachers for his one-week course called the *Ancient Secret of the Flower of Life Workshop*. I definitely recommend taking the course, if you can, from one of their certified teachers as they have been specifically trained to be conscious breathers. It took Drunvalo eight years to learn how to breathe properly because he had no one to teach him. Students in his course can learn to do so in only a week with the aid of an instructor who is a conscious breather. Instructions can also be found on the web. Activating your MerKaBA requires a sequence of seventeen breaths done in four phases incorporating specific intentions, visualizations, choreographed breathing, and mudras. Mudras come to us from Eastern science. They are the connecting of body circuits via finger and hand positioning to produce specific voltages thus propagating associated frequency patterns within the body. They are a simple and powerful way to work with your body. Putting your hands together for praying is a common mudra in the West.

Much of what Drunvalo developed for his incredibly informative workshop can be gained by reading the excellent books he wrote, which are titled with the same name as the workshop and issued as parts 1 and 2. Until you learn how to properly set up your MerKaBa it is helpful to set the intentionality that it be fully activated around you, then let your Higher Self see to the details. Once it is set up, you can also program your MerKaBa much like a crystal can be programmed. For instance, you can program it to protect you from harmful radiation such as microwave ovens or the 60-cycle hum from electrical lines. That subject is covered in a Dunvalo's follow-up seminar titled *Earth and Sky*.

From the perspective of augmenting our ability to learn, the other significant understanding associated with breathing in general, and MerKaBa breathing in particular, is that proper breathing increases your magnetic field, and hence increases your memory access and storage capability. According to Drunvalo Melchizedek,

> *Our memory is held together primarily by a magnetic field that exists around the brain – inside the skull and around the head. That field is further connected to every cell in the brain by individualized magnetic fields within each cell... Memory is dependent on a steady, living magnetic field, very much like a computer.*[8]

From a practical standpoint then, learning to breathe properly not only oxygenates your mind/brain/body system for maximum efficiency, it also increases the size and strength of the magnetic field upon which all of your memories are dependent. By the same token, this also means that your memories, whether cellular or aggregate, are subject to disruption by magnetic fields. It would be reasonable then to avoid living in strong magnetic fields such as those found around power lines. Be careful and sparing in your use of electric blankets and body magnets as they generate powerful magnetic fields that can be disruptive if you are subjected to them for too long. Anything strong enough to move a compass needle is strong enough to create a problem.[9]

The ultimate power of breathing can best be understood by looking at Kriya Yoga. Babaji, who gave us this knowledge again in modern times, restored this ancient but lost form of Yoga to consciousness. The Yogic promise of cosmic consciousness via breathing is epitomized by Kriya Yogi where a deeply developed yogi can in one half minute of breathing manifest one year of spiritual unfoldment. It is therefore feasible for the adept Kriya Yogi to use breath to manifest the equivalent of a thousand years of unfoldment in a single day. This incredible promise is further backed by Babaji who says that he will "Guard and guide all sincere Kriya Yogis in their path toward the goal."[10]

WATER

Water, water everywhere, nor any drop to drink.
Samuel Taylor Coleridge: *Rime of the Ancient Mariner*

Man in lifeboat on ocean – **"Miles and miles of water and not a drop to drink!"**

Hydrogen   Hydrogen

Oxygen
Figure 14.1

In dream analysis, water represents both your subconscious and your emotions. It is probably not an accident that the Walt Disney Corporation's Mickey Mouse symbol looks like the diagram of a water molecule.

The art of progress is to preserve order amid change and to preserve change amid order.
Alfred North Whitehead: *Forbes*, December 1, 1957

> *We must all obey the great law of change.*
> *It is the most powerful law of nature.*
Edmund Burke

Water as a subject could easily fill many books. We are only going to try to cover the essentials. First off, how essential is water? *You can last only days without water. All of our cells and cellular processes work with water as the transport medium and many of the molecules in our body also have water incorporated in them. The Earth mirrors this, as the water cycle is the foundation for all life on Earth. Water is so important that as a baby we begin life with 70 percent water as with the surface of the Earth.*[11]

Water is even more important to our brains because they are 90 percent water.[12] When you are dehydrated, what do you think gets sacrificed? Most likely it is the higher brain functions, your ability to think and learn, that shut down first. In order to think and learn, good hydration is essential. Milk, tea, coffee, soda pop, beer, wine, and anything else that isn't pure water, is a food in solution form. Solutes with caffeine in them, such as coffee, some teas, and most sodas, are diuretics. That means that not only do they require water to compensate for drinking them but they also cause you to further excrete water.

The pH scale goes from 0 to 14 or from acid to alkaline with 7 as neutral. It takes around 35 glasses of pH 10 water to compensate for drinking a Coke or Pepsi, a strong acid that has a pH of 2.[13] Because of what we drink and eat, and our lifestyle in general, almost everyone is dehydrated. However, this doesn't mean that other drinks do not have healthful uses, for instance, many herbal teas have healing or other properties that can call for their use, and the dilution factor is so great that in general herbal teas do not have the impact that something like a soft drink has on the body. However, the only healthful drink for thirst is water; all else requires more water to make up for the fact that you consumed it.

Exercise 14.2 – TESTING YOUR BODY FOR DEHYDRATION

There is a simple test to determine if you are dehydrated. Stand with your arms at your side and observe how the veins on the back of your hands stand out. Now elevate your arms until they are at shoulder height sticking straight out to either side. If you are properly hydrated your veils will stick out as much in this position as they did with your arms at your sides. If they deflate, you need more water.

CHARACTERISTICS OF VARIOUS WATERS

Is all water created equal? Water in nature would be healthful if we had not polluted it. There are 30,000 known pollutants and domestic water supplies are tested for only a few dozen. Bottled water is more typical now as a source of supply. However, bottled water is still not in a form that is healthful for us even if it is ultrapurified as in distilled or reverse osmosis water. The problem is that water that runs in pipes is stripped of its electrons, and hence energy.

The energy level in water is measured in Bovis Units, a scale of energy content developed by a French physicist. If it were environmentally healthy the Earth would naturally yield water with an energy range of 7,000 to 18,000 Bovis Units. After going through pipes water is reduced to as low as 3,000 Bovis Units of energy and this can happen once it passes through only 18 inches of pipe. Bottled water is seldom over 5,000 Bovis Units. Your body, as with other forms of life, requires water at 6,500 Bovis Units just to break even so the water we typically have available to drink brings our energy level below that which is healthy. Water that is healthful is in the range of 8,000 to 10,000 Bovis units. *Figure 14.2* lists the characteristics of various waters in order to help put this in context.

Figure 14.2 – CHARACTERISTICS OF VARIOUS WATERS

BOVIS UNITS	HEALTH	CHARGE	DESCRIPTION
0-100	Negative	Positive	Microwaved, distilled, or reverse osmosis water
3,000	Negative	Positive	Typical domestic water
5,000	Negative	Positive	Best of the bottled waters
6,500	Neutral	Neutral	Energy level of human body
8- to 10,000	Positive	Negative	Earth's natural healthy level
300,000	*Very positive*	*Very negative*	*Penta water*
400- to 500,000	Very positive	Very negative	Lourdes, France healing water

Besides being low in energy negative scale water clumps together into large molecular groupings until it becomes too large to pass readily through the membranes our body uses to organize itself into cells and organs. Most people's bodies are bloated with large cluster water that they cannot effectively move around. They are contending with water logjams preventing the cells of their bodies from working properly. *Unstructured water is dead water and it has been directly linked to the formation of disease. Healthy cells are always found to have structured water around them.* If you examine the cells of babies you discover that their water is structured in regular geometric shapes, pentagons or hexagons that are like snowflakes. This structure is slowly lost as the child grows.

In order to begin to understand what is happening scientists have examined water at the atomic level and found that the high-energy positive waters actually reverse their spin direction at the molecular level and start forming regular geometries rather than disorganized clusters. These geometric structures are much smaller in size than unclustered water clumps, thus allowing them to move easily across cellular boundaries. *Consequently, drinking high-energy water causes most people to automatically lose weight and become healthier as their body detoxifies and replenishes itself with structured water.*

As water goes up in energy it also has an associated gain in electrons to become super-ionized. Superionized water is super healthy for you. The water at Lourdes in France is super-ionized and yields Bovis measurements in the 400,000 to 500,000 range. Unfortunately this water does not have a stable configuration so that it can be taken from the region and retain this super Bovis reading.

PENTA WATER

Recently developed super water that is stable and readily available is pentagonal water. Water found in nature will have 3 percent to 5 percent penta water in it along with a full spectrum of other dynamically changing shapes including irregularly clustered water. Of the shapes that water molecules form in, penta water is the smallest geometric shape they organize into. Bill Holloway, the engineer who discovered penta water, was using it experimentally on his plants and seeing such dramatic results that he tried it on himself. In one month he effectively cured himself of fibromyalgia that he had lived with for 25 years and been debilitated by for 10.

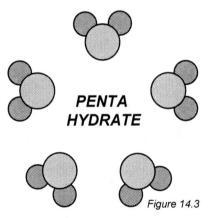

PENTA HYDRATE

Figure 14.3

The penta hydrate Bill engineered, using reverse osmosis water as a base and proprietary processes involving ultraviolet treatments, is more than 80 percent penta water in a stable configuration. He discovered that penta water was effective in accelerating the metabolic processes in his body and also clearing him of free radicals. Free radicals are a natural byproduct of stress and are directly related to aging. Free radicals are essential to our bodies' ability to kill germs and viruses so we need them in limited amounts. However, eliminating the excess of free radicals in the body will reverse the process of aging. Balance becomes the key. For example, it can be demonstrated that even if your body is cleared of excess free radicals, getting angry releases large amounts of free radicals and, in only a few minutes, overwhelms your body with them. That is why the emotions of jealousy, anger, and fear are so debilitating to the body with stress effects that are virtually irreversible if sustained over prolonged periods of time.

Aging is also directly related to how well hydrated your cells are. As babies we begin life with 70 percent water but as adults we are typically 45 percent to 50 percent water. As your hydration figure goes down your metabolic processes slow down, you age, and your body inches closer to the stopping point. If you can get water into the cells you reverse this process and effectively reverse aging. The statistics show that virtually everyone, except those who die violently, dies of dehydration. Some disease may have accelerated the process but none of it would have happened if you had proper hydration, as the cells would have cleaned up the mess.

Let us now delve into a rather sensitive area of the human experience – being overweight. Fat cells are lower in water content than muscle cells and fat is lighter than water. That is why obese people float easily and oil floats on water. Obese people are therefore dehydrated and metabolically slowed down thus tending to make them gain even more weight. Your body even plays a trick on you in this regard in that thirst and hunger are generated from adjacent nerve centers so they are often confused with each other. Consequently when you are most thirsty you can misinterpret it as hunger and thus make the situation even worse by eating. *Proper hydration is therefore the key to weight loss. All successful weight loss programs stress the necessity of drinking lots of water.* Water is in fact the ultimate solvent helping you to effectively dissolve the weight away. Many people using penta water have lost a great deal of unwanted weight while their skin gets younger and more wrinkle-free, their energy level goes up, and their body is able to heal the problems it previously could not deal with. Penta water also helps transport oxygen into your system so it aids not only in getting water into you but also vital oxygen to further support your metabolic processes.

Penta hydrate is also effective at completely eliminating hangovers. According to the manufacturer, that single effect alone has motivated a number of large investors to become interested in this new industry. It will also eliminate the soreness when you exercise and accelerate the rate at which you can exercise. Likewise, it will accelerate your recovery from operations.

DETOXIFYING WITH HIGH ENERGY WATER

Some people can feel the health of this water when it is in their body. In the beginning it is recommended that you take penta hydrate in the morning and not at night as it will so energize you as to keep you awake. You might also find that you have to dilute the water with regular distilled water, or alternate with glasses of unenergized water in order to keep your body from detoxifying too rapidly. If you heat penta water to a boil, you destroy its high energy properties, so regular bottled water is best to use for making tea or coffee.

There has been a long-standing debate as to whether or not drinking distilled water demineralizes your body. There is good evidence this is not actually a concern, however the statement is correct. The distilled water helps eliminate the harmful inorganic minerals from your body, which can cause a variety of diseases including arthritis, without robbing your body of the valuable organic minerals that are essential to life. The effect of drinking distilled water, and high-energy water such as penta hydrate, is therefore to help your body leach out that which it cannot incorporate in a healthful way. One of my friends has been drinking distilled water for decades without experiencing undesirable demineralization. In fact, distilled water is what the medical profession uses for dialysis. If it had negative demineralization properties it is unlikely it would still be used.[14]

My experience with this water supports this position. Overnight after first drinking it I found that my left knee, which has had three operations, functioned properly for the first time since I moved into our house three years ago. Now I can walk down the stairs normally rather than skip hopping to accommodate a knee joint that wouldn't bend well. I have also found that my energy level has gone way up, and need for sleep has greatly diminished. Pat, who attended my first presentation of the workshop based on this book, drank a bottle of Penta hydrate at the end of the day. By that evening, for the first time since he was diagnosed with debilitating arthritis twenty years ago, he was pain free. He also woke up without pain the next morning.

WATER OPTIONS

Water can also be imprinted with information. This is why tinctures work, as they are energy-based information imprinted in transport mediums such as water or alcohol. Alcohol has a chemical structure with a lot of water in it. Water can be thought of as liquid silicon that can be programmed much as the silicon chips in a computer accept their programming.

The producers of Penta Hydrate are not the only company marketing high-energy waters. Other processes, such as the Prell Beads, also apparently yield similar results. I drew heavily upon the Penta Hydrate Company material as it goes into the chemistry involved thus providing a firm foundation upon which to evaluate any water or process for generating water. If you do not wish to invest in high priced waters you can energize reverse osmosis or distilled water by either pouring it back and forth between containers or by half filling a water bottle and tumbling or percussing it 27 times, a figure arrived at empirically. These processes simulate the natural tumbling of water over rocks and energize it by adding electrons.

The other use for water, beyond drinking, is for bathing. Hot baths open your chakras and cleanse them. According to Leonard Orr in his book, *Breaking the Death Habit, the Science of Everlasting Life*, bathing twice a day would significantly increase our life span. Leonard also states that, "Meditating one hour per day in hot water can make anyone a spiritual master."[15]

FUEL

To avoid illness, eat less. To have a long life, worry less.
Chinese proverb

To lengthen thy life, lessen thy meal.
Benjamin Franklin

Cooked food is poison!
David Wolfe

Never eat more than you can lift.
Miss Piggy

Everybody who dies is killed by thoughts… Most people kill themselves with food.
Leonard Orr

You are what you eat.
Brian and Roberta Morgan

You can go for weeks without food. However, *because it has such high demands your brain suffers should it be chronically deprived of proper food and the energy it provides. As an adult your brain is 2 percent of your body weight, yet it uses 20 percent of the energy you develop.* If converted to electricity your brain uses as much energy as a 25-watt light bulb. It needs a high-energy diet in order to perform well. Along with the oxygen and water already discussed, plenty of fresh fruit and vegetables are needed in order to get the glucose your brain requires as an energy source. A complete discussion of nutrition is far beyond the confines of what can be said here. However, there are a few general rules that can be followed.[16]

GENERAL EATING RULES:
1. **Drink plenty of water. However, do not drink water either a half an hour prior to eating, or for an hour afterward, as it will dilute stomach acids and enzyme activity, thus making it more difficult for you to digest the food.**
2. **Chew your food thoroughly until you liquefy it.**
3. **Eat as many raw foods as you can because cooking destroys the enzyme content of foods and enzymes are the energy sources your body runs on.**
4. **Regular elimination is equally as important as assimilation. They are yin and yang to each other and in their balance is health. There are many doctors who believe proper elimination means a bowel movement with every meal or around three a day.**

On my mom's side of the family was my Grandpa Ross. He is a good example of what being conscientious about your diet can do for you. Gramps was head of the main post office in Los Angeles. The stress of this job eventually caused his heart to begin failing. He was forced to retire in his mid 50s with the prognosis of only a few years to live. He radically changed his diet to be as healthy as he could by eating wheat germ, blackstrap molasses, dates, and other health foods that were recommended in his day. He always said, "I want to wear out, not rust out!" He did. His heart eventually gave way and he died in bed, at the age of 94.

Dr. Norman Walker is an even better example of how effective following a few of these rules can be. At the age of 50 he found himself in poor health. Faced with this crisis he radically changed his diet by limiting himself to raw foods and chewing them so thoroughly that they were liquefied. His health and vitality returned and he was productive for many years afterward, finally noting in his last book, written when he was more than 100, that he still felt like a youth of 30. He lived to be 108.

If you want to change your diet to be more healthy, consuming organic produce is preferable because they have more than ten times the vitamins and minerals as regular produce and are as free of poisonous products, such as pesticides, as it is reasonable to achieve. Feeding lower on the food chain is always better than feeding higher. Consume the grains the cow eats and not the cow. There are two good reasons for this. First – plants, and plant products such as fruits, digest in only a few hours while animal meat takes more energy, and nearly ten times as long, to digest because it is so dense. Secondly – the higher you go on the food chain the more concentrated the environmental toxins become. Meat has more than ten times the concentration of toxins as the grass and grains it came from. If you do need to consume meat, and some people have a physiology such that for them this is probably necessary, then try to stick with the lighter meats such as fish. The best are the deep ocean fish as they generally live in less polluted waters.

The bottom line is your body is the best determiner of what you require. If you are a strict vegetarian and you are craving meat, then either you are deeply clearing old programming or your body is trying to tell you something you need to listen to. According to the book, *Eat Right 4 Your Type,* people with the blood type O usually need a little meat. NBA basketball star Bill Walton was a strict vegetarian but was not able to properly heal a broken ankle until he ate meat. I am not, however, advocating going back to the regular consumption of meat. Consume it only until your body says that is enough and then go back to being pure vegetarian. For example, for some that may mean consuming only a little fish every three months or so.

John Robbins listed in his groundbreaking book, *Diet for a New America,* many prominent examples of high performance athletes who are vegetarians. Examples are Dave Scott who won Hawaii's Ironman Triathlon a record four times, and Sixto Linares who broke the world record for a "double Ironman" in a single day by swimming 4.8 miles, cycling 185 miles, and running 52.4 miles. Other examples are Robert Sweetgal, at one time the world's best ultra-distance walker, Edwin Moses, the famous track star, and Andreas Cahling, the 1980 Mr. International in body building. Add to this list Dan Millman, an Olympic class athlete who eats a vegan diet, meaning he eats no meat or dairy at all. Decades after his college years when he became a vegan, I have seen Dan do athletic cartwheels in front of an audience. You do not perform at these levels unless your diet supports you totally. In his book, *Raw Power, Building Strength and Muscle Naturally*, Stephen Arlin explains how to eat a totally raw food diet with no meat and be a body builder and weight lifter.

One of the prevalent misunderstandings in America is regarding the need for proteins and supplements. You do not need as much of either as most people typically consume.[17] *Eating one of the super foods derived from plants and seaweeds, is more healthful and provides all the vitamins and minerals a person needs many times over. Proteins in particular are way over-consumed and for most people are not necessary if proper protein intake is achieved from plant-based sources.* For instance, a handful of sunflower seeds contains more protein than a steak. There is also evidence that eating meat contributes to osteoporosis as that disease occurs only in societies that eat meat. However, those statistics are generated for cooked meat, and some societies eat meat raw which is much more healthful. Meat from free-ranging grass fed animals such as cows and sheep, is also more healthful than grain-fed animals as they are significantly less fatty and also much higher in desirable Omega-3 fats. Therefore, if you eat meat or the products of animals such as milk or cheese, the best you can get is from organic, free-range, grass-fed animals.[18]

Most dairy is not healthful because milk and its products, such as cheese and butter, have been pasteurized, which kills the good properties of the milk, plus cows concentrate the toxins they consume in the milk much as they do in meat. All pasteurized dairy products are mucus-producing, which leads to congestion in various systems of the body. If your body or lifestyle dictates the need for cheese then it is best to eat feta cheese as unlike cows, goats produce the right magnesium to calcium ratio for humans to absorb the calcium in it. Feta milk, goat's milk, flocculates like human milk while cow's milk forms a single mass in the stomach making it difficult to digest.

If you eat the dairy products from cows, then get unpasturized organic whole milk from free-range grass-fed animals. If you eat the cheese from cows, then eat white cheese instead of yellow as the yellow cheeses have additives to give them their color. If you consume eggs, then consume those produced by organic free-range chickens. If you cannot eat 100 percent raw food, then eating 60 percent to 80 percent raw food is preferable to capitulating to all cooked food. If you eat cooked food, take enzyme supplements to aid your digestion. Always make the most healthful choices you can and you will aim your lifestyle toward good health. As with your breathing, become a conscious eater. One way to really raise your level of consciousness is to read *Eat Right 4 Your Type*, a book that explores our genetic heritage based on blood type and correlates that with what foods each type is tailored to consume.[19]

Another way to help your body is periodic fasting. Only a day every week or two is enough to do enormous good. Fasting cleanses your body and helps clarify your mind. While you are fasting your body can concentrate its resources on healing and cleansing rather than dividing its resources in order to supply the 50 percent of your energy that is normally required for digestion. There is some truth in the adage as it was originally worded, "Feed a cold to starve a fever." Starving for a few days gives your body the opportunity to redirect your energies toward the immune system. You also avoid the additional problem of having your vitamins and minerals going to feed the virus rather than yourself. The increase in body temperature experienced with a fever is the body's attempt to accelerate metabolic defenses that, as chemical reactions, are responsive to slight temperature increases. Taking aspirin or other drugs to reduce the fever is therefore counterproductive unless the fever goes too far. Fevers much beyond 105 degrees are dangerous because the chemical engines your body runs on begin breaking down. Fevers beyond 108 degrees are usually fatal for this reason.[19]

Another important point about healthful eating is to realize that it is always best to minimize the combining of foods unless you are knowledgeable about how to do so in a healthful way. Eating a few foods from the same class, such as all fruits for breakfast and carbohydrates for lunch, is the best way to help your digestive system. The Western practice of eating a heavy starch like potatoes with a meat, is actually hard on your digestive system as it is trying to simultaneously perform different types of digestive processes that cannot be done simultaneously, thus it does neither very well. The simplest set of healthy eating guidelines that I know of can be found in the book, *The Ancient Secret of the Fountain of Youth.*[20]

TIBETAN EATING GUIDELINES:

1. **If you are healthy and strong, eating starches and meat together is only a minor concern, otherwise, avoid this combination.**
2. **Drinking black coffee is okay if it does not bother you. If it does, don't drink it. (Note: Modern research indicates that coffee drinking is not recommended for pregnant women.)**
3. **Chew what you eat until it is a liquid and reduce your consumption of food.**
4. **Eat raw egg yolks once a day, every day. Eat them either prior or after, but not during a meal. (Note: The USDA recommends against the practice of eating raw eggs because of the potential for salmonella bacteria contamination.)**
5. **When you eat, reduce the variety of foods consumed at one meal to a minimum.**

What is the true promise of the Tibetan Eating Guidelines? There are many endorsements in *The Ancient Secret of the Fountain of Youth* that show the potential such an approach has. Besides Colonel Bradford whose body became healthy and hair returned to its natural color, we also have many testimonials of people who experienced the same phenomena. The ASFY book incorporates exercise with food, however, just the act of eating raw foods cannot be underestimated, it is key. The well-documented cases of Dr. Ann Wigmore and Dr. Gary Null prove this, for both ate chlorophyll rich diets and found their hair returning to its natural color along with their overall vitality. Dr. Gary Null even had new hair growing to replace that which he had lost.[20, 21, 22] The explanation for this is relatively easy to understand and well documented in many sources. The body as a chemical engine runs on a particular type of fuel, enzymes. Cooking kills enzymes as they are damaged by temperatures in the high fever range, anything above 105 degrees fahrenheit, and absolutely destroyed by cooking temperatures. *Enzymes are essential for proper digestion and assimilation of the food. Either you get those enzymes in the food you eat naturally in the raw state, you supplement your food with digestive enzymes purchased at a health food store, or your body pulls the enzymes required for digesting cooked food from your own body, thus running it down like a battery with an indicator we call aging. Reverse the process and you reverse aging. It is that simple.*[23]

Edgar Cayce recommended that if possible, *one should eat from his own back yard.* For many people having a garden is difficult because of both time and land constraints. In America, there are a growing number of fresh organic foods available in health food stores and small sections of conventional markets. There are also a number of mail order sources of organic foods to make healthful eating convenient. **Appendix J** is a listing of sources of organically grown foods and herbal medicines that should help make having a healthful lifestyle more reasonable. If you need to purchase digestive enzymes, they can be obtained from your local health food store.

Chapter 15 – EXERCISE and REST

God, I should say, has given men two arts: Music, and gymnastics.
Plato

Television Interviewer – *"What are the best exercises?"*
Dr. Harold J. Reilly – *"The ones you do!"*

The best exercise is walking.
Edgar Cayce

You grew it, you lift it!
Unknown

EXERCISE

EXERCISE in general is holistic because it stimulates both the body and the brain to new levels of unified capability. One of the very finest exercises you can do is walking. Edgar Cayce used to say, *"After breakfast walk a mile, after lunch rest a while." Walking is a cross-lateral exercise so it is effective for the mind and body, plus the primary lymphatic pump in the body is the tailbone which walking stimulates to maximum efficiency. Walking therefore both tones and cleanses your body while helping you to think. If you can walk in nature preserves, forest trails, or some other natural setting, you can also incorporate meditation with your exercise.*

Turning your exercise into a ritual can help you maintain it. I am named after my Grandfather Ross whom I mentioned in the previous chapter. He used to combine his morning prayers with sit-ups. He would say the name of a family member or friend for every sit-up he did until he had done 100 of them. One morning when he was in his 80s he came into breakfast looking rather spent. My mom turned to him and asked, "Pop, what's wrong?"

He replied, "I lost track of the names in the middle of my sit-ups and had to start over!"

The East in particular is rich with traditions of exercise that focus on unifying the mind, body, and spirit while increasing your prana, the energy flow which is also known as chi, qi, ki, ruach, or kundalini. The objective of exercise is therefore to increase balance and to energize. Hatha yoga is excellent for this and can be practiced anywhere. The eminent Swiss psychologist Carl Jung wrote this thoughtful tribute to yoga,

There is good cause for yoga to have many adherents. It offers the possibility of controllable experience and thus satisfies the scientific need for 'facts'; and, besides this, by reason of its breadth and depth, it venerable age, its doctrine and method, which include every phase of life, it promises undreamed of possibilities.[1]

The best simple set of yoga moves that I am aware of, which are formulated specifically to achieve health and longevity, is described in *The Ancient Secret of the Fountain of Youth.* Covered are five yoga-like exercises termed rites, that take only five minutes to do. If they are practiced daily they will energize your chakras in a balanced fashion thus fostering youthfulness and high energy levels.

The ASFY book begins with the story of a gray haired, balding, and lame British gentleman named Colonel Bradford in his late sixties, who early last century goes to Tibet letting a friend know that he is leaving. He returns four years later walking normally with his hair its natural color. He is so changed, being much younger in appearance, that his friend did not recognize him until he introduced himself. He brought back from Tibet their exercises and simple eating habits which, if practiced daily, have a transformative effect on the body. There is a video of these five exercises and how to practice them properly, which can be ordered by calling 888.855.5400, or writing to THE VIDEO, P. O. Box 2299, Gig Harbor, WA, 98335.[2]

Dan Millman also has a four minute set of simple exercises that he describes in his *Peaceful Warrior Workout Video*. You can order it by going to www.danmillman.com or calling 800.525.9000. The other set of exercises I would recommend is found in the book, *The Edgar Cayce Handbook for Health Through Drugless Therapy*. It is written by Dr. Harold J. Reilly, who for many decades was the foremost physiotherapist in the country, and Ruth Hagy Brod. It is a complete program for achieving health giving specific, easy to make, homeopathic approaches for many common problems such as: how to eliminate scars and handle other minor skin problems, how to reverse aging, beauty secrets, and the understanding of what constitutes a proper diet. One of the most impressive sections is a set of exercises that require nothing more than a towel. They take about a half hour to do and completely address all the muscles in your body. I did these exercises for a while and they were impressive in their thoroughness and the results I was seeing. *Another excellent exercise system that can be done, even if you are bed ridden or in a wheel chair, is Greer Childer's "Body Flex®" program. I found it doubly beneficial as the breathing she teaches is excellent preparation for the rigors of theta state breathing. You can order it by calling 800.852.9500.*

Reading and other forms of mental and physical activity stress our vision. Dr. Lawrence Sajdecki, an optometrist, developed a simple set of exercises that can be used to balance your vision, even if you currently wear heavy prescription glasses. When you do these exercises the prescription you require for glasses is likely to change to something weaker. Dr. Sajdecki required a prescription for nearsightedness most of his life until he went to a workshop on this subject from which he acquired these exercises. This technique is based on exercises that Dr. Bates developed near the beginning of last century. Because of its popularity his book, *The Bates Method for Better Eyesight Without Glasses,* is still available. Because the Bates method saved him from losing his eyesight, Aldous Huxley also wrote a popular book on the subject called, *The Art of Seeing.* Using his Bates derived exercises, in only a few months Dr Sajdecki went from requiring a –2.25 prescription, to not requiring glasses at all. Another excellent recent resource for improving your eyes is the *Yoga for Your Eyes* video by Meir Schneider.

Exercise 15.1 – Dr. LAWRENCE SAJDECKI'S DAILY EYE EXERCISES

1. Spend between five and a maximum of 20 minutes facing directly at the sun with your eyelids closed. You may experience seeing different colors as the sunlight refracts through your eyelids and stimulates your color receptors. This is stimulating therapy as sunlight is full spectrum, which is what your eyes were built to process.
2. As a yang to the yin of light stimulation, while in a darkened room, put the palms of your hands gently over your eyes. Do not press on your eyes. Do this for a length of time equal to your exposure to sunlight. This is dark therapy.
3. While performing exercise such as walking or running, go without glasses for about an hour to retrain your eye muscles for proper focus. If you are very nearsighted, you may have to limit your walks to areas you know well, or possibly even to your home. A treadmill would work well under those circumstances.
4. Practice what Dr. Jacob Liberman, a foremost expert in the field calls, "Open Focus Viewing." This is owl-eye or wide-eye viewing without focusing on anything. Be sure to relax and blink normally. In this mode you are not filtering your experience, just letting vision happen without judging what you are seeing. At first you may be able to do so only for five seconds at a time. You can intersperse this throughout your day in order to practice it often without having to dedicate a period of time to it.

BRAIN GYM® EXERCISES

Movement is the door to learning.
Paul E. Dennison

The correlation between movement and mental/physical balance is well known in the East. For instance, in Japan it is a common business practice to begin the workday with tai chi.[3] In the West, the Brain Gym® exercises have been developed to "tune you up" for learning. They are simple movements that use the holistic nature of the body to help remyelinate the brain. Dr. Paul Dennison developed them in the 1970s. The information I am presenting here is beautifully covered in Chapter 7 of Dr. Carla Hannaford's book, *Smart Moves, Why Learning is Not ALL in Your Head.* In the first and seventh chapters of her book Carla Hannaford explains what incidents alerted her to the power of these techniques.

The first incident involved a young man named Todd who was a 16-year-old sophomore in high school. Being 6 feet 2 inches tall the coach wanted him on the basketball team. Unfortunately he was clumsy, certified as learning disabled, and unable to read or write despite having attended many learning programs. At a conference that year his mother learned about the Brain Gym® exercises and had him, along with the whole family, doing one called the Cross Crawl® every morning and evening. Within six weeks Todd was reading at grade level and was able to join the basketball team.[4]

The second incident that got her attention happened when Carla accepted the challenge of taking the responsibility during recess for three children with learning disabilities. Two were eight-year-old boys and one was a 10-year-old girl named Amy. When she was six weeks old Amy had been abused. Consequently, she was taken from her biological parents to be adopted later. She was in loving environment when Carla began working with her but she still had physical damage from the earlier abuse. Consequently she could not effectively talk, read, or write, and had one leg that didn't work properly. Every day during the start of recess Carla did five minutes of the Brain Gym® exercises with her and the two boys. Within two months Amy's leg began working well enough that she could kick the ball straight when playing soccer with the boys, and she began speaking in complete sentences. After five months she caught up to second grade in her reading, and by the end of the year she was reading nearly at her grade level.[5]

One other incident in Carla's book adds compellingly to the Brain Gym® saga. In 1991 in Botswana, Africa, she was asked to work with the trainees of the Botswana Insurance Company. Historically, the best they had ever done when taking the annual mandated insurance exams was a pass rate less than 30 percent. She taught them the Brain Gym® moves in February and in May they had a 100 percent pass rate including one person who scored the first perfect ever in the history of the administration of the exam.[6]

Obviously, *people of all ages can benefit enormously from doing Brain Gym® movements, both in their physical and mental dexterity. It can help with sports, music, dance, art, focus, and academic performance in general.* Carla has many other examples of nearly miraculous cures of various learning disabilities including dyslexia, and impressive gains for even Downs Syndrome children. One particularly revealing point she notes is the nearly 100 percent correlation between learning disabilities and recurring incidents of childhood ear infections. The Brain Gym® movements apparently rectify these and other microtraumas.

Carla says that there are two obstacles to the use of these exercises. One is the fact that they are so simple that people question whether they can really help. They other is, being exercises, many people don't understand the holistic nature of the mind/brain/body well enough to accept that movement can help the brain. What I provide here is short descriptions of the reduced set of the Brain Gym® exercises presented by Carla Hannaford. If you want to explore the full set of exercises and the various ways they can be performed, you will have to investigate the source, Dr. Dennison and his groundbreaking investigative work and books on the subject, or the official web site, www.braingym.com.

Exercise 15.2 – LEARNING THE BRAIN GYM® EXERCISES [7, 8]

BRAIN BUTTONS®: Place one hand over your navel while your other hand stimulates the points between the first and second ribs directly under your collarbone. This activity stimulates your brain for incoming sensory input including visual. It helps with ocular lock (staring). It is great for bringing back focus during a test. It is also great for waking you up when you have been sitting a long time as in driving.

CROSS CRAWL®: Slow motion cross lateral walking in place while you touch your right elbow to your left knee, and vice versa. This helps your corpus callosum myelinate, thus enlarging and accelerating communication between the two hemispheres of your brain for high-level reasoning. It helps with writer's block, sports, and dance. If a person cannot do this movement but can do "same side" motions, it is an indication of the need for Dennison Laterality Repatterning with the help of a trained instructor. [9]

HOOKUPS®: First cross one ankle over the other. Next, cross your hands extended out front and clasp them together, then fold them down and inward to hold against your chest. Finally, rest your tongue on the roof or your mouth behind the teeth (hard palate). The energies of your body are thus cycled so that you energize and center in order to connect emotions with reason for a more integrative perspective. Teachers can use this to help with classroom stress levels. Two minutes of hook-ups cools down disruptive students.

LAZY-8'S FOR WRITING®: Draw big infinity symbols on large paper turned sidewise. Do five or more continuous repetitions with each hand, then with both hands. Dr. Hannaford says that this exercise is also great for writer's block or to help reduce the stress levels and increase the ability of students to find the answers in a classroom setting.

THE ELEPHANT®: Roll your head to lay your left ear on your left shoulder tightly enough to grip a paper, and then extend your left arm like a trunk. With your knees relaxed use your arm against your head to slowly draw Lazy 8 patterns in your mid-field in front of you. Do this three to five times, then repeat for the right arm. This movement helps with balance and is integrative. For full sensory stimulation, make elephant sounds. People who had chronic ear infections will find this a challenge.

THE THINKING CAP®: Use your fingers to massaging the outer edge of your ears from top to bottom several times. There are more than 128 acupuncture points on your outer ear that holistically map to the entire body, so this simple exercise stimulates your body and brain thus enhancing mental performance.

THE ENERGY YAWN®: Yawn while massaging the muscles around your temporal-mandibular joint (TMJ) which is where your jaw joins to your skull. The trunks of five major cranial nerves cross this point. This exercise will help your eyes and thus reading, plus hearing, verbalization, and thought processing while reducing stress.

THE CALF PUMP®: While standing up straight, take a step forward with one foot, and then lengthen the calf of your back leg while bending the knee of your front leg. Keep both feet flat on the ground. This is the leg "stretches" often done by runners. Perform on both sides. This increases the flow of cerebrospinal fluid and reduces stress. It helps with verbal skills and communication in speech-impaired or autistic children.

THE ENERGIZER®: Place your hands on a flat surface in front of you, and then lower your chin to your chest. Feel the stretch in the back of the neck and relaxed shoulders. Take a deep breath and scoop your head forward bringing it up and back allowing your back to arc slightly while opening your rib cage. Then exhale, curving your back and returning your chin to rest once again on your chest. This helps you energize and regain focus after long sessions sitting at the computer or a desk.

REST

Rest is the yang of the yin action exercise, and together they establish a pattern, which, like waves lapping on the beach, eventually moves mountains. Proper exercise sets you up for proper rest by helping your energy ebb and flow in a regular pattern. According to Paramahansa Yogananda:

> *The rejuvenating effects of sleep are due to man's temporary unawareness of body and breathing. The sleeping man becomes a yogi; each night he unconsciously performs the yogic rite of releasing himself from bodily identification, and of merging the life force with healing currents in the main brain region and in the subdynamos of his spinal centers. Unknowingly, the sleeper is thus recharged by the cosmic energy that sustains all life.*[10]

Eight hours of sleep every night is as much as most people will need, and less will be required as your body becomes more efficient. Meditation substitutes for sleep in about a three to one ratio so one hour of meditation is the equivalent of three hours of sleep. A good way to ground yourself after meditation is to bend over, put all ten fingers out, and touch the earth. This will quickly pull you out of even a long meditation session and ensure that you are back in your body. *The important thing, with both sleep and meditation, is to establish a pattern, then maintain it.*

Learn to be silent. Let your quiet mind listen and absorb.

Pythagorus

Although sleeping at night is the natural and best thing to do, if your job requires you to work at night and thus sleep during the day, then be consistent in this pattern even on your days off. The reason for this is because your body's circadian pattern, the 12-meridian pattern you cycle through every day, follows your rest and activity schedule in order to properly maintain your body, and it is not alterable in less than about a week. Therefore, if you are jet-lagged across many time zones, or pull an all-nighter, it can take a week for you to establish a regular pattern and recover from the disruption.

A powerful technique for re-energizing if you are depleted from a lack of sleep, or having worked for many hours beyond your norm, is to find the biggest tree you can and hug it, or sit down and lean against it for a while. Try to find one that has a trunk many feet in diameter. In only a few minutes this will help you enormously. Another quick way to energize is to trace the infinity sign on your forehead over the third eye, or behind your back with one hand tracing it over your coccyx, or tailbone. You can also trace it over your chest in the area of your thymus gland which is just above the sternum, as depicted in *Figure A.1* on Page 133 in *Appendix A* on Applied Kineseology. You can also thump yourself there which is one of the benefits gorillas receive by pounding their chests, and what special forces are trained to do when they need to energize quickly in order to survive an impending traumatic event like a grenade exploding near them or a high fall.

Sleep is the most common form of meditation for everyone - even birds.
The most important meditation. Not for Nirvana, but for survival!

Dalai Lama

SECTION V – SUMMARY OVERVIEW

YOU have finished at the automobile dealership and are driving away confidently and serenely in your beautifully refurbished automobile and refreshed understanding of how it works. Now all you need is a roadmap in order to navigate safely and quickly to where you desire to go.

Chapter 16 – A ROAD MAP

WE covered a lot of material in the previous 15 chapters. This chapter is meant to be an overview and quick reference to the most important concepts. It's something you can carry in your hip pocket as you navigate to success.

SECTION I – Chapter 1 – THE PROMISE OF A CHILD
Figure 16.1

☼ You were born with immense capabilities that were largely abandoned or suppressed in your desire for acceptance. ☼ Return to the lodestone of childhood in seeking your inspiration, for there lies your unborn genius potential. ☼ Make a new list of what you wish to release whenever it becomes necessary, and ceremonially burn it. ☼ Remember the letter you wrote to yourself, your new contract with the Universe, and honor it. Update it whenever a new understanding induces you to implement desirable modifications. ☼ Be the adult along with the child and you will find the genius within. 16.2

SECTION II – Chapters 2 through 6 – WHAT YOUR EQUIPMENT IS BUILT TO DO.
Figure 16.3

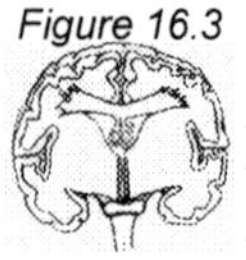

Phylogeny recapitulates ontogeny

Haeckel, E. 1899. *Riddle of the Universe at the Close of the Nineteenth Century*

Evolution, incarnation, and daily awakening all follow the same path of development.

A growing child mimes what evolution charted for the species and dawn brings for the day.

When we are conceived we begin life in the monistic delta state with spiritual vision.

Our foundation laid, we develop the androgyny of theta state and third eye vision where we perfect the art of sleeping and dreaming thus allowing our mind to learn with our brain.

When we are born we explore the alpha state and dual eyesight using our owl-like peripheral vision, thus firmly planting us in feminine space. *Figure 16.4*

Building patterns atop patterns, around the age of five we overlay all with the beta state of our perception and personality thereby gaining the laser-like foveal vision with which to dissect and judge with, thus planting us in masculine time and the sexual dichotomy of duality.

Each night we navigate the same waters that evolution and incarnation have acclimated us to; a course long ago charted by grand design.

What never goes away, but is often forgotten, is our foundation of knowing.

As we return to our source, individuality expresses itself as the basis for all diversity and the means by which each makes a unique contribution that synergistically advances the whole.

Our path has celestial origins with cosmic union as the endpoint. All paths lead to one.

SECTION III – Chapters 7 through 13 – LEARNING WITH MOM AND DAD
- **You Learn Best at Z^est^R_est_®**, the state of relaxed alertness, or wide-eye viewing, wide-ear listening, wide-open living, and holistic dreaming. Use largo music, reduced lighting, Superwords, mantras, relaxing rituals such as bathing, putting your consciousness in your abdomen, and the golden ball over your head, to put yourself into the optimal learning/remembering state, the zone of Supercompentency.
- **Re-LAX** into the theta state by coupling your inbreath with your eyes crossed and looking up, the three-finger mudra, and counting the **red** to **violet *rainbow*** chakra colors to your crown chakra. Breathe using the **(4,8,16,4) pattern** coordinated with the memory mantra:

(Inbreath) **I learn with zest!** (Hold) **I am in my gen ius zone where**
(Outbreath) **I am per fect mem o rey and I am per fect re call be cause** (Hold) **I am at rest.**

- **Re-TAIN** brackets what you SuperScan cadenced with the memory mantra and **(4,8,16,4) breathe pattern** used for **Re-LAX**. *Figure 16.3*
- **Re-CALL** also uses **(4,8,16,4)** breathing to activate your SuperMemory.

Superscan
With
OOwl-Eyes

- **Re-TURN** to the **beta state** by breathing in the **(4,4,4,4) pattern** and coupling your inbreath with eyes looking down at the earth while successively counting the chakras from seven to one. When you are finished, affirm using one of the following: **"I AM in my focus mode now!"** **"I AM fully awake, fully alert!"** or **"I AM awake, alive, alert enthusiastic!"**
- Master your mind at all levels. **Write down your manifestation list. Tell no one about it!** Use positive affirmations and decrees, such as those listed in **Appendixes F** and **G**, and/or **japa mala**, to reprogram your subconscious to be the perfect foundation and manifestation mechanism with which to live your life to its fullest potential and greatest happiness. You tie up the beta foveal-mind with positive affirmations and mantras that reprogram the alpha peripheral-mind. You shut down the beta foveal-vision with low light conditions. You shut down the beta hearing with low volume conditions such as subaudible background sound.
- Work with your dreams and visions:
- ❖ Address **PROBLEM SOLVING** with **VISUALIZATION-ACCEPTANCE-EXPECTANCY**
- ❖ Seek **INTUITIVE/PRECOGNITIVE SOLUTIONS** with **BELIEF-FOCUS-Re-LAXation**.
- ❖ Use the **Tibetan Waterfall** or **Net of Eir Visualizations** every time you go into the **SMART or GENIUS zones** either for SuperMemory tasks, or for sleep.
- Use the following key practices to develop your abilities and power rituals such as **abracadabra** and **arbadacarba**:

1st **KEY**	– *Awaken the child within and protect your inner child. Practice discernment*
2nd **KEY**	– *Develop your own, easy-to-do, healthful rituals*
3rd **KEY**	– *Practice, practice, practice!*
4th **KEY**	– *Keep a journal.* (Your dreams, plus SuperScan, Manifestation and Recall triumphs.)
5th **KEY**	– *Do it, with imagination, visualization, passion…. And LOVE!*

SECTION IV – Chapters 14 and 15 – REBUILDING YOUR FOUNDATION

Practice mindful breathing, hydrating, and eating. Consume the bounty of the earth to honor life. Exercise your eyes, body, and mind – for health. Use the Brain Gym®, and yoga-like exercises of your choice, to polish your golden vessel, for the treasure it holds is a promise with unlimited potential.

Appendixes A-K

Many useful skills such as energy kinesiology, are covered here, plus sources of information, lists of alpha state-inducing music, affirmations, useful mantras, and other information. Make copies of this chapter and any appendixes you need to assemble a traveling roadmap for healthful learning and living. Make it one of the first things you add to your super memory recall capability.

The automobile dealership idea used in this book yielded *"Great analogies, but – this is all technology. Remember that throughout the world, it was found that audiences burst into spontaneous applause when Luke Skywalker switched OFF the computer to deliver the missile to the Death Star."*

Douglas Buchanan

Figure 16.4

My apologies to any penguins I have offended. They are part of the great circle of life and help us see ourselves as we are, and as we can be. I am grateful.

Melvin Lewis Thomas

Appendix A – APPLIED KINESIOLOGY or MUSCLE TESTING (ENERGY TESTING)

There are more things in heaven and earth…
Than are dreamt of in your philosophy.
William Shakespeare: Hamlet

Listen to your body, and it will tell you what you need to know.
Wayne Dyer

The Chinese physician can detect imbalances in meridians by feeling the pulses,
but this a sensitive touch, and it may take 10 to 20 years to develop proficiency with it.
Touch for Health uses muscle testing to detect these same imbalances.
John Thie, *Touch for Health*

APPLIED kinesiology, or applied muscle testing, was developed by George Goodheart who founded the Applied Kinesiology organization. It was subsequently refined by his protégé, Alan Beardall and is now an established clinical procedure.[1] It is increasingly being used by the medical profession and laymen for expeditiously arriving at answers that would otherwise be difficult or time-consuming to obtain. Some doctors use this approach to test patients for negative reactions to drugs, or allergic reactions to any substance rather than resorting to the more traditional subcutaneous skin reaction testing. As a diagnostic tool it is something like the computerized engine analyzer used by the automobile dealership we spoke about at the beginning of this book. As a tool, how it works is somewhat mysterious, but the results are scientifically based and spectacular in their insightfulness and clarity. You quickly get to the root of the problem and obtain the answer you are seeking.

Applied kinesiology is based upon the energy characteristics of your body and the fact that your nervous system is sensitive to every part, from the mind/brain to the smallest cell and even the components of a cell, down to the molecules. Communicate with your brain and you communicate with the entire system. Communicate with your subconscious, even telepathically, and you tap into the entire system. Many studies, such as those conducted by the PSI Communications Project, demonstrate telepathically transmitted information that the physical body reacts to (bio-communication) without the conscious mind being involved in the process. For instance, blood flow associated with the fight or flight mechanism is affected, thus affecting the strength of the muscles.[2] You also have the added advantage of being able to test more than just "the physical." You can investigate the energy fields that comprise you or whomever is being tested, and thus arrive at trends prior to their showing up in the physical as disease, or not being at ease.

In her book *Energy Medicine*, Donna Eden devotes Chapter 2 to "energy testing" or "energy kinesiology" which she prefers as a term over applied kinesiology or applied muscle testing, because it addresses the root system being tested. Muscles are the intermediaries by which one interrogates the energy dynamics in the system. It is not the strength of the muscle being tested but rather the energy flow through the muscles that manifest as various levels of strength. Energy kinesiology is relatively easy to learn.[3] *When testing yourself or others, it is best that you be as balanced as possible. The Brain Gym exercises discussed in* **Chapter 15** *are formulated to achieve energy balance and are therefore part of the preparation. Also, make sure that you drink plenty of water to ensure that you are properly hydrated.*

Exercise A.1 – LEARNING APPLIED, or ENERGY KINESIOLOGY

In order to learn kinesiology it is best, but not essential, to work with someone who already knows it. A large muscle such as the deltoid, or shoulder muscle, is used for testing so the forces involved are easy to distinguish.

1. Both of you take a few deep breaths. As you exhale release all tension and expectations.
2. Use the Brain Gym exercises – Brain Buttons, Cross Crawl, and Hookups to balance your energies.
3. Have the person being tested agree to and say that "I give you permission to test."
4. Then have them extend either their right or left arm straight out to their side. Ask them to keep their arm firmly elevated and to pull against your pull as hard as they can.
5. Using two fingers on their wrist, pull down for one or two seconds to get a sense of how strongly they can resist this pull. Two pounds is the average maximum.
6. Phrase your queries as statements rather than questions, which are perceptually weaker.
7. Say: <u>Show me a strong muscle response or a "hold!"</u> *If they are feeling weak* and are unable to resist you adequately, have them do Brain Buttons to stimulate the K-27 acupressure points under each collar bone and separated by about three inches, then thump the thymus gland in the upper part of the sternum. Finally, touch the spleen neurolympahtic points centered just under each breast on a woman, or about three inches below the nipple on a man.[4]

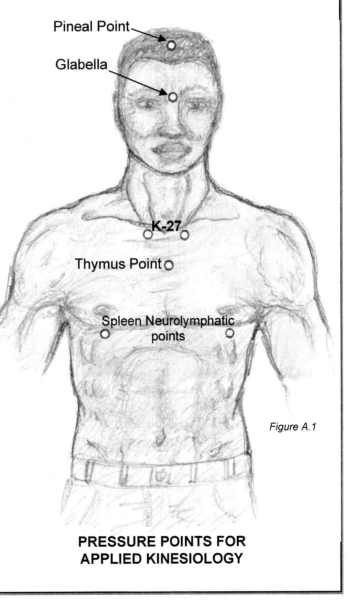

Figure A.1

PRESSURE POINTS FOR
APPLIED KINESIOLOGY

8. Say: <u>Show me a "break," or a weak muscle response such that the arm breaks lock and pulls down fairly easily to the side!</u> *If they are too strong* such that you cannot get their muscles to break lock, rubbing the top of the head between the typical hairline and the crown of the head will help reduce their ability to resist. This temporarily weakens them as you are stimulating the pineal gland at the pineal point, which helps you break their muscle lock. After rubbing this gland, use your index and middle finger combined to touch the glabella, the point just above the bridge of the nose, at which point their muscle will weaken enough to break lock. If they do not break lock, repeat this procedure until they do.[5]

Exercise A.1 – CONTINUED:

9. Set the intention for what you want a "hold" to represent, either a "Yes" or a "No." I have personally chosen to go with a hold being a "Yes."

Now you have a mechanism for asking "Yes" or "No" questions, or even counting by sequentially stating: 1 and not greater than 1 (No), 2 and not greater than 2 (No), 3 and not greater than 3 (No), and continuing until you get a "Yes" answer. Count by tens, hundreds, thousands, and so on for large numbers, then use successfully smaller ranges to narrow your answer down to an exact number if you wish. Use the following statements to test yourself on the accuracy of your answers by blindly (silently) stating them. You are calibrating for incorrect vs. correct responses so be sure to include questions that will yield an answer of "No!" For instance, you can fill in the name blank with a name different from that of the person you are testing in order to generate a No response:

1. You are (circle your choice) female/male!   Circle the response, either **Yes** or **No**
2. You name is (fill in the blank) _____!   Circle the response, either **Yes** or **No**
3. You are (circle your choice) right/left handed!   Circle the response, either **Yes** or **No**

Now, reverse roles so your partner has a chance to follow the same three steps above, and test accuracy with the same three statements issued silently

Dr. Hannaford contends that the answers obtained with energy kinesiology are the most accurate. When testing for a person's dominance profile there is a logical sequence that helps ensure that the answers will be reliable. The first question to answer is regarding which hand and associated arm is dominant. You do this by bringing attention to first one arm, and then the other, and thus determine which one locks up strongly and hence is the dominant one. Once the dominant hand and associated arm is determined, it is used to test for the remaining dominance profile characteristics by performing the following actions: [6]

TEST SEQUENCE TO DETERMINE SOMEONE'S DOMINANCE PROFILE:
1. EAR: Subject uses recessive hand to hold one ear, then the other.
2. EYE: Subject uses recessive hand to touch the outside corner of one eye, then the other.
3. FOOT: Subject uses recessive hand to touch one leg, and then the other.
4. HEMISPHERE: Subject uses recessive hand to touch one side of their head/brain, and then the other.
5. LOGIC/GESTALT MAPPING: Subject counts from one to five using recessive hand to touch one side of their head, then the other, to determine which side their logic function resides on. The other side is their gestalt function.

Chapter 6 in this book addresses dominance issues for everything but the feet and logic/gestalt hemispheric distribution. If you wish to delve into that level of complexity, Carla Hannaford's book *The Dominance Factor* will tell you everything you need to know as it goes considerably beyond the modest overview presented here. With all the factors addressed in her book taken into consideration, a person can be born with any one of 64 different learning combinations. Bear in mind that none of these combinations is inherently better than the others for each is a learning experience that cultivates individuality and diversity.

Applied kinesiology is a full-brain activity; therefore it helps develop the use of your latent mental abilities, including accessing the subconscious. Because the subconscious is telepathic you do not have to voice your statements aloud. That helps make certain that the ego of the person being tested isn't trying to influence the answers. Health issues are the most commonly addressed. You can test statements of a general physical, mental, emotional, or spiritual nature. The only testing I have found to be questionable is testing for future events. Answers about the future are based on the highest probability event happening. They are also dependent upon what you, and any other person or group of people involved, expect to happen. Prophecies about the future can be self-fulfilling, or self-defeating for that matter, as your ego and fears can drive your expectations in a variety of directions thus changing the outcome. The probable answer can therefore change many times before the actual event finally occurs.

One useful and quite reasonable variation to be aware of is surrogate testing, either in person or at a distance. The reason this works is because, as stated before, the subconscious is telepathic, Therefore; who, what, where, and when can all be addressed fairly easily. If a person is sick, or handicapped such that they cannot be tested directly, have a volunteer rest their hand lightly on the person being tested. Both of you then set the intention that the answers obtained will represent the person you want to test. You can test a baby or an animal in this way too. This form of testing also works at a distance if both you and the surrogate think of the person you want to test.

Once you are confident of your ability to perform applied kinesiology, you can also begin doing self-applied kinesiology. This will enable you to get answers without having to have a partner work with you. The principle is the same. In this instance you choose a muscle to stress with another muscle. For instance, you can extend the first finger of your left or right hand and extend the middle finger of the same hand over it. By pressing down with your middle finger while resisting with your first finger, you set up dynamic tension that you can use to establish yes/no answers. For me, a break is a no and a hold is a yes. This way I can single-handedly obtain kinesiological answers. Obviously you cannot use this technique to do blind muscle testing. This takes some practice to do because you have to be certain that you are not emotionally involved in the answers you are seeking thus influencing them, and confident enough in your technique to know that your answers will not be influenced by your ego.

Limitless like the ocean are your excellent qualities.
Dalai Lama

Figure B.1 – BRAIN DOMINANCE BUG[1]

Name _____

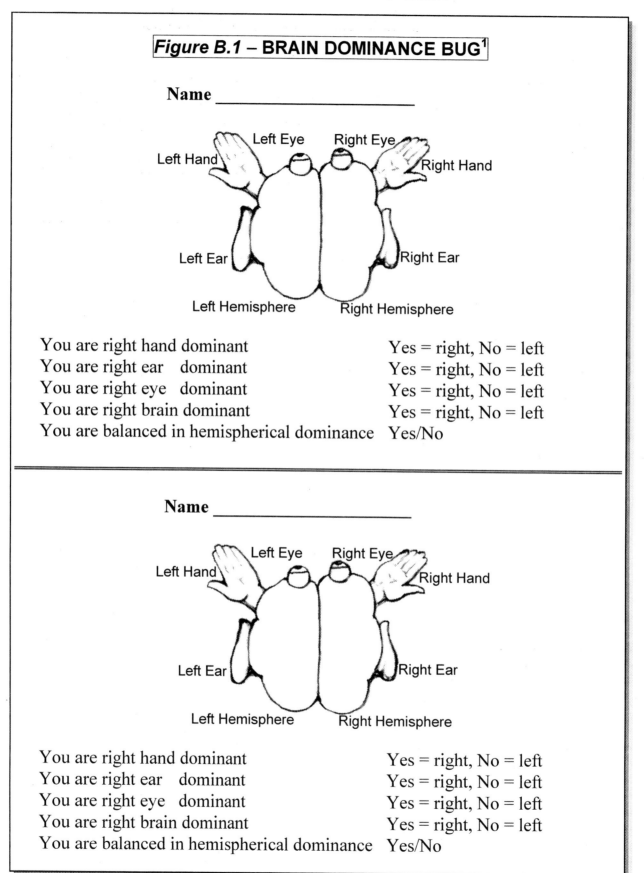

You are right hand dominant   Yes = right, No = left
You are right ear   dominant   Yes = right, No = left
You are right eye   dominant   Yes = right, No = left
You are right brain dominant   Yes = right, No = left
You are balanced in hemispherical dominance   Yes/No

Name _____

You are right hand dominant   Yes = right, No = left
You are right ear   dominant   Yes = right, No = left
You are right eye   dominant   Yes = right, No = left
You are right brain dominant   Yes = right, No = left
You are balanced in hemispherical dominance   Yes/No

Appendix C – Lozanov's Music for the Two "Concerts"[1,2]

The Dr. Georgi Lozanov method uses music in three distinct ways to accelerate learning:

1. Introductory music to relax participants and achieve the optimum state for learning. Such as Johann Pachelbel's *Canon in D.*
2. An "active concert," in which the information to be learned is read with the expressive music.
3. A "passive concert" in which the learner hears the new information read conversationally against a background of baroque music, to help move the information into the long-term memory.

ACTIVE CONCERT:

Beethoven
- Concerto for Piano and Orchestra No. 5 in B-flat major.
- Concerto for Violin and Orchestra in D major, Op. 61.
- Concerto No. 5 in E flat major for Piano and Orchestra, Op 73 (*Emperor*).

Mozart
- Symphony in D major, *Haffner*
- Symphony in D Major, *Prague.*
- Concerto for Violin and Orchestra in A major No. 5
- Concerto for Violin and Orchestra, Concert No. 7 in D major.
- Symphony in A major No 29.
- Symphony in G minor No. 40.

Haydn
- Concerto No. 1 in C major for Violin and Orchestra.
- Orchestra: Concerto No. 2 in G major for Violin and Orchestra.
- Symphony in C major No. 101, *L.'Horloge .*
- Symphony in G major No. 94.
- Symphony No. 67 in F major.
- Symphony No. 69 in B major.

Tchaikovsky
- Concerto No. 1 in B flat minor for Piano and Orchestra.

Brahms
- Concerto for Violin and Orchestra in D. major, Op. 77

PASSIVE CONCERT:

Vivaldi
- Five Concertos for Flute and Chamber Orchestra.
- The Four Seasons.

Handel
- Concerto for Organ and Orchestra in B-flat Major, Op 7, No. 6.
- The Water Music.

J. S. Bach
- Prelude in G major, *Dogmatic Chorales.*
- Fantasia for Organ in G. major, Fantasia in C minor.
- Fantasy in G Major, Fantasy in C minor and Trio in D minor.
- Canonic Variations and Toccata.

Corelli
- Concerti Grossi, Op. 6, No. 2, 4, 5, 8, 9, 10, 11, 12.
- Concerti Grossi, Op. 4, No. 10, 11, 12.

Couperin
- Sonatas for Harpisichord: *Le Parnasse* (Apotheosis of Corelli).
- L'Estree.

J. F. Rameau
- Concert Pieces for Harpisichord *Pieces de Clavecin* No. 1 and No. 5.

Appendix D – Additional Music Selections

I recommend:

- *Mozart For Meditation: Quiet Music for Quiet Times* (For inducing the alpha state).
- *Tune Your Brain With Mozart* – Energetic Music (For returning to the beta state).
- *Om Namaha Shivaya,* (alpha state Inducing).
- *Masterworks* – HEMI SYNC, developed by the Monroe Institute. Trademark is MetaMusic. www.MasterRep.com (Develops focused whole-brain awareness without the use of subliminal messages).

Dr. Jeannette Vos recommends:[1]

For creating a calm atmosphere

- Watermark by Enya.
- Most of Corelli's 12 concertos, from op. 6.
- Specialized, sequenced baroque music in OptimaLearning Classics, 303 and 601, from Barzak Institute.

For getting in the mood – Especially for cooperative learning activities.

- *Deep Breakfast* by Ray Lynch.

For "clustering" and fast writing

- *Antarctica* by Vangelis.
- *Brazilian* in the *Invisible Touch* album, by Genesis (Popular with teenagers).

For "poetry writing"

- *December* by George Winston.

For putting poems and whole language to raps.

- Hammer's tapes, but just the instrumental part.

For "state changes"

Vary the music depending on the age group, but generally any upbeat instrumental music will work, such as:

- *Planet of Light* by Deuter.
- *Run Away* by the Real McCoy (For teenagers).
- *I Need You* by Savage Garden (For teenagers).
- Elvis Presley music (For those from an earlier era).

For getting started with teenagers – right after a break:

- *Strike it up* by Black Box.
- *Sweet Harmony* by Beloved Conscience.

For goal setting

- *Chariots of Fire* by Vangelis.

For "visualizations"

- *Waterfalls* by Paul Lloyd Warner.
- *Sunsets* by Michael Jones.
- *December* by George Winston.

Appendix E

Name	Figure E.1 – Brain Bingo® Worksheet		Date	
	Lighting Up the Whole Mind/Brain/Body			

Front of brain ... **Back of brain**

Prefrontal cortex	Motor cortex	Temporal lobe	Parietal lobe	Occipital lobe
1	2	3	4	5
6	7	8	9	10
Limbic		Corpus callosum		Cerebellum
11	Left-brain, right side of the body	12	Right-brain, left side of the body	13
14		15		16
Medulla oblongata		Pineal gland or third eye		Brain stem
17	18	19	20	21
22	23	24	25	26 *Example* (x ⊗)

Appendix F – A SELECTION OF POSITIVE AFFIRMATIONS

AFFIRMATIONS to repeat either silently or aloud to yourself. For a real challenge and maximum positive benefits, do these affirmations while looking in a mirror at yourself. Do them two or three times a day until you can look yourself in the eye and not flinch, but accept what you are saying as part of you.

DR LOZANOV'S POSITIVE AFFIRMATIONS[1]

I can do it.
Now I am achieving my goals.
Learning is something I hugely enjoy.
Learning and remembering are easy for me.
My mind moves efficiently, effectively.
I am supremely calm.

Before an exam:
I recognize the right answers at the right time.
I remember all I need to know.
I am supremely calm and confident.
My memory is alert, my mind is powerful.

A selection of affirmations from, *You Can't Afford the Luxury of a Negative Thought,*
      By John Roger and Peter McWilliams
I am content.   – John Quincy Adams
I am the master of my fate; I am the captain of my soul.   – William Ernest Henley, 1888
Every day in every way, I'm getting better and better.   – Emile Coue, 1857-1926
I am absorbed in the wonder of earth and the life upon it.. – Pearl S. Buck
I am strong, I am invincible, I am woman.   – Helen Reddy
I feel warm and loving toward myself.
I am worthy of all the good in my life.
I am one with the universe, and I have more than I need.
I always do the best I can with what I know and always use everything for my advancement.
I forgive myself unconditionally.
I am grateful for my life.
I love and accept myself and others.
I treat all problems as opportunities to grow in wisdom and love.
I am relaxed, trusting in a higher plan that's unfolding for me.
I automatically and joyfully focus on the positive.
I give myself permission to live, love, and laugh.
I am creating and using affirmations to create a joyful, abundant, fulfilling life.

      and end your affirmations with:
…this, or something greater for my highest good, and the highest good of all concerned.

I unconditionally love and accept myself, just as I am, in all my magnificence!

Appendix G – Saint Germain's "I AM" DECREES

THESE decrees were given to us by Saint Germain, whose name means, "pertaining to the saints." According to the "I AM" books that detail this information, they are particularly effective for a couple of reasons. First off, their source is from the Ascended Master level and hence, above the duality of Earth. They are therefore perfect in their composition and intent. Consequently, they are far more powerful than the statements most of us are capable of making. Because they were given in English, they cannot be translated into any other language and still remain fully effective much as saying the Lord's Prayer is only fully effective in the language Jesus spoke, Aramaic. Secondly, unlike prayer as usually formulated in the Western Hemisphere, they are not supplication; they are decrees of stated intentionality. According to the "I AM" materials, the accumulative effect of using them is therefore a thousand times greater than that of normal prayer.[1] As you use these decrees remember the words of Jesus: "I have said, Ye are gods; and all of you are children of the most High."Psalm 82:6, John 10:34.

Upon Arising: "'BELOVED MIGHTY I AM PRESENCE!' Clothe me in Thy Violet Consuming Flame and keep It sustained and expanding through me throughout the day!"[2]

Prior to 8:00 a.m. and for the slightest disturbance:
Raise your hands to your "Presence" and say - "'Mighty I AM Presence,' pass your Violet Consuming Flame through my mental and feeling body; sweep out and dissolve all imperfection. Then pour Your Mighty Currents through, filling my body with Your Mighty Health, Strength, Courage and Buoyancy."[3]

Cleansing Mantra: "'I AM' a being of violet fire, 'I AM' the purity that God desires."[4]

To balance breath: "'I AM' the balancing-breath."[5]

To charge water:
"'I AM' the Presence charging this water with the Life-giving Essence which I absorb and which renews my body in Perfect Health and Eternal Youth."[6]
"'I AM' the Presence qualifying this water with the Electronic Precipitated Substance of Light from the Ascended Masters." Note: Stop long enough to feel it go into the water and as a self-luminous substance, go into your cells. This will bless both the water and your cells.[7]

Blessing for food:
"'Mighty I AM Presence,' accept this (all) food (under this radiation today) make it pure and holy. Transmute it into Thy Violet Golden Flame of Divine Love, and see that It purifies and perfects all our bodies with the speed of thought, forever Self-sustained."[8]

To clear the mind, eyes, and ears:
"'I AM' the Perfect Intelligence active in this brain.
'I AM' the Perfect Sight looking through these eyes.
'I AM' the Perfect Hearing through these ears."[9]

For the brain (yours or others): "'I AM' the quickening of the cells of (my or your) brain structure, causing it to expand and receive the Intelligent Direction of the Mighty Inner Presence."[10] "'I AM the Presence' thinking through this mind and body."[11]

To restore perfect memory:
"'Beloved Mighty I AM Presence,' I call for the restoration of my full Divine Memory."[12]

To learn information that you are seeking:
"'I AM' the illumining, Revealing Presence, and no outer activity that I need to know can be withheld from me, because 'I AM' the Wisdom, 'I AM' the Perception, 'I AM' the Revealing Power bringing everything before me – that I may see and understand, and be able to act accordingly." [13]

To perfect the physical body and its action:
"'Mighty I AM Presence," this is Your physical body. You take Perfect Command of it! Make it come into Perfect Order and Perfect Action."[14]

For perfect health: "'I AM' the Presence' of Perfect Health." [15]
"'I AM' Perfect Health now manifest in every organ of my body." [16]

To solve problems: "'God in me, the 'I AM Presence,' come forth! Govern and solve this situation harmoniously."[17]

To protect oneself while in an automobile:
"God is All-seeing and All-knowing, sees ahead, and will naturally avoid undesirable contact."[18]

To clear your world of undesirable conditions:
"'I AM,' 'I AM,' I KNOW 'I AM' free from this thing forever- no matter what it is." [19]
"'I AM' invincibly protected against any imperfect suggestion." [20]

To stop irritation in self: "'Mighty I AM Presence', govern this harmoniously!" [21]

When confronted with a frightening situation: Stand and say repeatedly, "I AM!" [22]

For determined accomplishment: "By the Power of Almighty God in me, I know that whenever I stand with determined desire to accomplish something constructive, it cannot fail." [23]

Enormously helpful:
"'I AM' the Miracle-Working Presence in everything I require to have done [24]

For financial freedom, say often:
"The 'Presence I AM' governs every existing channel in manifestation. It governs all." [25]

For a sense of tiredness: "I absorb the Mighty Presence and Energy of my God Self, and it expresses as alertness, joy, and abundant activity in my outer Life and affairs!" "God is my Energy, expressing in my outer activity right now!" [26]

For peace and rest during the night:
"'Mighty I AM Presence,' pass the Mighty Violet Consuming Flame through the mattress of my bed, and keep this Sustained Activity going through me." [27]

For manifesting via sleep whatever you have in your consciousness:
"'I AM' the quality of whatever I wish to use." [28]

Whenever commanding, end with: "I know it is acting with Full Power." [29]

Appendix H – DOUGLAS BUCHANAN – HIS BIOGRAPHY AND MONOGRAPHS [1,2]

DOUGLAS lives in a suburb of Chicago in a modest home with the street number of 360, a full circle, or completion. He was born in England more than 70 years ago and orphaned at the age of nine when his remaining parent, his father, died. He grew up with the austerity of WWII as his model for life. His intellect even then was considerable so despite poor health such that he nearly died, he recovered and won scholarships thus allowing him to obtain a fine education. He became a tutor at Wolsey Hall in Oxford where he wrote the courses on mathematics that were used there. He also has a fundamental mathematical proof to his credit. During his spare time as a teacher he helped the handicapped. He told them to give him two weeks notice and he would teach them any subject they wanted to know.

One day while eating fish and chips he saw an oily ring forming a perfect circle around a classified ad in the uncharacteristically intellectual newspaper his meal was wrapped in. It was for a teaching position. The synchronicity of the event captured his attention. He applied and was hired. He resigned his secure teaching positions and reduced a ten-room house to three trunks of possessions, mostly books, and set off to address his new challenge. In route to the remote region of Northwest Canada where his job awaited him, the Canadian National Railways lost his trunks, thus completely liberating him of possessions.

The school was in an extremely isolated place and the Indian children who lived there were in dire need of instruction. The church had taken away their religion and secular authorities had little to offer in substitution. There he became skilled at hunting and tracking. His path since then has led him to add many other skills to his list of abilities including songwriter and poet. He teaches locally to those who choose to seek his wisdom, and helped found the web site www.darshem.com.

When the document you are reading was a rough draft of 134 pages and 68,000 words, I dropped it off with Douglas seeking his review of the material. He received it at 6:45 in the evening while in the process of binding manuscripts for a class he was getting ready to teach the coming weekend. By 8:45 the next morning I received a detailed, single spaced, five page email from him giving me proofreading level feedback on errors, plus further enlightening comments about the contents. In only 14 hours he slept, did the work he had to do for his seminar and the myriad of other tasks that fill his every waking hour including the answering of 500 emails each week, and generated a review that most people would have had difficulty doing over the duration of days. That is the power of the techniques he employs and what this book is attempting to impart.

The Douglas Monographs can be purchased in Illinois at Practical Magick, or if out of state by contacting Douglas via email. There are seventeen monographs covering a variety of subjects. I have listed the ones directly applicable to what has been discussed in this book.

- Practical Magick, 663 N. LaGrange Rd., Frankfort, IL 60423. 815-464-4817.
- Out-of-staters may contact Douglas at ddvbuchanan@aol.com for mailed copies.

6. Meditation: The Bridge from the Apparent to the Real. This work addresses a very common problem that is not perceived as a problem by the novice meditator. The ego-mind complex of the practitioner is determined not to be dissolved by meditation, and uses various stratagems that make the meditators think that they are going deeper and deeper, when the reverse is actually true. Every one who has been fooled by the infinite videos that the mind plays for them should read this. It explains clearly what the major problems are, and details a time-tested way of avoiding every single one of the tricks of the ego-mind complex, whatever the current belief system or spiritual practice of the meditator.

14. Health Matters Lies you have been told about your diet and your health by the authorities. Truths that have been kept from you by government and industry in the name of profit. How health problems are dealt with in other countries whose medical professions are not dominated by the drug industries. More than two-dozen health articles from the thirty years of health writing of Douglas. These can help you become your own wellness coach.

16. Uses of the Japa Mala. This contains the manual presented to participants at the Practical Magick workshop on "Uses of the Japa Mala." It explains how to use the Mala for self-help, changing habits, healing, self-esteem, prosperity, as a tool for mundane welfare, and how to use it with powerful mantras to cultivate correct spiritual perspectives. The four Hindu goals of life: righteousness, Wealth, Pleasure and Liberation form the syllabus.

| Appendix I – Richard L. Welch's – Dynamic Brain Management and Mental Photography® |

25,000 Words Per Minute – No Less…. BRAIN MANAGEMENT

- By Richard Baker and Shannon Panzo

That man someday in the future would discover ways to access the diverse and incredible powers of the mind and thus begin utilizing "the other 90 percent" of the brain has never really been in question. That someday in the future the scientific community will have no alternative but to acknowledge the validity of proven scientific principles also has never really been in question. The only questions have been how and when. The answers to these questions are the topics of this article.

Imagine training your mind to be able to absorb information at the rate of hundreds of thousands of words per minute -- and to retain 100 percent of it, always accessible, for the rest of your life!

Imagine being able to program your subconscious mind to exert influence over your environment, including your physical body, to the degree of being able to fulfill your wishes, your needs and even giving you the ability to achieve and maintain good health!

Imagine increasing your mind's sensitivity to being able to perceive more information through all of your senses -- with full recall!

Imagine being able to program your dreams to solve problems you may have or those yet to confront you!

Imagine being able to keep current on reading everything in your areas of interest and specialization -- after you have finished absorbing the books in your library you never had the time to read!

All of these exceedingly desirable capabilities are now accessible as the result of the inexorable determination of Richard Welch, Founder and CEO of Subliminal Dynamics® Brain Management and the "Father of Mental Photography®". He spent millions of dollars and twenty-five years of research and discovery stripping the layers of obscuring misinformation, misunderstanding and disbelief from the path of unfettered learning and personal fulfillment by learning how to open the door to the subconscious mind.

In the beginning, after fifteen highly successful years in the financial planning industry, and one year of retirement at the age of thirty-four, Mr. Richard Welch bought the American Speed-reading Academy.

After two months of operating the school, Mr. Welch held a staff meeting and informed the teaching staff of his desire to innovate and improve the product. Within thirty days some startling things began to take place in the classroom. Several students were reading faster than 10,000 words per minute, and a few were exceeding 40,000 words per minute. Mr. Welch's initial reaction was skepticism, but following another staff meeting, he decided to re-write the course outline and implement into the course the innovations that appeared to contribute to the remarkable increase in reading speed.

He formed three pilot classes, ten students each. The classes included participants of many ages and occupations. Among the thirty people were a nine year old child and a seventy-two year old man. After ten weeks, the results were in -- and it astounded him! The average graduate had exceeded 40,000 words per minute and the average increase in rate of comprehension was 28 percent. Two students, a sixteen year old boy and a thirty-five-year-old accountant, exceeded 175,000 words per minute and were still climbing. The accountant, Bob Scott, decided to continue working with the method once a week to find his limit. A few weeks later, he peaked at an amazing 422,000 words per minute and tested with 85 percent comprehension on completely foreign material. Mr. Welch then felt sure he had found an entirely new method of speed-reading, or something like speed-reading, that when taught, produced unbelievable results with virtually anyone. He sent his speed-reading staff to libraries to read everything they could find on speed-reading, reading, the brain, and eye-brain coordination. He also continued working and testing his new methods in the classroom.

Arizona state University Psychology Department staff performed independent tests funded by Mr. Welch. Control groups from the campus and students provided by Mr. Welch were used in the testing. These tests confirmed that anyone with average intelligence can learn to read at astounding speeds up to 2,000,000 words per minute -- with increased comprehension. This was achieved by flashing information at forty milliseconds on a Tachistoscope. Tests performed by the Phoenix elementary school district confirmed that young children, fourth and fifth graders, could rapidly grasp his method. It raised their reading and vocabulary skills several years with only a few hours of using this method.

During research conducted from 1976 to 1978, Doctor Herbert Otto was consulted. Dr. Otto, Director of the Human Potentialities Research Project for the National Center for Exploration of Human Potential, in La Jolla, California, encouraged Richard Welch to continue his research and suggested he should protect it by using his own funds so that nothing could be published during the development of this amazing process.

In 1979, after moving the Company to San Jose, California, Mr. Welch began more testing and research to find new applications for the process now known as Subliminal Dynamics®. The speed-reading application was then re-named **Subliminal Photography®** and **Mental Photography®**, which more accurately described the phenomena. Mr. Welch also coined the phrase **"Welcome To Tomorrow®"**.

As the testing continued, it became obvious that the part of the brain being applied had remarkable abilities and it was primarily unexplored territory. The method of **Subliminal Dynamics Brain Management®** was then under a "trade secret" and put under lock and key for protection.

What came to life in 1975 was essentially a speed-reading course with more hidden potential than developer Richard Welch ever dreamed of. Like an exceptional child, it grew, developed ideas of its own, made friends in high places, acquired the name Subliminal Dynamics and reached adulthood in 1984. Now it is a new dimension way beyond any speed-reading course. As a whole-life enhancement training, its results are not limited to learning. Like the child prodigy it was, it continues to amaze people who find themselves shaking their heads in wonderment at the results.

People all over the world have learned this evolving process. In 1984, its simplification allowed the course to be taught in four three-hour sessions. IQs ranging from retarded to genius and ages ranging from 5 to 92 have been tested. Dyslexia is considered to be an attribute, not a deficit. The Mental Photography simply bypasses the dyslexic function. The success ratio is over 98 percent. As research is constantly being done and innovations are tested, the addition of new material has expanded the course to four 5-hour lessons.

Countless numbers of people from every corner of the globe that want to be taught the Brain Management Process have inquired through their internet site at http://www.subdyn.com. This instigated creation of the self-study format that is based on the past twenty-five years of Mr. Welch's research, development, and expertise. For the first time ever, people can learn the Brain Management Process in the comfort of their home or office. This training is presented in two-hour sessions for seven consecutive days. It is called **"Brain Management and Mental Photography®...made easy!"**

People from all backgrounds -- students, business and industry, education, professionals, law enforcement, military, scientists, and others -- learned the method successfully. The applications of this process are limitless -- and the implications are extraordinary.

Richard Welch, a world-renowned speaker and teacher, and his wife, Donna Welch, President, have appeared on numerous radio and television shows. Based in Aurora, Colorado, they and their fine staff commit to teaching Brain Management using the most innovative methods available. Brain Management is currently expanding worldwide and opening new foreign marketplaces.

To understand the operation of the process, the most necessary thing to realize is that while the four day intensive provides you with all you need to know and have: a student guide with instructions, practice routines, information, examples, tests, test results, relaxing tapes and the future ability to take FREE refresher courses. It does not provide the practice time which is necessary for this process to become second nature to us.

As it is with most skills, a substantial amount of exercise is required to become proficient at the process. Remember that the operative part of this process is accessing the subconscious and that is something for most people by maturity have lost. Actually, for most it takes approximately six weeks of daily organized practice as specifically outlined in the course and in the instruction manual before the habit is established. However, even during the course, the student is shown to have a surprising amount of natural skill at using the technique.

While the emphasis is placed on rapid book absorption, there are other very important areas which are covered in the classroom some of which are referenced at the beginning of this article. Imagine becoming accustomed to approaching all challenges with more confidence, more information, a greater sense of awareness and, to a probable considerable degree, a higher intelligence. Brain Management used daily as a natural part of living might well grant these.

Imagine living in a civilization filled with people in the fashion made possible by Brain Management. The differences would be great and the possibilities, awesome.

One of the first priorities for Brain Management is to introduce this process into the schools at the earliest level. All concepts of "gifted children" will have to be revised because all the children using this system will become "gifted". It is likely that present "gifted" people have in their own way discovered and used this process to a greater or less degree.

The work of this committed researcher, Richard Welch, demands the recognition, acceptance and utilization of his work at a level deserving of a Nobel Prize.

Welcome to Tomorrow?

For information, call 303.627.8793, or in the US: 800.869.1491

Appendix J – SOURCES FOR ORGANIC FOODS AND HERBAL REMEDIES

NATURE'S First Law – This Company sells many organic raw foods plus a supper food that if taken at the rate of a spoonful a day, will provide you with more than the adult daily requirements of vitamins and minerals, thus eliminating the need for pill based supplements. Their web site is: www.rawfood.com, and phone number is: **888-RAW-FOOD**

The American Botanical Pharmacy - Owned and operated by Dr. Richard Schultz. He also sells a super food that provides an adult with 2 to 5 times the vitamins and minerals needed each day. In addition, Dr. Schultz has a complete program and many products for effectively addressing any illness. Call **800-HERB DOC** to order one of their comprehensive catalogs and see for yourself how what is available can have a profoundly positive effect on both your health, and your ability to administer to yourself.

The next three companies I will discuss use multi-level distribution based selling. They are however excellent mail order sources of healthy organic foods that can help a person achieve a balanced diet. I therefore recommend them.

Cell Tech - Super Blue Green Algae is in many regards the most important food I would recommend. Douglas Buchanan says that taking only one pill of SBGA a day cleared his wife of allergies in only a few months. He has thoroughly investigated the company and their product and says that his friends who can see energies around people report being able to see the difference between people who take SBGA, and those who don't. The metaphysical literature says that SBGA will help children enormously, particularly the new Indigo Children who are arriving in such numbers now that most newborns are Indigo's.[1] SBGA is found in the pristine waters of Klamath Lake, Oregon, which is the only place in the world that this particular algae grows. **Cell Tech** is the company that pioneered the harvesting and selling of SBGA, and they have available a variety of foods and formulations including a bulk powder as a food additive for your pets. They can be contacted via: www.celltech.com, or their toll free number: **800-800-1300.** Our account number is **1025097**.

The Brain Garden - The next class of foods I would recommend is referenced in Daniel 1:11-20, which mentions a food called **pulse**. The story told is of Daniel and his friends, who were in the King's army, requesting a diet of pulse and water rather than "the King's meat." After 10 days the King found them healthier and stronger. After three years he found them 10 times better in wisdom than the most learned men in the kingdom. The **Brain Garden Company** sells foods based on the principles of preparation and formulation for pulse as discovered in an ancient document written by Socrates. Don Tolman, a man of considerable intellectual development with the ability to read at SuperScan speeds with photographic recall, is the founder. His foods are organic, raw, and dehydrated by parching so that they retain their full living energies. They are blended as balanced meals that promote a healthy strong body and full mind capacity. Because they are dehydrated, they are great for camping, traveling and emergency stores as they have a long shelf life and minimum size and weight. The Brain Garden also sells learning materials and whole living programs. Their web site is: www.thebraingarden.com, and their order number is **800-984-2263**. Our member number is **63344**.

Sunrider - Markets a line of organic foods, personal care, and household cleaning products that are healthy for you and the environment. The foundation of this system is the Chinese understanding of energy flow via your meridians and Yin/Yang. Eating as they advise addresses health issues by bringing your systems into balance while supplying you with proper organic nutrition based on foods dehydrated such that they retain their full enzymatic vitality. Many people lose a great deal of weight on this system along with regaining their health. The phone number to call is **888-278-6743** and our distributor number is **001299318.**

Appendix K –INTERNET AND CATALOG SOURCES

- **Accelerated Learning Systems,** Colin Rose, Accelerated Learning Systems Ltd., 50 Aylesbury Road, Aston Clinton, Aylesbury, Bucks, HP22 9AH, United Kingdom. Phone: 011-44-1296-63117, Fax 011-44-1296-631074, email: colinrose@globalnet.co.uk, www.accelerated-learning-uk.co.uk   United States: Malcom J. Nicholl, Accelerated Learning Systems Inc., 908 Crest Drive, Encinitas, CA 92024, Phone: 1-760-943-0762, e-mail: als@u-s.com, www.accelerated-learning.net.
- www.bachessences.com **Bach floral essences** for aromatherapy. Their web site lists contacts that are world wide. They have a wide variety of remedies including Clematis which helps one return to the present, or the Beta state.
- www.braingym.com**,** The **Brain Gym** web site.
- www.dreamkeepers.net, Recordings and books of indigenous wisdom.
- www.emode.com, *The Brain Test,* and *The IQ Test* are both worth taking.
- www.emissayoflight.com, **James Twyman's** web site including the *Spoonbender's Course.*
- www.lumiram.com, **Lumiram,** the number one maker of full spectrum lamps, and the original maker of "Neodymium" glass light sources since 1959. The company started in Sweden where the absence of light in the winter months induced the invention of a bulb to substitute for sunlight. They sell the Chromalux full spectrum bulb.
- **Light for Health corporation,** www.lightforhealth.com, Ph: 800.468.1104, 942 Twisted Oak Lane, Buffalo Grove, IL 60089. They sell a line of very high quality fluorescent bulbs that closely match the visible and near visible portions of the solar spectrum, and ballasts that operate at 20,000 cycles-per-second to eliminate the perception of 60 cps flicker observed in most fluorescent-based lighting. The ballasts will start the fluorescent lights in temperatures as low as -40C but they take an hour to warm up enough to function properly. At -18C they work fine. The lamps also operate in temperatures as high as 90C, or 183 degrees Fahrenheit.
- Dryden, Gordon; and Vos, Jeannette - *The book, the CD of presentation slides, and The Learning Revolution Companion 50 minute Video,* are all available via www.thelearningweb.net.
- **Learning Strategies Corporation,** (Photoreading® whole mind system) 900 East Wayuzata Boulevard, Wayzata, Minnesota, 55391-1836 USA. 952-476.9200, 800.735.8273. www.LearningStrategies.com
- **Lozanov's Suggestophobia® Institute** - web site is http://lozanov.internet-bg.net, or you can email him at dr_lozanov@yahoo.com.
- **Millman, Dan,** www.danmillman.com, *Peaceful Warrior Workout Video,* Ph: 800.525.9000**.**
- **The MASTERY of LEARNING** - My email is mel@themasteryseries.com. The Mastery Series web site is: www.themasteryseries.com. It covers this book and associated workshop, and others as they become available. There is a chat room for sharing learning experiences and more information about these techniques, and a schedule of upcoming workshops. You can take this workshop and those of other authors as on-line Internet courses by going to www.ConsciousOne.com.
- **Plow and Hearth** – www.plowhearth.com, Ph: 800.843.2509, POB 600, Madison, VA, 22727-1600. They sell a line of incandescent and fluorescent bulbs that are described as full spectrum.
- www.projectgutenberg.com is a repository containing hundreds of books online.
- 5790061.royalbodycare.com Bathcare products such as the Microhydrin Bath Salts (Helps immerse you in the alpha/theta state) "Bathe in your own 'Fountain of Youth' When you bathe in Microhydrin Bath Salts, you're bathing in 'living' water, immersing your skin in millions of supercharged hydrogen ions. Bask in the aromas of mandarin, grapefruit and lavender for a truly sensory experience." 22 Oz @$29 per bottle retail, $22 wholesale ($25 to become a member) They assigned me the web site listed above. It incorporates my membership number in it should you choose to become a member, or just order one of their products.
- www.youngliving.com 12662 South Redwood Road, Riverton, Utah 84065. Ph: 800.763.9963 to call in an order or enroll as a new member. An excellent product line of Essential oils including Lavender which helps induce the alpha state, and many other products aimed at healthy living. If you order from them, please do so under **our customer number: 27573.**
- **Perelandra,** Center for Nature Research, POB 3603, Warrenton, VA 20188. Phone: 800.960.8806. They sell a variety of excellent products including a line of floral essences. Two useful examples: 1) Eclipse: for Acceptance and insight. Enhances the individual's appreciation of his own inner knowing. Supports the mechanism that allows the body to receive the soul's input and insight 2) Zinnia: Reconnects one to the child within. Restores playfulness, laughter, joy and a sense of healthy priorities.
- *Yoga for Your Eyes* video by Meir Schneider. Available as #VT00012 from Sounds True Catalog, P.O.Box 8010 / Dept. W18, Boulder, CO /80306-8010. Ph: 800.333-9185, www.soundstrue.com, or from www.amazon.com.

GLOSSARY

- **Antahkarana** – Sanskrit for antar (interior) combined with karana (sense organ) or, interior sense organ. It is the energy cord or pillar of light by which our body receives all of its energy and through which we are connected to our puppeteer, more commonly called the Monad or Higher Self, and from there to God.
- **Astral Plane** – The next dimensional plane or level above the physical dimension. This level is still closely tied to duality consciousness. The astral plane is a layer above the earth's surface extending up approximately seven miles.
- **Avatara** – Sanskrit for *ava*, "down" and *tri*, "to pass" thus combining to mean, "descent." The word used in Hindu scriptures thus signifies the descent of Divinity into flesh. Examples of avatara would be Babaji, Yoganandna, Krishna, Rama, Buddha, Patanjali, and Jesus who became the Christ.[1]
- **Babaji** – Lord Shiva himself, or God the Father. *Baba* means "Father", *Ji* means "beloved" so combined they mean "Beloved Father" or "respected ruler." Babaji has appeared through the millennium as an eternal youth 16 to 18 years old. When he is in the human body, he calls himself Bhole Baba, which means, "Simple Father."[2]
- **Bushido** – Budo is Japanese for *the way of combat*, but *bu* also means to stop combat, so the word is inherently yin/yang.[3]
- **Chakras** –Sanskrit for spinning wheel as it was named for the ability of some to see the spinning energy vortexes that center on the primary glands of the human body. The occult cerebrospinal centers are also called astral lotuses. They are the primary energy centers of the body. There are seven traditional chakras arrayed from the crown of the head to the base of the spine. Many current books on metaphysics indicate that the number of chakras is growing from seven to twelve. For instance, Dar' Shem uses 12 symbols in its feminine Reiki because of the 12 activated chakras of a fully enlightened being. Dr. Joshua David Stone indicates in his writings that planetary ascension involves the eventual incorporation of 50 primary chakras into the human body.
- **Deosil** – Following the apparent direction of the sun as in the hands of a watch.
- **Dharma** – Sanskrit for "the best of all possible actions."
- **Dar' Shem** or **Darshan** – Quoting the web site, www.darshem.com, which was founded by Douglas Buchanan, "Dar' Shem is an ancient healing art in which the initiated channel energy through their bodies to help others. Like other forms of energy work, the ability to do this is transferred from Master to Student through a process of initiation and instruction. The attunement never wears off and cannot be lost. However, one's ability does grow from the time of the attunement onward through practice and repetition. As long as one is in Her service, one is in Her care."
- **Hara** – Japanese for "belly," referring to the energy in our belly, which is the energy center of the body or the abdominal chakra area a few inches below the navel.[4]
- **Japa** – To repeat, often associated with the practice of repeating a sacred mantra like the name of God. **Japa mala** is the repeating of a mantra while using a **mala.**
- **Karma** – Sanskrit for "action." Thus, karma accounts for the action in ones life as a consequence of a previous action in this or some prior lifetime. Karma is the effect based on some previous cause.[5]
- **Lama** – According to the Dalai Lama, "The actual meaning of lama or **guru** is something wise."
- **Mala** – This Hindi word literally translates as - "garland of flowers." It is a string of beads in multiples of 27. Thus it is either 27, 54, or 108 beads in a row forming a sacred number. It is therefore a counting device that predates, and probably was the model for, the Catholic Rosary.
- **Mantra** – A word or phrase that is repeated as a device to focus the mind on and hence, exclude other thoughts from forming. Some mantras go further by actually interacting with the body in ways to stimulate and purify it.
- **Mantram** – A word or phrase that is spoken out loud, like a decree. Putting *right now* at the end of a mantram makes it particularly effective as it puts the emphasis on the now.[6]
- **MerKaBa** – The LightSpiritBody; an Egyptian term describing the energy field which surrounds all matter from individual atoms, to cells, to your entire body as a composite field, and likewise the Earth and other planets, Solar system, and so on eventually aggregating to encompass galaxies in composite fields similar to the ones seen at every level. When spun to its full potential this energy field looks much like the typical depiction of a UFO, or something like to two cymbals placed together to form a solid shape. This is the same shape that the Milky Way Galaxy assumes.
- **Nirvana** – The deeper, permanent unchanging reality behind the reality most of us see, disguised in the mundane world by the illusory power of **maya.**
- **Om**– Means the same thing in Hindu that 'I Am' has come to mean in English.
- **Om Namah Shivaya** – The most common Mantra used in India and the one known best in the West. One translation would be, "I bow to Shiva, my Inner Self."

- **Prana** – Also known as **chi, qi, ki,** or **Kundalini.** This is the energy flow in your body, or the energy coming to you from your **antarkarana.** It is the energy of consciousness. Prana is stored in your **tan tien,** the reservoir in your subtle body. The **kundalini** is at the base of the spine as a spiral of 3 ½ turns. The practice of meditation awakens it.
- **Reiki** – A form of therapy using hands on healing and special symbols. It was restored to consciousness by the Japanese Master Mikao Usui, who late in the 1800's sought out the lost information on reiki and was guided to it.[7]
- **Rohun** – A form of therapy where the therapist puts the customer into a meditative state and together they explore each chakra. The initial rounds ferret out karma associated with having been abused and later sessions work on how the customer was the perpetrator. The objective is to acknowledge the lessons learned, then release and heal any residue from them. The final of seven sessions in total is for reintegration of all the chakras into a unified field. The result is effectively many years of therapy in a relatively short period of time.
- **Samadhi** – Complete awareness of God, or when your mind and the mind of the universe become one. It is the fulfillment of the meditative practice of Yoga.[8]
- **Samurai** – The Japanese warrior class.
- **Sanskrit** – The active language in India thousands of years ago. The closest modern equivalent to it is Malayalam, the dialect of the state Kerala in India.
- **Satori** – Japanese for a sudden awakening of awareness, an epiphany.
- **Sensi** – Japanese for master teacher.
- **Shaman** – A Central Asian Tungus word referring to someone who uses a heightened state of awareness to enter the normally hidden subtle realities of the spirit world in order to seek help for themselves or others.
- **Shiva** – Sanskrit for God
- **Tan Tien** – The energy reservoir in your subtle body at the location of the abdomen, behind your naval. It is the true seat of consciousness.
- **Tao** – The state of zero interference manifested by enlightened beings who have eliminated all of their internal duality programs. The concept comes from Lao Tze, sometimes spelled Lao Tzu, whose ancient text, *Tao Te Ching*, is all that survives today from this wonderful teacher.
- **Third eye** – The pineal gland located in the center of the head. It is referred to in the scriptures as the third eye, star of the East, inner eye, dove descending from heaven, eye of Shiva, eye of intuition, the one-eye, and so on.[9]
- **Turiya** – Sanskrit for what we call the delta state, although it is much more than that - it is the foundation for all the states the mind can operate in.
- **Widdershins** – Counterclockwise or goddess direction circle dancing.
- **Yin/Yang** – The opposites that are the substance that duality, what we think of as the real world, is made of. For instance, up/down, male/female, East/West, right/left, logic/gestalt, hot/cold, right/wrong, and so on.
- **Yoga** – Means union, from the Sanskrit *yuj,* meaning to join. Literally a joining by conscious effort of self-integration with the Universal Spirit in oneness. There are many forms of yoga such as **kriya yoga** – the form of yoga that gives us the ultimate power of breathing. Babaji, who gave us this knowledge again in modern times, restored this ancient but lost form of yoga to consciousness, **karma yoga** – right action through service, **bhakti yoga** – worshiping the Supreme Being, **Jnana yoga** – scholarly reflection leading to enlightenment, and **raja yoga** – Meditating to achieve mastery of the mind and consciousness. **Raja yoga** is further differentiated by **hatha yoga** – mastering the mind via the physical and vital bodies, **mantra yoga** – the use of japa or repetition of the names of God to achieve mastery, and **kundalini yoga** – achieving superconscious perception and mental illumination by arousing of the kundalini in the body via breathing and concentration on the chakras.[10]
- **Zen** – Quoting Taisen Deshimaru, "Ch'an in Chinese; dhyana in Sanskrit. True, profound silence. Commonly translated as objectless concentration or mediation; or, the original, pure human spirit."[11]

INDEX

REFERENCE NOTES

Front and Back Cover
1. Pages 117 & 123, Thomas, Charles B., *Water Gardens for Plants and Fish*, T.F.H. Publications Inc., 1988
2. Page 36, State of Illinois Department of Conservation, *Aquatic Plants, Their Identification and Management*, Department of Conservation, Division of Fisheries, Springfield, IL 62706, Revised 1994

Author's Background and Acknowledgements
1. Thomas, Melvin; Geltmacher, Hal, *Combat Simulator Display Development*, Society for Information Display (SID), Vol. 9, No 4&5, Apr/May 93
2. Thomas, Melvin L.; Reining, Gale; Kelly, George, The *Display for Advanced Research and Training: An "Inexpensive" Answer to Tactical Simulation*, Proceedings of the Society of Photo Instrumentation Engineers (SPIE), San Jose, CA, (24 February through 1 March, 1991)
3. September 18th, 1998, *The International Academy of Enzyme Nutrition.* Signed by Howard F. Loomis, Jr., DC.

Illustrations
1. Page 114, Dryden, Gordon; and Vos, Jeannette, *The Learning Revolution*, Available via www.learning-revolution.com 1999. Original Source - Buzan, Tony, *Make the Most Of Your Mind*, Published by Pan, London.
2. Ibid, Pg 118. Original Source - Healy, Jane M., *Your Child's Growing Mind*, Doubleday, 666 fifth Avenue, New York, NY, 10103
3. Ibid, Pg 122. Original source - Healy, Jane M., *Your Child's Growing Mind*, Doubleday, 666 fifth Avenue, New York, NY, 10103
4. Ibid, Pg 117
5. Pages 31, 55, 74, Hannaford, Carla, *Smart Moves, why Learning is Not All in Your Head*, Great Ocean Publishers, 1995
6. Pages 388 (gakushiki - learning, scholarship) and 516 (kiwameru - investigate thoroughly, study exhaustively, master) Halpern, Jack, Editor in Chief, *The Kodansha Kanji Learner's Dictionary*, Kodansha America, Inc, 575 Lexington Aven, New York, NY, 10022, 1999
7. Page 124 Dryden, Gordon; and Vos, Jeannette, *The Learning Revolution*, Available via www.learning-revolution.com 1999. Original source - Vitale, Barbara Meiser, *Unicorns Are Real*, Jalmar Press, P. O. Box 1185, Torrance, CA 90505
8. Ibid, Pg 124
9. Page 79, Hannaford, Carla, *Smart Moves, why Learning is Not All in Your Head*, Great Ocean Publishers, 1995
10. Page 44, Brennen, Barbara Ann, *Hands of Light*, Bantam New Age Books, 1988
11. Page 168, Dryden, Gordon; and Vos, Jeannette, *The Learning Revolution*, Available via www.learning-revolution.com 1999
12. Page 27, Meier, Dave, *The Accelerated Learning Handbook*, McGraw-Hill, 2000
13. Plate 116, Kapit, Wynn, and Elson, Lawrence M., *The Anatomy Coloring Book*, Harper and Roe, 1977
14. Ibid, Plate 137
15. Plate 123, Kapit, Wynn, and Elson, Lawrence M., *The Anatomy Coloring Book*, Harper and Roe, 1977
16. Page 181, Hannaford, Carla, *Smart Moves, why Learning is Not All in Your Head*, Great Ocean Publishers, 1995
17. Ibid, Pg 179
18. Page 120, Dryden, Gordon; and Vos, Jeannette, *The Learning Revolution*, Available via www.learning-revolution.com 1999. Original source - Rose, Colin, *Master it Faster*, published by Accelerated Learning Systems, Aston Clinton, Aylesbury, Bucks, England.
19. Page 27, Brennen, Barbara Ann, *Light Emerging, The Journey of Personal Healing*, Bantam New Age Books, 1993
20. Front Cover, Buchanan, Douglas, *Uses of the Japa Mala*, Self Published, 2002 (See *Appendix H*)
21. Page 46, Pearce, Joseph Chilton, *The Biology of Transcendence, A blueprint of the Human Spirit*, Park Street Press, 2002
22. Page 51, Eden, Donna; David Feinstein, *Energy Medicine*, Penguin Putnam Inc., 1999
23. Page 179, Hannaford, Carla, *Smart Moves, why Learning is Not All in Your Head*, Great Ocean Publishers, 1995

Chapter 1 – THE PROMISE OF A CHILD
1. Pages 97, 101, Dryden, Gordon; and Vos, Jeannette, *The Learning Revolution*, Available via www.learning-revolution.com 1999
2. Ibid, pages 148, 187
3. Page 315, Raye, Marina, *Do You Have an Owner's Manual for Your Brain?* Action Press, 1991
4. Story told on the internet by Lloyd Glen about 1994 incident involving his son Brian.
5. Pages 134, 135, Pearce, Joseph Chilton, *Magical Child*, Penguin Group, 1992
6. Ibid, Page 136
7. Page 48, Millman, Dan, *Sacred Journey of the Peaceful Warrior*, H. J. Cramer Inc., 1991

8. http://www.labyrinthina.com/coral.htm
9. Pages 161-170, 196, Pearce, Joseph Chilton, *Magical Child*, Penguin Group, 1992
10. Dong, Paul; Raffill, Thomas E., *China's Super Psychics*, Marlowe & Company, 1997
11. Page 154, Pearce, Joseph Chilton, *Magical Child*, Penguin Group, 1992
12. Page xiv, Frumker, Sanford "Buddy," *Mind Map, Your Guide to Prosperity and Fulfillment*, Health Associates, Ltd., P.O. Box 188009, University Heights, Ohio 44118, 1994
13. www.barbarabrennan.com
14. Page 187, Dryden, Gordon; and Vos, Jeannette, *The Learning Revolution*, Available via www.learning-revolution.com 1999
15. http://www.labyrinthina.com/coral.htm
16. Page 3, Pearce, Joseph Chilton, *Magical Child*, Penguin Group, 1992
17. Page 163, Williamson, Marianne, *A Return to Love*, Harper Collins, 1992

Chapter 2 – YOUR BRAIN
1. Page 13, Buzan, Tony, *Make the Most of Your Mind*, Simon and Schuster, New York, 1984
2. Savant, Marilyn Vos, *The Power of Logical Thinking*, St. Martin's Press, 1996
3. Carroll, Lee; Tober, Jan, *The Indigo Children*, Hay House, Inc., 1999
4. Pgs 51, 153, 171, 265, 290, in Kryon, *Kryon 2000, Passing the Marker*, The Kryon Writings Inc, 2000
5. Page 26, Hannaford, Carla, *Smart Moves, why Learning is Not All in Your Head*, Great Ocean Publishers, 1995
6. Page 115, Dryden, Gordon; and Vos, Jeannette, *The Learning Revolution*, Available via www.learning-revolution.com 1999
7. Page 169, Pearce, Joseph Chilton, *Magical Child*, Penguin Group, 1992
8. Page 31, Hannaford, Carla, *Smart Moves, why Learning is Not All in Your Head*, Great Ocean Publishers, 1995
9. Pages 17, 31, Healy, Jane M., *Your Child's Growing Mind*, Doubleday (A division of Random House) 1987
10. Pages 118, 122, Dryden, Gordon; and Vos, Jeannette, *The Learning Revolution*, Available via www.learning-revolution.com 1999
11. Pages 55, 74, Hannaford, Carla, *Smart Moves, why Learning is Not All in Your Head*, Great Ocean Publishers, 1995
12. Ibid, Pages 74, 75
13. Pages 115, 117, 119, 123, Dryden, Gordon; and Vos, Jeannette, *The Learning Revolution*, Available via www.learning-revolution.com 1999
14. Page 169, Pearce, Joseph Chilton, *Magical Child*, Penguin Group, 1992
15. Page 36, Hannaford, Carla, *Smart Moves, why Learning is Not All in Your Head*, Great Ocean Publishers, 1995
16. Ibid, pgs 51, 53
17. Page 129, Dryden, Gordon; and Vos, Jeannette, *The Learning Revolution*, Available via www.learning-revolution.com 1999
18. Page 554, Yogananda, Paramahansa, *Autobiography of a Yogi*, Self-Realization Fellowship, 1993
19. Ibid, pages 355, 389
20. Page 2, Vitale, Barbara Meister, *Unicorn's Are Real, A Right-brained Approach to Learning*, Jalmar Press, P. O. Box 1185, Torrance, CA 90505, 1982
21. Page 79, Hannaford, Carla, *Smart Moves, why Learning is Not All in Your Head*, Great Ocean Publishers, 1995
22. Ibid, pages 78, 79
23. Pages 124, 125, Dryden, Gordon; and Vos, Jeannette, *The Learning Revolution*, Available via www.learning-revolution.com 1999
24. Page 80, Hannaford, Carla, *Smart Moves, why Learning is Not All in Your Head*, Great Ocean Publishers, 1995
25. Page 23, Shlain, Leonard, *The alphabet Versus the Goddess*, Penguin/Compass, 1998
26. Page 80, Hannaford, Carla, *Smart Moves, why Learning is Not All in Your Head*, Great Ocean Publishers, 1995
27. Pages 8, 9, Vol 1 of Melchizedek, Drunvalo, *The Ancient Secret of the Flower of Life*, Light Technology Publishing, Published in 1998 for Vol 1, and 2000 for Vol 2
28. Page 80, Hannaford, Carla, *Smart Moves, why Learning is Not All in Your Head*, Great Ocean Publishers, 1995
29. Ibid, pages 84, 92
30. Pages 132, 133, Pearce, Joseph Chilton, *Magical Child*, Penguin Group, 1992
31. Page 98, Woolf, *A Room of One's Own*, Harvest Books; ISBN: 0156787334; Reissue edition, January 1990
32. Houston, Jean, *The Possible Human: A course in Enhancing you Physical, Mental, and Creative Abilities.* Los Angeles: J. P. Tarcher, 1982
33. Pages 24, 25, Webb, Terry Wyler and Douglas Webb, *Accelerated Learning with Music Trainer's Manual*, Accelerated Learning Systems, 2213 Georgetown, Denton, Texas, 76201, 1990

Chapter 3 – YOUR MIND
1. Page 185, Hill, Napoleon, *Think and Grow Rich*, Fawcett Crest, 1960
2. Moody, Raymond, M.D., *Live After Life*, Bantam Books, 1975

3. Page 32, Hannaford, Carla, *Smart Moves, why Learning is Not All in Your Head*, Great Ocean Publishers, 1995
4. Email from Rev Douglas Buchanan
5. Intro, Vitale, Barbara Meister, *Unicorn's Are Real, A Right-brained Approach to Learning*, Jalmar Press, P. O. Box 1185, Torrance, CA 90505, 1982

Chapter 4 – YOUR STATES OF BEING
1. Page 61, Brennen, Barbara Ann, *Hands of Light*, Bantam New Age Books, 1988
2. Page 314, Vol 1 of Melchizedek, Drunvalo, *The Ancient Secret of the Flower of Life*, Light Technology Publishing, Published in 1998 for Vol 1, and 2000 for Vol 2
3. Page 28, Braden, Gregg, *Awakening to Zero Point, The Collective Initiation*, Radio Bookstore press, 1997
4. Page 30, Ibid
5. Pages 396, 397, Vol 2 of Melchizedek, Drunvalo, *The Ancient Secret of the Flower of Life*, Light Technology Publishing, Published in 1998 for Vol 1, and 2000 for Vol 2
6. Page 28, Williamson, Maryianne, *A Return to Love, Reflections on the Principles of A course in Miracles,* Harper Collins, 1992
7. Page 54, Millman, Dan, *Sacred Journey of the Peaceful Warrior*, H. J. Cramer Inc., 1991
8. Page 181, Dryden, Gordon; and Vos, Jeannette, *The Learning Revolution*, Available via www.learning-revolution.com 1999
9. Page 429, Reed, Henry and Cayce, Charles Thomas, *On Mysteries of the Mind*, Gramercy Books, 1990
10. Email from Douglas Buchanan
11. www.bobfrissell.com
12. Page 71, Ferrucci, Piero, *What We May Be*, J. P. Tarcher, Inc., 1982
13. Dryden, Gordon; and Vos, Jeannette, *The Learning Revolution Companion 50 minute Video*, Available via www.learning-revolution.com, 1999
14. Page 176, Pearce, Joseph Chilton, *Magical Child*, Penguin Group, 1992
15. Page 311, Shlain, Leonard, *The alphabet Versus the Goddess*, Penguin/Compass, 1998
16. Page 27, Meier, Dave, *The Accelerated Learning Handbook*, McGraw-Hill, 2000
17. Email from Douglas Buchanan
18. Pages 378, 379, Shlain, Leonard, *The alphabet Versus the Goddess*, Penguin/Compass, 1998
19. Ibid, page 18
20. Ibid, page 26
21. Ibid, Chapter 4
22. Email from Douglas Buchanan
23. Page 314, Vol 1 of Melchizedek, Drunvalo, *The Ancient Secret of the Flower of Life*, Light Technology Publishing, Published in 1998 for Vol 1, and 2000 for Vol 2
24. www.llewellynjournal.com/article/301/
25. Pages 84, 210, Hannaford, Carla, *Smart Moves, why Learning is Not All in Your Head*, Great Ocean Publishers, 1995
26. Pages 382, 383, Shlain, Leonard, *The alphabet Versus the Goddess*, Penguin/Compass, 1998
27. Ibid, page 385
28. Ibid, pages 384, 385
29. Page 57, Dryden, Gordon; and Vos, Jeannette, *The Learning Revolution*, Available via www.learning-revolution.com 1999
30. Ibid, page 243.
31. Pages 54, 58, Hannaford, Carla, *Smart Moves, why Learning is Not All in Your Head*, Great Ocean Publishers, 1995
32. Ibid, page 67
33. Page 367, Reed, Henry and Cayce, Charles Thomas, *On Mysteries of the Mind*, Gramercy Books, 1990
34. Page 185, Hill, Napoleon, *Think and Grow Rich*, Fawcett Crest Book, 1960
35. Page 131, Raye, Marina, *Do You Have an Owner's Manual for Your Brain?* Action Press, 1991
36. Pages 106, 133 & 163, Hannaford, Carla, *Smart Moves, why Learning is Not All in Your Head*, Great Ocean Publishers, 1995
37. Page 316, Raye, Marina, *Do You Have an Owner's Manual for Your Brain?* Action Press, 1991
38. Page 214, Rich, Katherine Russell, *In a Single Stroke*, The Oprah Magazine, Oct, 2002.
39. Page 225, Dryden, Gordon; and Vos, Jeannette, *The Learning Revolution*, Available via www.learning-revolution.com 1999
40. Smith, Penelope, Advanced Interspecies Communication, When Animals Speak, Beyond Words Publishing, Inc., 1999.
41. Page 152, Hannaford, Carla, *Smart Moves, why Learning is Not All in Your Head*, Great Ocean Publishers, 1995
42. Pages 26, 27, Hannaford, Carla, *Awakening the Child Heart*, Hannaford, 2002
43. Yogananda, Paramanhansa, *Scientific Healing Affirmations*, Self-Realization Fellowship, Ninth Printing, 1990
44. Page 61, Nelson, Ruby, *The Door of Everything*, Devores Publications, (No publishing date)
45. Page 189, Knight, J. Z., *A state of Mind, My Story, Ramtha, The Adventure Begins*, A Warner Communications Book, 1987

46. Page 517, Yogananda, Paramahansa, *Autobiography of a Yogi*, Self-Realization Fellowship, 1993
47. Page 429, Reed, Henry and Cayce, Charles Thomas, *On Mysteries of the Mind*, Gramercy Books, 1990
48. Page 48, Dean, Douglas, J; Mihalasky S. Ostrander and L. Schroeder, *Executive ESP*, Englewood Cliffs: Prentice-Hall, 1974
49. Page 21, Raye, Marina, *Do You Have an Owner's Manual for Your Brain?* Action Press, 1991
50. Page 99, Pearce, Joseph Chilton, *Magical Child*, Penguin Group, 1992
51. Page 21, Morimitsu, Phil, *In The Company of ECK MASTERS*, Illuminated Way Publishing, 1987

Chapter 5 – YOUR VISION
1. Pages 42, 44, Buzan, Tony, *Speed-reading*, Plume, 1991
2. Pages 49, 54, 90, Musashi, Miyamoto, *A Book of Five Rings*, The Overlook Press, 1974
3. Page 45, Scheele, Paul R., *PhotoReading*, Learning Strategies Corporation, 900 East Wayzata Blvd, Wayzat, MN 55391-1836, 1999
4. Page 216, Pearce, Joseph Chilton, *Magical Child*, Penguin Group, 1992
5. Page 9, Musashi, Miyamoto, *A Book of Five Rings*, The Overlook Press, 1974
6. Pages 24, 25, Shlain, Leonard, *The alphabet Versus the Goddess*, Penguin/Compass, 1998
7. Email from Douglas Buchanan
8. Chapter 5, Key, Wilson Bryan, *Subliminal Seduction*, Penguin Group, 1974
9. Key, Wilson Bryan, *The Age of Manipulation*, Madison Books, 1989
10. Key, Wilson Bryan, *The Clam-Plate Orgy*, A Signet Book, 1980
11. Page 135, Dryden, Gordon; and Vos, Jeannette, *The Learning Revolution*, Available via www.learning-revolution.com 1999
12. Page 47, Scheele, Paul R., *PhotoReading*, Learning Strategies Corporation, 900 East Wayzata Blvd, Wayzat, MN 55391-1836, 1999
13. Page 179, Allegri, Renzo, *Padre Pio, Man of Hope*, Servant Publications, 2000
14. Page 7, Vol 1 of Melchizedek, Drunvalo, *The Ancient Secret of the Flower of Life*, Light Technology Publishing, published in 1998 for Vol 1, and 2000 for Vol 2
15. Preface, page x, *A Course in Miracles*, Foundation for Inner Peace, 1992
16. Page 289, *Stedman's Medical Dictionary*, The Williams & Wilkins Company, Baltimore, 22nd Edition, 1972
17. Page 1372, *Gray's Anatomy*, 35th British Edition, W.B. Saunders Company.
18. Page 48, Brennen, Barbara Ann, *Hands of Light*, Bantam New Age Books, 1988
19. Page 3, Vol 2 of Melchizedek, Drunvalo, *The Ancient Secret of the Flower of Life*, Light Technology Publishing, Published in 1998 for Vol 1, and 2000 for Vol 2
20. Chapter 14, Ostrander, Sheila; Schroeder, Lynn, *Psychic Discoveries Behind the Iron Curtain*, Bantam Books, 1970
21. Pages 218-226, Ostrander, Sheila; Schroeder, Lynn, *Super Learning*, A Laurel/Confucian Press Book, 1979
22. Page 221, Ibid
23. Pages 164, 165, Raye, Marina, *Do You Have an Owner's Manual for Your Brain?* Action Press, 1991
24. Page 614, Blake, William, *The complete Writing of William Blake*, Edited by Geoffrey Keynes, Oxford: Oxford University Press, 1966
25. Page 9, Foucault, Michel, *This Is Not a Pipe*, Berkley; University of California Press, 1983
26. Page 4, Pearce, Joseph Chilton, *The Crack in the Cosmic Egg*, Park Street Press, 2002

Chapter 6 – DIVERSITY IN LEARNING
1. Page 367, Dryden, Gordon; and Vos, Jeannette, *The Learning Revolution*, Available via www.learning-revolution.com 1999
2. Page 101, Pearce, Joseph Chilton, *The Biology of Transcendence, A blueprint of the Human Spirit*, Park Street Press, 2002
3. Page 181, Hannaford, Carla, *Smart Moves, why Learning is Not All in Your Head*, Great Ocean Publishers, 1995
4. Hannaford, Carla, *The Dominance Factor*, Great Ocean Publishers, 1997
5. Page 179, Hannaford, Carla, *Smart Moves, why Learning is Not All in Your Head*, Great Ocean Publishers, 1995
6. Ibid, page 195
7. Page 154, Hannaford, Carla, *The Dominance Factor*, Great Ocean Publishers, 1997
8. Page 345, Dryden, Gordon; and Vos, Jeannette, *The Learning Revolution*, Available via www.learning-revolution.com 1999
9. Pages 123-132, Healy, Jane M., *Your Child's Growing Mind*, Doubleday (A division of Random House) 1987
10. Chapter 15, Brennen, Barbara Ann, *Light Emerging, The Journey of Personal Healing*, Bantam New Age Books, 1993
11. Page 190, Hannaford, Carla, *Smart Moves, why Learning is Not All in Your Head*, Great Ocean Publishers, 1995
12. Pages 14, 33, Vitale, Barbara Meister, *Unicorn's Are Real, A Right-brained Approach to Learning*, Jalmar Press, P. O. Box 1185, Torrance, CA 90505, 1982

Chapter 7 – NATURAL LEARNING
1. Page 185, Hannaford, Carla, *Smart Moves, why Learning is Not All in Your Head*, Great Ocean Publishers, 1995
2. Page 27, Buzan, Tony, *Speed-reading*, Plume, 1991

3. Ibid, page 15
4. Ibid, page 57
5. Page 15, Scheele, Paul R., *PhotoReading*, Learning Strategies Corporation, 900 East Wayzata Blvd, Wayzat, MN 55391-1836, 1999
6. Ibid, pages 20, 58, 60 and 64
7. Page 70, Buzan, Tony, *Speed-reading*, Plume, 1991
8. Page 91, Ostrander, Sheila; Schroeder, Lynn, *Super Learning*, Dell Publishing Co., 1979
9. Ibid, page 134
10. Ibid, page 19
11. Ibid, page 13,14
12. Ibid, page 63
13. Ibid, pages 62, 70, 138
14. Ibid, page 64
15. Ibid, page 15, 134
16. Ibid, page 134, 135
17. Ibid, page 20
18. Ibid, page 68, Chapter 7
19. Pages 309-311, Dryden, Gordon; and Vos, Jeannette, *The Learning Revolution*, Available via www.learning-revolution.com 1999
20. Pages 34, 212, Ostrander, Sheila; Schroeder, Lynn, *Super Learning*, Dell Publishing Co., 1979
21. Webb, Terry Wyler and Webb, Douglas, *Accelerated Learning With Music*, Accelerated Learning Systems, 1990
22. Webb, Terry Wyler and Webb, Douglas, *Accelerated Learning with Music Trainer's Manual*, Accelerated Learning Systems, 2213 Georgetown, Denton, Texas, 76201, 1990
23. Page 378, Rose, Colin and Malcom J. Nicholl, *Accelerated Learning for the 21st Century, The Six-Step Plan to Unlock Your MASTER-mind*, Dell, 1997
24. Pages 176-181, 244, Ostrander, Sheila; Schroeder, Lynn, *Super Learning*, Dell Publishing Co., 1979
25. Page 38, Hannaford, Carla, *Smart Moves, why Learning is Not All in Your Head*, Great Ocean Publishers, 1995
26. Page 224, Pearce, Joseph Chilton, *Magical Child*, Penguin Group, 1992

Chapter 8 – SUPER RESULTS LIKE SUPER SCANNING
1. Email from Douglas Buchanan
2. Page 61, Dean, Douglas; J. Mihalasky, S. Ostrander, and L. Schroeder, *Executive ESP*, Englewood Cliffs: Prentice-Hall, 1974
3. Page 10, Buzan, Tony, *The Brain User's Guide*, E. P. Dutton, Inc., 1983
4. Pages 38-40, Looking Horse, Chief Arvol, *White Buffalo Teachings*, www.Dreamkeepers.net, 2001
5. Ibid
6. Email from Douglas Buchanan
7. Page 82, Buzan, Tony, *Speed-reading*, Plume, 1991
8. Page 92, Scheele, Paul R., *PhotoReading*, Learning Strategies Corporation, 900 East Wayzata Blvd, Wayzat, MN 55391-1836, 1999
9. Pages 50, 149, 151, Hannaford, Carla, *The Dominance Factor*, Great Ocean Publishers, 1997
10. Pages 47, 48, 112, 114, Russell, C. W., *The Life of Cardinal Mezzofanti*, London: Logman, Brown, and Co., 1858
11. Page 21, Shlain, Leonard, *The alphabet Versus the Goddess*, Penguin/Compass, 1998
12. Email from Douglas Buchanan
13. Ibid
14. Sugrue, Thomas, *There is a River: The Story of Edgar Cayce*, A.R.E. Press; Revised edition, February 1997
15. Stearn, Jess, *Edgar Cayce, The Sleeping Prophet*, Bantam Books; ISBN: 0553260855; Reissue edition, February 1990
16. Page 66 , Brennen, Barbara Ann, *Hands of Light*, Bantam New Age Books, 1988
17. Pages 115, 117, 121, 122, 127, 128, 133, 137, 149, 155, 168, Pearce, Joseph Chilton, *Magical Child*, Penguin Group, 1992
18. Pages 451, 452, Melchizedek, Drunvalo, *The Ancient Secret of the Flower of Life*, Light Technology Publishing, Published in 1998 for Vol 1, and 2000 for Vol 2
19. Page 18, 20, Buchanan, Douglas, *Uses of the Japa Mala*, 2002
20. Page 20, Shlain, Leonard, *The alphabet Versus the Goddess*, Penguin/Compass, 1998
21. Pages 38, 39, Frumker, Sanford "Buddy," *Mind Map, Your Guide to Prosperity and Fulfillment*, Health Associates, Ltd., P.O. Box 188009, University Heights, Ohio 44118, 1994
22. Ibid, page 37
23. Pages 18, 20, Buchanan, Douglas, *Uses of the Japa Mala*, 2002
24. Page 405, 406, Reed, Henry; Cayce, Charles Thomas, *Edgar Cayce on Mysteries of the Mind*, Gramercy Books, 1990 reprint

25. Page 171, Dryden, Gordon; and Vos, Jeannette, *The Learning Revolution*, Available via www.learning-revolution.com 1999
26. Page 13, Buchanan, Douglas, *Uses of the Japa Mala*, 2002
27. Page 70, Scheele, Paul R., *PhotoReading*, Learning Strategies Corporation, 900 East Wayzata Blvd, Wayzat, MN 55391-1836, 1999

Chapter 9 – WHAT LEARNING WITH MOM AND DAD MEANS

1. Email from Douglas Buchanan
2. Ibid
3. Ibid
4. Pages 129, 136, 158, 159, and Chapter XVII, Russell, C. W., *The Life of Cardinal Mezzofanti*, London: Logman, Brown, and Co., 1858
5. Email from Douglas Buchanan. Information in letter from Antonio Richard Hudson, Department of Phonetics and Linguistics,University College London,Gower Street,London WC1E 6BT. Source of information is Antonio Ruiz Mariscal. He granted permission to disseminate this information.
6. Pages 478, 479, Russell, C. W., *The Life of Cardinal Mezzofanti*, London: Logman, Brown, and Co., 1858
7. Page 97, Scheele, Paul R, *PhotoReading*, Learning Strategies Corporation, 900 East Wayzata Blvd, Wayzat, MN 55391-1836, 1999
8. Page 10, Pages 478, 479, Russell, C. W., *The Life of Cardinal Mezzofanti*, London: Logman, Brown, and Co., 1858
9. Pages 35, 36, Frumker, Sanford "Buddy," *Mind Map, Your Guide to Prosperity and Fulfillment*, Health Associates, Ltd., P.O. Box 188009, University Heights, Ohio 44118, 1994
10. Page 403, Reed, Henry; Cayce, Charles Thomas, *Edgar Cayce on Mysteries of the Mind*, Gramercy Books, 1990 reprint
11. Pages 86-90, Buzan, Tony and Dixon, Terence, *The Evolving Brain*, International Thompson Publishing, July, 1978
12. Page 439, Reed, Henry; Cayce, Charles Thomas, *Edgar Cayce on Mysteries of the Mind*, Gramercy Books, 1990 reprint
13. Pages 22-29, Hill, Napoleon, *Think and Grow Rich*, Renaissance Books; ISBN: 158063205X; October 2001
14. Email from Douglas Buchanan,
15. Page 2, Stone, Joshua David, *How to Teach Ascension Classes*, Light Technologies Publishing, 1998
16. Page 459, Reed, Henry; Cayce, Charles Thomas, *Edgar Cayce on Mysteries of the Mind*, Gramercy Books, 1990 reprint
17. Chapter 6, Ostrander, Sheila; Schroeder, Lynn, *Super Learning*, Dell Publishing Co., 1979
18. Page 124, Dean, Douglas, J; Mihalasky, S. Ostrander, and L. Schroeder, *Executive ESP*, Englewood Cliffs: Prentice-Hall, 1974
19. Junger, Sebastian, *The Perfect Storm*, Harper Mass market Paperbacks; ISBN: 006101351X; July 1998
20. *Anchorage Daily News*, August 26th, 2001
21. Robertson, Morgan, *Futility or The Wreck of the Titan*, Buccaneer Books, ISBN: 0899668216, 1991
22. Comparative information found at: http://members.aol.com/ken63728/morgan.htm
23. Russell, Walter, *The Secret of Working Knowingly with God*, The University of Science and Philosophy, 1993
24. www.philosophy.org
25. Page 146, Braden, Gregg, *Awakening to Zero Point, The Collective Initiation*, Radio Bookstore press, 1997
26. Page 22, 23, Ostrander, Sheila; Schroeder, Lynn, *Super Learning*, Dell Publishing Co., 1979
27. Email from Douglas Buchanan
28. Page 160, Page 22, 23, Ostrander, Sheila; Schroeder, Lynn, *Super Learning*, Dell Publishing Co., 1979
29. Page 98, Dean, Douglas, J; Mihalasky, S. Ostrander, and L. Schroeder, *Executive ESP*, Englewood Cliffs: Prentice-Hall, 1974
30. Email from Douglas Buchanan
31. Page 202, Pearce, Joseph Chilton, *Magical Child*, Penguin Group, 1992

Chapter 10 – DEVELOPING YOUR OWN RITUALS

1. Page 184, Dean, Douglas, J; Mihalasky, S. Ostrander, and L. Schroeder, *Executive ESP*, Englewood Cliffs: Prentice-Hall, 1974
2. Page 29, Gawain, Shakti, *Creative Visualization*, Nataraj Publishing, 1995
3. Page 185, Dean, Douglas, J; Mihalasky, S. Ostrander, and L. Schroeder, *Executive ESP*, Englewood Cliffs: Prentice-Hall, 1974
4. Pages 84, 101, Palmer, Harry, *Living Deliberately, the Discovery and Development of Avatar*, Star's Edge International, 1994
5. Page 127, Raye, Marina, *Do You Have an Owner's Manual for Your Brain?* Action Press, 1991
6. Page 50, Summer Rain, Mary, *Spirit Song*, Donning Company/Publishers, 1985
7. Page 61, Orr, Leonard, *Breaking the Death Habit, the Science of Everlasting Life*, Frog Ltd., 1998
8. Buchanan, Douglas, *Uses of the Japa Mala*, 2002
9. Page 8, Key, Wilson Bryan, *The Age of Manipulation*, Madison Books, 1989
10. Page 24, Key, Wilson Bryan, *Subliminal Seduction*, Penguin Group, 1974
11. Ibid
12. Key, Wilson Bryan, *The Clam-Plate Orgy*, A Signet Book, 1980
13. Gass, Robert; On Wings of Song, *Om Namaha Shivaya*, Spring Hill Music, 1996

Chapter 11 – PUTTING IT ALL TOGETHER

1. Page 272, Dryden, Gordon; and Vos, Jeannette, *The Learning Revolution*, Available via www.learning-revolution.com 1999
2. Page 152, Millman, Dan, *The Warrior Athlete, Body, Mind & Spirit*, Stillpoint Publishing, 1979
3. Pages 454, 455, Reed, Henry; Cayce, Charles Thomas, *Edgar Cayce on Mysteries of the Mind*, Gramercy Books, 1990 reprint
4. Page 12, Key, Wilson Bryan, *The Age of Manipulation*, Madison Books, 1989
5. Page 87, Dyer, Wayne, *Staying on the Path*, Hay House, Inc. 1995
6. Page 73, St. James, Elaine, *Inner Simplicity, 100 Ways to Regain peace and Nourish Your soul*, Hyperion, New York, 1995
7. Email, J. C. Gainer
8. Page 165, Williamson, Marianne, *A Return to Love, Reflections on the Principles of A course in Miracles*, Harper Collins, 1992

Chapter 12 – EXCELLENCE IN THE CORPORATE WORLD

1. Page 201, Pearce, Joseph Chilton, *Magical Child*, Penguin Group, 1992
2. Pages 130, 131, Covey, Stephen R., *The 7 Habits of Highly Effective People*, Simon and Schuster, 1989
3. Ibid, page 11
4. Page 185, Hannaford, Carla, *Smart Moves, why Learning is Not All in Your Head*, Great Ocean Publishers, 1995
5. Page 145, Hannaford, Carla, *The Dominance Factor*, Great Ocean Publishers, 1997
6. Executive Reports - You Can profit by Executive Hunches, *International Management*, March 1966
7. Mihalasky, John, "Extrasensory Perception in management," *Advanced Management Journal*, July 1967
8. "Question: What do Some Executives have More of? Answer: Intuition, Maybe." *Think*, Nov-Dec 1969
9. "How Extrasensory perception Can Play a Role in Idea Generation," *American Society of Mechanical Engineers Publication*, No. 72-De-5, 1972
10. Page 134, Covey, Stephen R., *The 7 Habits of Highly Effective People*, Simon and Schuster, 1989
11. Dean, Douglas, J; Mihalasky, S. Ostrander, and L. Schroeder, *Executive ESP*, Englewood Cliffs: Prentice-Hall, 1974
12. Page 198, Ostrander, Sheila; Schroeder, Lynn, *Super Learning*, Dell Publishing Co., 1979
13. Page 197, Dean, Douglas, J; Mihalasky, S. Ostrander, and L. Schroeder, *Executive ESP*, Englewood Cliffs: Prentice-Hall, 1974
14. Ibid, Page 4
15. Ibid, Page 4
16. Pages 198, 201-203, 207, Ostrander, Sheila; Schroeder, Lynn, *Super Learning*, Dell Publishing Co., 1979
17. Page 53, Dean, Douglas, J; Mihalasky, S. Ostrander, and L. Schroeder, *Executive ESP*, Englewood Cliffs: Prentice-Hall, 1974
18. Ibid, Page 7
19. Ibid, page 204
20. Ibid, page 97,
21. Ibid, page 46
22. Page 47, Dean, Douglas, J; Mihalasky, S. Ostrander, and L. Schroeder, *Executive ESP*, Englewood Cliffs: Prentice-Hall, 1974
23. Email from Douglas Buchanan
24. Page 46, Dean, Douglas, J; Mihalasky, S. Ostrander, and L. Schroeder, *Executive ESP*, Englewood Cliffs: Prentice-Hall, 1974
25. Ibid, Page 212
26. Page 149, Murphy, Dr. Joseph; Revised by Ian McMahan, Ph.D., *The Power of your Subconscious Mind*, Bantam Books, 2001
27. Page 150, Hannaford, Carla, *Smart Moves, why Learning is Not All in Your Head*, Great Ocean Publishers, 1995
28. Pages 21, 22, Berg, Yehuda, *The Power of Kabbalah*, The Kabbalah Centre, ISBN: 1-57189-180-3, September, 2000
29. Page 97, Dean, Douglas; J. Mihalasky, S. Ostrander, and L. Schroeder, *Executive ESP*, Englewood Cliffs: Prentice-Hall, 1974
30. Ibid, page 170
31. Laski, Margharita, *Ecstasy: A study of Some Secular and Religious Experiences*, Indiana University Press, 1962
32. Page 187, Pearce, Joseph Chilton, *The Biology of Transcendence, A blueprint of the Human Spirit*, Park Street Press, 2002
33. Page 150, Murphy, Dr. Joseph; Revised by Ian McMahan, Ph.D., *The Power of your Subconscious Mind*, Bantam Books, 2001
34. Page 189, Pearce, Joseph Chilton, *The Biology of Transcendence, A blueprint of the Human Spirit*, Park Street Press, 2002
35. Page 134, Pearce, Joseph Chilton, *Magical Child*, Penguin Group, 1992
36. Ibid, Page 204
37. Page 195, Pearce, Joseph Chilton, *The Biology of Transcendence, A blueprint of the Human Spirit*, Park Street Press, 2002
38. Page 67, Pearce, Joseph Chilton, *Magical Child*, Penguin Group, 1992
39. www.lightforhealth.com. Light for Health corporation, 942 Twisted Oak Lane, Buffalo Grove, IL 60089, 800.468.1104
40. Page 150, Hannaford, Carla, *Smart Moves, why Learning is Not All in Your Head*, Great Ocean Publishers, 1995

41. www.sei.cmm.edu
42. Deming, W. Edward, *Out of the Crisis*, MIT Press; ISBN: 0262541157; 1st edition, August 11, 2000
43. Page 253, Pearce, Joseph Chilton, *The Biology of Transcendence, A blueprint of the Human Spirit*, Park Street Press, 2002
44. Pages 65, 67, Dryden, Gordon; and Vos, Jeannette, *The Learning Revolution*, Available via www.learning-revolution.com 1999
45. Pages 74, 75, Dean, Douglas, J; Mihalasky, S. Ostrander, and L. Schroeder, *Executive ESP*, Englewood Cliffs: Prentice-Hall, 1974
46. Page 90, Buzan, Tony and Dixon, Terence, *The Evolving Brain*, International Thompson Publishing, July, 1978

Chapter 13 – OUR SUPER POTENTIAL

1. Page 199, Pearce, Joseph Chilton, *Magical Child*, Penguin Group, 1992
2. Page 105, Dryden, Gordon; and Vos, Jeannette, *The Learning Revolution*, Available via www.learning-revolution.com 1999
3. Ibid, page 497
4. www.subdyn.com
5. Scheele, Paul, *The PhotoReading Whole Mind System*, Learning Strategies Corporation, ISBN: 0925480533; 2000
6. Page 38, Ostrander, Sheila; Schroeder, Lynn, *Super Learning*, Dell Publishing Co., 1979
7. Page 46, Pearce, Joseph Chilton, *The Biology of Transcendence, A blueprint of the Human Spirit*, Park Street
8. Page 153, Hannaford, Carla, *The Dominance Factor*, Great Ocean Publishers, 1997
9. Page 51, Pearce, Joseph Chilton, *The Biology of Transcendence, A blueprint of the Human Spirit*, Park Street
10. Page 153, Hannaford, Carla, *The Dominance Factor*, Great Ocean Publishers, 1997
11. Page 81, Pearce, Joseph Chilton, *The Biology of Transcendence, A blueprint of the Human Spirit*, Park Street
12. Pages 35, 35, Russell, C. W., *The Life of Cardinal Mezzofanti*, London: Logman, Brown, and Co., 1858
13. Page xi, Prophet, Mark L & Elizabeth Claire, *Saint Germain on Alchemy, Formulas for Self-Transformation*, Summit University Press, 1993
14. Page 167, 'I AM' Activity, *"I AM" Fundamentals, Series I*, Saint Germain, Press, Inc., 1992
15. Page 64, Orr, Leonard, *Breaking the Death Habit, the Science of Everlasting Life*, Frog Ltd., 1998
16. Page 207, Allegri, Renzo, *Padre Pio, Man of Hope*, Servant Publications, 2000
17. Murphet, Howard, *Sai Baba, Man of Miracles*, Samuel Weiser, Inc., 1973
18. Baba, Sai: http://www.gurusim.com/lordsai.htm   http://www.askbaba.net/saibabagita/index.html http://members.ozemail.com.au/~vsivasup/sai/index.html Index to home pages about Sai Baba. His Address: Bhagawan Sri Sathya Sai Baba, Prashanti Nilayam, Puttaparthy, District Ananthapur, Andhra Pradesh 515134, INDIA
19. Page 261, 'I AM' Activity, 4-Ascended Master Saint Germain, Ascended *Master Instruction*, Saint Germain, Press, Inc., 1994
20. Pages 5, 110, Carroll, Lee; Tober, Jan, *The Indigo Children*, Hay House, Inc., 1999
21. Twyman, James; Neale Donald Walsch, *Emissary of Love: The Psychic Children Speak to the World*, Hampton Roads Publishing Co; ISBN: 1571743235; (March 2002)
22. Page 10, Carroll, Lee; Tober, Jan, *The Indigo Children*, Hay House, Inc., 1999
23. Ibid, page 7
24. Pages 249-253, Pearce, Joseph Chilton, *The Biology of Transcendence, A blueprint of the Human Spirit*, Park Street Press, 2002
25. Page 33, People Magazine, 10/3/94
26. http://leo.stcloudstate.edu/kaleidoscope/volume6/page8.html
27. Pages 37-43, Looking Horse, Chief Arvol, *White Buffalo Teachings*, www.dreamkeepers.net, 2001
28. Ibid
29. Ibid, page 35

Chapter 14 – AIR, WATER, and FUEL

1. Page 70, Ostrander, Sheila; Schroeder, Lynn, *Super Learning*, Dell Publishing Co., 1979
2. Page 146, Hannaford, Carla, *Smart Moves, why Learning is Not All in Your Head*, Great Ocean Publishers, 1995
3. Page xix, Orr, Leonard, *Breaking the Death Habit, the Science of Everlasting Life*, Frog Ltd., 1998
4. Edgar Cayce reading 1773-1. Found on page 110 of, Reilly, Harold J, Brod, Ruth Hagy, *The Edgar Cayce Handbook for Health Through Drugless Therapy*, MacMillan Publishing Co., 1975
5. Page 91, Orr, Leonard, *Breaking the Death Habit, the Science of Everlasting Life*, Frog Ltd., 1998
6. Pages 1, 25; Orr, Leonard, *Breath Awareness*, Published by Inspiration University, POB 118, Walton, NY, 13856, USA, ISBN 0-945793-02-2, 1988
7. Page 309, Vol 2 of Melchizedek, Drunvalo, *The Ancient Secret of the Flower of Life*, Light Technology Publishing, Published in 1998 for Vol 1, and 2000 for Vol 2
8. Ibid, Volume 1, pg 115
9. Page 352, Kryon, *Kryon 2000, Passing the Marker*, The Kryon Writings Inc, 2000
10. Pages 278, 279 & 552, Yogananda, Paramahansa, *Autobiography of a Yogi*, Self-Realization Fellowship, 1993

11. Much of the information from this section is taken from Bio-Hydration Research Lab's web site, www.hydrateforlife.com, and their informative CD, Penta Water CD - Water Myths and Water Magic, Facts everyone must know about the water they drink.

12. Page 138, Hannaford, Carla, *Smart Moves, why Learning is Not All in Your Head*, Great Ocean Publishers, 1995

13. Bio-Hydration Research Lab's web site, www.hydrateforlife.com, and their informative CD, Penta Water CD - Water Myths and Water Magic, Facts everyone must know about the water they drink.

14. Pages 4-7, 44, 87-89, Walker, N. W., *Water Can Undermine Your Health.*, Norwalk Press, POB 12260, Prescott, AZ 86304-2260, 1974

15. Page 12, Orr, Leonard, *Breaking the Death Habit, the Science of Everlasting Life*, Frog Ltd., 1998

16. Page 187, Dryden, Gordon; and Vos, Jeannette, *The Learning Revolution*, Available via www.learning-revolution.com 1999

17. Page 13, Buchanan, Douglas, *Health Matters*, Self Published, 2001 (See Appendix H)

18. Robinson, Jo, *Why Grassfed is Best*, Vashon Island Press, 29428 129th Ave, S.W., Vashon, WA 98070, (2000)

19. D'Adamo, Dr. Peter J., *Eat right 4 Your Type*, Putnam Pub Group; ISBN: 039914255X; January 1997

20. Page 127, Allegri, Renzo, *Padre Pio, Man of Hope*, Servant Publications, 2000

21. Page 63, 64 of Kelder, Peter, and Siegel, Bernie S., *The Ancient Secret for the Fountain of Youth*, Doubleday, 1998

22. Wigmore, Ann, *Why Suffer, How I overcame Illness and Pain Naturally*, Avery Publishing Group, inc, 1985

23. Page 271, Null, Gary, MD, *Gary Null's Ultimate Anti-Aging Program*, Kensington Publishing Corp., 1999

24. Howell, Edward, *Enzyme Nutrition, The Food Enzyme Concept*, Avery Publishing Group, inc., 1985

Chapter 15 – EXERCISE and REST

1. Page 264, Yogananda, Paramahansa, *Autobiography of a Yogi*, Self-Realization Fellowship, 1993

2. Part 1, Kelder, Peter, and Siegel, Bernie S., *The Ancient Secret for the Fountain of Youth*, Doubleday, 1998

3. Page 137, Hannaford, Carla, *The Dominance Factor*, Great Ocean Publishers, 1997

4. Page 108, Hannaford, Carla, *Smart Moves, Why Learning is Not All in Your Head*, Great Ocean Publishers, 1995

5. Page 14, Ibid

6. Page 116, Ibid

7. Pages 117-129, Ibid

8. Dennison, Paul E; Dennison, Gail E, *Brain Gym, Teacher's Edition*, Edu-Kinesthetics, Inc., 1989

9. Pages 129, 130, Hannaford, Carla, *Smart Moves, why Learning is Not All in Your Head*, Great Ocean Publishers, 1995

10. Page 280, Orr, Leonard, *Breaking the Death Habit, the Science of Everlasting Life*, Frog Ltd., 1998

Chapter 16 – A ROAD MAP

Appendix A – APPLIED KINESIOLOGY or MUSCLE TESTING (ENERGY TESTING)

1. Beardall, Alan G., *Clinical Kinesiology*, vols 1-5 (Lake Oswego, Oregon,: Alan G Beardall, 1980-1985)

2. Pages 17-19, 24, Dean, Douglas, J; Mihalasky, S. Ostrander, and L. Schroeder, *Executive ESP*, Englewood Cliffs: Prentice-Hall, 1974

3. Pages 44, 45, Eden, Donna; David Feinstein, *Energy Medicine*, Penguin Putnam Inc., 1999

4. Page 51, Eden, Donna; David Feinstein, *Energy Medicine*, Penguin Putnam Inc., 1999

5. Bio-Polarity Technique (BPT) and Emotional Polarity Technique (EPT). Doctors Ron and Annette Cargioli, 1239 South 10th, Street, Noblesville, IN 46060, 317-773-6646

6. Pages 43-46, *Appendix A*, Hannaford, Carla, *The Dominance Factor*, Great Ocean Publishers, 1997

Appendix B – BRAIN DOMINANCE BUG

1. Page 179, Hannaford, Carla, *Smart Moves, why Learning is Not All in Your Head*, Great Ocean Publishers, 1995

Appendix C – Lozanov's Music for the Two "Concerts"

1. Lozanov, Georgi; Gateva, Evalina, *The Foreign Language Teacher's Suggestopedic Manual*, Published by Gordon and Breach, New York, 1988

2. Pages 172, 180, 322, Dryden, Gordon; and Vos, Jeannette, *The Learning Revolution*, Available via www.learning-revolution.com 1999

Appendix D – Music Selections

1. Page 172, Dryden, Gordon; and Vos, Jeannette, *The Learning Revolution*, Available via www.learning-revolution.com 1999

Appendix E – BRAIN BINGO®

Appendix F – A Selection of Positive Affirmations

1. Page 102, Ostrander, Sheila; Schroeder, Lynn, *Super Learning*, Dell Publishing Co., 1979

Appendix G – Saint Germain's "I AM" Decrees

1. Pages 22, 49, 'I AM' Activity, *"I AM" Fundamentals, Series II*, Saint Germain, Press, Inc., 1998

2. Page 103, 'I AM' Activity, *"I AM" DECREE BOOKLETS * ONE *,* Saint Germain, Press, Inc., 1994
3. Page 41, 'I AM' Activity, 6-The Ascended Masters, *Ascended Master Discourses,* Saint Germain, Press, Inc., 1999
4. Insert, Prophet, Mark L., *Kuthumi, Studies of the Human Aura,* Summitt University Press, 1985
5. Page 134, 'I AM' Activity, 3-Ascended Master Saint Germain, The *"I AM" Discourses,* Saint Germain, Press, Inc., 1998
6. Page 123, Ibid
7. Page 97, 'I AM' Activity, *"I AM" DECREE BOOKLETS * TWO *,* Saint Germain, Press, Inc., 1994
8. Page 90, 'I AM' Activity, 5-Chanera, *"I AM" Adorations and Affirmations, "I AM" Decrees,* Saint Germain, Press, Inc., 1998
9. Page 58, 'I AM' Activity, 3-Ascended Master Saint Germain, The *"I AM" Discourses,* Saint Germain, Press, Inc., 1998
10. Page 154, Ibid
11. Page 191, Ibid
12. Page 91, 'I AM' Activity, 4-Ascended Master Saint Germain, Ascended *Master Instruction,* Saint Germain, Press, Inc., 1994
13. Page 140, 'I AM' Activity, 3-Ascended Master Saint Germain, The *"I AM" Discourses,* Saint Germain, Press, Inc., 1998
14. Page 104, 'I AM' Activity, 6-The Ascended Masters, *Ascended Master Discourses,* Saint Germain, Press, Inc., 1999
15. Page 198, 'I AM' Activity, 3-Ascended Master Saint Germain, The *"I AM" Discourses,* Saint Germain, Press, Inc., 1998
16. Page 58, Ibid
17. Page 309, Ibid
18. Page 56, Ibid
19. Page 238, Ibid
20. Page 285, 'I AM' Activity, 2-Godfre Ray King, *The Magic Presence,* Saint Germain, Press, Inc., 1993
21. Page 301, 'I AM' Activity, 3-Ascended Master Saint Germain, The *"I AM" Discourses,* Saint Germain, Press, Inc., 1998
22. Page 12, 'I AM' Activity, *"I AM" Fundamentals, Series II,* Saint Germain, Press, Inc., 1998
23. Page 119, 'I AM' Activity, 4-Ascended Master Saint Germain, Ascended *Master Instruction,* Saint Germain, Press, Inc., 1994
24. Page 132, 'I AM' Activity, 3-Ascended Master Saint Germain, The *"I AM" Discourses,* Saint Germain, Press, Inc., 1998
25. Page 178, Ibid
26. Page 269, 'I AM' Activity, 4-Ascended Master Saint Germain, Ascended *Master Instruction,* Saint Germain, Press, Inc., 1994
27. Page 337, 'I AM' Activity, 6-The Ascended Masters, *Ascended Master Discourses,* Saint Germain, Press, Inc., 1999
28. Page 132, 'I AM' Activity, 3-Ascended Master Saint Germain, The *"I AM" Discourses,* Saint Germain, Press, Inc., 1998
29. Page 180, Ibid

Appendix H – Douglas Buchanan - His Biography and Monographs
1. Emails from Douglas Buchanan
2. Additional clarifying input as an email from Jim Saul

Appendix I – Richard Welch's Subliminal Dynamics and Dynamic Brain Management
1. This information can be found at: http://www.subdyn.com

Appendix J – Sources for Organic Foods and Herbal Remedies.
1. Page 189, Carroll, Lee; Tober, Jan, *The Indigo Children,* Hay House, Inc., 1999

Appendix K – Listing of Internet and Catalog Sources

Glossary
1. Pages 345, 346, Yogananda, Paramahansa, *Autobiography of a Yogi,* Self-Realization Fellowship, 1993
2. Page 50, 51, Orr, Leonard, *Breaking the Death Habit, the Science of Everlasting Life,* Frog Ltd., 1998
3. Page 114, Deshimaru, Taisen, *The Zen Way to the Martial Arts,* E. P. Dutton, 1982
4. Pages 9-11, Stein, Diane, *Essential Reiki, A complete Guide to an Ancient Healing Art,* Crossing Press Inc., 1995
5. Page 180, Watson, Donald, *The Dictionary of Mind and Spirit,* Avon Books, 1991
6. Part V, Kelder, Peter, and Siegel, Bernie S., *The Ancient Secret for the Fountain of Youth,* Doubleday, 1998
7. Pages 9-11, Stein, Diane, *Essential Reiki, A complete Guide to an Ancient Healing Art,* Crossing Press Inc., 1995
8. Page 301, Watson, Donald, *The Dictionary of Mind and Spirit,* Avon Books, 1991
9. Footnote, page 180, Yogananda, Paramahansa, *Autobiography of a Yogi,* Self-Realization Fellowship, 1993
10. Pages 390, 391, Stearn, Jess, *Yoga, Youth, and Reincarnation,* Harper and Roe, 1965
11. Page 120, Deshimaru, Taisen, *The Zen Way to the Martial Arts,* E. P. Dutton, 1982

Questions and Answers from Seminars and Emails
1. Pages 99-109, Pearce, Joseph Chilton, *The Crack in the Cosmic Egg,* Park Street Press, 2002
2. Pages 141, 151-154, 156-160, Pearce, Joseph Chilton, *Magical Child,* Penguin Group, 1992
3. Ibid, page 223

BIBLIOGRAPHY

1. *A Course in Miracles*, Foundation for Inner Peace, 1992
2. Bio-Polarity Technique (BPT) and Emotional Polarity Technique (EPT). Doctors Ron and Annette Cargioli, 1239 South 10th, Street, Noblesville, IN 46060, 317-773-6646
3. "Executive Reports - You Can profit by Executive Hunches," *International Management*, March 1966
4. *Gray's Anatomy*, 35th British Edition, W.B. Saunders Company, 1973
5. "How Extrasensory perception Can Play a Role in Idea Generation," *American Society of Mechanical Engineers Publication*, No. 72-De-5, 1972
6. "Question: What do Some Executives have More of? Answer: Intuition, Maybe." *Think*, Nov-Dec 1969
7. "Revelation, A commentary Based on a Study of Twenty-Four Psychic Discourses by Edgar Cayce," *Association for Research and Enlightenment (A.R.E.)* Press, 1992
8. *Stedman's Medical Dictionary*, The Williams & Wilkins Company, Baltimore, 22nd Edition, 1972
9. "The Teeth and the Body, Energetic Inter-Relation," *Academia Latin Americana De Medicina Biologica (The Latin American Academy of Biological Medicine)*, Ebinciones Los Robles, P. O. Box 627, Popayan, Columbia, South America.
10. Allegri, Renzo, *Padre Pio, Man of Hope*, Servant Publications, 2000
11. Andrews, Ted, *Animal-Speak: The Spiritual and Magical Powers of Animals Great and Small*, Llewellyn Publications, ISBN: 0875420281; 1993
12. Arlin, Stephen, Dini, Fouad, and Wolfe, David, *Nature's First law: The Raw-Food Diet*, Maul Brothers, 1997
13. Arlin, Stephen, *Raw Power, Building Strength and Muscle Naturally*, Maul Brothers Publishing, 1998
14. Baba, Sai: http://www.gurusim.com/lordsai.htm   http://www.askbaba.net/saibabagita/index.html http://members.ozemail.com.au/~vsivasup/sai/index.html   Index to home pages about Sai Baba. His Address: Bhagawan Sri Sathya Sai Baba, Prashanti Nilayam, Puttaparthy, District Ananthapur, Andhra Pradesh 515134, INDIA
15. Bach, Richard, *Illusions, The Adventures of a Reluctant Messiah*, A Dell/Eleanor Friede Book, 1977
16. Bates, William Horatio, *The Bates Method for Better Eyesight Without Glasses*, Henry Holt (Paper); ISBN: 0805002413; Revised edition (December 1986)
17. Beardall, Alan G., *Clinical Kinesiology*, vols 1-5 (Lake Oswego, Oregon,: Alan G Beardall, 1980-1985)
18. Berg, Yehuda, *The Power of Kabbalah*, The Kabbalah Centre, ISBN: 1-57189-180-3, September, 2000
19. Berber, Richard, M.D., *Vibrational Medicine*, Bear and Co., 1988
20. Beyers, Dwight C., *Better health With Foot Reflexology, Including Hand Reflexology*, Ingram Publishing, Inc., 1983
21. Blake, William, *The complete Writing of William Blake*, Edited by Geoffrey Keynes, Oxford University Press, 1966
22. Boone, J Allen, *A Kinship With All Life*, Harper Inc., 1954
23. Braden, Gregg, *Awakening to Zero Point, The Collective Initiation*, Radio Bookstore press, 1997
24. Brennen, Barbara Ann, *Hands of Light*, Bantam New Age Books, 1988
25. Brennen, Barbara Ann, *Light Emerging, The Journey of Personal Healing*, Bantam New Age Books, 1993
26. Bro, Harmon H, *Edgar Cayce on Dreams*, Bonanza Books, crown Publishers, 1986
27. Brown Jr., Tom, *Grandfather*, Berkley Publishing Group, 1993
28. Brown Jr., Tom, *The Tracker*, Berkley Publishing Group, 1996
29. Brown Jr., Tom, *The Way of the Scout*, Berkley Publishing Group, 1995
30. Buchanan, Douglas, *Health Matters*, Self Published, 2001 (See Appendix H)
31. Buchanan, Douglas, *Meditation, the Bridge from the Apparent to the Real*, Self Published, 1996, 2001 (See Appendix H)
32. Buchanan, Douglas, *Uses of the Japa Mala*, Self Published, 2002 (See Appendix H)
33. Buzan, Tony, *The Brain User's Guide*, E. P. Dutton, Inc., 1983
34. Buzan, Tony and Dixon, Terence, *The Evolving Brain*, International Thompson Publishing, July, 1978
35. Buzan, Tony, *Make the Most of Your Mind*, Simon and Schuster, New York, 1984
36. Buzan, Tony, *Speed-reading*, Plume, 1991
37. Carroll, Lee; Tober, Jan, *The Indigo Children*, Hay House, Inc., 1999
38. Carter, Mildred, *Hand Reflexology: Key to Perfect Health*, Parker Publishing Co., Inc., 1975
39. Chopra, Deepak, *Ageless Body, Timeless Mind*, Harmony Books, 1993
40. Condron, Daniel R., *Permanent Healing*, SOM Publishing, 1995
41. Covey, Stephen R., *The 7 Habits of Highly Effective People*, Simon and Schuster, 1989
42. Critchlow, Keith, *Order In Space*, Thames & Hudson, 1969
43. D'Adamo, Dr. Peter J., *Eat right 4 Your Type*, Putnam Pub Group; ISBN: 039914255X; January 1997
44. Dean, Douglas, J; Mihalasky, S. Ostrander, and L. Schroeder, *Executive ESP*, Englewood Cliffs: Prentice-Hall, 1974
45. Deming, W. Edward, *Out of the Crisis*, MIT Press; ISBN: 0262541157; 1st edition, August 11, 2000

46. Dennison, Paul E; Dennison, Gail E, *Brain Gym, Teacher's Edition*, Edu-Kinesthetics, Inc., 1989

47. Deshimaru, Taisen, *The Zen Way to the Martial Arts*, E. P. Dutton, 1982

48. Dong, Paul; Raffill, Thomas E., *China's Super Psychics*, Marlowe & Company, 1997

49. Doreal, M, *The Emerald Tablets of Thoth-the-Atlantean*, Source Books, POB 292231, Nashville, TN 37229-2231, USA, (No date listed)

50. Dryden, Gordon; and Vos, Jeannette, *The Learning Revolution*, Available via www.learning-revolution.com 1999

51. Dryden, Gordon; and Vos, Jeannette, *The Learning Revolution Companion 50 minute Video*, Available via www.learning-revolution.com, 1999

52. Dyer, Wayne W, *Manifest Your Destiny*, Harper Collins, 1997

53. Dyer, Wayne, *Staying on the Path*, Hay House, Inc. 1995

54. Eden, Donna, *Energy Medicine*, Penguin Putnam Inc., 1998

55. Ferrucci, Piero, *What We May Be*, J. P. Tarcher, Inc., 1982

56. Fields, Rick; Taylor, Peggy; Weyler, Rex; Ingransci, Rick, *Chop Wood, Carry Water*, Jeremy P. Tarcher, Inc., 1984

57. Foucault, Michel, *This Is Not a Pipe*, Berkley; University of California Press, 1983

58. Frumker, Sanford "Buddy," *Mind Map, Your Guide to Prosperity and Fulfillment*, Health Associates, Ltd., P.O. Box 188009, University Heights, Ohio 44118, 1994

59. Gass, Robert; On Wings of Song, *Om Namaha Shivaya*, Spring Hill Music, 1996

60. Gawain, Shakti, *Creative Visualization*, Nataraj Publishing, 1995

61. Grover, Linda, *August Celebration, A Molecule of Hope for a Changing World*, Gilbert, Hoover & Clarke, 1993

62. Halpern, Jack, Editor in Chief, *The Kodansha Kanji Learner's Dictionary*, Kodansha America, Inc, 575 Lexington Aven, New York, NY, 10022, 1999

63. Hannaford, Carla, *Awakening the Child Heart*, Hannaford, 2002

64. Hannaford, Carla, *Smart Moves, why Learning is Not All in Your Head*, Great Ocean Publishers, 1995

65. Hannaford, Carla, *The Dominance Factor*, Great Ocean Publishers, 1997

66. Hay, Louise, L., *You Can Heal Your Life*, Hay House Inc., 1999

67. Healy, Jane M., *Your Child's Growing Mind*, Doubleday (A division of Random House) 1987

68. Hill, Napoleon, *Think and Grow Rich*, Renaissance Books; ISBN: 158063205X; October 2001

69. Houston, Jean, *The Possible Human: A course in Enhancing you Physical, Mental, and Creative Abilities.* Los Angeles: J. P. Tarcher, 1982

70. Howell, Edward, *Enzyme Nutrition, The Food Enzyme Concept*, Avery Publishing Group, inc., 1985

71. Huxley, Aldous, *The Art of Seeing*, Creative Arts Book Co; ISBN: 0916870480; Reprint edition (October 1, 1982)

72. 'I AM' Activity, *"I AM" Fundamentals, Series I*, Saint Germain, Press, Inc., 1992

73. 'I AM' Activity, *"I AM" Fundamentals, Series II*, Saint Germain, Press, Inc., 1998

74. 'I AM' Activity, Godfre Ray King, *The Magic Presence*, Saint Germain, Press, Inc., 1993

75. 'I AM' Activity, Ascended Master Saint Germain, The *"I AM" Discourses*, Saint Germain, Press, Inc., 1998

76. 'I AM' Activity, Ascended Master Saint Germain, Ascended *Master Instruction*, Saint Germain, Press, Inc., 1994

77. 'I AM' Activity, Chanera, *"I AM" Adorations and Affirmations, "I AM" Decrees*, Saint Germain, Press, Inc., 1998

78. 'I AM' Activity, The Ascended Masters, *Ascended Master Discourses*, Saint Germain, Press, Inc., 1999

79. 'I AM' Activity, Beloved David Lloyd, *The "I AM" Discourses*, Saint Germain, Press, Inc., 1993

80. 'I AM' Activity, *"I AM" DECREE BOOKLETS * ONE *,* Saint Germain, Press, Inc., 1994

81. Jensen, Eric, *Super Teaching*, The Brain Store Inc., 1995

82. Junger, Sebastian, *The Perfect Storm*, Harper Mass market Paperbacks; ISBN: 006101351X; July 1998

83. Kapit, Wynn, and Elson, Lawrence M., *The Anatomy Coloring Book*, Harper and Roe, 1977

84. Key, Wilson Bryan, *The Age of Manipulation*, Madison Books, 1989

85. Key, Wilson Bryan, *The Clam-Plate Orgy*, A Signet Book, 1980

86. Key, Wilson Bryan, *Subliminal Seduction*, Penguin Group, 1974

87. Kelder, Peter, and Siegel, Bernie S., *The Ancient Secret for the Fountain of Youth*, Doubleday, 1998

88. Knight, J. Z., *A state of Mind, My Story, Ramtha, The Adventure Begins*, A Warner Communications Book, 1987

89. Kraft, Dean, *A Touch of Hope*, Berkeley, 1998

90. Kryon, *Kryon 2000, Passing the Marker*, The Kryon Writings Inc, 2000

91. Lama, Dalai, and Cutler, Howard C., *The Art of Happiness*, Penguin Putnam Inc, 1998

92. Laski, Margharita, *Ecstasy: A study of Some Secular and Religious Experiences*, Indiana University Press, 1962

93. Levine, Mel, *A Mind at a Time*, Simon & Schuster, 2002

94. Lockhart, Douglas, *SAVAZIUS - The Teachings of a Greek Magus*, Harper Collins - UK; ISBN: 1852309709; 1997

95. Looking Horse, Chief Arvol, *White Buffalo Teachings*, www.dreamkeepers.net, 2001

96. Lozanov, Georgi; Gateva, Evalina, *The Foreign Language Teacher's Suggestopedic Manual*, Published by Gordon and Breach, New York, 1988
97. Manning, Jeane, *The Coming Energy Revolution*, Avery Publishing Group, 1996
98. Meera, Mother, *Mother Meera Answers*, Mother Meera Publications, 1991
99. Meier, Dave, *The Accelerated Learning Handbook*, McGraw-Hill, 2000
100. Melchizedek, Drunvalo, *The Ancient Secret of the Flower of Life*, Light Technology Publishing, Published in 1998 for Vol 1, and 2000 for Vol 2
101. Mihalasky, John, "Extrasensory Perception in management," *Advanced Management Journal*, July 1967
102. Millman, Dan, *Everyday Enlightenment, the Twelve Gateways to Personal Growth*, Warner Books, 1999
103. Millman, Dan, *Sacred Journey of the Peaceful Warrior*, H. J. Cramer Inc., 1991
104. Millman, Dan, *The Warrior Athlete, Body, Mind & Spirit*, Stillpoint Publishing, 1979
105. Moody, Raymond, M.D., *Live After Life*, Bantam Books, 1975
106. Morimitsu, Phil, *In The Company of ECK MASTERS*, Illuminated Way Publishing, 1987
107. Murphet, Howard, *Sai Baba, Man of Miracles*, Samuel Weiser, Inc., 1973
108. Murphy, Dr. Joseph; Revised by Ian McMahan, Ph.D., *The Power of your Subconscious Mind*, Bantam Books, 2001
109. Musashi, Miyamoto, *A Book of Five Rings*, The Overlook Press, 1974
110. Naisbitt, John, and Aburdene, Patricia, *Megatrends 2000*, Avon, 1991
111. Nelson, Ruby, *The Door of Everything*, Devorss Publications
112. Null, Gary, *Gary Null's Ultimate Anti-Aging Program*, Kensington Publishing Corp., 1999
113. Orr, Leonard, *Breaking the Death Habit, the Science of Everlasting Life*, Frog Ltd., 1998
114. Orr, Leonard, *Breath Awareness*, Published by Inspiration University, POB 118, Walton, NY, 13856, USA, ISBN 0-945793-02-2, 1988
115. Ostrander, Sheila; Schroeder, Lynn, *Psychic Discoveries Behind the Iron Curtain*, Bantam Books, 1970
116. Ostrander, Sheila; Schroeder, Lynn, *Super Learning*, A Laurel/Confucian Press Book, 1979
117. Oz, Mehmet, *Healing from the Heart*, Penguin Group, 1998
118. Palmer, Harry, *Living Deliberately, the Discovery and Development of Avatar*, Star's Edge International, 1994
119. Pearce, Joseph Chilton, *The Biology of Transcendence, A blueprint of the Human Spirit*, Park Street Press, 2002
120. Pearce, Joseph Chilton, *The Crack in the Cosmic Egg*, Park Street Press, 2002
121. Pearce, Joseph Chilton, *Magical Child*, Penguin Group, 1992
122. Praagh, James Van, *Talking to Heaven*, Penguin Books Ltd, 1997
123. Prophet, Mark L., *Kuthumi, Studies of the Human Aura*, Summitt University Press, 1985
124. Ramtha, Mahr, Douglas James, *Voyage to the New World*, Masterworks, Inc., 1985
125. Reed, Henry; Cayce, Charles Thomas, *Edgar Cayce on Mysteries of the Mind*, Gramercy Books, 1990 reprint
126. Ray King, Godfre, *Saint Germain's, Ascended Master Instruction*, Saint Germain press, Inc, 1985
127. Raye, Marina, *Do You Have an Owner's Manual for Your Brain?* Action Press, 1991
128. Reilly, Harold J, Brod, Ruth Hagy, *The Edgar Cayce Handbook for Health Through Drugless Therapy*, MacMillan Publishing Co., 1975
129. Rich, Katherine Russell, *In a Single Stroke*, The Oprah Magazine, Oct, 2002.
130. Robinson, Jo, *Why Grassfed is Best*, Vashon Island Press, 29428 129th Ave, S.W., Vashon, WA 98070, (2000)
131. Robertson, Morgan, *Futility or The Wreck of the Titan*, Buccaneer Books, ISBN: 0899668216, 1991
132. Rose, Colin and Malcom J. Nicholl, *Accelerated Learning for the 21st Century, The Six-Step Plan to Unlock Your MASTER-mind*, Dell, 1997
133. Rose, Colin, *Master it Faster*, published by Accelerated Learning Systems, Aston Clinton, Aylesbury, Bucks, England.
134. Russell, C. W., *The Life of Cardinal Mezzofanti*, London: Logman, Brown, and Co., 1858
135. Russell, Walter, *The Secret of Working Knowingly with God*, The University of Science and Philosophy, 1993
136. Savant, Marilyn Vos, *The Power of Logical Thinking*, St. Martin's Press, 1996
137. Scheele, Paul R., *PhotoReading*, Learning Strategies Corporation, 900 East Wayzata Blvd, Wayzat, MN 55391-1836, 1999
138. Shlain, Leonard, *The alphabet Versus the Goddess*, Penguin Group, 1998
139. Smith, Penelope, *Animal Talk, Interspecies Telepathic Communication*, Pegasus Publications, 1989
140. Smith, Penelope, *Advanced Interspecies Communication, When Animals Speak*, Beyond Words Publishing, Inc., 1999
141. Solzhenitsyn, Alexander, *The Gulag Archipelago*, Harper & Row, 1973, 1974
142. St. James, Elaine, *Inner Simplicity, 100 Ways to Regain peace and Nourish Your soul*, Hyperion, New York, 1995
143. State of Illinois Department of Conservation, *Aquatic Plants, Their Identification and Management*, Department of Conservation, Division of Fisheries, Springfield, IL 62706, Revised 1994
144. Stearn, Jess, *Edgar Cayce, The Sleeping Prophet*, Bantam Books; ISBN: 0553260855; Reissue edition, February 1990
145. Stearn, Jess, *Yoga, Youth, and Reincarnation*, Harper and Roe, 1965

146. Stein, Diane, *Essential Reiki, A complete Guide to an Ancient Healing Art*, Crossing Press Inc., 1995

147. Stone, Joshua David, *How to Teach Ascension Classes*, Light Technologies Publishing, 1998

148. Stone, Joshua David, Dr, *The soul's Perspective on How to Achieve Perfect Radiant Health*, Writers Club Press, 2001

149. Sugrue, Thomas, *There is a River: The Story of Edgar Cayce*, A.R.E. Press; Revised edition, Feb 1997

150. Summer Rain, Mary, *Mary Summer Rain's Guide to Dream Symbols*, Hampton Roads Publishing Co., Nov 1997

151. Summer Rain, Mary, *Spirit Song*, Donning Company/Publishers, 1985

152. Tesla, Nikola; and Childress, David, *The Fantastic Inventions of Nikola Tesla*, Adventures Unlimited Press, 1993

153. Thomas, Charles B., *Water Gardens for Plants and Fish*, T.F.H. Publications Inc., 1988

154. Thomas, Melvin; Geltmacher, Hal, *Combat Simulator Display Development*, Society for Information Display (SID), Vol. 9, No 4&5, Apr/May 93

155. Thomas, Melvin L.; Reining, Gale; Kelly, George, The *Display for Advanced Research and Training: An "Inexpensive" Answer to Tactical Simulation*, Proceedings of the Society of Photo Instrumentation Engineers (SPIE), San Jose, CA, (24 February through 1 March, 1991)

156. Thurston, Mark A., *How to Interpret Your Dreams*, Edgar Cayce Foundation, 1978

157. Twyman, James; Neale Donald Walsch, *Emissary of Love: The Psychic Children Speak to the World*, Hampton Roads Publishing Co; ISBN: 1571743235; (March 2002)

158. Vitale, Barbara Meister, *Unicorn's Are Real, A Right-brained Approach to Learning*, Jalmar Press, P. O. Box 1185, Torrance, CA 90505, 1982

159. Walker, N. W., *Water Can Undermine Your Health.*, Norwalk Press, POB 12260, Prescott, AZ 86304-2260, 1974

160. Walsch, Neale Donald, *Conversations With God, Book 1*, G. P. Putnam's Sons, 1996

161. Watson, Donald, *The Dictionary of Mind and Spirit*, Avon Books, 1991

162. Webb, Terry Wyler and Douglas Webb, *Accelerated Learning with Music*, Accelerated Learning Systems, 1990

163. Webb, Terry Wyler and Douglas Webb, *Accelerated Learning with Music Trainer's Manual*, Accelerated Learning Systems, 2213 Georgetown, Denton, Texas, 76201, 1990

164. Wegscheider-Cruise, Sharon, *Learning to Love Yourself, Finding Your Self-Worth*, Health Communications Inc., 1987

165. Wigmore, Ann, *Why Suffer, How I overcame Illness and Pain Naturally*, Avery Publishing Group, inc, 1985

166. Williamson, Marianne, *A Return to Love, Reflections on the Principles of A course in Miracles*, Harper Collins, 1992

167. Wolfe, David, *The sunfood Diet Success System, 2nd Edition*, Maul Brothers Publishing, 2000

168. Woolf, *A Room of One's Own*, Harvest Books; ISBN: 0156787334; Reissue edition, January 1990

169. Wright, Machaelle Small, *Behaving As if the God in all Life Mattered*, Perelandra, 1997

170. Zukav, Gary, *The Seat of the soul*, Simon & Schulster Inc., 1989

171. Yogananda, Paramahansa, *Autobiography of a Yogi*, Self-Realization Fellowship, 1993

172. Yogananda, Paramahansa, *Scientific Healing Affirmations*, Self-Realization Fellowship, Ninth Printing, 1990

QUESTIONS AND ANSWERS FROM SEMINARS AND EMAILS

Q: How long does it take to develop the ability to read at 25,000 words per minute with perfect recall?

A: You develop at the rate you chose. How soon your abilities become fully functional is dependant upon many factors. The most important factor is your openness to these concepts and willingness to practice. For a few, the skill of reading at a minimum of 25,000 words per minute (60 pages a minute) with perfect recall, will manifest in weeks. In most it takes months. In some cases it takes years. All of us have perfect memories. Few of us have perfect recall. The real trick is dealing with the layers of separation you have built as walls between the forgetfull person you appear to be now and the perfect fountain of memory you were naturally as a child. Along the way you have learned to read and write thus giving you another medium for perfect recall. Practice is the key - what you concentrate on, you become.

Q: Can everyone do this or are some just not capable?

A: If you can see, read, and write, then you already have the tools necessary to awaken this skill. You do not have to be able to see perfectly, nor read and write perfectly. Just well enough to be able to comprehend and do the exercises presented in the *The Mastery of Learning Seminar* and *Book*.

Q: How can I work with my dreams as you recommend when I never remember them?

A: Those who don't remember their dreams have chosen to not remember and probably live a lifestyle that supports that decision. Intentionality and a few simple steps allow you to begin remembering them. I also used to never remember my dreams. Once I decided that I wanted to and began recording what little I began to remember, in only a few months I was remembering whole dreams every night and eventually eight or nine dreams each night.

Q: If everyone has this ability as you say, why don't I know anyone who can do this?

A: It is well documented by Dr. Joseph Chilton Pearce and others that in places like Greece, Africa, South America, and Asia, firewalking is a common nonordinary phenomena. The children learn from watching their elders and eventually join them in walking across a pit of blazing coals so hot that it melts aluminum on contact. In Ceylon the pit is typically 20 feet long, six feet wide, and many feet deep with hot coals at temperatures measured at 1400 degrees Fahrenheit. Annually, a few die trying this. The vast majority raised in the cultures that practice firewalking cross the blazing hot pit barefoot and unscathed; their cloths unsinged even, because they know they can do it. You probably don't know anyone who does firewalking, yet fire walking is common around the world.[1,2] What I am teaching takes far less commitment and failure is not fatal. You can do it because as a child you once did it. I am not teaching you a skill so much as helping you remember what you once did naturally. The skill I teach merely awakens your own latent ability.

Q: If this is so great, why don't they teach it in school?

A: A few schools teach some of the abilities I discuss and honor a child's potential to a far greater degree than most public education demonstrates. Examples are *Montessori* and *Waldorf Schools*, *Sylvan Learning Centers*, and in particular, Dr. Lozenov's *Suggestophobia Institute* and the seminars and books developed by Dr. Richard Welch and Paul Scheele. Once the general public begins to understand and acknowledge the far greater potential all of us have and the tools currently available from many sources, then this will enable most school systems to start incorporating techniques like those presented in *The Mastery of Learning* in forms they find culturally acceptable.

Q: Can you do what your book teaches?

A: I am still learning. *The Mastery of Learning* covers many techniques such as remembering your dreams, being able to see auras, wide-eye viewing, Brain Gym and Tibetan exercises, positive affirmations, and reading at a minimum of 25,000 words per minute. I practice most of these skills every day. I am pretty good at remembering my dreams, accessing my subconscious, and integrating my right and left brain for holistic thought. All were essential for writing *The Mastery of Learning!* I practice reading at 25,000 words per minute every day. I have reached the 100th time goal for my ReLAX and ReTAIN rituals. My ReCALL ritual needs more work as my Superscanned knowledge currently comes overnight after sleeping on it and is in the form of intuitive hunches. Perfect ReCALL in only minutes, which is what Douglas Buchanan and others demonstrate that we all are capable of, is my goal.

Q: (Typical question at *Magical Child Seminar*): **Okay, what do we adults do now about our child and our own split selves?**

A: (Answer from Dr. Joseph Chilton Pearce): Bonding is the issue, regardless of age…. Anything that blocks bonding should be avoided. Hospitals for delivery, bottles for feeding, cribs for sleeping, playpens and strollers for isolation, day-care centers for not caring, nursery schools for not nurturing, preschools – all create abandonment and weaken the bond. Surely, a parent would do everything possible to protect the child from premature literacy and be warned about television. To nurture a magical child is a full-time responsibility.[3]

The memory flower is a four petaled forget-me-naught with a shining golden center.
Melvin Lewis Thomas

All the world's a stage and all the men and women merely players; they have their exits and their entrances; and one man in his time plays many parts, his acts being seven ages.
William Shakespeare

The MASTERY of LEARNING CD

By Melvin Lewis Thomas

The CD is packaged with this booklet

It contains new information and guides you through the essential exercises

The MASTERY of LEARNING CD

By Melvin Lewis Thomas

TABLE OF CONTENTS

Note: Track descriptions in normal text are explanations and *in italics are exercises*.

Thank you for purchasing the **The MASTERY of LEARNING** book and **CD**.

This booklet appended at the back of the main book is the script by which the CD is narrated and assembled. Supplementary information, assembly instructions, and actions are in *italics,* and the voiceovers are in normal text. The voiceovers have been performed by Mel Thomas. For some, reading this booklet while listening to the audio will be more effective than listening to the audio by itself. For others, the audio alone will be sufficient. One way or the other, virtually everyone will have the tools necessary to understand the intent of this audio and the system of instruction known as:

The MASTERY of LEARNING

The Mastery Series Inc. wishes you the very best in your learning progression based on what is offered in **The MASTERY of LEARNING.**

Respectfully

Melvin Lewis Thomas - CEO
The Mastery Series Inc.
POB 640
Beecher, IL 60401
Mel@themasteryseries.com

Web Site
www.themasteryseries.com

Track 1 – INTRODUCTION (10:44)

Begin with the Mastery of Learning Music as a lead in with this narrative starting as the music ends.

Welcome to a new way of learning that will reawaken the exemplary way you learned as a child.

You can follow the CD's auditory instructions by also reading the accompanying booklet thus employing auditory, visual, and kinesthetic activities so that all learning preferences are addressed.

The purpose of these instructions is to aid you in developing a set of techniques that will place your memory at your command.

These techniques and exercises are explained in the main body of the book, *The Mastery of Learning.*

Reading the book or attending the seminar is essential for understanding the purpose of these exercises and the terminology used.

These instructions will help you regain the ability to learn with a child's sponge like absorption.

Once you have mastered the techniques that these instructions cover, the artificial support mechanisms that this CD's audio provides will no longer be required.

These instructions are based on four key exercises covered in the main body of the book, *The Mastery of Learning.*

Two of these exercises have been separated into yet two more related exercises thus yielding a total of six different exercises.

Each of the exercises is introduced with an audio track and printed script of setup instructions.

It is best to place yourself in a relaxing and distraction free environment while listening to this CD.

Even if you find auditory instruction difficult to follow, being relaxed will greatly increase your ability to learn and absorb the full effect.

I strongly recommend against listening to these audio exercises while you are driving as it could be dangerous and certainly is not conducive to being able to execute them properly.

However, if someone else is driving while you sit in a passenger seat, then a portable CD player and this booklet provide you with an excellent opportunity to productively immerse yourself.

Thus, you may gainfully employ the time often lost during long automobile trips or while using other forms of transportation.

Doing the **Brain Gym**® exercises prior to listening to any part of these exercises will also substantially increase your ability to learn.

They are found in **Chapter 15** of *The Mastery of Learning.*

The best preparatory exercises are: **Brain Buttons**®, **Cross Crawl**®, **Hookups**®, and the **Thinking Cap**®.

Performing each exercise for about two minutes for a total of eight to ten minutes, will prepare you properly.

If you have particular problems that one of the other exercises address, then adding it to the list will accelerate progress towards achieving your fully integrated mind, brain, and body capabilities.

You begin with **Exercise 1.1** from *The Mastery of Learning's* **Chapter 1**.

It is recorded on **Track 2** of this CD.

By listening to it as a guided meditation you may be able to tap into memories of some of your suppressed childhood potential.

Those memories are the golden nuggets you began life with.

Most of us placed them in a bag which we stored in a vault secured with a long forgotten combination.

Exercise 1.1 will help you open your vault and once again behold the brilliant golden glimmer of your own unique talents.

It is only necessary to do to this exercise a single time although you may wish to listen to it on occasion just as a reminder.

Exercise 8.1 is the second one taken from the book.

This exercise is meant it to develop your **ReLAX** and **ReTAIN** abilities while practicing SuperScanning.

Track 3 is an introduction to both of these exercises which are covered using **Tracks 5, 6, and 7.**

Performing the **ReLAX** exercise is typically only required once in a session whereas the **ReTAIN** exercise is required for the duration of a SuperScan session and thus may be looped through a number of times so that its ten minute duration covers the time you wish to SuperScan.

When you have finished SuperScanning you skip forward past the remainder of the ten minute **Track 5** session to **Track 6,** and terminate your SuperScan session by saying the concluding word: **Tain**.

The third exercise is the second one found in **Chapter 8**.

It is *Exercise 8.2*.

Its purpose is to develop your **ReCALL** and **ReTURN** abilities which are on **Tracks 8** and **9** so that they immediately follow the **ReLAX** and **ReTAIN** exercises.

Track 4 is an introduction to the **ReCALL** and **ReTURN** exercises

The **ReCALL** exercise also gives you the option of being tested on **25** simple words typically found in a dictionary or thesaurus to aid you in accessing your vision based photographic memory.

The **ReLAX, ReTAIN, ReCALL**, and **ReTURN** exercises have been sequenced one after another so that you can practice them as a set.

If you practice these exercises two times a day you will reach the critical 100th repetition and program these powerful trigger words into your subconscious in only 50 days, or less than two months.

You will also, along the way, accumulate many valuable minutes of SuperScanning practice during which you can acquire knowledge that soon you will effortlessly access.

If you chose to practice these exercises four times a day you will be able to program your subconscious with the four different **Re** based trigger words in only 25 days, comfortably less than a month.

Track 10 and the associated write-up introduce you to your final exercise.

It is *Exercise 9.1*, the **Net of Eir Visualization**, which follows immediately on **Track 11**.

Using this exercise daily prior to going to sleep is an excellent way to cleanse internal negativity and reprogram yourself for perfect vibrant health, vitality, and success.

Track 12 is the conclusion

It guides you though scoring your **Brain Bingo**® **Exercise** and also has a few suggestions for how to increase your effectiveness while doing all of these exercises.

Now, let us return to the way you began, as a child.

Our objective is to set your house in order.

Your current situation can be summed up with two quotes:

> The first is from Martin Burber, a theologian, "In fetal existence, we were in communion with the universe." [1]

> And the second is from Harville Hendrix, a well published therapist, "In thousands of ways, both subtly and overtly, our parents gave us the message that they approved of only a part of us. In essence, we were told that we could not be whole and exist in this culture." [2]

Now is your time to return to wholeness, which has the same root as holiness and holistic.

That is the underlying purpose of *The Mastery of Learning*.

What you are really learning about is yourself.

Rather than learning, you are actually remembering, the opposite of dismembering which is what as a child you did in order to fit in your culture.

Now you are almost ready for *Exercise 1.1*.

The only preparation necessary it to place yourself in a relaxing and distraction free environment with some assurance that you will be able to complete this, and any subsequent exercises that you plan on doing, without interruption.

If the options are available to you, it would be advantageous to take the phone off the hook and dim or turn off the lights.

You may advance to the next audio track, which is *Exercise 1.1*, when you are ready.

This is **Exercise 1.1, Remembering your Childhood Potential.**
It is a self-guided meditation, a journey of remembrance to the closet, basement, and attic places where your childhood memories are stored.
Please take a few deep breaths and relax. Let your mind drift back to the way your life began…
What were you as a child that you have forgotten?
What gifts and abilities did you abandon in your race for acceptance and understanding?

If you observe babies you will see that they seem to look both at and around you, for along with the physical they see both the vibrant colors of your aura and the light of your being.
Sensing thoughts and feeling emotions are natural for infants.
Most mothers know that even in the womb their child is distressed by discordant conditions around them, or at peace and harmonious when that is the environment they are immersed in.
Young children sometimes see the spirits of departed loved ones, fairies, or their own angel guides.
If they can speak they may call what they see *birdies* among other names, being limited in how they can communicate.
Most parents are aware that their young children have exceptional memories.
They only have to read a book to them to verify this.
They usually will be corrected for any mistake or deviation from prior readings.

Time has no meaning to small children so they live in the ever present now which holistically includes the past, the present, the future, and portals most of us no longer see except perhaps in our dreams.
Therefore, they can have awareness of past events, potential futures, and other realities.
Sometimes in their reality the name they apply to themselves is different from the one you have given them.
In the year 2000, Mike, my wife's 19-year-old nephew, fell four stories onto concrete thus sustaining major head injuries and a broken back.
Even with full life support in a modern trauma center he was not expected to live for more than a few hours.
Then a miracle changed that dire prognosis.
After a few weeks he finally came out of his coma.
As is typical of massive head injuries, he began the process of rebuilding his brain and mind much like a child.
When he first awakened he asked, "Where is Giovanna?" and he thought his name was Tony.
His mother and my wife then remembered that when he was very young he used to think that he was Tony.
In the early stages of his recovery he could see a girl in the hospital room that the rest of us could not.
His brain and mind quickly recovered and soon he answered to Mike rather than Tony, but he could still remember his refreshed childhood remnants and the girl none of us could see who sat with him.
To this day we have no idea who she or Giovanna were.
They were part of a reality different from the one we have in common with Mike, who nine months after his accident recovered sufficiently to run in Chicago's 5K Beverly Ridge run.
Soon he was back in college and he recently graduated as a Certified Public Accountant.

Because it is acceptable in their cultures much of the world's population has children who openly speak of their knowledge of other civilizations and times, and parents who do the same.
My wife learned from a client about her son Randy who lives in the Chicago area and sometimes mentioned to his mom his Indian friends.
She thought he was fantasizing.
One day his class went on an outing to the Field Museum in downtown Chicago.

His mom was one of the chaperones.

When their guide stood in front of a grouping of Native American artifacts and asked if anyone knew what one of the implements was, five-year-old Randy spoke up with both its name and an explanation of its use.

He then further astounded everyone by accurately naming and describing the function of everything else in the same display.

Particularly enchanting is the story told by Dan Millman of four year old Sachi, who wanted time alone with her baby brother when he was newly arrived.

Her parents finally agreed, while wondering if this could be sibling rivalry.

As a precaution, they listened at the crack of the partially open door to the baby's room.

They were stunned to hear her earnestly ask her brother to tell her again what God felt like because she was beginning to forget.

The movie *Fairy Tale, a True Story,* is about children who photographed real fairies at the Great Houdini's request.

In the actual event this movie is based on, Houdini wasn't involved.

The man who brought the affair into prominence was Sir Arthur Conan Doyle, the author of the Sherlock Holmes classics.

The grownups that tried to witness the fairies could not see them, but were amazed by the photos.

After seeing this movie both my wife Carol and our daughter Gina were visited by the fairies during the night.

What they saw correlated well with the movie but went far beyond in vivid detail.

Gina was so startled she screamed, thus scaring them away.

My wife also saw the fairies in the twilight of awakening, but she likewise overreacted and has been visited only one time since then.

My wife and I have a doctor friend named Jeanne who remembers a precious moment years ago when she was flying a kite with her five year old son Charlie.

The kite and string got so tangled in a tree that they couldn't free it.

Charlie said, "Don't worry mom, I know I can get this kite out of the tree!"

Then he closed his eyes, put his forehead to the ground, and moments later the kite floated gently away from the tree.

Sometimes adults retain or regain such abilities.

Using similar levitation techniques Edward Leedskalnin, who weighed only 100 pounds, single handedly quarried and raised blocks of stone weighing as much as 28 tons to build his residence, a Coral Castle on ten acres.

Now his home is a tourist attraction just South of Miami, Florida.

The fitting of the stones astounds engineers and is so precise as to remind one of the Great Pyramids and Machu Pichu.

When Uri Geller demonstrated on national television his ability to bend a spoon with his mind, what was never brought to the nation's attention were the thousands of children, and a few adults, who duplicated this feat because they saw him do it.

A well documented case was that of eleven year old Juni who is Japanese.

Just hearing the broadcast was all the impetus he needed.

A few years ago my son Matt met James Twyman, the author of *Emissaries of Light* and ten other wonderfully enlightening books.

He learned in his travels how to bend a spoon with his mind and personally taught Matt the same skill.

If you go to his web site: www.emissaryoflight.com, you can also learn from James Twyman how to develop your own spoon bending ability.

China has recently begun to openly support the development of such abilities and now has hundreds of thousands of children with extraordinary capabilities because they are not limiting themselves.

4

Many books, TV shows, and prominent personalities are giving us an expanded understanding, such as medium James Van Praagh, who has been on more than 5,000 radio and TV shows.

In April of 2002, he was portrayed by Ted Danson in a made-for-TV movie that was broadcast by ABC.

In 1997 I was at the Whole Life Expo in Chicago.

While I was there James was scheduled to address a randomly assembled audience of thousands, much as he has done more publicly on his recent nationally televised show, *Beyond*.

I arrived with the auditorium one third filled, but ended up seated in the front row because friends had unexpectedly saved me a seat.

James started off by relaying the words from a man who was killed in a fire that was a surprise to him.

I stood up because when I was very young, that is how my father died.

After I gave him permission to come to me, James proceeded to describe scene after scene he was seeing, all recent incidents in my life.

Then he described a handsaw I had used a month earlier that had my family's name marked on it.

I learned for the first time that this tool had actually been my father's, and not my grandfather's as I had thought until that moment.

At the end of my public session with James Van Praagh, it was obvious that my father had been watching over me for the more than 40 years since his body died.

Maybe during the early stages of his recovery my wife's nephew Mike could see as James Van Praagh sees thus revealing to him the presence of a young girl who was invisible to the rest of us.

In his initial childlike recovery Mike could articulate what it is possible many children sometimes see.

Unlike Mike they cannot explain their perception to the grownups around them nor the greater reality they experience.

These gaps in comprehension limit in other ways.

My wife was born with a knowingness that her hands were meant to heal. As a child she would pretend to be a doctor, with local cats and dogs as patients, because she didn't know of any other form of healer or healing.

Now she is a clinical esthetician and Reiki master, both professions where you "heal" with your hands.

At one of his *Magical Child* seminars, Dr. Joseph Chilton Pearce had a man share what for him had been a "disorientating and confusing" experience.

His eight-year-old son had been whittling with a knife, slipped, and cut the arteries in his left wrist.

He was screaming as the blood sprayed.

Without thinking the panicked father grabbed his son's face, "looked into his eyes, and commanded, 'Son, let's stop that blood!'

The screaming stopped, the boy beamed back, said 'okay,' and together they stared at the gushing blood and shouted, 'blood, you stop that!'"

The blood stopped, the wound healed quickly, and the father nearly came unhinged by the unexpected assault on what he thought of as reality.

The Menninger Foundation has scientifically documented adult Jack Schwarz, who retained his childhood ability such that he can heal deep wounds instantly.

It is my hope that this journey via the exceptional experiences of a few adults, and the childhoods of others, has awakened memories of your childhood reality and the potential you began with.

This concludes **Exercise 1.1**

Track 3 - INTRO to *Exercise 8.1* – SuperScanning Using the Douglas Technique (13:34)

Open with the Mastery of Learning song with the words: When you look with a song, it stays with you the best. Your mind, it will hold on! *Fade the song out to a low background level to play out while this narrative is spoken:*

This is the introduction to **Exercise 8.1** where you learn how to SuperScan using the Douglas Technique.

It is intended to help you develop your **ReLAX** and **ReTAIN** exercises, which are covered in sound **Tracks 5, 6, and 7** respectively.

When you are performing these exercises, you can remove your glasses if you wish, even if you normally wear them for reading, as they will not be required.

If you wear contact lenses and require them for reading, it is best to leave them in as they will be necessary for one of the exercises immediately following the **ReLAX** and **ReTAIN** exercises.

When performing these first two exercises, the way you will be using your eyes will eliminate the need for being able to read conventionally.

That is because you will be using your eyes and body as a five year old does rather than the way you do now that you are older.

The shoulders back, erect posture, wide-eyed openness of a baby is the ideal.

Your body and eyes thus synergistically support the freely open acquisition of knowledge while proper posture also allows you to breath openly, which is essential.

At the beginning of **Chapter 5** in *the Mastery of Learning* is a description of how to properly use your eyes.

You are asked to view the book with the borders of your vision with your eyes in soft focus owl-eye mode.

You do this by looking over and focusing well beyond the book, which can be upside down to aid you in not latching onto words on the page.

Another approach is to dim the lights until you are not able to see the words well enough to read them.

It is best to use natural lighting such as moonlight or diffuse daylight in a darkened room.

If neither is available, your next best choices are either a candle or dimmed incandescent lighting.

The type of lighting to avoid is fluorescent as most have a 60 hertz flicker that will be distracting to you and thus hinder your ability to perform these exercises; plus it typically cannot be dimmed.

In this instance, if you require glasses to read, you will actually have an advantage as removing them will probably prevent you from being able to read conventionally, which is what we are trying to avoid.

However, if you are using the approach of working in dim light you will also have to be able to easily increase the light level so that you can see well enough to write in order to perform the **ReCALL** exercise that immediately follows the **ReLAX** and **ReTAIN** exercises.

For these exercises, the **memory mantra** you will be using is: "I learn with Zest! I am in my gen ius zone where I am per fect mem o ry and I am per fect **Re Call** be cause, I am at Rest."

It is the "song" that puts your mind into the proper mode for super learning tasks and positively reinforces perfect retention and retrieval of the information that you SuperScan.

An explanation of this **memory mantra** can be found in **Chapter 8** of *The Mastery of Learning*.

It is two sentences containing a total of 32 syllables.

These sentences have been carefully crafted to have this number of syllables because that is the total number of seconds in a theta state inducing breath cycle of 4, 8, 16, and 4 seconds.

Synchronizing the **memory mantra** with theta inducing breathing firmly establishes the perfect state of being for super memory tasks.

The objective is to develop these exercises as a form of self hypnosis, which is really what all hypnosis is.

You therefore induce the conditions that you naturally experienced as a five year old while retaining the knowledge and discernment of the older person you are now.

Thus - you are in control at all times!

The **memory mantra** begins with an energizing sentence ending in the word zest: "I Learn with Zest!"

It is intended to conjure up the enthusiasm you had as a five year old when your mind was naturally in the theta state.

The theta state is normally associated with dreaming.

It is therefore a state of creative rest.

Beginning the **memory mantra** with enthusiastic "Zest," and ending it with "Rest," simulates the state of being you were in as a child.

This combination of opposites, **Zest** and **Rest**, or **ZestRest®**, is the uniting of duality to oneness thus allowing you to be energized and dreamy at the same time.

Unions of this nature are very powerful as they encapsulate the whole of experience between their extremes.

An example is found in relationships.

It is summed up in the common expression, "Opposites attract!"

Many psychologists and therapists have noted that married couples often have opposite characteristics.

According to therapist Harville Hendrix, these conflicting character traits are really different strategies for dealing with the same childhood wound thus plumbing the range of human response choices.

Quoting the Roman poet Ovid, "We two form a multitude." [3]

In their union a couple gives each other the opportunity to heal the problem they have in common by finding balance via the opposing strategy of their mate.

A second less well known example can be found in the ancient healing art of **Dar'Shem**.

It is a technique known as **Ghazism Pye'**, which translates as "Fire and Ice."

It is therefore the union of opposites.

For instance, you sooth and help heal a burn from fire by putting ice on it.

All of reality as we know it can be characterized as polarized opposites such as fire and ice, male and female, up and down, good and bad, strong and weak, and so on.

In the union of opposites can be found the totality of experience and hence, both balance and strength.

A third example can be found in Japan.

The martial art of **Aikido** is also founded on the principle of the union of opposites.

When performed correctly, a defender using **Aikido** will blend perfectly with their opponent such that the attacker will experience no opposition thus finding all of their exertion returned.

The attacker's energy becomes both the attack and the defense.

They nullify because the defender gets out of the way while guiding the energy flow of the attacker.

In its name, **Aikido** presents the key to understanding this advanced defensive art.

Ai means harmony, **Ki** means energy, and **Do** means path.

When read from right to left as is the custom in Japan, **Aikido** therefore translates as, "The path of energized harmony."

Energized harmony is analogous to **ZestRest**.

There is great power in **ZestRest** just as there is great power in **Aikido**.

That is the intent of the structure formed with the **memory mantra's** bracketing **Zest** introductory sentence and **Rest** inducing concluding phrase.

The internal sentence in the **memory mantra** is:

"I am in my gen ius zone where I am per fect mem o ry and I am per fect **Re Call**."

These are two affirmations that as "I AM" statements, address the highest level of your being with the intention of restoring your childhood genius potential and super memory competence.

Constant repetition of such powerful declarations will eventually result in you embodying their truth.

That truth is really a healing to regain your childhood super proficiency which originally enabled you to learn an entire culture, including the complexities of its language, in an amazingly short period of time.

In his ground breaking book, *Crack in the Cosmic Egg*, Joseph Chilton Pearce discusses a Stanford University Professor by the name of Hilgard who "spent ten years in research on one question: why can only about twenty percent of the population undergo a deep trance experience?" [4]

Dr. Pearce reveals that the answer Hilgard found was that, "As children, all those capable of deep trance as adults had shared in fantasy play and imaginative ventures of some sort with their parents." [5]

These adventures were the result of either having been read to, or told tales of fantasy.

Dr. Pearce further reveals that if they are not supported, "Trance abilities are lost somewhere in early adolescence," that is, around the age of 12 to 14.[6]

To address that issue the exercises you will be learning have been developed as compelling broad spectrum approaches for self-inducing the desired trance or hypnotic state of being.

Many will not respond to a minimalist approach because they are in the deep trance resistant group.

It is therefore expected that around one person in five will require only the key critical elements, while the other four will eventually experience the desired effect by persistently using every element.

Your **ReLAX exercise** is track 5 on this CD.

Immediately following it are two tracks which cover the **ReTAIN** exercise.

You will need to have one or more books easily within reach to SuperScan while doing this exercise.

Also, if you intend to practice developing photographic **ReCALL** in the subsequent exercise, one of those books needs to be either a dictionary or thesaurus.

Whatever book you are using for SuperScanning practice, make sure that you turn its pages at a metered pace that matches the **memory mantra** cadence so that you turn a page every two seconds.

That way you have a scanning pace of a page per second and are easily able to maintain this pace.

While doing these exercises, mentally repeat the **memory mantra** after practice has enabled you to memorize it.

In order to aid you in following the theta state inducing breathing pattern, there is a repeating sequence of timed tuba tones that will queue you for the inbreath, hold, outbreath, and closing hold.

Complete tonal sequence with voice over: They are an **Inbreath** E tone for 4 seconds, a **hold** middle C tone for eight seconds, an **outbreath** low E tone for 16 seconds which may require developing your lung power to sustain this because that is a fairly long length of time, and a **hold** low G tone for 4 seconds.

That same tonal sequence will repeat for the **ReLAX, ReTAIN,** and **ReCALL exercises** in order to help you maintain the foundation theta state inducing 4, 8, 16, and 4 second cadence that they require.

You will also be listening to a one or more voices guiding you dependant upon the complexity of the exercise.

The critical elements of this learning system are the foundation theta state inducing breathing, the **memory mantra**, and an enthusiastic attitude.

The reinforcing elements, which also help induce the theta state, are visualizations, a mudra, and specialized eye movements.

When beginning these exercises they are easier to learn if you concentrate first on doing the critical breathing tones and **memory mantra**, and then add the reinforcing elements after you have mastered the foundation.

With everything these exercises require, performing them may initially seem difficult.

In only a few repetitions you will have mastered all that is being requested of you.

With practice, soon they will feel like second nature and be very calming.

Before long you will have successfully completed 100 repetitions of each trigger word encapsulating exercise.

Then **ReLAX** and **ReTAIN** will become personal power words that when you utter them; will activate your subconscious to place you in the perfect state of being for the super memory feats you chose to accomplish.

Repeat listening to this audio explanation until you are comfortable with what has been explained here.

When you are ready, listen to the next audio track which explains your **ReCALL** and **ReTURN** exercises.

Track 4 – Intro to *Exercise 8.2* – ReCALL with BRAIN BINGO® and ReTURN (07:10)

This is the introduction to **Exercise 8.2** where you learn how to **ReCALL** SuperScanned material and other subconscious information using the Douglas Technique, and then **ReTURN** to full consciousness.

Examples of what you might wish to **ReCALL** are the books that you have SuperScanned and also names, dates, numbers and other information often found just beyond conscious access.

Your subconscious is also the gateway to your genius level so you can use your **ReCALL** ability to access creative information.

For instance, you can use **ReCALL** to retrieve dreams that upon awakening seem to have been lost.

Your subconscious has all of your dreams stored for you to retrieve when you have learned how to do so.

As you have already learned, the key is to still be conscious when you place yourself in the theta state and while in this deep reverie with your subconscious, ask questions that you desire answers to.

Any question is fair game.

You can thus retrieve books that you have SuperScanned, and any other information you require such as answers to problems that you need to solve.

The answers that you get will be as creative as the questions you are able to formulate.

It is said, that if you know enough to ask a question, you already know the answer.

Your subconscious can put you in contact with any level of intelligence that you are prepared to hear.

There is a Belgium Teacher of the Photoreading School of Instruction by the name Marion Ceyssens whose abilities are at mastery level.

She holds a book in her hands, shakes it for a couple of seconds, and she has read it.

Douglas Buchanan says that this skill is also found as a Rosicrucian technique.

It is based on the premise that if you have read one book, you have read them all.

What that means is, when a book is read properly you tap into the mind of the author whose creative source is the universal mind from which all thought comes.

Therefore, upon reading a single book properly you have the ability to access all books.

Knowing where this can lead should give you an additional incentive for continuing this work.

The **ReCALL** exercise is on **Track 8** immediately following the **ReLAX** and **ReTAIN** exercises so you will still be in the theta state.

It begins with a single theta state breathing cycle and accompanying **memory mantra** during which you focus on the information that you wish to retrieve.

After that are two more theta state breathing cycles, with **memory mantra** accompaniment, to give you the opportunity to **ReCALL** properly what you are focused on accessing via your subconscious.

You can then either skip to the next track to practice your **ReTURN** exercise, or allow the **ReCALL** track to progress to the **Brain Bingo® Practice Test**.

The simple words used for this test have been selected to cover 25 of the 26 letters in the English Alphabet with the exception of the letter X, which contains very few words anyway.

If you plan on practicing this visual memory development exercise you will need to make a copy of the **Brain Bingo® Practice Sheet** found on page 20 of this booklet.

The 25 words that you will be tested on have already been filled in thus eliminating the need for you to write in the words in order to maximize your opportunity to **ReCALL** their page positions.

Blank **Brain Bingo® Practice Sheets** can also be found at the end of **Chapter 8** and as **Appendix E** in the main body of *the Mastery of Learning.*

Xeroxing copies would be preferable to writing on the practice sheets in your book or booklet as that will give you the option of practicing **Brain Bingo®** many times using different reference books.

Each new dictionary or thesaurus you practice with can be tested using the same words as their specific page locations change between books.

You will also need a pencil to write with.

Finally, be prepared to put on your glasses if you require them for reading, and if you are working in a dimmed environment, increase the light level so that you can see to write.

After the **Brain Bingo**® example test is **Track 9** which guides you through developing your **ReTURN** exercise.

This exercise requires no support materials.

It uses beta state inducing breathing in four second intervals of **Inhale, hold, exhale**, and **hold.**

These foundation breathing tones are generated by a flute and they are sequenced in the reverse order of the tuba tones used for the **ReLAX, ReTAIN**, and **ReCALL** theta state breathing.

In the beta state your mind is fully conscious and your mental activity is accelerated to the level that most people typically operate in while awake.

I recommend that you always end a practice session with the **ReTURN** exercise.

This exercise is also a great way to wake up in the morning should you find that a challenge.

That way you are assured of being in the beta state of full wakefulness prior to going on with your day.

This helps avoid finding yourself operating at your inner child level when you, for instance, drive your automobile or speak to your spouse.

Subconscious based abrupt frankness is not necessarily conducive to harmonious interactions.

Now you are almost ready to begin practicing your **ReLAX, ReTAIN, ReCALL** and **ReTURN** sequence of exercises.

The next track you will listen to is the **ReLAX** exercise.

Immediately following it is the **ReTAIN** exercise.

While you are performing the **ReTAIN** exercise and reach the end of a book, either reverse directions or put it down and pick up another book to continue SuperScanning.

If the **ReTAIN** exercise track ends, either loop back to its beginning or choose to end your session by allowing your CD player to transition naturally to the next track.

You can also end your **ReTAIN** session at any point you chose by using your CD player's skip forward button to advance to the next track.

Likewise, you will also have the option of ending your **ReCALL** exercise by skipping to the following track without performing the **Brain Bingo**® **Practice Session.**

If you have chosen to perform a **Brain Bingo**® **Exercise,** scoring it is explained at the end of **Chapter 8** in the main body of *The Mastery of Learning*, and also by the concluding track of this CD.

If you have understood what these instructions are guiding you to do, and have made the necessary preparations, you are ready to move on to the next track and begin the **ReLAX** exercise.

Otherwise, listen to these instructions again, and if it helps, practice listening to the exercises they cover until you are comfortable with what you are being asked to do.

When you feel that you understand well enough to begin performing the exercises, then you only need to make final preparation to be ready to advance to the **ReLAX** exercise on the next track.

The final preparations required are that:

- You have all of your books ready and within easy reach for SuperScanning,
- If you plan on practicing **Brain Bingo**®, you have a pencil and practice sheet ready to use.
- If you are using this approach, you have set the illumination levels around you to be dim enough that you cannot read, and you also have the ability to easily return your lighting to comfortable viewing levels.
- If you wear them, you have removed and set your reading glasses within easy reach.
- And most importantly, you are seated comfortably and upright with your shoulders back so that you can inhale and exhale deeply, using your diaphragm and pelvis.

Final preparations made, you are now ready to move on to the next track and begin practicing the four exercises forming the extraordinarily **Re-Warding** reading system that Douglas developed and that you can learn to use to great effect as he does.

Track 5 - ReLAX Exercise (04:48)

This is **Exercise 8.1** for programming yourself to **ReLAX**.
Begin with a deep **Inbreath** vocalizing *(Uptone)* **Reeeeeeeeeeeeee-**
With a slow out breath and slow breathing:

 OOwl-eyes

- State that: "'**I AM**' the **balancing-breath!**"
- Put your **eyes into soft focus owl-eye mode.**
- Put your **consciousness at the center of your body**, behind and two inches below your navel.
- Put your **hands in a centering mudra** such as thumb+index+middle fingers together.
- Set the intention of doing this exercise with the **enthusiasm of a wide eyed child.**

*What comes next are cycles of the theta state breathing tuba tones coordinated with the **memory mantra** and associated supporting narrative describing the actions required.*

4 sec High E with voiceover: **Inhale** strongly and deeply:
Second voiceover: **I learn with zest!**
8 sec Middle C with voiceover: **Hold** while **crossing your eyes** and **looking up:**
Second voiceover: **I am in my gen ius zone where**
16 sec Low E with voiceover: **Exhale** slowly while you **look level, close your eyes, visualize your red** charka, and mentally track with the **memory mantra:**
Second voiceover: **I am per fect mem o rey and I am per fect re call be cause**
4 sec Low G with voiceover: **Hold** until the next cycle.
Second voiceover: **I am at rest.**

4 sec High E with voiceover: **Inhale** strongly and deeply:
Second voiceover: **I learn with zest!**
8 sec Middle C with voiceover: **Hold** while **crossing your eyes** and **looking up:**
Second voiceover: **I am in my gen ius zone where**
16 sec Low E with voiceover: **Exhale** slowly while you **look level, close your eyes, visualize your orange** charka, and mentally track with the **memory mantra:**
Second voiceover: **I am per fect mem o rey and I am per fect re call be cause**
4 sec Low G with voiceover: **Hold** until the next cycle.
Second voiceover: **I am at rest.**

4 sec High E with voiceover: **Inhale** strongly and deeply:
Second voiceover: **I learn with zest!**
8 sec Middle C with voiceover: **Hold** while **crossing your eyes** and **looking up:**
Second voiceover: **I am in my gen ius zone where**
16 sec Low E with voiceover: **Exhale** slowly while you **look level, close your eyes, visualize your yellow** charka, and mentally track with the **memory mantra:**
Second voiceover: **I am per fect mem o rey and I am per fect re call be cause**
4 sec Low G with voiceover: **Hold** until the next cycle.
Second voiceover: **I am at rest.**

4 sec High E with voiceover: **Inhale** strongly and deeply:
Second voiceover: **I learn with zest!**
8 sec Middle C with voiceover: **Hold** while **crossing your eyes** and **looking up:**
Second voiceover: **I am in my gen ius zone where**
16 sec Low E with voiceover: **Exhale** slowly while you **look level, close your eyes, visualize your green** charka, and mentally track with the **memory mantra:**
Second voiceover: **I am per fect mem o rey and I am per fect re call be cause**
4 sec Low G with voiceover: **Hold** until the next cycle.
Second voiceover: **I am at rest.**

4 sec High E with voiceover:	**Inhale** strongly and deeply:
Second voiceover:	**I learn with zest!**
8 sec Middle C with voiceover:	**Hold** while **crossing your eyes** and **looking up:**
Second voiceover:	**I am in my gen ius zone where**
16 sec Low E with voiceover:	**Exhale** slowly while you **look level, close your eyes, visualize your blue** charka, and mentally track with the **memory mantra:**
Second voiceover:	**I am per fect mem o rey and I am per fect re call be cause**
4 sec Low G with voiceover:	**Hold** until the next cycle.
Second voiceover:	**I am at rest.**
4 sec High E with voiceover:	**Inhale** strongly and deeply:
Second voiceover:	**I learn with zest!**
8 sec Middle C with voiceover:	**Hold** while **crossing your eyes** and **looking up:**
Second voiceover:	**I am in my gen ius zone where**
16 sec Low E with voiceover:	**Exhale** slowly while you **look level, close your eyes, visualize your indigo** charka, and mentally track with the **memory mantra:**
Second voiceover:	**I am per fect mem o rey and I am per fect re call be cause**
4 sec Low G with voiceover:	**Hold** until the next cycle.
Second voiceover:	**I am at rest.**
4 sec High E with voiceover:	**Inhale** strongly and deeply:
Second voiceover:	**I learn with zest!**
8 sec Middle C with voiceover:	**Hold** while **crossing your eyes** and **looking up:**
Second voiceover:	**I am in my gen ius zone where**
16 sec Low E with voiceover:	**Exhale** slowly while you **look level, close your eyes, visualize your violet** charka, and mentally track with the **memory mantra:**
Second voiceover:	**I am per fect mem o rey and I am per fect re call be cause**
4 sec Low G with voiceover:	**Hold** until the next cycle.
Second voiceover:	**I am at rest.**
4 sec High E with voiceover:	**Inhale** strongly and deeply.
8 sec Middle C with voiceover:	**Hold** your breath as you prepare for a long exhale.
16 sec Low E with voiceover:	**Exhale** very slowly and deeply while saying **Laaaaaaaaaaaaaaaaaaaaax!**
4 sec Low G with voiceover:	**Hold** until the next cycle.
4 sec High E with voiceover:	**Inhale** while saying *(Uptone)* **Reeeee!**
8 sec Middle C with voiceover:	**Hold** while you prepare your book for SuperScanning.
16 sec Low E with voiceover:	**Exhale** slowly while you:

visualize a **golden ball of light over your crown charka,**
put your **consciousness at the center of your body,**
and **look over and beyond your book with soft focus owl-eyes.**

4 sec Low G with voiceover:	**Hold** while the next track takes over.

Visualizing a **golden globe** over your crown chakra

Track 6 - ReTAIN Exercise (10:08)

*High E **Inhale** tone for 4 seconds with voiceover* <u>I learn with zest!</u>
Inhale

*Middle C **Hold** tone for 8 seconds with voiceover* <u>I am in my gen ius zone where</u>
Hold

*Low E **Exhale** tone for 16 seconds w/voiceover* <u>I am per fect mem o rey and I am per fect re call be cause</u>
Exhale

*Low G **Hold** tone for 4 seconds with voiceover* <u>I am at rest.</u>
Hold

This pattern repeats for a total of 19 times which is 19x32 = 608 seconds, or 10 minutes, 8 seconds.

Normal book appearance

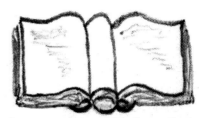

Book appearance while SuperScanning

Your subconscious cave of knowledge wealth

Track 7 – Conclusion to ReTAIN Exercise (00:32)

High E tone for 4 seconds with voiceover: **Inhale** strongly and deeply.
    Second voiceover: **I learn with zest!**
Middle C tone for 8 seconds with voiceover: **Hold** while you place the books you SuperScanned in your lap.
    Second voiceover: **I am in my gen ius zone where**
Low E tone for 16 seconds with voiceover: **Exhale** slowly while you look at the title of each book to lock in what you have SuperScanned, then end with **Taaaaaaaaaain!**

    Second voiceover: **I am per fect mem o rey and I am per fect re call be cause**
Low G tone for 4 seconds with voiceover: **Hold** while the next track takes over.
    Second voiceover: **I am at rest.**

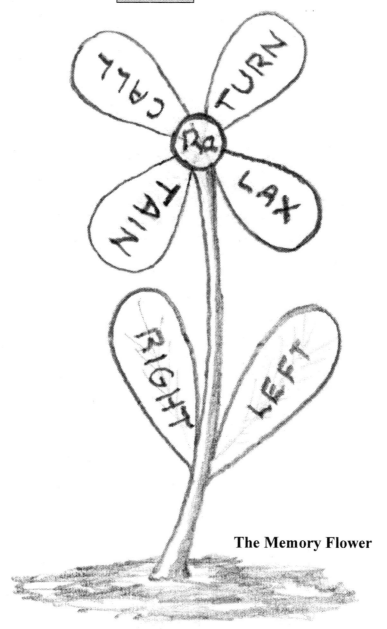

The Memory Flower

Track 8 – Exercise 8.2, Your ReCALL exercise including a BRAIN BINGO® Session (07:34)

*The 4 theta state breathing tones and **memory mantra** are in the background throughout this exercise:*
*High E **Inbreath** tone for 4 seconds with voiceover (Uptone):* **Say Reeeeeeeeeeee-**
*Middle C **Hold** tone for 8 seconds with voiceover:* Visualize a **golden ball of light over your crown charka**
*Low E **Outbreath** tone for 16 seconds with voiceover:* Focus on the information you wish to retrieve. End by
saying **Caaaaaaaaall!**
*Low G **Hold** tone for 4 seconds*

*High E **Inbreath** tone for 4 seconds*
*Middle C **Hold** tone for 8 seconds with voiceover:* If needed, write notes on the information you have recalled.
*Low E **Outbreath** tone for 16 seconds with voiceover:* Continue in this theta state breathing pattern as long as
it is necessary to record your information.
Low G Hold tone for 4 seconds

*High E **Inbreath** tone for 4 seconds*
*Middle C **Hold** tone for 8 seconds with voiceover:* Skip to the **ReTURN** exercise on the next track when you are done.
*Low E **Outbreath** tone for 16 seconds with voiceover:* Or wait for the next breath pattern during which you
will prepare for the **Brain Bingo® Exercise.**
*Low G **Hold** tone for 4 sec*

*High E **Inbreath** tone for 4 seconds*
*Middle C **Hold** tone for 8 seconds with voiceover:* Place your **Brain Bingo®** sheet and pencil in front of you.
*Low E **Outbreath** tone for 16 seconds with voiceover:* Continue in this breathe pattern as the **Brain Bingo®**
practice words are called out.
*Low G **Hold** tone for 4 sec*

Word #1 is In, ReCALL and write I N, then mark an X where it is located on one of the representative book pages. Your first inclination is usually correct.
Word #2 is Big, ReCALL and write B I G, then mark an X for your first inclination for its position on the page.
Word #3 is Green, ReCALL and write G R E E N, then mark an X for its page position.
Word #4 is Toe, ReCALL and write T O E, then mark an X for its page position.
Word #5 is Up, ReCALL and write U P, then mark an X for its page position.
Word #6 is Now, ReCALL and write N O W, then mark an X for its page position.
Word #7 is Hair, ReCALL and write H A I R, then mark an X for its page position.
Word #8 is Eye, ReCALL and write E Y E, then mark an X for its page position.
Word #9 is Yes, ReCALL and write Y E S, then mark an X for its page position.
Word #10 is Zip, ReCALL and write Z I P, then mark an X for its page position.
Word #11 is Apple, ReCALL and write A P P L E, then mark an X for its page position.
Word #12 is Care, ReCALL and write C A R E, then mark an X for its page position.
Word #13 is Dig, ReCALL and write D I G, then mark an X for its page position.
Word #14 is Find, ReCALL and write F I N D, then mark an X for its page position.
Word #15 is June, ReCALL and write J U N E, then mark an X for its page position.
Word #16 is Kind, ReCALL and write K I N D, then mark an X for its page position
Word #17 is Lap, ReCALL and write L A P, then mark an X for its page position.
Word #18 is Post, ReCALL and write P O S T, then mark an X for its page position.
Word #19 is Olive, ReCALL and write O L I V E, then mark an X for its page position.
Word #20 is Mix, ReCALL and write M I X, then mark an X for its page position.
Word #21 is Wise, ReCALL and write W I S E, then mark an X for its page position.
Word #22 is Vise, ReCALL and write V I S E, then mark an X for its page position.
Word #23 is Sand, ReCALL and write S A N D, then mark an X for its page position.
Word #24 is Quiet, ReCALL and write Q U I E T, then mark an X for its page position.
Word #25 is Race, ReCALL and write R A C E, then mark an X for its page position.
This concludes the **Brain Bingo® Exercise.** You can score it after you have done the **ReTURN** exercise on the next track which you will transition to in a moment.

Track 9 - Your ReTURN Exercise: (02:52)

Now you will perform the **ReTURN** exercise for being fully awake in the beta state. During the outhbreath with each charka, say the words spoken by the voiceover as this makes the exercise more powerful.

4 pulse Low E with voiceover: **Inbreath** while saying *(Uptone)* **Reeee-**
4 pulse Low G with voiceover: **Hold** while you look down
4 pulse High E with voiceover: **Outbreath** and look level. *Simultaneous voice speaking:* **Cha kra 7 now!**
4 pulse Middle C with voiceover: **Hold** for four seconds

4 pulse Low E with voiceover: **Inbreath** deeply and quickly
4 pulse Low G with voiceover: **Hold** while you look down
4 pulse High E with voiceover: **Outbreath** and look level. *Simultaneous voice speaking:* **Cha kra 6 now!**
4 pulse Middle C with voiceover: **Hold** for four seconds

4 pulse Low E with voiceover: **Inbreath** deeply and quickly
4 pulse Low G with voiceover: **Hold** while you look down
4 pulse High E with voiceover: **Outbreath** and look level. *Simultaneous voice speaking:* **Cha kra 5 now!**
4 pulse Middle C with voiceover: **Hold** for four seconds

4 pulse Low E with voiceover: **Inbreath** deeply and quickly
4 pulse Low G with voiceover: **Hold** while you look down
4 pulse High E with voiceover: **Outbreath** and look level. *Simultaneous voice speaking:* **Cha kra 4 now!**
4 pulse Middle C with voiceover: **Hold** for four seconds

4 pulse Low E with voiceover: **Inbreath** deeply and quickly
4 pulse Low G with voiceover: **Hold** while you look down
4 pulse High E with voiceover: **Outbreath** and look level. *Simultaneous voice speaking:* **Cha kra 3 now!**
4 pulse Middle C with voiceover: **Hold** for four seconds

4 pulse Low E with voiceover: **Inbreath** deeply and quickly
4 pulse Low G with voiceover: **Hold** while you look down
4 pulse High E with voiceover: **Outbreath** and look level. *Simultaneous voice speaking:* **Cha kra 2 now!**
4 pulse Middle C with voiceover: **Hold** for four seconds

4 pulse Low E with voiceover: **Inbreath** deeply and quickly
4 pulse Low G with voiceover: **Hold** while you look down
4 pulse High E with voiceover: **Outbreath** and look level. *Simultaneous voice speaking:* **Cha kra 1 now!**
4 pulse Middle C with voiceover: **Hold** for four seconds

4 pulse Low E with voiceover: **Inbreath** deeply and quickly
4 pulse Low G with voiceover: **Hold** while you look down
4 pulse High E with voiceover: **Outbreath** and look level.
          Simultaneous voice speaking quickly: **"I am awake, alive, alert and enthusiastic now!"**
4 pulse Middle C with voiceover: **Hold** for four seconds

4 pulse Low E with voiceover: **Inbreath** deeply and quickly
4 pulse Low G with voiceover: **Hold** while you look down
4 pulse High E with voiceover: **Outbreath,** look level and say Tuuurn!
4 pulse Middle C with voiceover: **Hold** for four seconds

This concludes the **ReLAX, ReTAIN, ReCALL,** and **ReTURN** set of exercises.
You can breathe naturally now.

Track 10 – Introduction to the Net of Eir Visualization (01:54)

This is the introduction to **Exercise 9.1**, the **Net of Eir Visualization**.
It is the last one covered by this CD.
The optimal time to perform it is just prior to drifting off to sleep because that gives this message to your
     subconscious as something to integrate while you sleep.
You can either perform the **ReLAX** ritual, or once it is effective, say **ReLAX** as a trigger word to
     properly prepare you for the **Net of Eir Visualization** and peaceful sleep afterwards.
Historically the **Net of Eir** comes from the Norse.
Eir was the physician to the Norse Gods.
Her **golden net** was woven so fine that it had spacing of molecular dimensions that would hold water.
It was used to extract mental and physical garbage by walking through it in spirit form.
As you walk through it you are asked to look up at the mountains in the distance.
This way your eye movements support putting you into the low alpha or high theta state where you
     subconscious dwells.
After walking through you are asked to scrape off the gunk on the net using the flint knife provided, put it
     into the bowl, and point your "power hand" at it so that you purify the gunk.
Your power hand is your dominant hand.
Think of it as being able to project a laser beam of powerful light that does your bidding.

By consciously performing this exercise you reprogram your subconscious to reflect the health and purity
     that you desire to be.
Use a portable sound system to enable yourself to listen to this exercise after you have retired for the night.
Using earphones will allow you to do so without disturbing others.
When you are properly prepared, say **ReLAX** to yourself to reinforce the use of that trigger word for
     instant relaxation into the alpha/theta state.
The **Net of Eir Visualization** will
     begin in a moment.

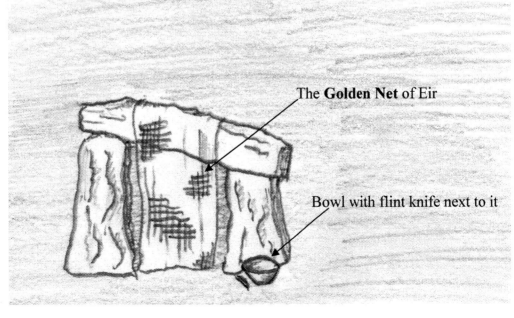

The **Golden Net** of Eir

Bowl with flint knife next to it

Track 11 - *Exercise 9.1* – THE NET OF EIR VISUALIZATION (02:07)

This is **Exercise 9.1**, the **Net of Eir Visualization**.

Visualize yourself going to a great plain with mountains on the horizon.

In front of you are two upright megalithic stones of different heights.

The one on the right is the lower but it is still taller than you.

Across these stones is a third megalith thus completing a construct forming the rune UR, the rune of healing.

Thrown over this structure is Eir's ultrafine net of gold mesh.

Holding the intention of healing while looking at the mountains beyond, walk through the net in spirit form.

Then return to the front of the monolithic structure by going to your right around it.

Collected on the net will be the dense, negative material that is lower in vibration than spirit so it could not get through.

It often looks like black molasses.

At the base on the right side of the structure is a stone or silver bowl.

There is a flint knife lying to the left of it.

Use the knife to scrape the gunk off the net into the bowl.

Then point your "power hand" at the gunk and set it on fire in order to purify it, thus clearing it of all negativity.

In moments the contents will be rendered into something looking like a collection of fireflies or sparklers.

Empty the bowl over your head letting the points of light enter into your body to return to their original positions.

Feel yourself balanced and at peace.

This concludes **Exercise 9.1,** the **Net of Eir Visualization**

Track 12 – CONCLUSION (03:13)

End with the Mastery of Learning music and this voiceover:

Congratulations, you have reached the conclusion of this CD.

If you performed the **Brain Bingo®️ Exercise**, then you will probably want to score yourself.

You will need to look up each word read to you in the book you SuperScanned.

Put a circle around every X you placed in the correct position the word was located in as illustrated by **Brain Bingo®️** example space #26, which has the italicized word "*example*" in it.

If you SuperScanned the book upside down, then you will have two acceptable positions for the word, the conventional location, and the location the word is in when the book is upside down.

Either is correct from the perspective of the subconscious mind.

The purpose of this exercise is to give you the sense of lighting up your entire mind and brain while demonstrating that your intuitive capacity for word location is working even though you have only begun to reawaken your innate ability.

Write down the number of correct answers you had out of a possible 25, then multiply that number by four to get the percentage you had correct.

Had you been randomly guessing, you would have gotten only a few of them correct or around 10 percent for a small two-column dictionary.

Even the first time they perform this exercise, most people do better than what random guessing accounts for.

Now you have a technique you can practice for strengthening your fledgling photographic **ReCALL** ability.

If you have followed this audio instruction in sequence, you also covered the other key exercises.

The first one helped you restore lost memories from your childhood.

It is another contrast of opposites for in uniting with yourself as a child you grow more quickly as an adult.

The next four exercises helped you learn how to store and access SuperScanned material so that you can eventually achieve photographic **ReCALL**.

The last exercise helps you end your day with a cleansing guided visualization.

Unless you write it down, you are likely to forget when you started doing these exercises and be less aware of your regained capabilities.

Keeping a journal will give you a sense of progress and self encouragement with each metered success.

It will also aid you in understanding what is happening as you change with the forces in you that these exercises will release.

Record your score every time you perform a **Brain Bingo®️ Exercise**.

By using different dictionaries, the same words can be practiced as their locations will have changed.

Remember that enthusiasm, practice, and persistence are the keys to developing proficiency.

Performing these six exercises are all that you need to do in order to flawlessly integrate SuperScanning and SuperReCALL into your daily life.

They are however, merely tools to take you back to what you had in the beginning.

The true miracle of what you began life as merely has to be awakened for it was there all along.

I wish you the best in your endeavors to regain your childhood luster.

Thank you for doing this work for your successes inspire others to succeed.

Thus, we help each other regain a valuable legacy that all have as a birthright and that most of us lost somewhere along the way during our earthly adventure.

REFERENCE NOTES:

173. Page 16, Hendrix, Ph.D., Harville, *Getting the Love You Want, A guide for Couples*, Henry Hold and Co., 1988
174. Ibid, Page 23
175. Ibid, Page 45
176. Page 110, Pearce, Joseph Chilton, *The Crack in the Cosmic Egg*, Park Street Press, 2002
177. Ibid, Page 112
178. Ibid, Page 115

Exercise 8.2 – Continued

Figure 8.7 – Brain Bingo® Worksheet

Name · · · Date

Lighting Up the Whole Mind/Brain/Body

Front of brain · · · Back of brain

Prefrontal cortex	Motor cortex	Temporal lobe	Parietal lobe	Occipital lobe
1 IN	2 BIG	3 GREEN	4 TOE	5 UP
6 NOW	7 HAIR	8 EYE	9 YES	10 ZIP
Limbic	Left-brain, right side of the body	**Corpus callosum**	Right-brain, left side of the body	**Cerebellum**
11 APPLE		12 CARE		13 DIG
14 FIND		15 JUNE		16 KIND
Medulla oblongata		**Pineal gland or third eye**		**Brain stem**
17 LAP	18 POST	19 OLIVE	20 MIX	21 WISE
22 VISE	23 SAND	24 QUIET	25 RACE	26 *EXAMPLE*

Mel's Mastery of Learning ReWORDs Journal

Conclusions based on my experience so far:

1. I have been doing Greer Childer's "Body Flex®," program exercises for many months prior to attempting this. They helped enormously and I highly recommend them if you find *the Mastery of Learning* exercises initially too challenging. Even someone confined to a wheel chair or bed can do many of the Body Flex® exercises. They can be ordered by calling **800.852.9500**. *Breath is life, and inspiration as a word is based on respiration*, or breath, for that is spirit in physical form. When were born, you breathed your first breath. When you expire someday you will breathe your last breath. In between, inspiration is based on your ability to breathe. When you begin you will likely find *the Mastery of Learning* exercises stressful. They will probably even cause you to sweat. They are cardiovascular exercises that develop lung capacity. It takes time to acclimate your body to this new level of capability. Once you do, you will find that this *breathing cleanses your mind and helps you in many other ways physically, mentally, emotionally, and spiritually.* This is a holistic program with full spectrum benefits. *Breathe in and out with your nose* if you can as it will be sufficient for most people and that way you have good control over breath flow.

2. *Doing these exercises either late at night when it is dark and you have been sleeping, or the first thing upon arising in the morning, is advantageous.* If late at night then don't do the **ReTURN** exercise until you get up in the morning. By doing these exercises during quiet hours there is no phone to contend with, your stomach is empty thus allowing for full chest expansion, and having just awakened you are still in the alpha state thus making it easier to get into the theta state. Also, when you conclude your exercises in the morning you wake yourself up properly by going into the beta state with the **ReTURN** exercise thus beginning your day naturally.

3. *Choose a book to practice with that will be easy to work with.* I chose Webster's Encyclopedic Dictionary because it has over 1300 pages printed on good quality thick paper that is easy to grasp and turn. Also, because of the print density on a page it gives me a scanning speed of 75 to 100 thousand words per minute.

4. It is best if you mentally track with the **memory mantra** and not try to subvocalize the words as that depletes your air too rapidly unless you have a very well developed lung capacity.

5. Visualize the charkas when you are asked to see the colors for the **ReLAX** exercise. That way you count the **Rainbow Bridge** to your crown charka.

6. The **ReTAIN** and **ReCALL** exercises are the most stressful because not only are you breathing, but you are also turning the pages of a book or trying to write. It is likely that they will be the last ones you are capable of doing properly.

7. If you activate your CD's forward skip button at the beginning of the last four second hold on the theta state breathing cycle of 4, 8, 16, and 4 seconds, a typical CD player will take approximately four seconds to begin the next track and you will be kept on cycle for your breathing. This gives you the flexibility of being able to skip out of the **ReTAIN** and **ReCALL** exercises at the end of any breathe cycle you choose.

8. While you are first learning how to do this, short cycle the **ReTURN** and **ReCALL** exercises until you can breathe perfectly through the entire set, then lengthen your **ReTURN** exercise until you can go for the full ten minutes. Begin doing the **ReCALL Brain Bingo**® work once you are able to maintain proper breathing while writing down the words being called out. This way you avoid practicing improper procedure and build up slowly to being able to the do the entire process correctly and in a stress free manner.

9. During the exhale portion of the breathe cycle of the **ReTURN** exercise, say "Cha kra 7 now!" and so on for the other six charkas and concluding affirmation. It is much more powerful if you reinforce the action with your own voice.

10. *The prime objective of the CD is for you to develop your expertise to the point where you don't need the CD.* Once you have memorized the elements of each exercise and can perform them in sequence without the aid of the CD, you will do better with the **ReTAIN** and **ReCALL** exercises by doing them on your own. The CD causes some stress as it is difficult to follow an unvarying pattern precisely. The body is flexible and slight changes in breathe length are not a problem. Being natural while honoring the pattern is the objective. Once you have memorized the pattern you can also become creative in how you mix the elements for efficient use of your time. For instance, beginning your inbreathe with a quick "Re!" combined with "I learn with Zest!" allows you in a single inbreathe to do what takes two theta state breathe cycles on the CD. Likewise, you don't need the CD for practicing **Brain Bingo**®. Write the words down ahead of time on a **Brain Bingo**® practice sheet prior to SuperScanning a reference book and you will be able to take the test without any assistance. If you want variations, chose new words, write them on a **Brain Bingo**® sheet, then supserscan your reference book and take the test. You can have stacks of tests prepared ahead of time. Seeing the words ahead of time does not affect the outcome as long as you use a new reference book for your superscan test. This is great for road trips or other idle times.

11. ***Practice theta state breathing by itself by using the memory mantra to maintain timing.*** Once you have memorized the **memory mantra** and associated breathe pattern, you will be able to practice while driving in low task load **conditions** *(Do not attempt this until you can do so without stress or danger of passing out, and also do this only for the ReTAIN and ReCALL exercises without actually trying to SuperScan as you are, after all driving. Finally, only attempt this when you are essentially alone on the road and it is easy to drive. I practice while driving straight and deserted backroads that are alternate routes to my destination).* **This is very relaxing and quickly develops lung capacity so that the entire set of exercises became much easier to do.**

12. ***Be patient and persistent in doing these exercises and you will be richly ReWarded!***

Monday, June 14th, 2004 (1)

This is my first attempt at doing *the Mastery of Learning* exercises as they have been reformulated with the addition of the theta and beta state inducing breathe cycles. Previously I had however, listened to all of them prior to doing the seminar that I gave at Practical Magick bookstore two days ago. I decided to SuperScan a Webster's unabridged dictionary as that will give me plenty to work with and is good info to commit to memory.

I found the first exercise, **ReLAX**, doable with the exception of trying to subvocalize **the memory mantra** as that depleted my air too rapidly. I discovered that if I did not completely evacuate my air I was able to keep going relatively well. Also, the activities of this exercise made it relatively easy to do, possibly because I was busy enough so that I was trying to follow rather than be concerned about my air supply.

The **ReTAIN** exercise was more difficult to do for some reason. It is different somehow, as if the theta breath cycle is suddenly more stressful. I was able to go for about four minutes and had to cheat some with quick breathes. I became overheated with sweat on my brow from doing this while trying to SuperScan my dictionary. I gave up completely any thought of subvocalizing the **memory mantra**. I made it to page 271 in the dictionary.

The **ReCALL** exercise is okay, more like the **ReLAX** exercise because my mind is occupied. There is one of the breathe prompts that is not easily heard because my accompanying sentence is timed to launch precisely the same point and it drowns out the prompt. However, the tones seem to work well as prompts and I believe that this is workable once a person gets used to it. In subsequent releases this is something to work to avoid as a problem, but it is still only a minor problem.

I found the **ReTURN** exercise easy to do and reasonably well balanced.

My overall impression is that they are doable as formulated with the exception of subvocalizing. I also found it best to have some breath reservoir left in my lungs or else I began having a panicky feeling during the four second hold prior to the next inbreath, and thus sometimes had to take a cheater breath. It is absolutely critical that the inbreath be very deep so that I have filled my lungs or else this is not doable.

Tuesday, June 15th, 2004 (2)

My second attempt. I still find theta breathing in general a challenge. It generates an enormous charge of energy in me. I believe that the energy being generated is an indication of Chi being ingested, and possibly is kundalini in nature. Therefore, it is likely that this breathing is purifying my body as it ramps the energy up. It will take my body awhile to acclimate to this energy level. I always feel alert, refreshed, and invigorated after doing the exercise, as if I have done a very aerobic workout. This is a good sign.

Once again I only did the **ReTAIN** exercise for a few minutes. This shortens the overall cycle time for the set of exercises. I have done this because I find myself sometimes fighting the breathe cycle. However, it also sometimes works and I know that when I find the proper pattern, with deep cycle breathing that is natural and nearly completely evacuates my lungs, and then I will have it. This time I made it to page 397 in my dictionary. Because of truncating the **ReTAIN** exercise I do this entire cycle of exercises very quickly, and that is desirable as it means that in less than fifteen minutes I practice all of them. I can therefore, once I have habituated, in a thirty minute time frame do this twice thus halving the time it takes to program my trigger words. This still appears to be feasible and the exercises, as formulated, work with the small modification of not doing the subvocalization. I also noted that it would have been better for me to have mentioned to the class that a person is supposed to visualize the blue charka, for instance, rather than just the color blue which is all that I am asking for. That would naturally move a person's thought system up the charka rainbow rather than the way it is now where you have the make the association in your mind. I can teach around this for the moment and the current exercise is still workable with that point in mind.

Wednesday, June 16th, 2004 (3)

I am doing these exercises the first thing up arising in the morning so that I am still in the alpha state thus giving myself a head start on going into the theta. Today I made it through five cycles of the **ReTURN** exercise plus the ending cycle for a total of three minutes and 16 seconds. I also discovered that the **ReCALL** cycle can be skipped through after a single breathe cycle as the first breath cycle is a complete **ReCALL** exercise. Later when I have acclimated to this procedure, and finished SuperScanning my big dictionary, I will do the **Brain Bingo**® exercise. It was not necessary to do any cheating breaths this time as I was able to fill my lungs enough to make it through each theta state breath cycle. The transition from the **ReTAIN** conclusion to the **ReCALL** was a little difficult. It is better to skip forward at the beginning of the final hold tone and voiceover thus making that transition the four seconds it is supposed to be. It is necessary to make sure that I sit properly so that I can fill my diaphragm completely in the four second inbreath. I am using my nose for inbreaths and outbreaths. Finally, I noticed that I can say the "**Cha Kra 7 Now**", and so on for each breath cycle of the **ReTURN** exercise, and that this makes it both easier to do and more powerful. This time I made it to page 576 in the dictionary. This is becoming easier to do and I am not overheating as much as I did in the beginning. The **ReTURN** exercise also definitely seems to be working as I feel much more awake after doing it.

Thursday, June 17th, 2004 (4)

I had a big meal yesterday evening so it was more difficult doing this today as I am still somewhat full and cannot breathe as deeply as I need to. This will stop one from gluttony. I made it to page 737 of my big dictionary. I had to do some cheater breathes today but I still managed to adhere pretty well to the protocol. I still find the **ReLAX** and **ReTURN** exercises the easiest and the **ReTAIN** exercise a challenge.

Friday, June 18th, 2004 (5)

I am still fighting it and occasionally having to take cheater breathes. I will continue to do this until my body habituates. This is a form of aerobic training to reteach my body to be comfortable with long breathes rather than the short, shallow breathing that I, and most everyone else, have done most of their lives. I made it to page 822 in my dictionary. I have found that I can do all of the exercises by breathing through my nose and that this works pretty well.

Saturday, June 19th, 2004 (6)

I am still fighting it and occasionally having to take cheater breathes. Only did one cycle of the **ReTAIN** exercise so I only made it to page 854 in my dictionary. This was the shortest a session could be. It totaled 9 minutes and 48 seconds and was a complete session having performed all four exercises. That means that in thirty minutes one could practice doing this three times. However, it is probably best to do the **ReTAIN** exercise for at least six minutes which would make this a fifteen minutes exercise that could be done twice in thirty minutes. That is good practice without much demand on one's time.

Sunday, June 20th, 2004 (7)

The **ReLAX** and **ReTURN** exercises worked great this time. The **ReLAX** ritual was actually ReLAXing and the **ReTURN** ritual really feels efficient at getting me back into the beta state. The **ReTAIN** and **ReCALL** rituals still required cheater breathes, but not nearly as much and this is the first time that I have not felt overheated from doing these exercises. It is apparent to me that the **ReLAX** and **ReTURN** exercises require physical activity and that small amount of extra exertion is what is making them more taxing. However, my body has more than half way acclimated and within a few more days of practice I expect to be able to do this as it is meant to be performed. I have been doing this for one week now, and it is working!!! Made it to page 988 and then page 107 of the supplemental section at the end of the dictionary. This is further than I have made it in any previous attempts.

Monday, June 21st, 2004 (8)

Almost made it without error this time, only a couple of cheater breathes during the inhale portions of theta state breathing. I made it to page 187 of the supplement.

Tuesday, June 22nd, 2004 (9)

I only messed up the **ReCALL** breathe cycle this time which was the final theta state breathing cycle. I made it to page 213 of the supplement. I should be able to do it correctly tomorrow. I also practiced **ReTAIN** breathing while driving using the memory mantra to time myself. I was in a situation on a freeway with little or no traffic and I found that I could therefore practice and still drive. It was very refreshing although obviously I was not trying to read while driving, only practice the breathing. I did so for seven breathe cycles, or just over three and a half minutes.

Wednesday, June 23rd, 2004 (10)

I made it all of the way this time with a minimum time set of the four **Re** based rituals and did so with proper breathing and no significant errors. I made it to page 243 of the supplement. From this point forward I will begin to lengthen the time during which I do the **ReTAIN** ritual until I can do if for the full ten minutes without stress.

Thursday, June 24th, 2004 (11)

Fudge, I messed up the outbreathe on the **ReTAIN** concluding breathe cycle. Other than that I got it right. I did seven breathe cycles of SuperScanning. This went well in general and I made it to the end of my big dictionary, page 319, and started back the other direction making it to page 309.

Friday, June 25th, 2004 (12)

Once again I messed up the **ReTAIN** exercise, only this time it was the necessity of taking a cheater breathe on the inbreathe. I did two **ReTAIN** breathe cycles and I made it back to page 239. I again practiced the **ReTain** exercise using the **memory mantra** to time myself for seven cycles while driving today on a deserted back road on my way to an appointment. I of course did not try to read, only practice the pattern. It worked.

Saturday, June 26th, 2004 (13)

Again I messed up, two breathe cycles this time. I did a minimum time set of exercises until I can get it correct. I will make it tomorrow. I made it back to page 207 in the supplement.

Sunday, June 27th, 2004 (14)

It seems that I will continue to have slight breath errors, mostly in the inbreath, until practice eliminates them. The **ReLAX** and **ReTURN** exercises are easy enough to do but **ReTAIN** and **ReCALL** have enough extra elements that I still feel rushed and I am not breathing quite as smoothly or naturally, and consequently I have some difficulty with them. I also coughed in the middle of an inbeath which I take as an indication of a clearing. However, I believe that these minor difficulties would be eliminated if I were not also trying to locate a skip forward button on my computer using the mouse. In the future I may develop a single track exercise that includes all four exercises and is short cycle, another that is long cycle, and a third that is long cycle with **Brain Bingo**® added. That will eliminate the necessity for breaking my focus to look for a button. Alternatively, I may just transition away from using the CD and having memorized the pattern by now, do this on my own. That is really the ultimate objective anyway. Either way this will work once my reserve capacity exceeds demand. For today, I made it back to page 184 in the supplement.

Monday, June 28th, 2004 (15)

A cough and a few minor interruptions during inbreathe portions, but otherwise I had a good run and I made it back to page 155. I am going to start lengthening the time I do this from this point forward. *I did 13 theta state breathe cycles while driving today. Once again I caution, do not attempt this until you can do so without stress or danger of passing out, and also only for the* **ReTain** *and* **ReCall** *exercises without actually trying to SuperScan as you are, after all, driving. Finally, only attempt this when you are essentially alone on the road and it is easy to drive. I practice while driving straight and deserted backroads that are alternate routes to my destination.* I have found this to be well worth doing having passed 100 cycles of theta state breathing and finding my body doing this somewhat naturally, and also this gives me great cardiovascular practice that clears my mind and increases the kundalini flow up my spine and into the back of my brain.

Tuesday, June 29th, 2004 (16)

A cough or two during practice but good breathe control this time. I made it back to page 124 in the supplement. Also, I was able to practice **ReTAIN** breathing and **memory mantra** while driving and did so two different times for a total of around 26 breathe cycles. I am finding this an excellent exercise to do while driving in low task load situations as it is good practice, calming, and great cardiovascular exercise too. Using the **memory mantra** to time my breathing is working very well.

Wednesday, June 30th, 2004 (17)

It is working well now. I made it back to page 49 in the supplement and now I have enough reserve to do this correctly for all of the exercises. I practiced for 20 minutes while driving today and I will continue doing this until I have achieved 100 repetitions of each exercise done correctly.

Thursday, July 1st, 2004 (18)

It is working well now. I made it back to page 959 in the main portion of the dictionary.

Friday, July 2nd, 2004 (19)

I practiced a short cycle again today and I made it back to page 933 in the main dictionary. I also practiced breathing for about three minutes while driving. This approach is working very well.

Saturday, July 3nd, 2004 (20)

I practiced a short cycle again today and I made it back to page 905 in the dictionary. I also practiced theta state breathing and the **memory mantra** for four minutes while driving today.

Sunday, July 4th, 2004 (21)

I made it back to page 852 in the dictionary and I practiced breathing for four minutes while driving.

Monday, July 5th, 2004 (22)

I made it back to page 822 in the dictionary. I also tried theta state breathing while walking today at the forest preserve. I couldn't do it for more than one cycle as it was too demanding while exercising that hard. I will have to work up to this.

Tuesday, July 6th, 2004 (23)

I made it back to page 791 in the dictionary.

Wednesday, July 7th, 2004 (24)

I made it back to page 717 in the dictionary and did 3.5 minutes of theta breathing while driving.

Thursday, July 8th, 2004 (25)

I made it back to page 518 in the dictionary and did 4 minutes of theta breathing while driving. I have begun lengthening the amount of time that I SuperScan. I did so for six cycles this time.

Friday, July 9th, 2004 (26)

I made it back to the front of the dictionary thus doing properly 9 minutes of SuperScanning and around 530 pages of material. I still occasionally begin to feel the "panicked" feeling during the last hold before the next big inbreath, however, I am able to maintain the pattern and resist interrupting it. The next major step will be to have enough capacity so that I remain relaxed throughout the entire **ReTAIN** exercise. I also did 5 minutes of theta state breathing while driving (**T-cycles**). It felt very good and refreshed me.

Saturday, July 10th, 2004 (27)

I made it to page 675 in the dictionary. With the 20 introductory pages in the beginning, that is 695 pages of material. I SuperScanned for the entire duration of the **ReTAIN** exercise, or slightly more than ten minutes for a total of 20 minutes overall. When I began it was easy to do. By the time I reached the last two cycles I was struggling such that quick cheater exhales were necessary on the inbreath cycle to clear my lungs and keep going. I was also beginning to perspire so I overheated a little, but not nearly as much as I experienced the first week of doing this. However, I essentially made it the entire distance through everything but the complete **ReCALL** exercise. As soon as I can do this in a relaxed fashion, I will add the **Brain Bingo**® portion of the **ReCALL** exercise.

Sunday, July 11th, 2004 (28)

I made it all the way through the dictionary and back to page 197 in the supplement. That is approximately another 700 pages as I did yesterday. Once again I overheated a little and I had to exhale and inhale during an inbreathe cycle a few times. Overall, a good session though. I need to practice more theta state breathing independently of the CD, while driving for instance, in order to take myself to the next level. It is becoming obvious to me that as soon as I can become independent of the CD I will do this more naturally, at least for the **ReTAIN** and **ReCALL** portions which are done for extended periods of time. The **ReLAX** and **ReTURN** exercises are easy to follow with the CD and probably still best done that way until the 100 repetition programming threshold is obtained, then after that they are power words that take only a moment to invoke.

Monday, July 12th, 2004 (29)

20 minute session. I made it to page 424 once again covered 700 pages of material. I only barely overheated this time and I only needed cheater exhale/inhales a couple of times. I am getting close to being able to do this as intended.

Tuesday, July 13th, 2004 (30)

20 minute session, 700 pages, and getting easier to do. I still haven't quite done it right though.

Wednesday, July 14th, 2004 (31)

10 minute short cycle session because I didn't get to it until late in the afternoon after eating a big meal. Big mistake, I was barely able to the do the session. An empty stomach makes this much easier to do.

Thursday, July 15th, 2004 (32)

20 minute session, 700 pages, and a good practice session but far from perfect. Done on an empty stomach upon first arising, and consequently much easier to do.

Friday, July 16th, 2004 (33)

20 minute session, 700 pages done well. Also did 20 minutes theta breathing (**T-cycles**) while driving.

#	Day	Date	Session	T-Cycles	Comments
34	Sat	07-17	20 min	0 min	I almost have it, only two quick-breath cycle breaks this time.
35	Sun	07-18	20 min	10 min	Still cannot quite do it correctly, but getting there.
36	Mon	07-19	20 min	22 min	Practiced mid morning prior to eating too much so not a problem.
37	Tue	07-20	20 min	42 min	Drove a lot today so I was able to get in quite a bit of practice
38	Wed	07-21	20 min	0 min	Humid day, I overheated and needed many cheater breathes.
39	**Thu**	**07-22**	**17 min**	**0 min**	*Did the ReTAIN exercise freeform (without CD) and it helped a lot.*
40	Fri	07-23	17 min	0 min	Difficult to do today, high humidity warm day.
41	Sat	07-24	20 min	0 min	Cool day, low humidity, free form worked pretty well this time.
42	**Sun**	**07-25**	**20 min**	**0 min**	*Did all of the exercises correctly, however, transitions still rough.*
43	Mon	07-26	20 min	0 min	Did well except for transitions while fumbling with buttons.
44	**Tue**	**07-27**	**20 min**	**42 min**	*Breathing almost easily today and Owl-Eye vision is starting to work.*
45	**Wed**	**07-28**	**20 min**	**0 min**	*Last night I had a vision of seeing a book through opaque glass.*

I take this to be confirmation that my Owl-Eye vision is awakening.

#	Day	Date	Session	T-Cycles	Comments
46	Thu	07-29	20 min	0 min	Didn't use headphones this time, and working hard on posture.
47	Fri	07-30	20 min	20 min	Was able to practice while driving to a conference.
48	Sat	07-31	11 min	0 min	Camping today – at conference, not much time.
49	Sun	08-01	11 min	0 min	Camping today – at conference, not much time.
50	Mon	08-02	11 min	0 min	Last day of conference. Superscanned a book loaned to me.
51	Tue	08-03	20 min	0 min	Back home and back to normal practice regimen.
52	Wed	08-04	20 min	0 min	Hard to do, hot and muggy in the house, on generator overnight.
53	Thu	08-05	20 min	0 min	An okay session as the weather has turned cooler and the air is dry.
54	**Fri**	**08-06**	**20 min**	**0 min**	*Easiest session I have ever had. Virtually a perfect set of exercises.*
55	Sat	08-07	14 min	0 min	Hard to do the exercises today. I was short of breath this time.
56	Sun	08-08	20 min	0 min	Good set today, but not perfect. Compelling feeling while superscanning.
57	Mon	08-09	18 min	0 min	Tried exercises in the tub. Too hunched over and too hot to do properly.
58	Tue	08-10	20 min	20 min	A number of cheater breaths necessary today, but otherwise an okay set.
59	Wed	08-11	20 min	0 min	Tough to do today, my body is tight thus making breathing difficult.
60	**Thu**	**08-12**	**20 min**	**22 min**	*I SuperScanned 900 pages of a Pre-Calculus teacher's edition math*

book. After a noon nap I had a vision of a single bookshelf divided down the middle, with three shelves on each side. The PreCalculus book was in the middle of the top shelf on the right hand side along with a number of other books. I wasn't able to quite see the left side yet although the whole structure was there along with books in place. I interpret this to mean that my right brain has the info and my left brain focus mode is built but I am not yet seeing the right brain info. The structure is in place waiting for my vision to gain access.

#	Day	Date	Session	T-Cycles	Comments
61	Fri	08-13	31 min	0 min	*Did Brain Bingo® today. Scored 20%, well above chance.* I found the

exercise difficult to do. I was not able to maintain my breathing while listening to the Brain Bingo® exercise. I will try this again using the **Memory Mantra** to cadence to. I believe this will work better and improve my score.

#	Day	Date	Session	T-Cycles	Comments
62	Sat	08-14	20 min	20 min	Caught in traffic on my way to do the "Mastery of Learning Seminar" in

South Bend, IN. I did the **Memory Mantra** and theta state breathing thus putting me into the "Now." While in this state I mentally asked how long I would be stuck in traffic, and immediately got an answer of ten minutes. My subconscious response turned out to be correct which I confirmed because I was timing my practice session.

#	Day	Date	Session	T-Cycles	Comments
63	Sun	08-15	20 min	0 min	Superscanned more pre-Calculus material and an Edgar Cayce book.
64	Mon	08-16	20 min	0 min	Saw a vision this morning of a flickering light, as if a florescent light had

a bad connection. I interpret this as saying that my ability is cutting in and out. More practice is the answer. Superscanned three books this morning during my ten minutes of ReTAIN practice.

#	Day	Date	Session	T-Cycles	Comments
65	Tue	08-17	20 min	0 min	2 new books superscanned.
66	Wed	08-18	20 min	0 min	SuperScanned the math book again.
67	**Thu**	**08-19**	**20 min**	**11 min**	*Did my exercises early in the morning while it was still dark. I left the*

lights off. I found SuperScanning very natural under these conditions. I SuperScanned a different math book.

#	Day	Date	Session	T-Cycles	Comments
68	Fri	08-20	20 min	0 min	SuperScanned 4 books. Rainy & overcast, a subconscious kind of day.
69	Sat	08-21	20 min	0 min	SuperScanned 4 books.
70	Sun	08-22	20 min	0 min	SuperScanned 2 books.

71	Mon	08-23	20 min	0 min	SS'd 4 books including Flower of Life material. Rainy & overcast again.
72	Tue	08-24	20 min	10 min	SS'd 3 books.
73	Wed	08-25	20 min	0 min	SS'd 4 books. Rainy, overcast, & tornado type of day.
74	Thu	08-26	20 min	14 min	SS'd 1.5 books. Early AM session in dark w/ ReTURN later in day.
75	**Fri**	08-27	20 min	14 min	SS'd 3.5 books. *Awakening vision of barely illuminated green neuron tree. Whole tree was there, just very thin. I need more practice to myelineate the structure better.*
76	Sat	08-28	20 min	0 min	SS'd 3 books.
77	Sun	08-29	20 min	5 min	SS'd 4.5 books. Rainy & cool this morning, the subconscious reigns.
78	Mon	08-30	20 min	0 min	SS'd 3.5 books 2 of which were Jane Robert's books.
79	Tue	08-31	20 min	19 min	SS'd 4 Jane Robert's books.
80	Wed	09-01	20 min	0 min	SS'd 4 JR books. Day is cool and crisp. Exercises easy to do.
81	Thu	09-02	20 min	20 min	SS'd 3.5 JR books. Another cool and crisp day. Easy to breathe.
82	**Fri**	09-03	20 min	0 min	SS'd 4 James Redfield books. **My waking dream last night was of a left Eye-of-Horus formed out of six inch wide sheet metal followed by an Egyptian woman doing a hand motion over it from left to right. According to Drumvalo Melchizedek the left Eye of Horus is the symbol for the Egyptian feminine-body school of emotion (Pg 264 in the Ancient Secret of the Flower of Life.) It is worth noting that I SS'd this book on 8-23-04.**
83	Sat	09-04`	20 min	0 min	SS'd 4.5 books. Finished Kryon except 1, started Sister Thedra books.
84	Sun	09-05	20 min	0 min	SS'd 5 books. Finished Kryon, Sister Thedra, & Solara books.
85	Mon	09-06	20 min	0 min	SS'd 4.5 books. Misc collection of books in bathroom.
86	Tue	09-07	20 min	0 min	SS'd 2 books. Cool day, low humidity, good day for SSng.
87	Wed	09-08	20 min	0 min	SS'd 2 books, both on Egypt
88	Thu	09-09	20 min	20 min	SS'd 3.5 books, on Orion, Pleiades, and HAARP.
89	**Fri**	09-10	20 min	20 min	SS'd 4 books, on Pleiades and 3 Richard Bach books. **Did this session at 5 AM while it was still dark. Once again I note that at night it is much more focused and compelling.**
90	**Sat**	09-11	20 min	0 min	SS'd *The Learning Revolution* **in darkness so complete that for most pages I could not even tell if there was print on the page. I am seeking feedback from my subconscious to know if this was too dark a level to be working at.**
91	Sun	09-12	20 min	0 min	SS'd 4 books. *Mind Map, Indigo Children, Magical Child & Cosmic Egg.*
92	Mon	09-13	20 min	0 min	3 books. *Photoreading, Super-Learning, Psychic Discoveries in USSR.*
93	Tue	09-14	20 min	15 min	4.5 books. Nidle's, Essene's, Bringers of Dawn, & Barbara Hand Clow
94	Wed	09-15	20 min	0 min	1.5 books. Pre-Calculus answer book & TI-83 Instruction manual.
95	**Thu**	09-16	20 min	20 min	1.5 books. Finished Pre-Calc and **redid** *The Learning Revolution.* **In the twilight of awakening this morning I asked if the book SS'd in session 88 in darkness such that I could not consciously see words on the page, was retained. I saw a vision of incompletely formed letters indicating that it was only partially acquired by my subconscious.**
96	**Fri**	09-17	20 min	20 min	4 bks, *Bashar, Unfinished Symphonies,* 2 *Lazaris* 2 bks. **Noticed today how much more sensitive my peripheral vision is all of the time. Sometimes I seem to notice even a leaf falling hundreds of feet away and other small movements that before I mostly missed.**
97	Sat	09-18	20 min	0 min	5 bks, 4 Og Mandino bks and *Unseen Hands & Unknown hearts.*
98	Sun	09-19	20 min	36 min	3 bks, *Creating Love, The Family, & Ageless Body, Timeless Mind.*
99	Mon	09-20	20 min	0 min	1/5th of *The Layman's Parallel Bible.* It is a total of 3035 thin pages. They are hard to turn which slows me down considerably.
100	Tue	09-21	20 min	20 min	1/5th of *The Layman's Parallel Bible.* **Graduation day! I am now completely independent of the CD. My subconscious has been programmed with the format of all four rituals thus making them power words for me. From this point forward I can invoke the ReLAX, ReTAIN, ReCALL, and ReTURN exercises that I have practiced by just saying the words. Now I can SuperScan material at will by saying "ReLAX," after which I begin theta state breathing with the memory mantra by saying "Re," then I SuperScan whatever I need to, I end theta state breathing by saying "TAIN," and then I end my session by saying "ReTURN." Later, when I need to access this new material I say "ReLAX," and then "ReCALL" When I am done accessing I say "ReTURN" to end my subconscious probing of what I have previously SuperScanned.**
101	Wed	09-22	20 min	0 min	2/5[ths] of *The Layman's Parallel Bible.* This time I treated all Re-words as power words so I was able to do almost exclusively SuperScanning practice.

04/09/09

#	Day	Date	Session	T-Cycles	Comments

ReWORDS Practice Journal   Name: Pg